PUNK ART HISTORY

intellect Bristol, UK / Chicago, USA

GLOBAL PUNK

Series editors: Russ Bestley and Mike Dines

Produced in collaboration with the Punk Scholars Network, the Global Punk book series focuses on the development of contemporary global punk, reflecting its origins, aesthetics, identity, legacy, membership, and circulation. Critical approaches draw upon the interdisciplinary areas of (amongst others) cultural studies, art and design, sociology, musicology, and social sciences in order to develop a broad and inclusive picture of punk and punk-inspired subcultural developments around the globe. The series adopts an essentially analytical perspective, raising questions over the dissemination of punk scenes and subcultures and their form, structure, and contemporary cultural significance in the daily lives of an increasing number of people around the world. To propose a manuscript, or for more information about the series, please contact the series co-editors Russ Bestley and Mike Dines (contact details available at www.intellectbooks.com).

The Punk Reader: Research Transmissions from the Local and the Global
Edited by Russ Bestley, Mike Dines, Alastair Gordon and Paula Guerra
Trans-Global Punk Scenes: The Punk Reader Vol. 2
Edited by Russ Bestley, Mike Dines, Alastair Gordon and Paula Guerra
Punk Identities, Punk Utopias: Global Punk and Media
Edited by Russ Bestley, Mike Dines, Matt Grimes and Paula Guerra
PUNK! Las Américas Edition
Edited by Olga Rodríguez-Ulloa, Rodrigo Quijano and Shane Greene
Blank Canvas: Art School Creativity From Punk to New Wave
Simon Strange
Punk Pedagogies in Practice: Disruptions and Connections
Edited by Francis Stewart and Laura Way
Punk Art History: Artworks From the European No Future Generation
Marie Arleth Skov
In Search of Tito's Punks: On the Road in a Country that No Longer Exists
Barry Phillips

PUNK ART HISTORY

ARTWORKS FROM THE EUROPEAN NO FUTURE GENERATION

MARIE ARLETH SKOV

First published in the UK in 2023 by Intellect, The Mill, Parnall Road, Fishponds, Bristol, BS16 3JG, UK

First published in the USA in 2023 by Intellect, The University of Chicago Press, 1427 E. 60th Street, Chicago, IL 60637, USA

Produced in collaboration with the Punk Scholars Network

A catalogue record for this book is available from the British Library.

Copy editor: MPS Limited
Cover designer: Russ Bestley
Indexing: Marie Arleth Skov
Production manager: Sophia Munyengeterwa
Typesetting: Russ Bestley

Part of the Global Punk series
ISSN 2632-8305 | ONLINE ISSN 2632-8313

Hardback ISBN 978-1-78938-747-6
Paperback ISBN 978-1-78938-700-1
ePDF ISBN 978-1-78938-701-8
ePUB ISBN 978-1-78938-702-5

Printed and bound by Gomer

To find out about all our publications, please visit www.intellectbooks.com. There, you can subscribe to our e-newsletter, browse or download our current catalogue and buy any titles that are in print.

This is a peer-reviewed publication.

Opening image: VÆRST (WORST), *Im Eimer* (Done for), 1985, from *Das Zeug* (*The Stuff*), 1986. Courtesy of Christian Lemmerz and Michael Kvium.

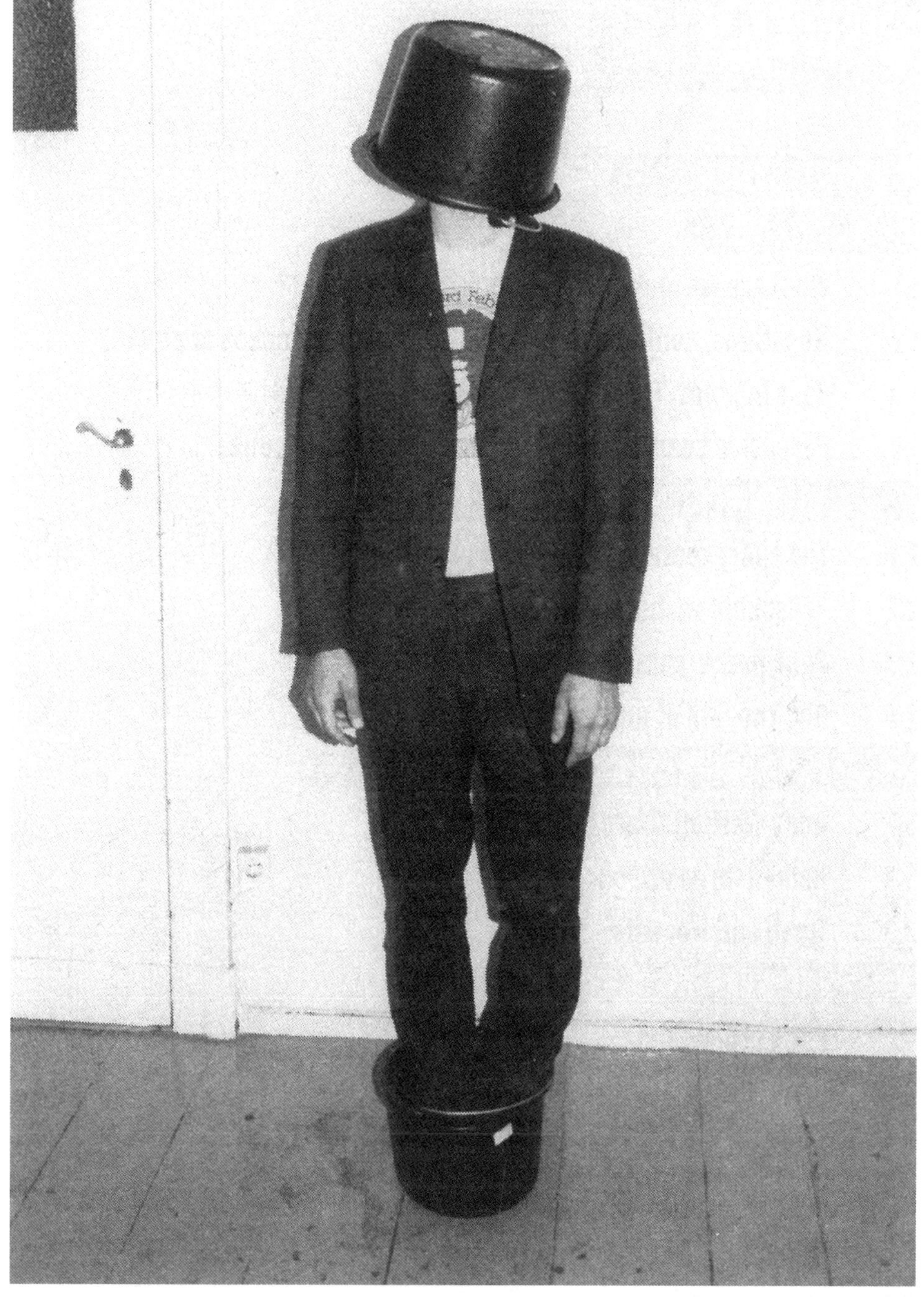

CONTENTS

ACKNOWLEDGMENTS 9

1 PRELUDE 11

1.1 What are we looking at? A punk art movement? 12

1.2 Negations, conflicts, and swindles: The elusiveness of punk 24

1.3 Case in point: The first *Punk Art* exhibition, 1978 32

1.4 Forty-five years of trying to capture the art in punk 41

2 ART ORIGINS IN THE STORY OF PUNK 51

2.1 The short version: From proto to post 51

2.2 Art school vs. hard school 61

2.3 Punk precursors: 1919, 1966, and 1968 63

2.4 DIY: The DNA of punk 71

3 POP MULTIPLES, CAMP AFFIRMATIONS 85

3.1 Andy Warhol: "Hero of the Punks" 86

3.2 Hedonism as attack 94

3.3 Trash and travesty 100

4 THE WEAPONS OF THE UNDERDOG 113

4.1 Punk propaganda 113

4.2 Punk poetry 121

4.3 Crime as art, scandal as art 131

5 ART WITH NO FUTURE? 145

5.1 Originality and appropriation 145

5.2 Modernity in extremis 152

5.3 Avant-garde vs. rear-guard 159

6	**CHILDREN RUN RIOT: THE ART OF THE INFANTILE**	164
6.1	Dead end kids	164
6.2	*The Life of Sid Vicious*: The sad, dead boy	171
6.3	"Infancy conforms to nobody"	174
7	**WORK VS. PLAY**	180
7.1	Punk's *homo ludens*	180
7.2	Ingenious Dilettantes	184
7.3	"The Baby Wagner Lullaby," or Brilliance blackout	189
8	**SEX**	197
8.1	Queer punks and dykes in high heels	198
8.2	Defiant prostitutes, porn artists and well-dressed whores	206
8.3	Sadism and submission	214
8.4	Punk feminism: Vamp up!	223
9	**PAIN AND PRESENCE**	237
9.1	Performances and punches	238
9.2	"It hurts and looks cool!": Fetish fashion	241
9.3	Real romance?	249
10	**DYSTOPIAN WITH A TWIST**	254
10.1	It's the end of the world	254
10.2	The Grand Downfall Show	259
10.3	Broken heroes, aces of failure	263
11	**THE LAWS OF THE LAWLESS**	271
LIST OF INTERVIEWS AND ARCHIVES		283
BIBLIOGRAPHY		285
INDEX		303

ACKNOWLEDGMENTS

The print of this book was supported by the New Carlsberg Foundation.

The PhD research on which this book builds was funded by a Mads Øvlisen PhD Scholarship within Art History from the Novo Nordisk Foundation.

Thank you to all of the artists who talked to me, showed me their archives, and to the artists, archives, and estates who gave me permission to print their artworks in this book: Anna Banana, Tabea Blumenschein/Townes Archive (Shoko Kawaida and Fetisch Terranova), GENESIS BREYER P-ORRIDGE, the estate of BREYER P-ORRIDGE and Benjamin Tischler, Neke Carson, Luciano Castelli, Cosey Fanni Tutti, Anno Dittmer, Estate of Leo Dohmen, Elmer, Gilbert & George, Jutta Henglein-Bildau, Allen Jones, Estate Birgit Jürgenssen, Hugo Kaagman, Per Katchetowa, Estate of Martin Kippenberger, Käthe Kruse, Michael Kvium, Christian Lemmerz, Marc Miller, Wolfgang Müller, Lars Nørgård, Knud Odde, Tom Otterness, Diana Ozon, Jamie Reid, Steen Møller Rasmussen, Ilse Ruppert, Jon Savage, Pennie Smith, Nina Sten-Knudsen, Ian Townson Archive, David Wise, and Xavier from Timeless Editions.

Thank you to the supervisors of my co-tutelle PhD thesis, Martin Schieder (Universität Leipzig) and Mikkel Bolt Rasmussen (Københavns Universitet). Thank you to Russ Bestley, Mike Dines, and the Punk Scholars Network. Thanks to the team at Intellect Books, especially Sophia Munyengeterwa. Thank you to my family and my friends, Laura, Aneta, Rie, Henrik, Morten, Emil, and Jens.

Shorter segments of this book have previously been published here:

Skov, Marie Arleth. "The Art of the Enfants Terribles: Infantilism and Dilettantism in Punk Art." *RIHA Journal*, 0201 (15 November 2018).

Skov, Marie Arleth. "The 1979 American Punk Art Dispute: Visions of Punk Art between Sensationalism, Street Art and Social Practice." *Punk & Post-Punk* 9, no. 3 (2020), 443–66.

Skov, Marie Arleth. "Surrealism and Punk: The Case of COUM Transmissions." In *Radical Dreams: Surrealism, Counterculture, Resistance*, edited by Elliott King and Abigail Susik, 207–33. University Park: Penn State University Press, 2022.

Skov, Marie Arleth. "The Copenhagen Punk Years: Art with No Future?" In *A Cultural History of the Avant-Garde in the Nordic Countries 1975–2000*, edited by Benedikt Hjartarson, Camilla Paldam, Laura Schultz, and Tania Ørum, 643–61, Leiden, Boston: Brill Rodopi, 2022.

1 PRELUDE

Sometimes, punk is art. And sometimes, art is punk. Punk as a movement was not only just as visual as it was musical but also highly concerned with art as a concept and, specifically, with art history. In this book, the punk movement of the late 1970s to early 1980s is examined as an art movement through archive research, interviews, and art historical analysis. It is about pop and pain, poetry and presence. It is also about artists refusing to become the next artworld ism. Instead, the protagonists of the punk movement adopted and appropriated elements of history, especially art history, and in the process rendered meaningless formalist concepts of originality. Central to the book is the analysis of how punk themes are transported through art: themes like hedonism and (anti-)heroization, trash and fame, splendor and brokenness. Often, these artworks touch on contrarieties, and paradoxically turn them around: the artificial is the authentic, the guilty is the innocent, failure is success, and destruction is creation.

The punk movement rejected the tale of endless advance, progress, and prosperity in post-war western society. This sentiment evidently manifested itself in punk visual art too: it was about decadence, decline, and death. This stance, however, made the way for some very vivid artworks. Punks placed themselves as the rear-guards, not the avant-gardes, a statement which was actually made by Danish punks in 1981, when they called themselves "bagtropperne." Behind the rear-guard watchword was the rejection of the inherent notion of progress that the avant-garde name brings with it; how could a "no future" generation want to lead the way? In art history—parallel to political and social history—the tale of progress was coming to an end, too, most prominently disseminated in Arthur C. Danto's essay "The Death of Art" (1984). Like a seismograph, the punk movement of the late 1970s and early 1980s made the art-to-end-all-art, somehow an echo of past times and the epitome of its own time, anachronistic and zeitgeisty at the same time. In this book, we will take a look at what that meant: the role of conscious retrogression and chosen infantilism, of a youth movement between Oliver Twist realism and Peter Pan escapism.

It is my intent to show it, not tell it: this means we will be going through many (many!) examples and stories. Through these examples and stories, together we will move in on the topic area "punk art history," in the sense of: punk in relation to art and in relation to art history—"punk" times "art" times "history." An explosive equation. The book has eleven chapters: the first two will set the scene, followed by eight chapters exploring the themes of *Punk Art History* in depth, and finally ending with one chapter to boil it all down. Each chapter begins with a short overview of what is to come. Here is the first one, because Chapter 1 starts NOW: In the first part of this chapter—"What are we looking at? A punk art movement?"—we will do just that, that is to determine what it is we are looking at, the material of this book. Secondly, we will be dealing with "Negations, conflicts, and swindles: The elusiveness of punk," an elusiveness that is notorious, but then again punks were generally not set on being understood. With punk, we are dealing with a movement that was often in opposition to itself, full of conflicts and battles. As a case in point, we will, thirdly, be looking at the first exhibition actually named *Punk Art*, which took place in Washington, DC in 1978 and later traveled to Amsterdam, where it was bound for trouble with the local punk artists there. Finally, I will try to recap what fated those before me: "45 years of trying to capture the art in punk."

A very short introduction, this was. It is punk, after all, so speed is of the essence. *Hey, ho, let's go.*

1.1 What are we looking at? A punk art movement?

The punk movement was hybrid as hell: punk rock bands blurred the lines between stage shows and performance art, punk girls and boys and in-betweens changed their bodies into artworks, painting their faces like a Mondrian (like Jordan in London) or dressing up like a dream (like Gudrun Gut in Berlin), and hedonistic punk bashes invoked Surrealist theater staging. The etymology of the word "punk" goes all the way back to the late 1500s, when it meant "prostitute" (or, today: sex worker). It was later used either for "a young inexperienced person or beginner," "a usually petty gangster, hoodlum, or ruffian," or as slang for "a young man used as a homosexual partner especially in a prison."[1] Echoes of these concepts—sex, money, crime, youth, and abused power—can be found in the art of punk.

Punk was characterized by intermedia performances and collaborations between visual artists, poets, and musicians to a new degree—sure, such crossings had flourished in the 1960s already; Andy Warhol and the Velvet Underground, Yoko Ono's angry poetry, Mike Kelley's Destroy All Monsters—but the fusion of art forms reached a new high in punk, as did the transfers between different media: from music track to film to artwork to performance, and back again.

The French art/punk group Bazooka declared: "Mon papi s'appelle art moderne / Mais je ferai mieux que lui" ("My daddy is called modern art / But I will do better than him").[2] That statement might be read as a sideswipe at the predominant maleness and occasionally father-figure-esque admiration of the protagonists of modern art: Picasso, Dalí, Duchamp. The influence of modern art is recognized, but the defiant line "je ferai mieux" likewise expresses a rebuttal: we will not fall into the same traps, the artists of Bazooka seem to say. Though punk was from the very beginning a highly visual movement, the artists involved with punk were also highly aware of the pitfalls of the all-consuming artworld. "It was image, not sound, that defined the early days of Dutch punk," writes Jerry Goossens.[3] But that imagery was meant for another audience (punk kids and a few elderly revolutionary diehards) and for another time (now!) rather than high art for collectors and museums to hoard for eternity. As P-Orridge explains:

> We wanted to go into popular culture, away from the art gallery context, and to show that the same techniques that had been made to operate in that system could work. We wanted to test it out […] at a more street level—with young kids who had no education in art perception […]. A little mini-Dada movement, eh?[4]

Artists who were involved with the punk movement drew on the early twentieth century radical avant-garde—Futurism, Dada, Surrealism—but deferred these strategies to their own time and their own desires. "We wanted COUM Transmissions to have an effect like Dada, and PoP and other movemeants [*sic*]," P-Orridge declared.[5] That is the effect of rattling things up. Radical avant-garde ideas of dissemination, fragmentation, and crossover were revisited, but implemented in adapted ways. In the cultural time lapse between the emergence of Futurism, Dada, Surrealism, and the emergence of punk, lay an explosion of rock 'n' roll, teenage culture, diverse neo-Dada manifestations, TV, mass media, and a pop/sex revolution on top. The game had changed.

As one of the first to write about punk and art (in a chapter of his 1979 master's thesis), Hollow Skai claimed that while punk was understood as an art movement in the USA, in the UK, it was understood as a youth movement (and one with a stronger working-class ethos).[6] In essence, punk was somehow both and that was a part of what made the movement special. Hardly any other art movement of the twentieth century reached that level of cultural shock and awe, or mass media hype, or establishment hysteria. Punk was at the same time youth rebellion and a subversive art movement. Few other modes can compare (if any at all, perhaps the student revolt in Paris in 1968 and its Atelier Populaire). All the while, only few punks identified their work as "art"—not even as "anti-art"—despite the obvious links. One reason for that was to avoid ending up as the newest ism, just another page in the book of art novelties. Punk refused to be forced into the casting mold of previous art movements. The protagonists we deal with here were much too aware of (art) history and the cooptation and musealization of formerly radical art groups for that. The "No Future" generation was, thus, curiously old souls and young rebels at the same time. Standing at the end of the long twentieth century looking back, the promise of doing something "new," of changing everything, had in itself become old.

Abandoning the very idea of innovation (including its business overtones) was part of what was (ironically) new about punk.

Though never established as a term, "punk art" occurs a few times in the late 1970s and early 1980s. In 1978, the first *Punk Art* exhibition took place in Washington, DC, and around the same time, a group of artists and poets in Amsterdam called their work punk art. When the Americans came to Amsterdam with their *Punk Art* show, however, this caused a great row. We will dive into that conflict later in this chapter. In 1984, Bill Gaglione wrote about his art zine: "The aim of Dadazine is to publish the art and artists of the Neo-Avant-Garde; Dada, Correspondence Art, Fluxus, Concretism, Lettrism, Conceptual Art, Bruitism, Simultaneous Poetry, Happenings/Events, Punk Art, etc."[7] His listing shows in which context he sees punk. As we shall see, he is both right and wrong: the neo-avant-garde (of the 1950s–60s) plays an especially intricate role in punk art, it is both revered and refuted, it is reproduced and ridiculed. This is one of the tasks of this book: to go through the art origins of punk, especially beyond the often-dropped reference of Dada and the Situationist International, because, as Daniel Kulle points out: "the influence of other European as well as American art movements of the 1960s has hardly been researched at all."[8]

Anyhow, to attempt an exact definition of that term "punk art" would be ludicrous. Nobody knows. After all, that is one of the magic tricks of punk: to be *so* overt, *so* present, *so* extreme—yet so elusive. This elusiveness is punk's *Credo, quia absurdum est* ("I believe, because it is absurd"). A paradox. A code not meant to be cracked. Although, of course, we will undauntedly have a go at it anyway! Not to arrive at an exact definition of "punk art"—but, at the other end of this book, to have a better idea of the entangled meanings of *Punk Art History*, or: punk multiplied by art multiplied by history. To understand the roots and the strategies and the subject matter of punk, which is art, and art, which is punk. To do so, we will be looking at so many examples. The examined materials cover almost all media: paintings, drawings, bricolages, collages, booklets, posters, zines, installations, sculptures, Super 8 films, documentation of performances and happenings, Body Art, and street art. A 2-year-old boy running down the streets of Berlin dressed up as the Sex Pistols' Sid Vicious. A woman with flames coming out of her vagina. A live mouse, graffiti, and a broken statuette. Dental braces made of pearls; a necklace made of needles. A cigarette vending machine with art and smoke bombs inside. A shaved and naked punk poet with wings. At the heart of the book are the analysis of these works of art. Thus, a word on my material and how this book came about.

Material Grrrl: From Europe with love

Writing this book has been an inductive process. Nine years ago, I started researching for my PhD thesis on punk art. As an art historian with a love for punk (that came via a teenage love for grunge), the topic almost gave itself, especially as what was at first more intuition proved to be traceable and it became increasingly clear just how much punk had to do with art and with history (and how relatively superficial the research hitherto had been).

Now, there could have been many ways to go about researching the liaison between punk and art history. As a Copenhagener, who moved to Berlin as a 19-year-old, I decided to include art from those two cities. Amsterdam, too, had an interesting punk art scene and was accessible to me, and finally, although I was trying to move beyond the familiar US–UK axis, London was too important to ditch. I furthermore decided to focus on artists groups, as these to some degree reproduced the concept of a punk rock band within art. While I was writing my PhD thesis, I interviewed members of Die Tödliche Doris (i.e. the Deadly Doris: Tabea Blumenschein, Käthe Kruse, and Wolfgang Müller), as well as members of Værkstedet Værst (i.e. the Workshop Called Worst: Christian Lemmerz, and Lars Nørgård), and the KoeCrandt group (roughly translated "dirty rim on a toilet seat": Hugo Kaagman, and Diana Ozon). As I dived further into the material, I complemented interviews with artists Nina Sten-Knudsen and Elmer, as well as curator and artist Marc Miller, and with e-mail correspondences with Jon Savage, Anna Banana, and GENESIS BREYER P-ORRIDGE[9] (the latter of COUM Transmissions/Throbbing Gristle). For a full overview, see "List of Interviews and Archives" towards the end of this book.

A substantial part of the material was researched in the private archives of these protagonists, while some public collections and archives, such as the Tate Archive, the MoMA Queens Archive, and The Fales Library & Special Collection, were drawn upon as well. The recorded interviews were primarily conducted while the interviewees were going through their personal archives, meaning that there are many sound bites such as the following: "This is me, with dreadlocks [paper rustling]. These are dead insects."[10] Though that is at times both quite entertaining and quite charming, an appendix of complete transcripts did not seem worth it. All quotations used here, however, have been approved by the interviewees.

London, Amsterdam, West Berlin, Copenhagen: this is a very north-western European focus, I am aware. New York features time and again, because, well, you really cannot write about punk and art, without writing at least a little bit about New York. Southern Europe is missing, Eastern Europe is almost completely missing (East-Berlin features with some poetry), although both Southern and Eastern Europe had a strong punk rock scene, and—yes, I know!—a very strong punk art vein, too. Not to mention: South America, Asia ... There are thus still plenty of fields left for future researchers to take away. Even within the scenes that I am describing, positions are missing: there were more, there were others. In the end, I have chosen to concentrate on this material, which did seem to be more than enough to build my case. Write what you know, as a wise man once said. OK, it was Mark Twain, and he might not have had punk in mind, but hey.

Whereas my PhD thesis presented the four chosen artists groups (and their respective scenes) one after another, I have chosen to break it up here. The main reason is that I wanted to be able to synthesize the content, to point to overarching topics. The structure of this book mirrors that approach: each chapter is focused on a theme, which is then explained and supported through examples, meaning primarily (but not only!) artworks by the artists I interviewed. Although the respective punk scenes, which I write most about, are thus all interspersed in this new structure, thus highlighting shared features, it is important to underline that there are local differences. Each local punk scene drew from the historical and cultural specifics of that place, from the language, from a musical and artistic tradition, from the social and political structure. Each punk scene had its own preoccupations, and punk thus manifested, as Gerald Matt put it, "differently yet consistently"[11] in different cultural spheres, not unlike—say—Dada's diverse manifestations, in Zurich, Berlin, Paris, etc.

The second choice I made was to concentrate the book on the timeframe of the late 1970s to early 1980s. Arguably, punk changed even within that timeframe, as we shall see: by 1979, the first punks were already moving on. In retrospect, however, some of the subdivisions and very early post-positions of punk are hard to sharply divide. Over time, it rather becomes clear how much these positions actually (still) had in common. Outside of London (as the epicenter of European punk), this effect is even more pronounced. When punk arrived in West Berlin, for example, it was with a slight delay: the first seeds of Neue Deutsche Welle were already sprouting and these two modes crossed and rubbed off on each other. Nonetheless, I argue, the late 1970s to early 1980s, roughly, were the quintessential punk years in Europe.

At that point in time, the artists were primarily working and exhibiting each in their own spheres and were scarcely interconnected with each other. In one incidence, two members of Die Tödliche Doris were in the audience when Throbbing Gristle (formerly COUM Transmissions) played at SO36 in 1980. When Genesis P-Orridge screamed "Dis-ci-pliiiine!!!!" into the microphone and then held it toward the crowd, Wolfgang Müller screamed back "Aaaaargh!!!!" as can be heard on the Throbbing Gristle album *Live in Berlin* (1980, Figure 1.1). "Throbbing Gristle were important to us," says Müller, "the Sex Pistols

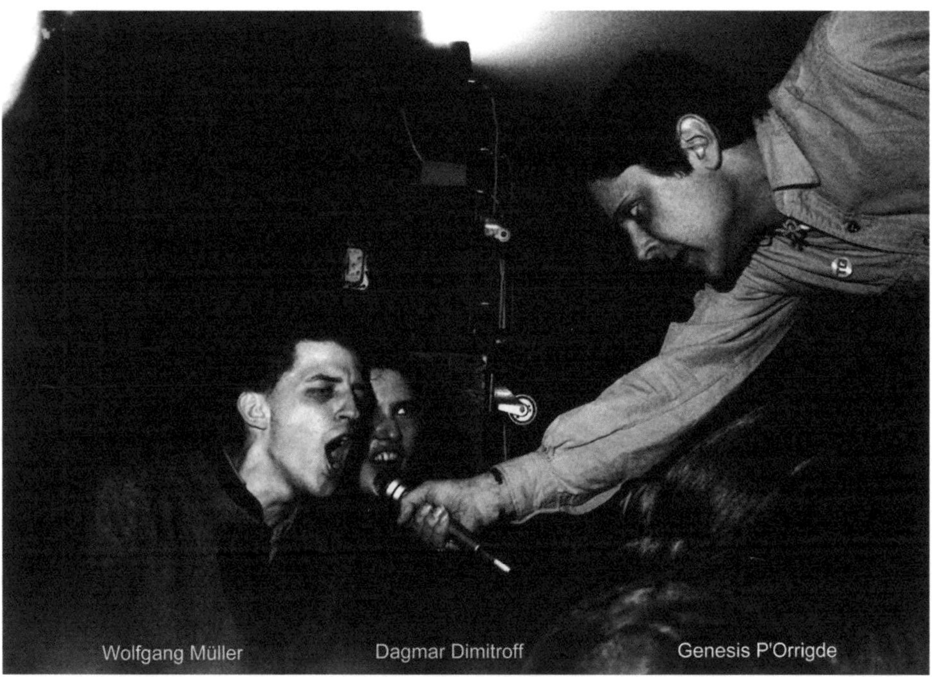

Figure 1.1: Throbbing Gristle performing in SO36 in West Berlin, 7 November 1980, with Die Tödliche Doris, photograph by Richard Gleim, postcard from the Archiv der Tödlichen Doris. Courtesy of Wolfgang Müller.

too, with their affirmation, with their humor. To this day, I find John Lydon an intriguing character."[12] The Sex Pistols remain the first and the most repeated reference point in the interviews. Hugo Kaagman, too, when talking about the inauguration of Beatrix in 1980 and the major battles between police and punk protesters in Amsterdam, quotes the Sex Pistols: "You know, 'fuck the queen, fascist regime', we had that too. In 1980, we had the slogan: 'geen woning, geen kroning' ('no housing, no coronation')."[13]

There are differences between the structure of the artists groups: COUM Transmissions was a gang, Die Tödliche Doris a concept, KoeCrandt a collective, and Værkstedet Værst was indeed a workshop. COUM and Die Tödliche Doris were the only two groups who were active both as musicians and artists. "Doris saw her music as the result of a creative process, which could have brought forth a painting, a sculpture, or a concept,"[14] writes "Monika Reich," the fictive PR secretary of Doris. The works themselves often generate an almost synesthetic experience. As recipients, our visual and auditory impressions correspond. Genesis P-Orridge, meanwhile, as a reaction to punk's infamous "three chords" stated: "You can start with no chords. Why not just say 'form a band' and it doesn't matter what it sounds like or whether you even make a noise, if you stand there silent for an hour."[15] The statement, in its John Cageian radicality, points to

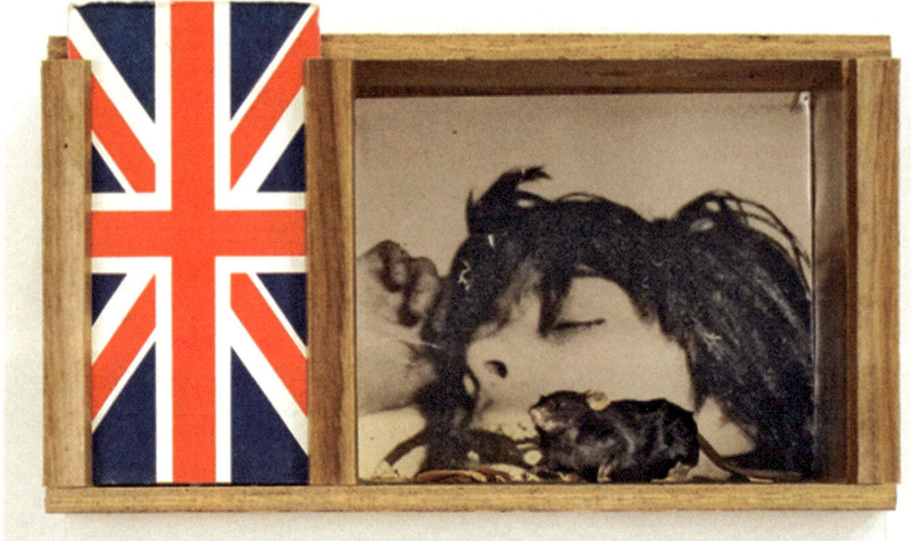

Figure 1.2: COUM Transmissions, The British Government, *1975. Courtesy of the estate of GENESIS BREYER P-ORRIDGE and New Discretions.*

COUM's antagonistic style. To Wolfgang Müller, too, punk was about the transgression of limits, but of a specific kind:

> Not in the sense of, I puke somewhere or spit on the floor or at the camera, that does not have so much to do with punk. Those are only macho gestures, that is not transgressive, just bad behavior. If you reduce punk to bad behavior, well, that is not very interesting. I think it is something else.[16]

That interpretation of punk as "something else" did not always go down well (more on this in the section "Art school vs. hard school"). For example, punk in the KoeCrandt group version consisted of poetry, collage, improvised theater and happenings, concerts, installations, and graffiti. All their quoting of CoBrA and Fluxus, however, made Peter Panic from the Amsterdam-based punk band PANIC call them "intellectual sacks of shit, performing little plays that make me want to vomit."[17] And with that seditious statement by Peter Panic, wouldn't you think that we are on the exactly right path into a discussion of the topic of punk art ...

Punk art samples

We are, then, dealing with punk that is art and art that is punk. More than anything punk art is defined by punk attitude. Since that alone is a fairly unclear statement, let us instead

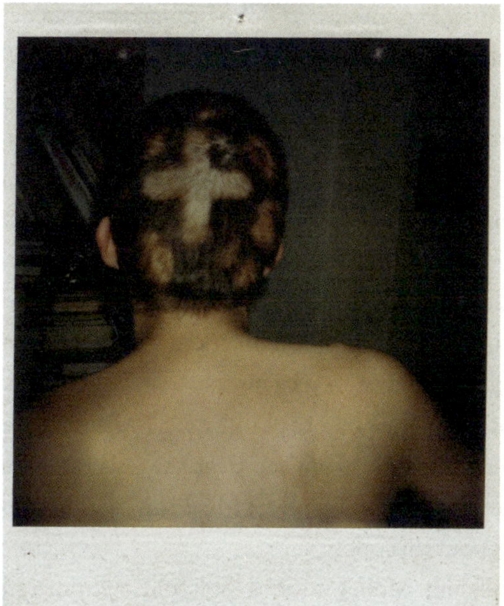

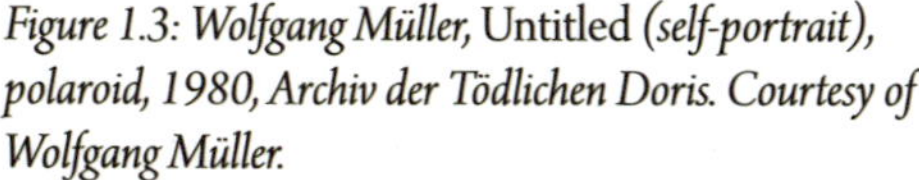

Figure 1.3: Wolfgang Müller, Untitled *(self-portrait), polaroid, 1980, Archiv der Tödlichen Doris. Courtesy of Wolfgang Müller.*

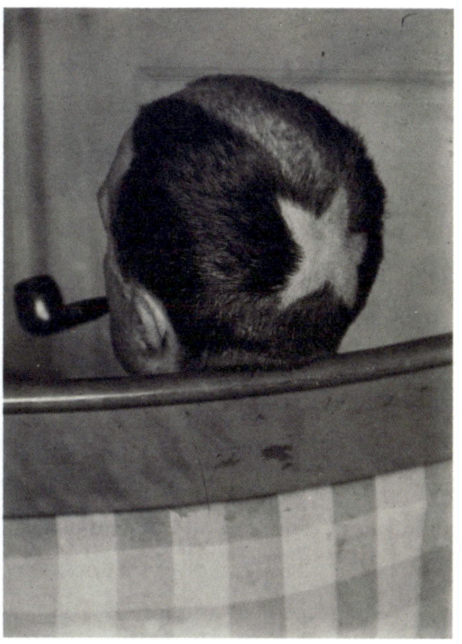

Figure 1.4: Marcel Duchamp, Tonsure, *1919 or 1921, photograph by Man Ray. © Man Ray Trust/ ADAGP, Paris. © VG Bild-Kunst, Bonn 2022.*

look at three quick examples that give a more concrete impression of what it is we will be examining in this book. A wooden box with a photo of a gagged boy and the Union Jack. A polaroid of an artist with a shaved crown in a flat in Berlin, that invokes another shaved crown of an artist in a bathtub in Paris from 60 years before. And a huge neo-Expressive painting imitating a music record sleeve. One, two, and one two three …

In October of 1975, the artists group COUM Transmissions participated in the *Ninth Paris Biennale* at the Musée d'Art Moderne. The centerpiece was their work *The British Government* (Figure 1.2). P-Orridge explains: "There were six boxes in *The British Government*. Two had photos of my girlfriend Akiko Hada, two had photos of boys by Sleazy and two had photos from my archives of fearful faces."[18] In the box depicted here, we see one side containing an upended cardboard Union Jack flag and next to it, a transparent box containing a grainy, black-and-white photograph (taken by Peter "Sleazy" Christopherson) of a young, gagged boy with a live mouse running back and forth in front of his face. The setup calls to mind a scene in room 101 in Orwell's *1984* where the main protagonist Winston Smith is tortured by his own worst nightmare: to be slowly eaten alive by rats. The work thus addresses topics of entrapment and abuse of power while also comparing Britain to the Orwellian Oceania.

COUM Transmissions turn the British flag into a symbol of abhorrence, an act that resonates within the history of radical art: Dada artists defecated on the flags of all consulates at the Cabaret Voltaire in Zurich.[19] In the first Surrealist manifesto of 1924, Breton wrote: "Everything remains to be done, every means must be worth trying, in order to lay waste the ideas of family, country, religion."[20] In June 1968, the Vienna Actionists disrupted a lecture at the University of Vienna to stage an action in which they sang the Austrian National Anthem while covering themselves in excrement, vomiting, and whipping each other. In all cases, nationalism and national pride are attacked and sabotaged. The installation by COUM, *The British Government*, hijacked the Union Jack a year before Jamie Reid did so in his seminal[21] Sex Pistols designs for *Anarchy in the UK* (1976). We might call it zeitgeist; we might call it punk before punk broke. Either way, we are, beneath the overturned flag, looking at youth, pain, sadism, trash, travesty, and the malevolent circumvention of an official setting (the Musée d'art Moderne)—all topics which we will repeatedly encounter throughout this book.

A second example: in 1980, Wolfgang Müller took a polaroid self-portrait with a shaved cross as tonsure, surrounded by holes (Figure 1.3). The old avant-garde undertaking—to tear down the borders between art and life—was invoked in punk's lifestyle performances and bodily styles. Here, Müller's point of reference is Marcel Duchamp's five-pointed star tonsure (with comet-like tail), as photographed by Man Ray in 1919 or 1921 (Figure 1.4). Duchamp's self-staging touches on several roles; the star (Duchamp as a celebrity, a work of art in himself), the leader (as the incarnation of a star to be followed), the artist (though Man Ray took the photo, Duchamp credited himself as the artist, i.e. a conceptual artist), and the simultaneously emasculated and powerful, sacrificing and privileged priest. In light of Duchamp's *Rrose Sélavy*, the tonsure also seems to play with the notion of an alternative masculinity, as Giovanna Zapperi has argued.[22] Duchamp's tonsure thus signified a quite early dealing with the subversive potential of body and style.

In punk culture, apart from Müller's self-portrait polaroid, Anna Banana also ran a feature on haircuts and shavings in *VILE*,[23] which included an "homage to Duchamp" with Buster Cleveland, who kept his hair long, but shaved a five-pointed star on his crown. Wolfgang Müller's polaroid gives a first impression of how artists involved with the punk movement leaned into art history, especially the art of the early twentieth century radical avant-gardes, that is: Futurism, Dada, and Surrealism. His is a distinctly punk rendition: shabby, anti-aesthetical, no silver gelatin print, but a quick polaroid, no star to be followed, but a cross looking more like a stigma. We will be returning to this approach of quoting, but reinterpreting art history time and again throughout this book.

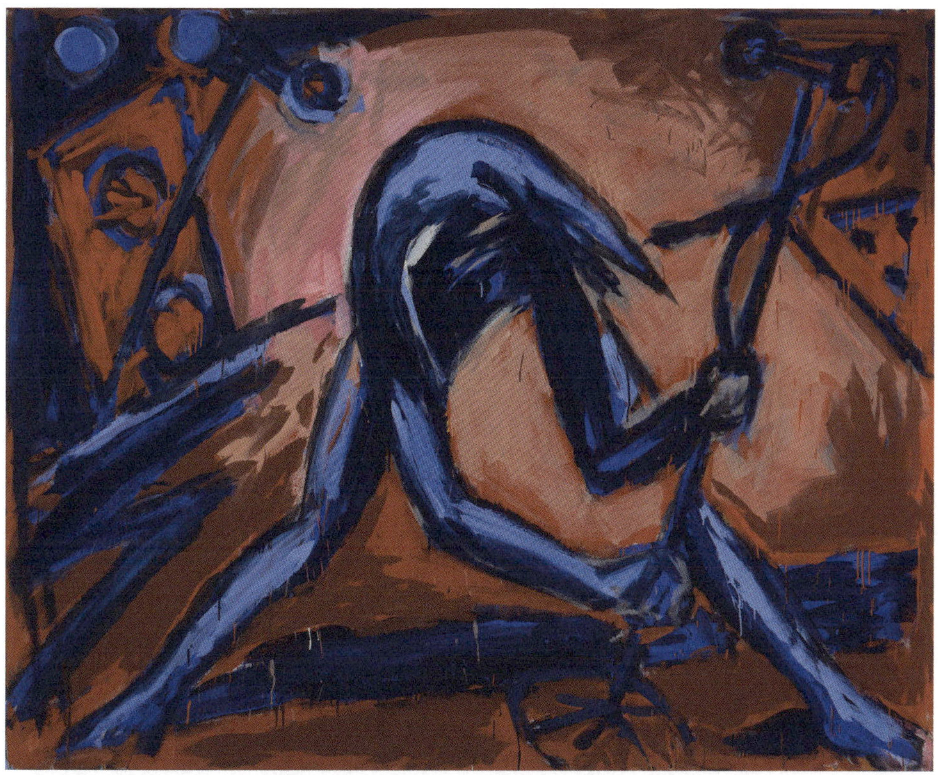

Figure 1.5: Helmut Middendorf, The Singer, *1981, ARoS Aarhus Kunstmuseum. Photograph by Ole Hein Pedersen. © VG Bild-Kunst, Bonn 2022.*

We will attempt to understand what this appropriation meant. What happens when 1970s underground artists imitate and redo modern art?

A third example of how we might look at the connection between punk and art is *The Singer* (1981, Figure 1.5). Helmut Middendorf painted his version of Pennie Smith's iconic photo of Paul Simonon of the Clash smashing his guitar on stage at the Palladium in New York (Figure 1.6). The Clash used the photo for the cover of *London Calling* (1979) together with a font that replicated the writing on Elvis Presley's debut cover. The photo itself captures a moment of rage, of losing it, of sheer physicality, and of the powerfulness of letting-it-go. In Middendorf's version, the guitar becomes a microphone, but the pose of the bent-over figure and the composition are the exact same. In an interview in 1984, Middendorf describes how he experienced SO36 and punk. He reminisces about how everyone danced by themselves:

> With regard to communication, it was dead certain the coldest joint that ever

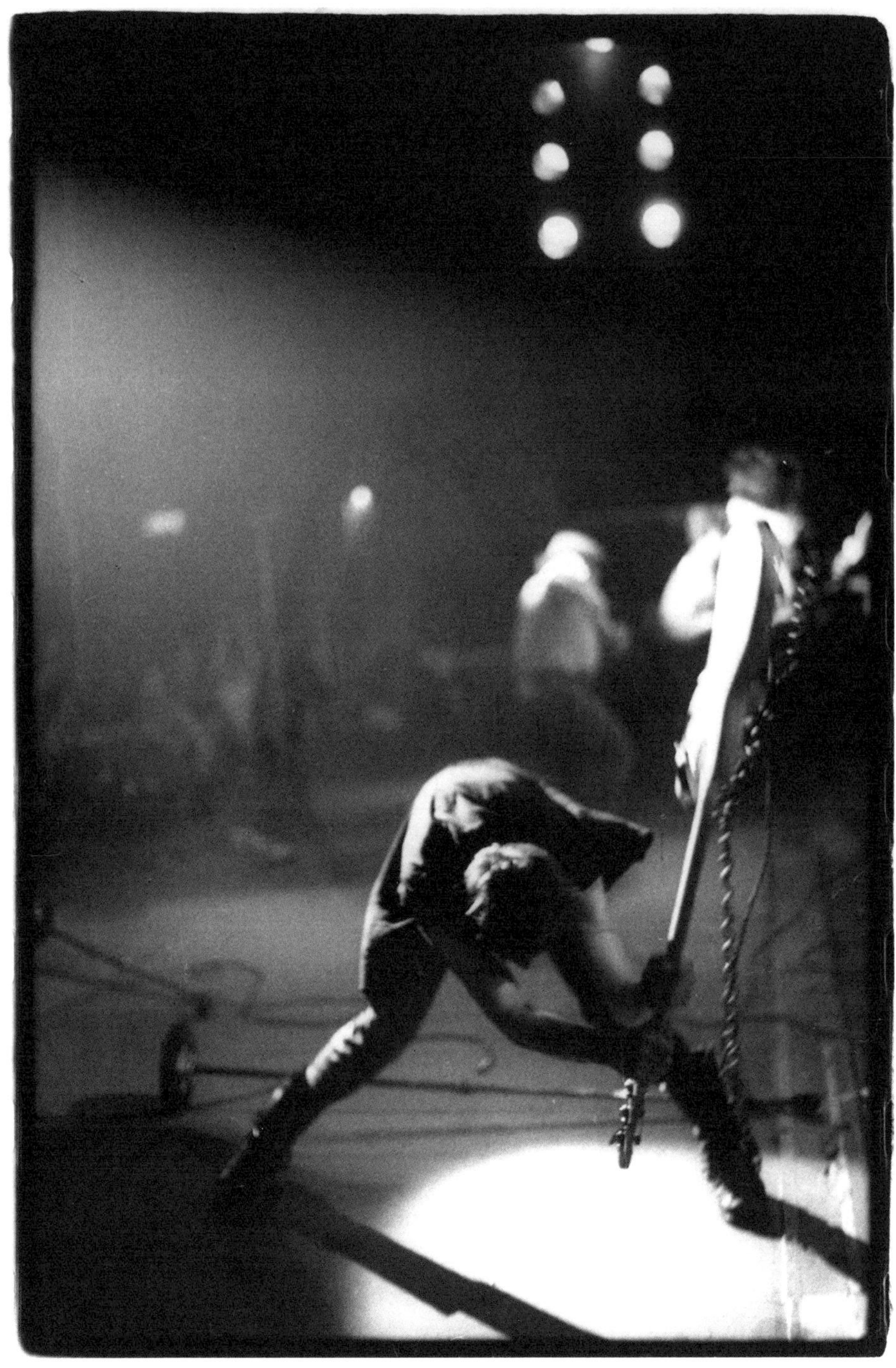

Figure 1.6: Pennie Smith, Paul Simonon performing on stage, image used for the Clash, London Calling, *1979.*

> existed. But that was something unbelievably honest […] The music was reduced, naked, direct, and that was a parallel to the pictures that we wanted to do, they were also to be pure, direct, straightforward […] The first concerts back then in SO36 and in New York, they were so intense, so tremendously intense, that I had to react in my paintings. That intensity, at the time, was not present in art, it had to be created first.[24]

The "wild" painters, gathered under the collective term the Neue Wilde ("New wild ones"), were trying to reproduce that intensity in their art. Characteristically, the Neue Wilde made no sketches, but painted directly onto either canvas or untreated cotton with acrylics or latex paint, instead of oils. The very large formats gave the act of painting an almost physical, performance-like quality. The paintings were deliberately done haphazardly and hastily, with paint splatters, raw brushstrokes, and kitschy colors in cheap materials. The other name this style was given, was thus "bad painting." The artists played up their de-skilled approach, in an attempt to transfer the accessibility of performance art into the once-elevated medium of painting.

The expression *Die Neuen Wilden* can be traced back to Wolfgang Becker's exhibition of that name in Aachen in 1980. It alluded to the French expressionist group *Les Nouveaux Fauves* and was supposed to refer both a wild aesthetic style and a wild lifestyle, which in the case of the West Berlin scene was transported in subjects like night clubs and deviant sexual practices. Middendorf, together with other key figures of the Neue Wilde in West Berlin (the so-called "Moritz Boys") established a self-help gallery at Moritzplatz in Kreuzberg in 1977 to show their paintings. The Neue Wilde were part of an international phenomenon. Comparable neo-Expressionist styles developed primarily in Italy, Scandinavia, and the USA in the late 1970s and early 1980s.[25] "The art before, especially the 70s conceptual art, it was so aseptic, so bloodless. Our generation fought that. We thought everything was sterile and boring," says Christian Lemmerz of the Danish scene.[26] This is an upheaval that took place in many genres at the time—music, art, poetry—a need to rattle things up.

These three short samples—a bricolage, a self-portrait cum Body Art, and a 180 × 200 cm large painting—give an impression of the range of cases, we are looking at. The scene is set for amateurism, provocation, appropriation, speed, destruction, sadism, and much more. The attempt here, however, is to not primarily look for parallels (in the sense of, this is what was happening in punk rock, and here is an example of something similar going on in art), but instead to look for fusions. In the years we are looking at, late 1970s to early 1980s, punk was a lifestyle that was art, a lifestyle that—in the old avant-garde sense—tried to break down the barriers between art and life as two separate categories and that furthermore invoked scandals, events, trials as artistic situations, much in the tradition of Dada and, even more, Surrealism. In punk, poetry and art coalesce, music and art coalesce, activism and art coalesce. The argument here is that in punk the separation of these entities was rendered meaningless. In *Sympathy for the Devil: Art and Rock and Roll since 1967*, Dominic Molon makes the point that the fusion of art and rock is often tied to community, noting the "insistently social nature of the convergence of art and rock music."[27] Early punk was in this sense a social movement, a shared identification as a group of outlaws and outsiders, even if nobody could really define what that shared identification meant exactly. This notorious elusiveness of punk caused quite a few misunderstandings, when diverging interpretations clashed. In the next two sections, "Negations and swindles: The elusiveness of punk" and "Case in point: The first *Punk Art* exhibition," we will take a closer look at these battles.

1.2 Negations, conflicts, and swindles: The elusiveness of punk

No cultural movement is easy to define. Punk, however, does seem a "notoriously amorphous concept," as Roger Sabin emphasizes in his anthology on the cultural legacy of punk.[28] Punk was a fusion, adapting practices from avant-garde art and political activism, as well as from rock 'n' roll youth culture. Indeed, as Jon Savage notes, "Punk brought together suburban stylists, Bowie victims, teenage runaways, hardened sixties radicals, gay men and women, artists, disco dollies, criminals, drug addicts, prostitutes of all persuasions, football hooligans, intellectuals, big beat obsessives, outcasts from every class."[29] Maybe that spectrum laid the seed for the many inherent conflicts of punk: originality vs. plagiarism, school vs. street, artificiality vs. authenticity, humor vs. seriousness, and naïveté vs. cynicism.

But punk had no great wish to be "understood" and most certainly not to be defined. Part of this resistance was perhaps due to punk's all-consuming starting point: negation. At the backbone of punk culture lies the wish to do exactly the opposite of whatever the audience, or the media, had come to expect. Anger at the status quo can be found in all of punk's early manifestations. In April of 1976, Malcolm McLaren released the Sex Pistols' first press handout: "Teenagers from London's Shepherd's Bush and Finsbury Park: 'We hate everything.'"[30] "No feelings, no future, no fun" were the essential Sex Pistols lyrics.[31] The Californian hardcore punk band Black Flag added "No values": "I've got no values / Might as well blow you away / Don't you try pretendin' / Telling me it's all right / I might start destroyin' / Everything in my sight! / No values."[32]

There is an echo here of the Dada manifesto: "Let each man proclaim: there is a great negative work of destruction to be accomplished."[33] The historical backgrounds for both movements, Dada/Surrealism and punk, were societies in moral crisis; crisis that to a certain degree was not being acknowledged. To negate was thus a way to expose: "Negation is not nihilism. Nihilism is the belief in nothing and the wish to become nothing [...] Negation is the act that would make it self-evident to everyone that the world is not as it seems," Greil Marcus stated in 1983, adding that "creation may occupy the suddenly cleared terrain."[34] Punk's negation was primarily a *tabula rasa* method; punk's NO had a purifying effect. This distinction between negation and nihilism is important yet has often been disregarded. As Kevin Mattson observes: "The mass media tried to pin one exclusive meaning on the movement by stressing its nihilistic elements."[35]

Dada and disco: True blankness

In punk's unwillingness to be comprehensible (and thereby more manageable), the movement is again not unlike Dada. "I write this manifesto to show that people can perform contrary actions together while taking one fresh gulp of air," Tristan Tzara wrote in 1918: "The contradiction and unity of poles in a single toss can be the truth."[36] Politically, punk's negation was linked with its radical disposition, although the initial pure negation gave way after some time. Jon Savage tellingly quotes George Grosz:

> We demanded more. We did not quite know how to say what that more was; but many of my friends and I did not find any solution in the merely negative, in the rage at having been deceived and in the denial of all previous values. And so we were driven more and more to the left.[37]

Grosz's description of the politicization of Dada resounds in at least one version of punk. On the reverse of the *White Riot* sleeve, for example, the Clash cite Stuart Christie and Albert Meltzer's *The Floodgates of Anarchy*: "Youth, after all, is not a permanent condition, and a clash of generations is not so fundamentally dangerous to the art of government as would be a clash between rulers and ruled."[38] As one of the first teenage movements, punk turned its rage not only towards parents but "right where it belongs, at the rich and powerful," as Robert Christgau notes.[39] Anarchism to some was an actual political philosophy, to others more of a slogan.[40] Although punk is often given left-wing political credentials, it was, as a movement, first and foremost radical and critical. Punks took pleasure in ostracized positions, including reactionary lumpen-proletarianism or skinhead aggression.

Punk attempted to escape annexation by the cultural elite and to avoid being defined. One manifestation of this was punk pranksterism, or the "swindle." In his essay on Julien Temple's 1980 Sex Pistols mockumentary *The Great Rock 'n' Roll Swindle*—a prime example of punk's determination to deceive, confuse, and obscure, and the great delight taken therewith—David Huxley tellingly concludes: "The closer punk is examined [...] the more elusive it becomes."[41] Or—as punk musician Marco Pirroni put it in 2005:

> It [punk] was just a big promo to sell trousers, it was a working-class social revolution, it was an art school prank, it was a posey fashion experiment, it was all about the music, man, it was a record company marketing campaign, it was left-wing, it was neo-Nazi, it was fascist, it was apolitical, it was an anti-drug, pro-amphetamine anti-sex shag-fest, it was racists who loved reggae, it was against disco, but danced to Donna Summer, we came not to praise Elvis, but to dress like him, we hate Pink Floyd, we love Pink Floyd [...] Boredom with a passion, the worse it is, the better it is [...] If I have to explain, you can't understand."[42]

Regarding "[t]he fiction of a punk movement that was neither organized nor produced (yet shared and globalized) by members of the working class in good faith, honest and not bookish," Eloy Fernández Porta notes: "This has been, for a long time, the greatest of the punk 'swindles', in many cases maintained against all evidence."[43] Perplexed by punk's inner contradictions, however, the broader society and media often reacted by reducing punk to exactly that rock cliché it never wanted to be.

Punk's fear of being coopted, however, sometimes lead to choosing the wrong enemy. When, for example, Debbie Harry of pioneer punk band Blondie performed the disco-infused "Heart of Glass" on NBC's *The Midnight Special* (in October 1979), she was accused of betrayal, of losing her artistic integrity, of being a sell-out. The punk community also showed its chauvinist side in targeting Harry specifically, portraying her, rather than co-founder Chris Stein, as the one "freaking" under the strains of success, not capable of managing herself.[44] Yet Blondie as a band had always been open-minded, and the affinity with disco was not new: they had played Donna Summer's "I Feel Love" at CBGB's in 1978. Although they were later conceived as opposites, there were at the time several elements binding disco and punk together: they were "low" culture, "low" art, defying the canon. They were inclusive of the oppressed. From the outset both punk and disco were closely intertwined and partly originated in the gay community (of New York of the 1970s). Both were urban, hedonistic, artificial. Both did not require high skill, and there was almost no separation between performer and audience. Savage has even portrayed disco as more blatant in its societal critique. "The dancing steps required of a Disco champion are so formulaic that to excel he must become an automaton," he writes of John Travolta's character in *Saturday Night Fever* (1977): "This was the true blankness to which the punks never came close. The hedonism propagated by Disco was more immediately subversive of established morality."[45]

The depiction of rock as particularly profound in contrast to, for example, R'n'B and disco tunes can at times have a taste of that old "lone wolf" or "lone genius" trope, often implicitly male too. There can be a breathtaking arrogance in the judgmental attitude within not only punk, but rock more generally, against more flashy, danceable, and gregarious styles. This is a point that Shane Greene touches upon too, in the introduction to *Punk! Las Américas Edition*, when he criticizes how McNeil and Holmstrom (of *PUNK* magazine) position punk in opposition to disco: "They did so by appropriating rock's long-standing claim toward musical 'authenticity,' which is too often a masquerade for expressing racial, class, and gendered anxieties about other bodies and bodily movements."[46] In 1979, artist Dan Graham wrote about Ohio punk band Devo's discordant, disco-beat style that "the group is deliberately playing on the assumption that punks are against disco and are thus anti-lower-class Black/ Italian/ Hispanic music [...] The corporate rock industry prefers to divide minority groups into separate markets."[47] Devo opposed that prejudiced, stereotypical confinement, Graham reasons. Likewise, being a first-generation punk band, like Blondie, and then to play "Heart of Glass" on TV, at a time when both punk and disco were about to solidify into mutual opponents, might thus be considered a very punk thing to do. "Punk and everything punk called for the opposite," as Munuera argues.[48] Blondie and Devo thus also moved against that alleged deepness of (punk) rock vs. the alleged superficiality of other musical genres. Surely, the point which Dan Graham makes is of the essence: Punks turning not against the multi-racial and queer communities of disco, but rather against that very superficial way in which both punk *and* disco were being "sanitized" into the mainstream.

The inner conflicts of punk were of course also present when it came to art. We will take a closer look at the "Art school vs. hard school" conflict in the next section. For now, let us focus on two short anecdotes that underline this tension in punk and the misunderstandings among different punk fractions. One story took place in West Berlin in a clash between Martin Kippenberger and Rat Jenny; another story took place in Copenhagen in a clash between punks at the Ungdomshuset (Youth house) and the band Einstürzende Neubauten.

Dialogue with the youth of today

Currents and countercurrents ran between and within the factions of squatters, street punks, post-punks, artists, and the first formations of the left-wing autonomist scene in West Berlin in the late 1970s and early 1980s. The half-city was small, and everybody went to the same few alternative venues, where all these groups both cross-fertilized and clashed with one another. One of those venues was the SO36 in Kreuzberg, named after its postal code Süd-Ost 36 (South-East 36), a hub for the synergetic mix of art and music in West Berlin at the time.

In 1978, artist Martin Kippenberger moved to West Berlin and rented SO36. For about a year, he managed the place with a caustic sense of arrogance. He aggravated the punk regulars with "Luxus in SO36"[49] posters, wore a coat and tie, and raised the price of beer, which he also sold on tap instead of in the aluminum cans that the punks preferred for their trashiness, cheapness, and throw-away aesthetic. Together with his gallerist-to-be Gisela Captain, he opened Kippenbergers Büro (Kippenberger's office) on a factory floor in Kreuzberg.[50] Kippenberger was not trying to cut out the middleman, but rather to be one himself. He consciously played (with) the role of grand provocateur, parodying the greedy impresario. But the irony was lost on some. At a WIRE concert at SO36 in 1979, a group of masked and hooded punks, the so-called Kommando gegen Konsumterror (Commando against consumerist terror) attacked the SO36, vandalized it, stole the cash box, and distributed a flyer that read: "Destroy SO36! Punx gegen Konsumscheisse! Eine Mark für eine Dose Bier! Raus mit der Ku-Damm Schickeria!" (Punx against consumerist shit! One mark for a can of beer! Out with the KuDamm jet set!—KuDamm being the prominent West Berlin shopping street Kurfürstendamm).[51]

The culmination of the SO36 conflict was the night when Kippenberger was beaten up so badly by Ratten-Jenny (Rat-Jenny, aka Jenny Schmidt) that he ended up in hospital. She was one of the punks who had been turned down at the doors of SO36. There are many versions of the story, including Kippenberger's,[52] Rat-Jenny's, and journalist Guido Schirmeyer's.[53] In one version, Rat-Jenny and a pack of punks ambushed Kippenberger; in another, it was just the two of them fighting and he hurt her first. In the third version, he called her a "cunt" and she then attacked him with a broken beer bottle. In any case, Kippenberger subsequently turned Jutta Henglein's photo of his bandaged visage (Figure 1.7) into a now-iconic painting with the title *Dialog mit der Jugend* (*Dialogue with the Youth of Today*, 1981, Figure 1.8), the centerpiece of his *Berlin bei Nacht* (*Berlin at Night*) triptych. After the incident, Kippenberger moved to Paris, "where art does not collide as fiercely with punk," as Wolfgang Müller viciously notes.[54]

The incident of Rat-Jenny beating up Kippenberger is more nuanced than the clichés of a berserk punk who resorted to violence because she was upset about the price of beer, or of an unworldly artist who did not understand what he had gotten himself into. Rat-Jenny (at least in hindsight) was angry about Kippenberger's "brutal" treatment of women.[55] In Wolfgang Müller's account, Kippenberger was ignorant of his

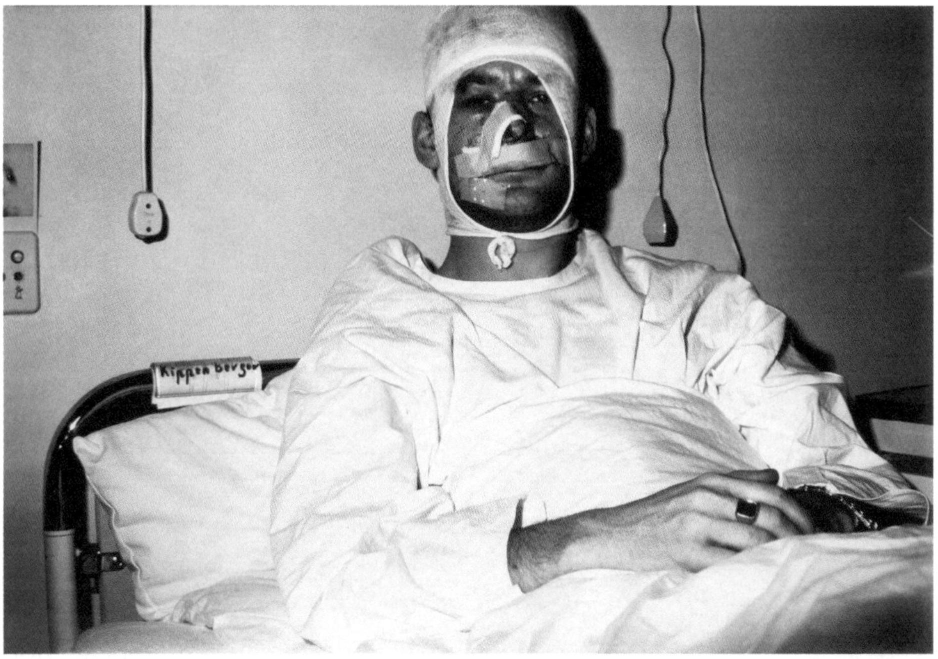

Figure 1.7: Martin Kippenberger at the hospital, 1981. Photograph by Jutta Henglein-Bildau. Courtesy of Jutta Henglein-Bildau.

own privileges, and accordingly his provocations were unfiltered and insensible: "He was running around name-calling, what's up, you faggot, what's up, you negro. But as a white male, you are not in opposition if you do that, you are just right in the middle of society."[56]

On the other hand, Kippenberger's tendency to self-sabotage, his persistent mocking of not only everyone (indiscriminately!) around him but also himself makes the story a bit more complicated. His direct, yet theatrical handling of the attack by Rat-Jenny incorporated punk elements. The title of the painting, *Dialogue with the Youth of Today*, shows Kippenberger's use of one-liners and wry humor. Kippenberger was in his late 20s at the time of the incident, only about three years older than Rat-Jenny. The work simultaneously mocks the brutality of violence (the "dialogue" in the title) and spins it into a myth (oil on canvas! The artist-martyr!). As Marcus Verhagen writes: "Martin Kippenberger liked to overplay his hand. He did it on principle, turning comedy into farce and grand drama into *opéra bouffe* [...] When confronted with exalted reputations or principled positions, Kippenberger responded like a person with Tourette's Syndrome."[57] Kippenberger carried both his wounds and his weaknesses openly. In his re-versioning of Beuys' aphorism, Kippenberger inverted the message to "Jeder Künstler ist ein Mensch"

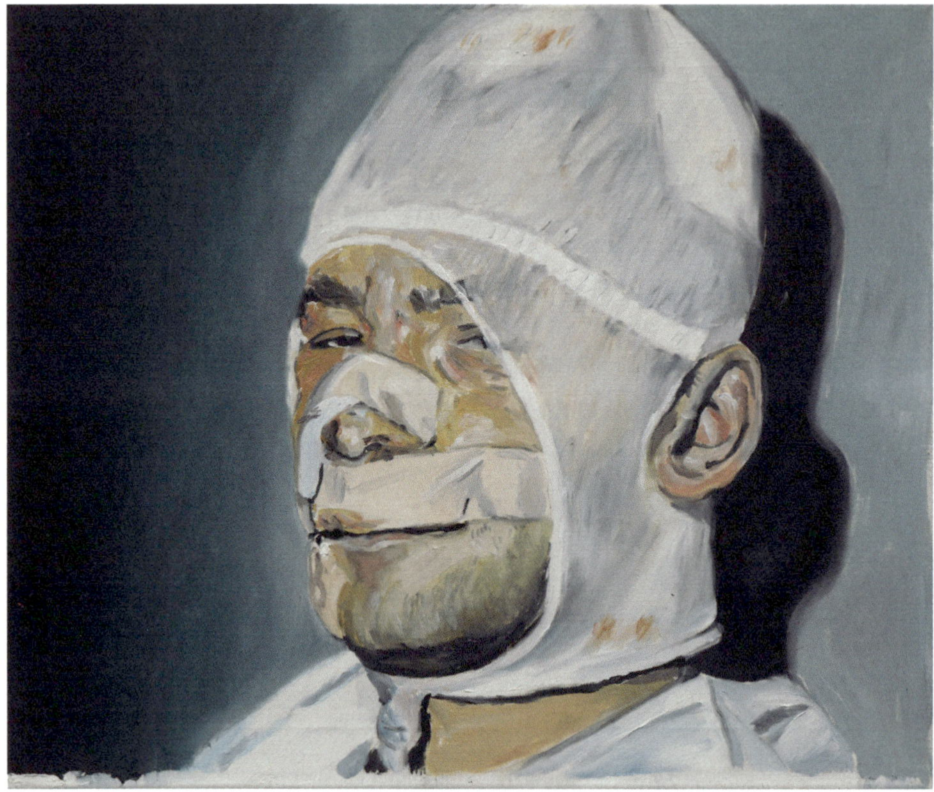

Figure 1.8: Martin Kippenberger, Dialog mit der Jugend (Dialogue with the Youth of Today)*, 1981. Part of the triptych* Berlin bei Nacht (Berlin at Night). *Courtesy of the Estate of Martin Kippenberger, Galerie Gisela Capitain, Cologne. Photograph by Simon Vogel.*

(every artist is a human, instead of every human is an artist).[58] This embrace of failure and human shortcomings does have a punk feeling to it.

"In the Louvre, they asked me to sign the hole!"

Some years later in Copenhagen, another clash between punk and art occurred, when the Einstürzende Neubauten played at Ungdomshuset. This time, the story is also about history: destruction of history, understanding of history, and identity through history.

In the early 1980s, many from the punk movement moved on to the BZ (squatter) movement, which really gained momentum after a playground (*byggeren*) was torn down to refurbish the so-called "black square" at Nørrebro. An activist group calling for a youth house was put together. A major feature of the urban renewal planning of the 1960s and 1970s was the tearing down of older buildings to build new housing blocks, a policy which the social democratic mayor Egon Weidekamp came to embody. He had trouble understanding the squatters; "Do you know what I have fought for my whole life? To give workers a home with their own toilet and bath and hot water, so that no one would have to live like my family out in Viborggade!" he exclaimed at one debate.[59] After extensive discussions and street battles, however, he did give the squatters the right to use the former Folkets Hus (The People's House) for that purpose. As Sune Carlsson Kølster writes, the punks were the first to come and the last to leave at the Youth House.[60]

The former People's House had a history. Like other housing for workers, it was built in the late 1870s during the second wave of industrialization. It was funded by workers from Nørrebro, had been used by Kvindeligt Arbejderforbund (The Association of Women Workers), and in 1910, had been visited both by Lenin and by Rosa Luxemburg.[61] This historical background was fitting to this milieu, which was more political than the first generation of punks. Decisions were made at meetings every Monday, where topics were debated until an agreement was reached; there was no voting. Several queer festivals and cross-dressing parties took place in the house.[62] Furthermore, street art and graffiti were a key part of the Youth House culture, and several artists, such as Ulrik Crone and later Rose Eken, exhibited there. The rules in the self-proclaimed anarchistic Youth House were "no sexism, no homophobia (later changed to: no heterosexism), no violence, no hard drugs."[63] The Youth House was a beloved house, and the people involved with the house saw themselves in a specific historical tradition that was connected with that house.

When Einstürzende Neubauten played a concert at the Youth House in 1984, however, they were not aware of the history of the house. N.U. Unruh smashed some stucco off a balcony with a Kango hammer, onto which he had also mounted a microphone to use as an instrument, as in many other concerts. "My thought was to redesign the stucco on the balcony, which was already broken. It is a critique of bourgeois architecture," N.U. Unruh stated years later.[64] The episode, nevertheless, led to serious trouble with the punks at the Youth House, who confiscated the Kango hammer, threw bottles at N.U. Unruh, hitting him on the forehead, and smashed the windows and slashed the tires of Einstürzende Neubauten's tour car. "I didn't think anyone loved that house so much," N.U. Unruh explains, "Never before and never again did I experience a reaction like at the Youth House. When I used the Kango hammer in the Louvre in Paris, they asked me to sign the hole!"[65] When a compilation of the best concerts at the Youth House was released in 2005, Einstürzende Neubauten only agreed to be involved on the condition that a subtitle was added behind their track, in brackets: "('we want the Kango-hammer back!')."

1.3 Case in point: The first *Punk Art* exhibition, 1978

Kippenberger being beaten up by Rat-Jenny and the Youth House punks slashing the tires of N.U. Unruh's tour car point to the cultural clashes within punk culture. At the same time, they point toward a culture that revered clashes: the humor in the tackling of these conflicts is inherently punk, too. Artist Nina Sten-Knudsen, after describing a fight she had had with poet Søren Ulrik Thomsen (see section 4.2 "Punk poetry"), sums it up: "[It] was all about pushing each other."[66] How fittingly then, that the very first *Punk Art* exhibition, which was first shown in Washington, DC, and in New York in 1978 and then traveled to Amsterdam in 1979, likewise caused a collision. This case is likewise interesting, because it shows the diverging perceptions of what punk art was or should be.[67]

The curators of the East Coast show, Marc Miller and Bettie Ringma, were rolling with the early New York punk crowd at CBGB. Their ideas about punk art were influenced by that scene, leaning on pop and hype, whereas the punk art scene in Amsterdam stood in the tradition of art activist groups. But first things first. The impetus for the *Punk Art* exhibition came from the finding that the New York punk scene was full of visual artists. About choosing what work to include, Marc Miller explains:

> We were just artists who were hanging out at CBGBs. And it became clear that there were a lot of visual artists there, so the show we did drew 80-90 percent out of the people that were at CBGBs. That was before it really opened up, so it was a small group of regulars. So much of it was just obvious, you didn't even need to think about it! We started with *Punk* magazine, because they kind of named the movement, you know. They came out of the School of Visual Arts, were cartoonists, they were connected with all the groups. They were at the center of the scene, even though they were very young kids. John [Holmstrom] and Legs [McNeil], they were just looking for action. […] We didn't have a very big roaster [*sic*] there, so it filled up pretty quickly.[68]

The "not very big roaster" was the Washington Project for the Arts, an art space led by Alice Denney. Denney had been an important advocate of Pop Art in the 1960s, and when Miller and Ringma approached her with the idea of a punk art exhibition, she saw punk art as a similar faction. In an interview with Howard Smith, she recounted: "A lot of people are upset. Many of the board members obviously don't even consider it a valid art form. But I knew better than to be put off by pejorative responses. I did the first Pop Art show down here back in '66, long before that was considered acceptable."[69] At 50, the press dubbed her the "Doyenne of Punk," a role she gladly embraced (Figure 1.9).

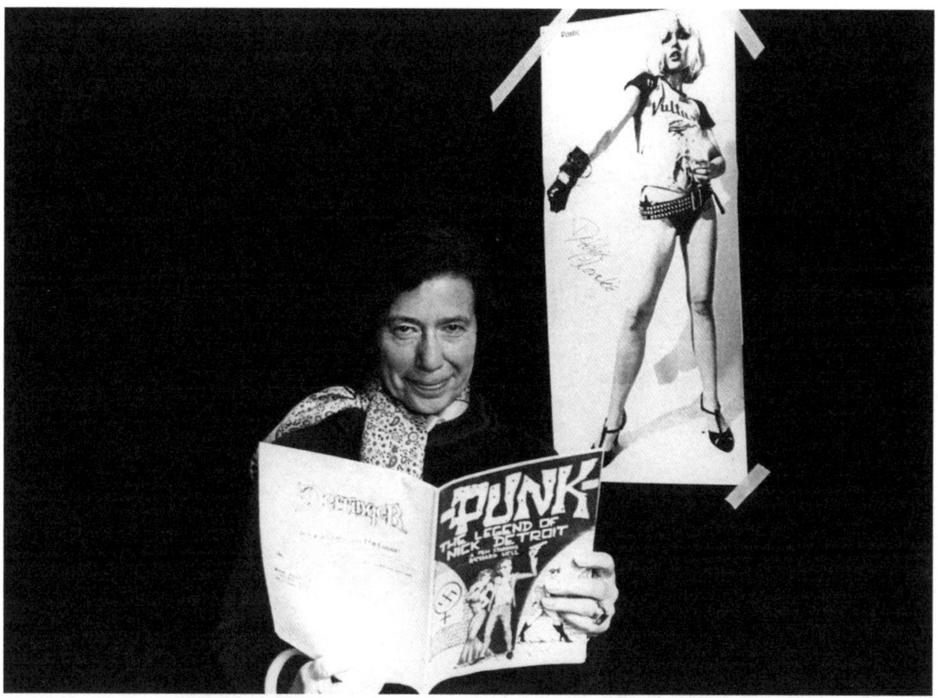

Figure 1.9: Alice Denney with PUNK *magazine, 1978. Archive of Marc Miller. Courtesy of 98Bowery.com.*

The *Punk Art* exhibition comprised 30 artists working in diverse media: drawing, bricolage, painting, installation, cartoon, film, photography, and fashion. The artists came from both inside and outside the artworld. Some were represented in the hip galleries of the art district of SoHo, and others distanced themselves from that scene. "There was a lot of hypocrisy," Miller remembers,

> Everybody was pretending to be anti-art, especially the ones most connected to the artworld. Well, they did not want to be playing that artworld game anymore. […] There was a rebellion against art, but because at that time there was so much art-for-art's-sake around and a kind of formalism.[70]

In their press release, the curators recreated the rock 'n' roll excitement of punk:

> What is it? Why is it? Where is it? When is it? *Punk Art* is the most ambitious show ever mounted at the Washington Projects for the Arts […] The Punk movement is the most energetic statement of the seventies. It stems from a generation of artists which grew up with television as their best friend where they viewed violence, sex, and cigarette commercials daily.[71]

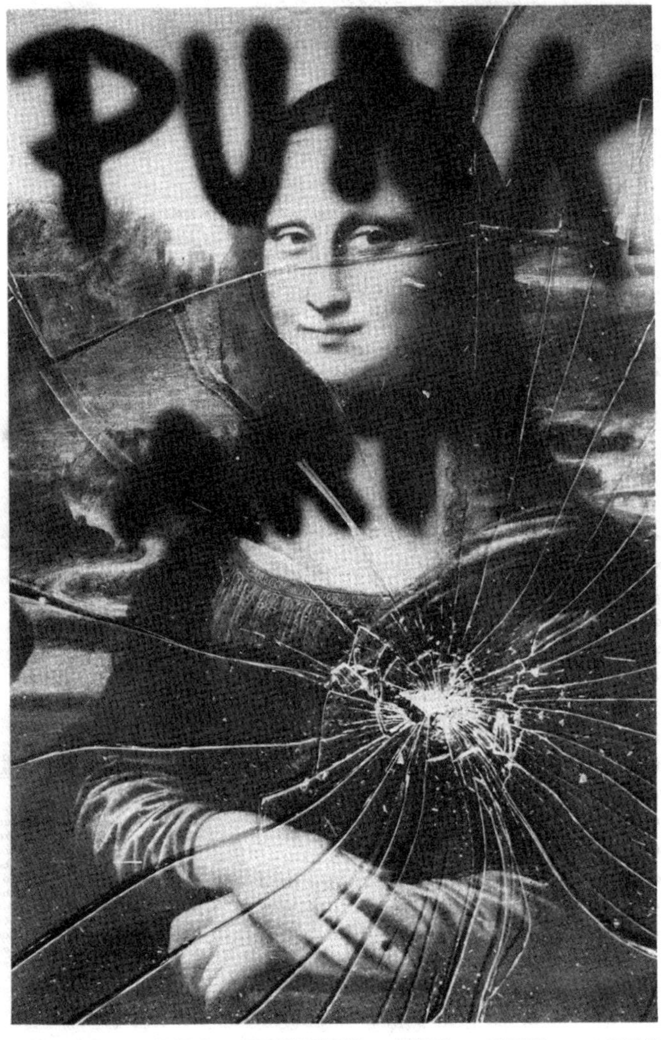

Figure 1.10: March H. Miller, Bettie Ringma, and Curt Hoppe, Smashed Mona, *1978. Front cover of the catalogue of the* Punk Art *exhibition, Washington Project for the Arts, Washington DC, May 15–June 10, 1978. Archive of Marc Miller. Courtesy of 98Bowery.com.*

Punk was thus equated with bored, antisocial, and mass-media-consuming teenagers. Toward the press, the curators represented the punk movement as all boldness and action. "It was a little bit of hype, a little bit of manipulation," says Miller:

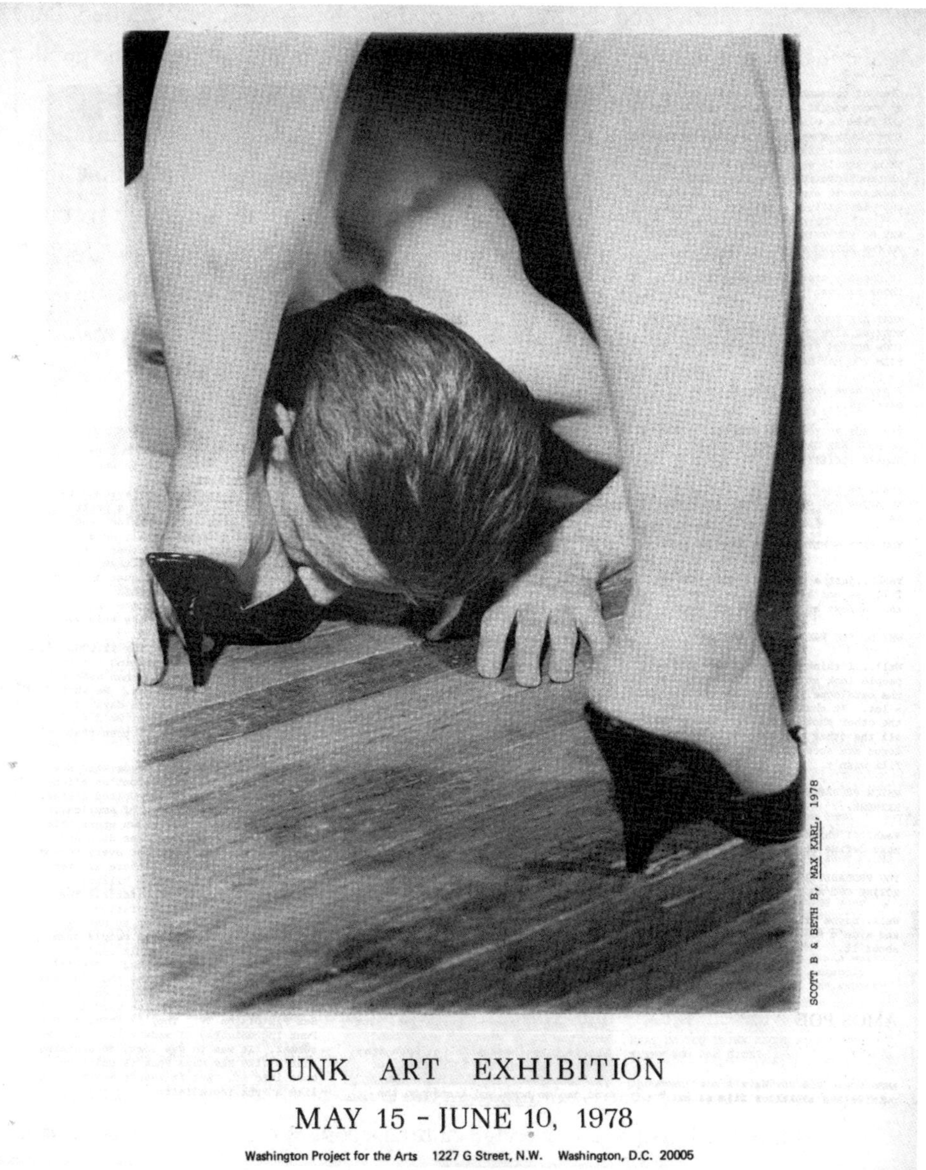

Figure 1.11: Scott B & Beth B, Max Karl*, 1978. Front cover of the catalogue of the* Punk Art *exhibition, Washington Project for the Arts, Washington DC, May 15–June 10, 1978. Archive of Marc Miller. Courtesy of 98Bowery.com.*

Just coming up with ways to personify the concept of punk. We knew that the term punk art was ripe for attention [...] There were some we left out, although they would have fit in. Just because it did not match the public perception of punk [...]. We did not want to confuse people too much.[72]

The more contemplative and doubting sides of punk thus were largely omitted. Punk's social criticism, self-destruction, and pain were not in focus, at least not in the publicity for the show (in the works themselves, however, these sentiments often were).

Instead, the PR emphasized provocation. "We phrased it as an invasion of Washington. We were not just gonna do a punk art show, we were gonna invade Washington. That had a lot to do with Legs [McNeil], who was a terrific provocateur," Miller recounts.[73] The image of punk art invading Washington worked. Howard Smith, for example, writes how the exhibition is within "throw-up distance from the White House."[74] In a release from Associated Press, which was picked up by many local newspapers, the "bizarre outfits" of the "several hundred guests" present at the vernissage were described extensively.[75] The coverage thus mostly affirmed an image of punk that was about attention-seeking fashion and provocation. The key visual used on the invitation, the poster and the catalogue was a work by Bettie Ringma and Marc Miller themselves, in collaboration with Curt Hoppe: *Smashed Mona* (1978). It showed a black-and-white reproduction of Leonardo da Vinci's *Mona Lisa* (*c.*1503–06) behind smashed glass, with the title "PUNK ART" spray-painted across the image, above and beneath Mona Lisa's face (Figure 1.10). It was a fairly simple gesture of destruction, outbreak, and Duchamp reference. The image seemed to suggest that, whereas Duchamp in *L.H.O.O.Q.* (1919), had only bestowed the Mona Lisa with a moustache and suggested her ass were on fire (*L.H.O.O.Q. = Elle a chaud au cul*), punk art would simultaneously break her free of the museum glass and more irreversibly and recklessly demolish the Old Masters. The back side of the *Punk Art* catalogue was a work by Scott B. and Beth B. called *Max Karl*: A naked man kneeling on the floor to kiss the black lacquer stiletto pumps of a standing woman (Figure 1.11). In combination with the title, we have here an ironic commentary on power relations.

Legs McNeil, meanwhile, was also pursuing another goal: to distance US punk from UK punk, especially the likes of the Clash, who had recently released their socio-critical "I'm so bored with the USA" (1977 in the UK), formulating a punk version of the 1970s leftwing rejection of a perceived US cultural, economic, and military imperialism. McNeil wrote a "Punk Manifesto" (Figure 1.12) which he not only distributed to the press, but also wrote on the walls of the art space:

> [Punk is not] asexual faggot hippie blood-sucking ignorant scum as the media would have you believe. Elements of that behavior pattern has infiltrated this country from England. The English bands with their uncool need for media attention have perverted the term punk […] Everyone knows shit flows to the top.[76]

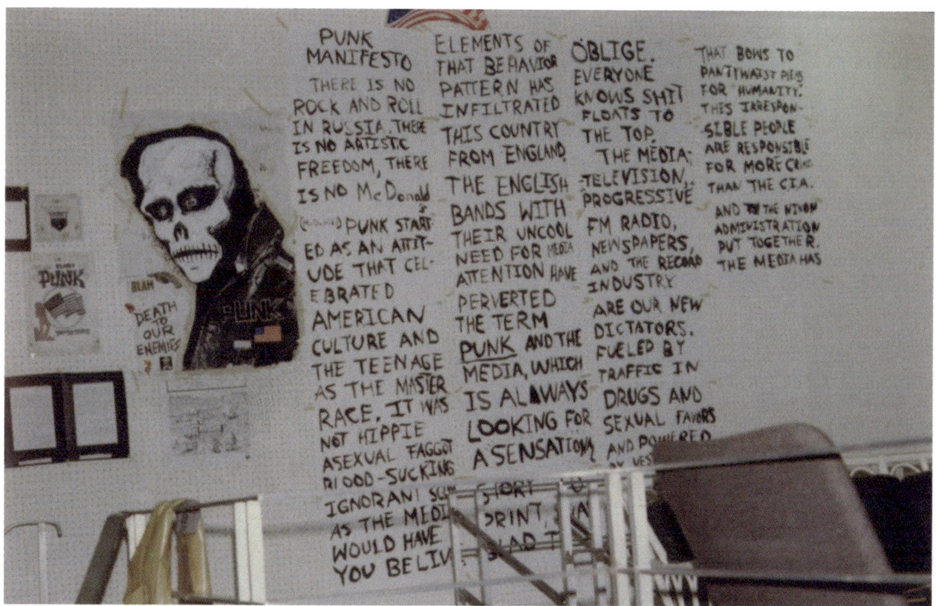

Figure 1.12: Legs McNeil, "Punk Manifesto," 1978. Archive of Marc Miller. Courtesy of 98Bowery.com.

McNeil's statement was not included in the *American Punk Art* exhibition in Amsterdam (he did not travel there to write it on the wall), but that looming conflict between different perceptions of punk, and the rejection of what was regarded as American cultural imperialism, just added to the circumstances that altogether guaranteed this show was bound for a battle.

The reason Marc Miller and Bettie Ringma had the idea to go to Amsterdam was that Ringma was Dutch and knew Karen Kvernenes, who owned Art Something. After the shows in Washington and New York, punk art had momentum. The exhibition had to be reduced to avoid shipping costs, but it still featured most of the key names from the US show: Holmstrom and McNeil, Curt Hoppe, Tina L'Hotsky, Ruth Marten, Robert Mapplethorpe, Tom Otterness, Marcia Resnick, Screaming Mad George, Arturo Vega, among others. The flyer accompanying the exhibition announced a series of events at the Kunsthistorisch Centrum (Art Historical Center), including a panel discussion with Ringma and Miller with the title "punk art: sex, geweld, geld, en sensatie" (punk art: sex, violence, money, and sensation) on June 8, 1979.

This focus on hype alone did not go down well with the social involvement that had arisen within the punk movement and which the artists of the KoeCrandt group held high. The KoeCrandt group was a loosely structured group centered around two squat houses on Sarphatistraat, which were used to live and work in, and which over the years became known as the punk club DDT666, Gallery ANUS, Gallery Ozon, and Zebra House. The mouthpiece of the group was their zine *KoeCrandt*, which Hugo Kaagman started together with punk musician Ludwig Wisch, aka Lulu Zulu. By early 1978, the poets Kristian Kanstadt and Diana Ozon and graffiti artist Dr Rat had joined in. Their house, at the time called Gallery ANUS, was a multipurpose space. The artists showed punk objects as what could be described as objets trouvés, willfully fetishizing the everyday remains of punk and connecting themselves to a Dada tradition of leftover bricolage, as we can find, for example, in the work of Kurt Schwitters, or the Surrealists browsing flea markets for the objects of yesterday. ANUS also hosted the editorial offices of *KoeCrandt* and it was an open workshop where visitors could use the stencils or sewing machines, where concerts were organized, leaflets printed, zines sold, bikes repaired. Young runaways came to the gallery and were helped out with official forms. With this kind of merging of social activism and art, the ideas of the KoeCrandt artists, especially Ozon and Kaagman, about punk art were fundamentally different to the ones of Ringma and Miller.

This divide was further enhanced by a large article in the art section of *Het Parool*. Under the headline "Punk Art: schreeuw om aandacht" ("Punk art screams for attention"), Miller and Ringma were interviewed, and Ringma stated, "The emphasis in all this art, and also the music, which we call punk, lies on violence, sensation, ego-tripping, and attention-grabbing."[77] Furthermore, the two curators dismissed the local scene in the interview. Miller admits:

> We did not know anything. We did not know there were any punks in Amsterdam. We knew there were punks in England, we had met The Damned. But there were punks in Amsterdam, it turned out, and some of our quotes in *Het Parool* did not go down well with them, we said like 'there is no punk in Amsterdam' which was just ignorance, so they got rattled up. But ok, in the show in Washington, we had a punk band playing against a disco band, you know, you want a battle, you want a fight, you want a little tension. This time it was not deliberately, but, you know, it got us a lot of write-ups, and nothing bad happened. The punks put a note on our door, and we got some negative reviews.[78]

Miller also explains the addition of *American* to the *Punk Art* title of the show;

> Around that time, it was becoming increasingly clearer that a lot was happening in London, and it was different. So that was why we tagged on *American* to *Punk Art* in the title, which annoyed a lot of people! I think, maybe they could've given us a pass.

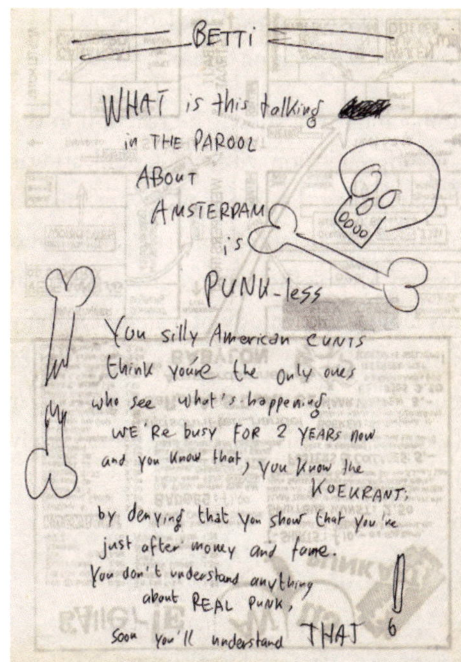

BETTI

WHAT is this talking in THE PAROOL ABOUT AMSTERDAM is PUNK-less

You silly American CUNTS think you're the only ones who see what's happening

WE'RE busy FOR 2 YEARS now and you know that, you know the KOEKRANT;

by denying that you show that you're just after money and fame.

You don't understand anything about REAL PUNK,

Soon you'll understand THAT 6

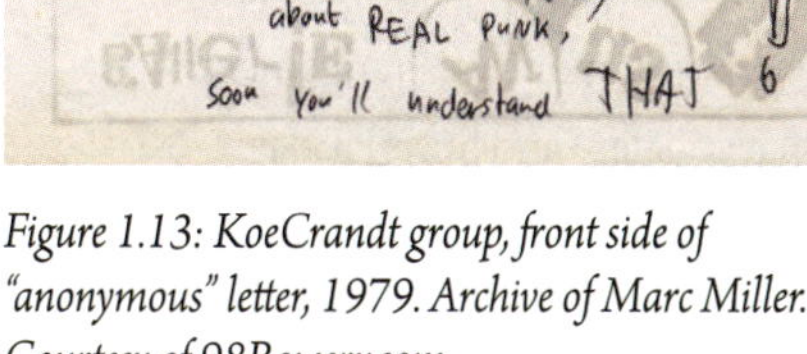

Figure 1.13: KoeCrandt group, front side of "anonymous" letter, 1979. Archive of Marc Miller. Courtesy of 98Bowery.com.

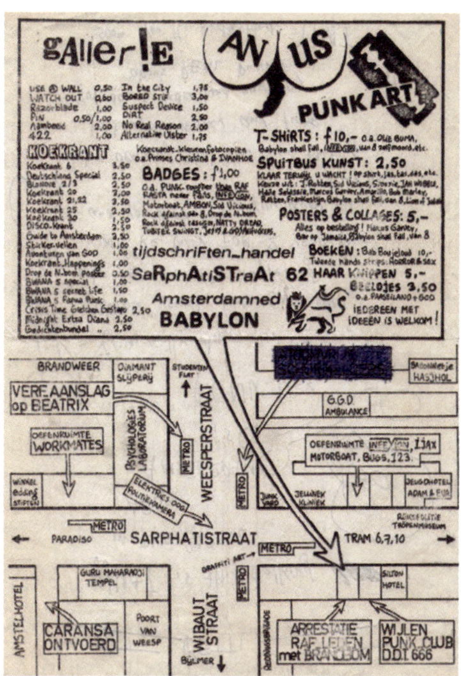

Figure 1.14: KoeCrandt group, back side of "anonymous" letter, 1979. Archive of Marc Miller. Courtesy of 98Bowery.com.

No such thing would happen. Instead, a threatening letter (Figure 1.13), unsigned, but written on the back of a Gallery ANUS flyer (Figure 1.14), was posted on the door of Art Something one night. It read "You silly American CUNTS think you're the only ones who see what's happening [...] You don't understand anything about REAL PUNK, soon you'll understand THAT!"[80]

"We thought it was posh American art which had nothing to do with punk. And indeed, it had nothing to do with the kids here in the streets," says Ozon, "But they were saying 'this is how it is' [...] it was such an arrogance."[81] Thus the problem lay in the representation of punk, in the attention it got in the local media, and also in the lack of interest for punk in Amsterdam. Kaagman states:

> Sure, we wrote that "anonymous" note. We were non-commercial, both the musicians and the artists. [...] And why did they not come to us? They never came to us, we had to go them! Who the fuck do they think they are? We were not jealous, but we thought they were stealing our movement! Typical American. They think they know better. And they know nothing about what is going on here, about

squatting, or anything. [...] We went to the opening but we never talked to them. They had no roots here, they did not check out what was going on here.[82]

It was not only the punks who were complaining about the show. The reaction in the established *Museum Journal* gives a hint of the incomprehension with which punk art was met. Feminist art historian Rosa Lindenburg complained that the works were "macho art" and among others criticized Robert Mapplethorpe as an "anti-feministic" artist, who "glorifies the male body," which—in the context of Mapplethorpe's progressive, liberal stance and his fight for LGBTQ rights—seems almost like parody of a stereotypically bigoted feminist position.[83] Lindenburg thus exemplifies the lack of understanding of some older feminists towards punk in particular, and more generally of the younger generation's understanding of sex and gender (which we will also be looking more closely at in the section "Punk feminism: Vamp up!").

On a note of self-reflection, Miller admits,

> The review that stung the most was by Gerard Pas in *Artzien*. [...] He was our first friend in Amsterdam but his negative review caused a temporary estrangement. It contained more than an ounce of truth and it still resonates (and hurts) today.[84]

Under the title, "The Great Art Swindle???," Pas writes:

> This brings us to the reason for this criticism and that is the "American Punk Art" exhibition. I believe that the premises of such an exhibition are quite justified although I find that the way in which this collection of material has been compiled under the title "American Blah Blah" is truly facinorous and that they who have been involved in expressing the product of their labor over the last years would be saddened by the lapidicolous manner in which their works have been handled by the organizers whose names fill the pages of *Het Parool*.[85]

Pas asserted that it was not the artists in the exhibition, but rather the makers of the show, who were "ego-tripping and attention-grabbing," as Ringma had put it. The integrity of the artists, Pas argued, was compromised by the superficial branding of their work. If we go back to the original exhibition in Washington, an Associated Press reporter quoted one "Helen, an art gallery owner who uses no last name" and who had a "crayon tattoo" (not a real one) in demonstrating the kind of horror Pas envisions: "Punk Art [...] may be misunderstood, but it should not be ignored," the woman stated: "In ten years everyone will want to own some punk art."[86] If ever there were a hope in punk's "No Future" it would be the avoidance of ending up as one more "at first misunderstood, but now acclaimed" eccentric art label, as celebrated by Helen, art gallery owner with fake tattoo. The PR done by Ringma and Miller did nothing to prevent that, but rather bought into it.

Forty years later, the dust has settled. There was more common ground between the artists in Amsterdam and New York than the battle between them at first suggests. "We were total outsiders when we did that show. Later I learnt more about the context," Miller recognizes,[87] whereas Kaagman now concedes "Well, perhaps the art itself was not that bad. Some of it I actually really liked, it was pretty sick."[88] Like the whole punk movement, punk art is also a self-contradictory and mutating phenomenon. It can be the affirmation of trash culture, the adulation of fast food, teenage sex, beer cans, cheap dollars, cartoon excitement, tabloid hype. Andy Warhol's provocations loomed in this affirmation—we will dive deeper into this question in Chapter 3: "Pop Multiples, Camp Affirmations." It is an important point that this hype and trash strategy was not without critical edge: it was about overthrowing the bloated self-righteousness of high culture and formalism; it was about punctuating the bubble of l'art pour l'art. Regardless of its relevance, such a stance might however be misunderstood as hollow. Another artistical strategy was the one of the KoeCrandt artists, in which the social aspect was pronounced. As we shall see, both these sides of punk manifested within punk artistical output, and both were tied to the history of art. Before we go further into the different topics and strategies of punk art, however, I will try to do a fairly quick run-though of the attempts to catch the "art" in punk hitherto.

1.4 Forty-five years of trying to capture the art in punk

Roughly half a century after its first manifestations, the history of punk is being written, and this means the involvement of universities and museums. To some, any sort of academic or curatorial examination of punk is an affront. To others, it is a question of whether it is done with sincerity. As this historical and scholarly review intensifies, it is becoming clear how complex a task that is. Relative to the scope of the movement, the state of research must be described as quite inadequate, despite the increased academic interest in recent years. For example, the Punk Scholars Network[89] began its work in 2012, and the journal *Punk & Post-Punk* began publishing in 2011. Different fields and different scenes are being examined—from Cuba to Indonesia to Ireland, from aesthetic to political to philosophical questions. The focus then, is widening to span beyond the UK/US mid 1970s music/fashion versions of punk. This welcome expansion goes hand-in-hand with an expansion of viewpoints regarding gender, sexuality, languages, origins. Most recently, *Punk! Las Américas Edition* was published in the Global Punk book series (Intellect, 2021), and a few months later, the podcast *Punk in Translation: Latinx*

Origins was released by Audible. Feminist perspectives on punk and a more balanced representation of the role of women in punk have been getting underway, too, in the writings of, for example, Rebecca Binns, Maria Elena Buszek, Helen Reddington, etc. Furthermore, punk scholarship has seen a shift in generations, mixing contemporary witnesses of punk's onset with younger scholars (like myself). This distance can both benefit and blur our perspective. Historization always carries the pitfall of heroization.

If we go back in time, punk has from the very beginning been subject to some academic interest. In the 1970s, the theorization of subcultures and youth cultures, for example in the work of John Clarke, Stuart Hall, Dick Hebdige, and Paul Willis, became increasingly influential. The Centre for Contemporary Cultural Studies (CCCS) at the University of Birmingham became a model for the interdisciplinary, critical approach to this new field, in which punk was among the first case studies. The late 1980s and the early 1990s saw the publication of some of the most authoritative works on punk: Dave Laing's *One Chord Wonders* (1985), Greil Marcus' *Lipstick Traces* (1989), Jon Savage's *England's Dreaming* (1991), Craig O'Hara's *The Philosophy of Punk* (1995), and Legs McNeill and Gillian McCain's *Please Kill Me* (1996). Furthermore, original source material was made more easily available: for example, the reprint of V. Vale's *Search and Destroy*, numbers 1–6 (1977–79), in 1996.

By the late 1990s to early 2000s, though, it had become increasingly clear that many aspects of the punk movement had still not been examined. Roger Sabin emphasizes this in *Punk Rock: So What?* (1999): "The aim of the book is not to be comprehensive but to re-start the process of questioning, and to point up new areas for research."[90] That is exactly the process that has been unfolding in the last two decades, and art history is one of the areas where the investigation of punk is still new, compared to the work already done within the fields of musicology, sociology, and cultural studies. In 1999, Sabin complained: "Most histories are content to limit themselves to discussion of what happened within the fields of music and fashion."[91] Since then, a number of efforts have been undertaken to broaden the scope of research. Acknowledgment and analysis of punk as an artistic movement has been one result. Perhaps not surprisingly, most contributions to our understanding of punk within art history have been through art exhibitions. Most of these however, only illustrate the visual side of punk—with a more design-minded focus on record sleeves, posters, and zines[92]—while others attempt to uncover what "art" might have meant in the punk movement more broadly.

One of the first to do the latter was the exhibition *Zurück zum Beton: Die Anfänge von Punk und New Wave in Deutschland 1977–'82* (*Back to Concrete: The beginnings of Punk and New Wave in Germany 1977–'82*) at Kunsthalle Düsseldorf in 2002. As curator

Ulrike Groos herself noted, it was a fragmentary and polyphonic compilation of artefacts and pictures,[93] confined to a five-year-period and in West Germany only. Its achievement, nonetheless, was an expanded conception of what punk might be, as the exhibition looked not only at punk music, but also at language and image. Some five years later, in 2007, Mark Sladen and Ariella Yedgar put together *Panic Attack! Art in the Punk Years*, at the Barbican Art Gallery in London, with a focus on artworks made in the UK and USA in the late 1970s to early 1980s. "[T]he primary focus here is not music but art," Sladen explained, "and the argument is that much of the best British and American art of this time was also punk in spirit."[94] The exhibition focused on this notion of a "punk spirit," which is presented as confrontational, angry, independent, and intelligent—and included examples from three categories: social-critical art (e.g. Gordon Matta-Clark, John Stezaker, Tony Cragg), divergent Body Art (e.g. Adrian Piper, COUM Transmissions, Paul McCarthy, David Wojnarowich), and DIY art (e.g. Linder, Jon Savage, Jamie Reid), all from the years 1974 to 1984.

One year later, in 2008, the exhibition *Punk: No One Is Innocent: Kunst–Stil–Revolte* in the Kunsthalle Wien presented punk artworks from three cities: London (e.g. Derek Jarman, Vivienne Westwood, Bill Woodrow), New York (e.g. Lynda Benglis, Robert Longo, Tony Oursler), and West Berlin (e.g. Die Tödliche Doris, Jörg Buttgereit, Salomé). Two conceptual features made *No One is Innocent* a particularly convincing interpretation of punk art: first, the curatorial implementation of punk's genre-defying mixture of methods, and second, the contributors' descriptions (Jon Savage on London, Glenn O'Brien on New York, and Wolfgang Müller on West Berlin) of how punk manifested itself in each of those spheres.

More problematic was Éric de Chassey's *Europunk: The Visual Culture of Punk in Europe 1976–1980*, which was first shown at the Villa Medici in Rome in 2011. *Europunk*'s individual contributions—among others those of Jon Savage, Jerry Goossens, and de Chassey himself—provide thoughtful insight into the punk art scenes not only in London but also in Paris, Rotterdam, Amsterdam, Manchester, Pordeone, and other places, and thus expand our awareness beyond the New York–London axis. The argumentation in the catalogue introduction, however, is hardly insightful. Here, de Chassey generalizes that "punk artists [...] never ceased to proclaim their opposition to the notion of art, at least in the movement's early years, which are the only years that can be considered true to the punk spirit."[95] This statement is neither adequately substantiated nor further explained. Indeed, the ambiguity and diversity of punk art and anti-art are not reflected upon, and the antagonisms within punk are reduced to right and wrong, true and untrue. "Our aim was never to display a given work because it was pretty or interesting in the punk context only," de Chassey explains in offering a rationale for the selection of objects, "but rather because it incorporated something of the urgency presiding over its creation—and thus, a certain beauty, even if paradoxical, that might earn its rightful place in museums."[96] This criterion of "beauty"—paradoxical or not—as being on the threshold of a "rightful place in museums" exposes a surprisingly reactionary concept of art. "Urgency," too, however fitting in some cases, is something of a one-sided cliché of punk creativity.

In contrast, the small CHELSEA space in London presented *Red White and Blue: Pop Punk Politics Place* in 2012, which investigated "relationships, influences and appropriations from political, pop, and punk imagery" in Britain only, ranging from 1968 to 2012.[97] It was a concentrated show, only a few rooms, but one that managed to capture some image of the multidimensionality of punk, and, with Michael Bracewell, had a superb writer of the introduction: "A hybridization, then, of intense social realism and equally dedicated Romanticism," he describes punk.[98]

Also in 2012, the *College Art Association Annual Conference* in Los Angeles dedicated two sessions to "Punk Rock and Contemporary Art on the West Coast" and "Towards a Rock and Roll History of Contemporary Art."[99] Both sessions built on the work of Greil Marcus, Jon Savage, and others, while emphasizing the need to "[broaden] our understanding of aesthetic influences and regional models for punk,"[100] for example by including figures such as Bruce Conner, Wallace Berman, and the San Francisco Beats when looking at punk in California.

Greil Marcus' *Lipstick Traces* was also the starting point for the exhibition *PUNK: Its Traces in Contemporary Art*, curated by David G. Torres, which was shown at Museu d'Art Contemporani de Barcelona (MACBA) in 2016. The goal of the exhibition was "to pinpoint how punk has left its mark on contemporary art, on many artists, works, and proposals" and to show how punk "extends beyond the seventies, beyond the Anglo-Saxon context and beyond the music scene."[101] Just as Marcus traces the origins of punk back through the twentieth century, Torres traces punk's influence on contemporary art, with works from the 1960s to the 2010s (e.g. VALIE EXPORT, COUM Transmissions, Die Tödliche Doris, Nan Goldin, Guerrilla Girls, Douglas Gordon, Mike Kelley, Dan Graham).

Most recently, the journal *Punk & Post-Punk* (vol. 9, no. 3, 2020) guest-edited by Rebecca Binns and Ian Trowell, dedicated a special issue to punk design and punk art. The most prominent artists who have been associated with punk art in the UK are known for their collages for punk bands: Jamie Reid for the Sex Pistols, Linder Sterling for Buzzcocks, and Gee Vaucher for Crass. This was reflected in the issue, but other perspectives were included as well, among others a highly interesting investigation into

"Ladies' Auxiliary of the Lower East Side: Post-Punk Feminist Art and New York's Club 57" by Maria Elena Buszek.

It is clear then that the work of writing the art history of punk has begun. However, punk's resistance to definition, curation, and academization, requires us to proceed carefully. The history of perceptions of punk is full of misapprehensions. On the one side, disparagement from conservative media and politicians, on the other, pandering from (liberal) cultural elites. For different reasons both sides have not been able or willing to understand the motivation of punk. Or rather, many conservatives were not so far from understanding, but they just did not agree with the values or anti-values of punk; that (mutual) hatred was always intended, even desired by punks. The love from the established culture industry, less so. "Culture vultures forever circling in an ominous sky," is how Bob Nickas described the crowd at the opening of the *Chaos to Couture* exhibition at The Metropolitan Museum of Art in New York in 2013, remarking that the organizers "wouldn't know what punk is or was if it bit them on the ass."[102] Similar comments might apply to the 2016 Punk London festival, "celebrating" 40 years since punk's outburst in London in 1976. The festival was funded by the Lottery Grant and organized with support from the Mayor of London (the conservative Boris Johnson), together with "some of the most cutting edge cultural organisations and businesses."[103] "Hi folks," the cliché-ridden, condescending newsletters would begin, "Lots of awesome stuff going on this month." These and other comparable misuses of punk imitate its habitus with supposedly "raw" and "edgy" language and design. Punk is transmuted into a bourgeois excitement commodity, a thrilling but ultimately harmless danger. "Punk has become another marketing tool to sell you something you don't need. The illusion of an alternative choice," complained Joe Corré, the son of Malcolm McLaren and Vivienne Westwood, before burning punk memorabilia worth around five million pounds in a spectacularized act of defiance.[104] This act was widely discussed and many proposed Corré could perhaps have put the money to work more progressively. As an image—a boatload full of culture money going up in flames on the Thames—it was not bad.

From my perspective, one deficiency in the present literature is that there are few to no in-depth analyses of the artworks. Statements about the characteristics of punk art often rely on overviews, which at times advance the significance of aesthetics over meaning, form over content. Furthermore, positions outside of the US–UK axis (and particularly so if we focus on what has been published in English) are underrepresented. And finally: the artists involved in punk were highly aware of history, especially of art history. On the whole, the punk movement was quasi steeped in art historical references, be they anti-art or not. And so, the next chapter will be about tracing those art history stimuli.

Notes

1. "Punk," Merriam-Webster, accessed July 8, 2017, https://www.merriam-webster.com/dictionary/punk.

2. Bazooka quoted in *Europunk: The Visual Culture of Punk in Europe (1976–1980)*, ed. Éric de Chassey (Rome: Drago, 2011), 126.

3. Jerry Goossens, "A Black and White Statement: The Imagery of Dutch Punk," In *Europunk: The Visual Culture of Punk in Europe (1976-1980)*, ed. Éric de Chassey (Rome: Drago, 2011), 202.

4. Genesis P-Orridge quoted in *RE/search*, "Throbbing Gristle," in *RE/search Issue 6–7: Industrial Culture Handbook*, eds. V. Vale and A. Juno (San Francisco: RE/Search Publications, 1983), 15–16.

5. GENESIS BREYER P-ORRIDGE, e-mail to the author, October 26, 2018.

6. Hollow Skai, *PUNK: Versuch der künstlerischen Realisierung einer neuen Lebenshaltung* [1979], Wissenschaftliche Reihe, vol. 3 (Berlin: Archiv der Jugendkulturen Verlag, 2008), 180.

7. Michael Crane and Mary Stofflet, eds., *Correspondence Art* (San Francisco: Contemporary Arts Press, 1984), 493.

8. Daniel Kulle, "Alle Macht der Super-8: Die West Berliner Super-8-Film-Bewegung und das Erbe des Punks," in *Punk in Deutschland: Sozial- und Kulturwissenschaftliche Perspektiven*, eds. Philipp Meinert and Martin Seeliger (Bielefeld: transcript, 2013), 271.

9. In the case of GENSESIS BREYER P-ORRIDGE, who identified as nonbinary in the latest two decades, I have for strictly textual reasons chosen to call them by the name they used at the time in question and which therefore is used in all contemporary source materials, that is: Genesis P-Orridge and refer to them as he/him, as that was how they identified in those years. BREYER P-ORRIDGE read my PhD in October 2018 to double check all factual matters and they agreed.

10. Diana Ozon, interview with the author, November 24, 2017.

11. Gerald Matt, "Vorwort," in *Punk: No One is Innocent; Kunst – Stil – Revolte*, eds. Kunsthalle Wien, Gerald Matt, and Thomas Mießgang (Nuremberg: Verlag für Moderne Kunst, 2008), 7.

12. Wolfgang Müller, interview with the author, May 23, 2013.

13. Hugo Kaagman, interview with the author, November 22, 2017.

14. Wolfgang Müller and Martin Schmitz, eds., *Die Tödliche Doris – Kunst (The Deadly Doris –Art). Band 3* (Berlin: Martin Schmitz Verlag, 1999), 54.

15. Genesis P-Orridge quoted in Simon Reynolds, "Ono, Eno, Arto: Nonmusicians and the Emergence of Concept Rock," in *Sympathy for the Devil: Art and Rock and Roll since 1967*, ed. Dominic Molon, (Chicago: Museum of Contemporary Art, 2007), 91.

16. Müller, interview, 2013.

17. Peter Panic quoted in Goossens, "A Black and White Statement," 200.

18. GENESIS BREYER P-ORRIDGE, e-mail to the author, October 26, 2018.

19. David G. Torres, "Traces of a Punk Attitude in Contemporary Art," in *PUNK: Its Traces in Contemporary Art*, ed. David G. Torres (Barcelona: Museu d'Art Contemporani de Barcelona, 2016), 46.

20. André Breton, "First Manifesto of Surrealism [1924]," in *Manifestoes of Surrealism* (Ann Arbor: University of Michigan, 1969), 128.

21. A note on the word "seminal": This word has been criticized in later years, the argument being that because men have "semen," the notion is bound to an image of a male artist ejaculating his influence like semen onto the rest of art history. The origin of "seminal" however comes from Latin: *semen* (and not

from Latin *sperma*) or going even further back, from proto-indo-European *she* (to sow; plant). See https://www.etymonline.com/word/seminal (accessed April 10, 2022). That is how I use the word: seminal as a metaphor for seed, for ideas which spread with the wind, or are carefully planted, and grow into a harvest of ideas, one day.

22. Giovanna Zapperi, "Marcel Duchamp's 'Tonsure': Towards an Alternate Masculinity," *Oxford Art Journal* 30, no. 2 (2007): 291–303.

23. Anna Banana, *About VILE: Mail Art, News and Photos from the Eternal Network* (Vancouver: Banana Productions, 1983), 49–50.

24. Helmut Middendorf quoted in Heinrich Klotz, *Die Neuen Wilden in Berlin* (Stuttgart: Klett-Cotta, 1984), 143.

25. See for example Götz Adriani and Museum für Neue Kunst Karlsruhe, eds., *Obsessive Malerei – ein Rückblick auf die Neuen Wilden* (Ostfildern: Hatje Cantz, 2003) and Nina Ehrensmann, *Paint Misbehavin'. Neoexpressionismus und die Rezeption und Produktion figurativer, expressiver Malerei in New York zwischen 1977 und 1984* (Berlin: Peter Lang, 2005).

26. Christian Lemmerz, interview with the author, March 27, 2018.

27. Dominic Molon, "Experimental Jet Set: The New York Scene," in *Sympathy for the Devil* (Chicago: Museum of Contemporary Art, 2007), 10.

28. Roger Sabin, "Introduction," in *Punk Rock: So What? The Cultural Legacy of Punk*, ed. Roger Sabin (London: Routledge, 1999), 3.

29. Jon Savage, *England's Dreaming: The Sex Pistols and Punk Rock* (London: Faber & Faber, 2005), xiv.

30. Savage, *England's Dreaming*, 162.

31. The track "No Feelings" was released on *Never Mind the Bollocks, Here's the Sex Pistols*; "No future" is a line from "God Save the Queen," and "No Fun" was a cover of The Stooges (original from 1969).

32. Black Flag, "No Values, The First Four Years" (SST Records, 1980).

33. Tristan Tzara, "Dada Manifesto 1918." Quoted from: Robert Motherwell, *The Dada Painters and Poets: An Anthology* (Cambridge: Harvard University Press, 1981), 81.

34. Greil Marcus, "Gulliver Speaks," in *Artforum*, November 1983, accessed December 10, 2017, https://www.artforum.com/print/198309/gulliver-speaks-35454.

35. Kevin Mattson, "Did Punk Matter? Analyzing the Practices of a Youth Subculture During the 1980s," *American Studies* 42, no. 1 (Spring 2001), 70.

36. Tzara, "Dada Manifesto 1918," 76–77.

37. Georg Grosz in *A Little Yes and a Big No*, 1946. Quoted in Savage, *England's Dreaming*, 477.

38. Stuart Christie and Albert Meltzer, *The Floodgates of Anarchy* (Oakland, CA: PM Press, 1970), 107.

39. Robert Christgau, "Avant-Punk: A Cult Explodes … and a Movement Is Born," in *Village Voice*, October 24, 1977, accessed December 10, 2017, https://www.robertchristgau.com/xg/music/avantpunk-77.php.

40. See Lisa Sofianos, Robin Ryde, and Charlie Waterhouse, *The Truth of Revolution, Brother: An Exploration of Punk Philosophy* (London: Situation Press, 2014).

41. David Huxley, "'Ever Get the Feeling You've Been Cheated?' Anarchy and Control in The Great Rock 'n' Roll Swindle," in *Punk Rock: So What?*, ed.Roger Sabin (London: Routledge, 1999), 97.

42. Marco Pirroni, 2005, quoted in Kugelberg and Savage, *Punk: An Aesthetic* (New York: Rizzoli, 2012,) 144.

43. Eloy Fernández Porta, "The Artist in the Mosh Pit," in *PUNK*, 163.

44. See Iván López Munuera, "I Don't Know Where I Am Going but I Promise It Won't Be Boring: The Political Specificity of Punk," in *PUNK*, ed. Torres, 194–214.

45. Savage, *England's Dreaming*, 434.

46. Shane Greene, "Introduction: ¿Otro Punk es Posible?" in *Punk! Las Américas Edition*, eds. Olga Rodríguez-Ulloa, Rodrigo Quijano, and Shane Greene (Bristol: Intellect Books, 2021), 15.

47. Dan Graham, "Punk as Propaganda," in *Sympathy for the Devil*, 124. Originally published as "Punk: Political Pop" in *Southern California Art Magazine*, no. 22, 1979.

48. Munuera, "I Don't Know Where I Am Going," 219.

49. Luxus (Luxury) was the no wave band in which Martin Kippenberger played.

50. Petra Reichensperger, "Schlau sein – dabei sein," in *Lieber zu viel als zu wenig: Kunst, Musik, Aktionen zwischen Hedonismus und Nihilismus (1976–1985)*, ed. Neue Gesellschaft für Bildende Kunst e.V. (Berlin: NGBK, 2003), 21.

51. See Robin Jahnke, "Merhaba S.O. 36," in *SO36. 1978 bis heute*, ed. SUB OPUS 36 e.V (Berlin: Ventil Verlag, 2016), 99 and Frank Apunkt Schneider, *Als die Welt noch unterging: Von Punk zu NDW* (Mainz: Ventil, 2007), 185.

52. Susanne Kippenberger, *Kippenberger: Der Künstler und seine Familien* (Berlin: Berlin Verlag, 2007).

53. Wolfgang Müller, *Subkultur Westberlin 1979–1989: Freizeit* (Hamburg: Philo Fine Arts, 2013), 268–77.

54. Wolfgang Müller, "Das Chaos reist mit dem Schönen Wochenende," in *Punk: No One Is Innocent*, 160.

55. Müller, *Subkultur Westberlin*, 274.

56. Müller, interview, 2013.

57. Marcus Verhagen, "There's No Success Like Failure: Martin Kippenberger," in *Failure: Documents of Contemporary Art*, ed. Lisa Le Feuvre (London: Whitechapel Gallery, 2010), 43.

58. Wall text, *Martin Kippenberger: sehr gut | very good*, Hamburger Kunsthalle Berlin, February 23–March 18, 2013.

59. Jens-Emil Nielsen, *Ung i 80'erne* (Copenhagen: Her&NU, 2005), 21.

60. Sune 'Køter' Carlsson Kølster, "Punk," in 69, ed. Helle Hansen (Copenhagen: Verve Books, 2008), 24.

61. René Karpantschof and Flemming Mikkelsen, "Kampen om Byens rum. Ungdomshuset, Christiania og husbesættelser i København," in *Kampen om Ungdomshuset: Studier i Oprør* (Copenhagen: Frydenlund og Monsun, 2009), 21–44 and Grethe Jensen, "Folkets Hus," in 69, 8–13.

62. Jørgen Callesen, "Dunst i ungeren: kønspolitik, punk og sexuelt anarki," in 69, 122–23.

63. Andreas Karker, *Jagtvej 69: Historien om et hus* (Copenhagen: Lindhardt og Ringhof, 2007), 63.

64. N.U. Unruh quoted in Simon Jeppesen, "Einstürzende Ungdomshus," in *69*, 44.

65. N.U. Unruh quoted in Simon Jeppesen, "Einstürzende Ungdomshus," in *69*, 44.

66. Marc Miller, interview with the author, April 16, 2018 and Nina Sten-Knudsen, interview with the author, May 17, 2018.

67. Parts of this subchapter were previously published in my article in *Punk & Post-Punk* in 2020.

68. Miller, interview, 2018.

69. Denney quoted in Howard Smith, "Clash Bash," in *Voice*, May 1, 1978.

70. Miller, interview, 2018.

71. Press release, Washington Project for the Arts, April 4, 1978, private archive of Marc Miller, Brooklyn, NY.

72. Miller, interview, 2018.

73. Miller, interview, 2018.

74. Smith, "Clash Bash."

75. Associated Press (AP) release, May 17, 1978, private archive of Marc Miller, Brooklyn, NY.

76. Howard Smith, "Boy Scouts of Rock," in *Voice*, May 8, 1978.

77. *Parool Kunst*, June 8, 1979, private archive of Marc Miller, Brooklyn, NY.

78. Miller, interview, 2018.

79. Miller, interview, 2018.

80. Letter in the private archive of Marc Miller, Brooklyn, NY.

81. Ozon, interview, 2017.

82. Hugo Kaagman, interview with the author, November 22, 2017.

83. Rosa Lindenburg in the *Museumsjournaal* (*Museum Journal*), press clip in the archive of Diana Ozon.

84. Marc Miller, "Punk in Amsterdam," accessed May 8, 2018, https://98bowery.com/idyll-in-holland/punk-in-amsterdam.

85. Gerard Pas, "The Great Art Swindle???," *Artzien: A Monthly Review of Art in Amsterdam* 1, no. 8 (June 1979).

86. Associated Press (AP) release, May 17, 1978.

87. Miller, interview, 2018.

88. Kaagman, interview, 2017.

89. Punk Scholars Network, "About the Punk Scholars Network," accessed July 8, 2022, https://www.punkscholarsnetwork.com/about-punk-scholars-network

90. Sabin, "Introduction," 9.

91. Sabin, "Introduction," 4.

92. For an interesting overview on the topic of design, see Russ Bestley and Alex Ogg, *The Art of Punk: The Illustrated History of Punk Rock Design* (London: Voyageur Press, 2012).

93. Ulrike Groos, "Zurück zum Beton," in *Zurück zum Beton: Die Anfänge von Punk und New Wave in Deutschland 1977–'82*, ed. by Kunsthalle Düsseldorf and Ulrike Groos (Cologne: Walther König, 2002),109.

94. Mark Sladen, "Introduction," in *Panic Attack! Art in The Punk Years*, 10–11.

95. de Chassey, "Introduction," in *Europunk*, 9.

96. de Chassey, "Introduction," in *Europunk*, 10.

97. Donald Smith, "Curator's Foreword," in *Red White and Blue: Pop Punk Politics Place*, ed. Chelsea Space (London: University of the Arts, 2012), 3.

98. Michael Bracewell, "Some Notes for the Exhibition," in *Red White and Blue*, 13.

99. Matthew Jesse Jackson and Robert Slifkin, "Towards a Rock and Roll History of Contemporary Art," and Adam Lerner and Steven Wolf, "Punk Rock and Contemporary Art on the West Coast," CAA sessions, Los Angeles, February 23, 2012, accessed January10, 2018, http://www.collegeart.org/pdf/caa_2012_abstracts.pdf.

100. Lerner and Wolf, "Punk Rock and Contemporary Art on the West Coast," 76.

101. Exhibition flyer, *PUNK: Its Traces in Contemporary Art*, curated by David G. Torres (Barcelona: MACBA, 2016).

102. Bob Nickas, "Komplaint Dept: Never Mind the Bollocks, Here's Anna Wintour," accessed July 8, 2017, https://www.vice.com/en/article/9bneje/kompbrlaintbrdeptbr-never-mind-the-bollocks-anna-wintour.

103. "About," Punk London, accessed July 8, 2017, no longer online.

104. Quoted in "Punk Funeral: Joe Corré Burns £5m of Memorabilia on Thames," accessed July 8, 2017, https://www.theguardian.com/music/2016/nov/26/punx-not-dead-joe-corre-burns-memorabilia-worth-5m-on-thames.

2 ART ORIGINS IN THE STORY OF PUNK

In all honesty, this chapter is a bit fragmented. But important! (Nevertheless, or exactly for that reason, as it does highlight the truly fragmented nature of art history writing. You decide). As the title goes, the chapter sets out to find the "art origins in the story of punk"—a question, one could approach from so many different angles, only to find so many different answers. Thus, this chapter effectively only highlights *some* art origins. What is significant is to show that the history of the punk movement is about music, yes, most definitely! But also about so much more ...

The first part of the chapter is thus a short version of the story of punk, from proto to post. It begins with the first mentioning of a rebellious punk subculture in Detroit and New York in the 1950s, continues through the punk rock explosions 1975–76 and the change of the movement through the political backdrop in the UK, to Crass' track "Punk is Dead" in 1979, and ends with the subsequent survival and diversification of the movement.

Afterwards, the "art school vs. hard school" conflict in punk is delineated, though not overestimated: after all, to think that the opposite of *art* must be *hard* might just point to a somewhat limited perception of art. This awareness is juxtaposed with examples of the hard/art history origins of many of punk's concepts, among others the radical compositions of Dadaist Erwin Schulhoff, the visual language of the Motherfuckers and King Mob, the auto-destruction of Gustav Metzger, Yoko Ono's tabloid taunts, and William S. Burroughs' cut-ups. The chapter ends with the recognition of do-it-yourself (DIY) as a key method and medium of punk in *all* its manifestations: art, music, film, poetry, and fashion.

2.1 The short version: From proto to post

The beginning and the end of punk are topics of debate. One reason for this might be its closeness to a myriad of related styles and circles: no wave, new wave, dark wave, industrial, hardcore, queercore, etc. Few other movements are so deeply embedded in "pre-" and "post-" areas. The timeframe most incontrovertibly associated with punk spans no more than a couple of years in the mid to late 1970s, the two fixed points being New York in 1975 and London in 1976. "This is the history of the flash. But the fire is much greater," David G. Torres argues.[1] Punk developed as it spread to local scenes all over the world. Skinheads, anarcho-punks, and riot grrrls all found inspiration in punk, interpreting it in contrasting ways. A too-limited standpoint on punk might then amount to what Roger Sabin calls "a kind of orthodoxy"[2] in punk studies, which would be detrimental to the purpose of understanding the motivation and effects of punk. This applies not only to the time period chosen for research but also to questions of identity and genre. However, in the following short introduction aimed to profile punk's history, these two fixed points do serve as important signposts.

Detroit and New York's proto-punk

In the USA in the 1950s, the first mentions of "punk" in relation to a rebellious troublemaker lifestyle, can be found. In the June 1956 volume of *The Lowdown*, under the caption "Sewer Street of America: PUNK STREET, NEW YORK CITY," David A. Loehwing reports:

> Each city in the world has a punk street. Some are vicious. And some are soft. In New York, Punk Street is a little bit of love, a little more of V.D., somewhat more of kick 'em where it hurts most.[3]

A second example can be found in the 1957 book *The Young Punks*, which was billed as "The savage, frightening story of the teen-age jungle," next to a grainy photo of a bar fight on the cover.[4] In various ways, 1950s mods, teddy boys, and the Beat Generation, all influenced punk. Just as twenty years later, subcultures of the 1990s (such as grunge) looked to the 1970s,[5] the 1970s saw a return to the 1950s. For example, Joey Ramone quoted *The Wild One* as inspiration for wearing a leather jacket,[6] and no less than two punk bands (Circle Jerks and the Violators) recorded tracks with the title "Live Fast, Die Young."

Punk was also a continuation of that part of the 1960s counterculture that posed an aggressive, alternative undercurrent to the dominant surface of flower power. Proto-punk bands such as the Fugs, the Stooges, Death, or Suicide, and underground publications such as *Fuck You: A Magazine for the Arts*, stood for outrage and anger. In 1966, for example, song titles such as "Shut Up" and "I Hate You" by the Monks, and graphics proclaiming "ANARCHY + APOCALYPSE + AFRAISAMERICA" in the teen magazine *Resurgence*, exposed a dark side of the US youth culture. In European and UK punk, there are strong links back to anarchist groups of the 1960s and radical publications, such as Jeff Nuttall's *My Own Mag* (1960–67). *Oz* magazine specifically links post-war Surrealism to the British counterculture of the late 1960s, as David Hopkins has shown the impact of *Oz* might just have played a more significant role in the (underground) dispersion of Surrealist thought, than the blockbuster books and exhibitions displaying the smoothed, sellable big names of Surrealist painting.[7]

Punk—as a way of life and an artistic/musical statement—started drawing on these notions of aggression, anger, and outrage in the early 1970s, most notably in Detroit and New York. The term "punk rock" was first used by journalist Dave Marsh in

Creem Magazine in 1971, in reference to the Mexican-American Detroit/Bay City band Question Mark and the Mysterians.[8] The first eruption, then, was in the summer of 1975 in New York, visible through punk rock, such as the New York Dolls, Patti Smith, Blondie, and Ramones, playing at music venues like CBGB and Max's Kansas City, and the Mercer Arts Center. It was also in 1975 that Richard Hell wrote "Blank Generation"[9] (not released until 1977 however). The loft scene of lower Manhattan with its weird and violent body performances—the Kipper Kids, Mike Kelley, Jack Smith, and Laurie Anderson—was closely entwined with the punk movement.[10] Various characters surrounding Velvet Underground and Andy Warhol's factory also blended in. On the cover of the first issue of *PUNK*—which was advertised by "punk is coming!" flyers downtown in December 1975—is thus a cartoon drawing of Lou Reed by John Holmstrom.[11]

West End, London

Meanwhile in London, Vivienne Westwood and Malcolm McLaren had opened their shop SEX on 430 King's Road in London's West End. They sold fetish, S&M, and bondage gear as well as self-made clothing heavy with historical and literary references: for example, ripped shirts with gay sex fantasies in the style of Tom of Finland, portraits of Karl Marx, handwritten descriptions of rape, CHAOS and ANARCHY stencils, swastikas (sometimes inverted), and slogans from France's May of '68 and the Situationists, such as "Be Reasonable, Demand the Impossible" and "Prenez vos désirs pour la réalité" (Take your desires for reality). At 430 King's Road, a small group of (very young) individuals started finding each other—the first generation of "punks" in England, though the name was not in use yet. "A large number of those first agitators of punk," Servando Rocha points out, "were neither musicians nor truly interested in music."[12] Like the epitome of the twentieth-century avant-gardist's wish to unify art and everyday life, punk at this point was most of all a way to live and a way to make art, in whichever form or genre. This attitude was exemplified by Jordan, one of the first protagonists of the scene, who had, in Savage's words, "turned her own body into an art object."[13] In Derek Jarman's early fictional punk film, *Jubilee* (1978) Jordan plays the nihilist and violent Amyl Nitrate (Figure 2.1), who symbolically incorporates Britannia, in one scene performing a pastiche of the song "Rule Britannia." Her alias, Amyl Nitrate, is a depressant, which slows the user down, and involuntary relaxes the muscles, especially the anal and vaginal sphincter—her role a taunting sideswipe at British patriotism.

McLaren and Westwood visited New York on several occasions between 1973 and 1975, among other reasons to work with the New York Dolls. Richard Hell made a big impression on both McLaren and Westwood—his lyrics, his style (he was the one

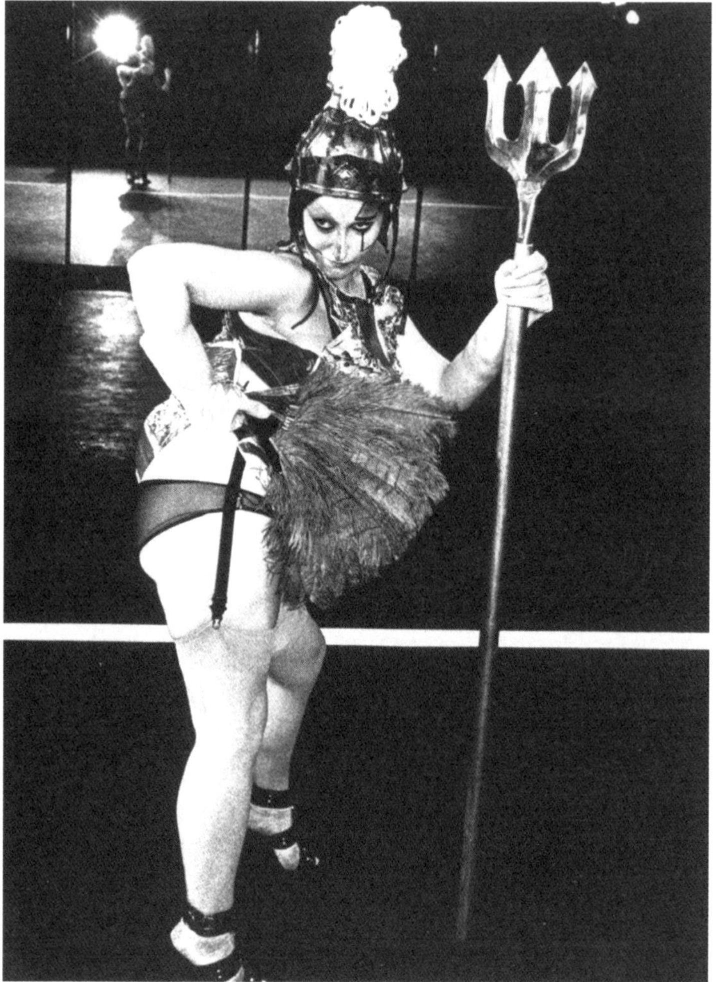

Figure 2.1: Jordan as Amyl Nitrate as Britannia during the filming of Derek Jarman's Jubilee*, 1978. Courtesy of Megalovision, Whaley-Malin Productions, Ronald Grant Archive, and Mary Evans.*

to start wearing safety pins)—and in 1975, McLaren tried to persuade Hell to come to England "to front the group he had back home."[14] When Hell was not interested, McLaren returned to London. Here, he found that a group of teenage boys had started hanging out in the SEX shop. The four—all working-class, all called John, as Savage notes—were, in the words of John Lydon (aka Johnny Rotten), "all extremely ugly people. We were outcasts, the unwanted."[15] McLaren took on the role of manager and impresario. He gave the band a name, Sex Pistols—an advertisement for the King's Road shop, and bordering on the ridiculously Freudian—and set them to practicing and writing songs. Soon after, he booked their first two gigs: St. Martin's School of Art on November 6, 1975, and one day later at the Central School of Art and Design in Holborn.

Together with Westwood and Jamie Reid—whom he knew well from their time together in Croydon Art School—McLaren transferred the concept of "punk" to the UK. They took the living art shock tactics already applied at SEX to the field of rock music. McLaren saw this as an opportunity to "operate as the catalyst for chaos, as a cultural terrorist," as Simon Reynolds describes the role.[16] McLaren envisioned himself as "a shock conceptualist," and respectively "an artist, who happened to work with music."[17] The Sex Pistols, to him, were "a work of art [...] an idea, not a band."[18] However, the Sex Pistols themselves and the reach of their music—then and now—obviously do challenge the completeness of this delineation.

McLaren, Reid, and Westwood placed punk in an art/shock conjunction reminiscent of historical avant-gardes. The difference was that punk—and in the UK, in 1976, primarily the Sex Pistols—reached an unprecedented amount of attention from mainstream society, the mass market, and the yellow press. One reason for that was probably the sensitivity of a society that was already looking for the signs of the coming collapse, and found those signs in punk, as the embodiment of the coarsening of youth.

The other side of town: COUM in East End

Jon Savage argues that there were three key formations of punk in London in the mid 1970s: Sex Pistols, the Clash, and COUM Transmissions/Throbbing Gristle (TG).[19] What they all had in common—despite their differences—was that they did not think the rich, powerful, glamorous London was the true London. Each in their own way, they pointed to the poor, violent, downtrodden London. Punk at this point was about truth, about the exposure of the truth. Whereas the Sex Pistols was darkly romantic, and the Clash was socially conscious, COUM/TG was engaged in a more basic exploration of human malice.

London was a "paranoid place" in those years, Jon Savage notes.[20] The heightened sentiments of dystopia and apocalypse in COUM's work in the mid 1970s also reflected these surroundings. The artists lived and worked in Hackney in London's East End (thus, on the other side of town from the Sex Pistols): their studio, the so-called "Death Factory" was in Martello Street and their home was a squat on Beck Road, a street filled with destroyed working-class houses, then occupied by artists, bohemians, and activists. At the time, large parts of London consisted of devastated and decaying areas, but in Hackney, there was nothing transitory about poverty. The miserable situation of the area worsened in the mid to late 1970s, due to the economic crisis. However, not only

Hackney but London's entire East End had been the epitome of impoverishment for centuries. The area had been the home of religious rebels, industrial workers in the "stink industries," and political radicals; it had suffered cholera, pest, and riots, and had been heavily bombed in both World War I and World War II.[21] From the infamous Ratcliffe Highway Murders to Jack the Ripper, the East End had acquired a reputation for savagery and violence and was thus depicted by Charles Dickens, Oscar Wilde, and Arthur Conan Doyle. Hackney in particular was notorious for its anti-authoritarianism, which in the 1970s was embodied, among other things, in groups like the so-called "ranting poets" with their *Stand Up and Spit* poetry performances.

The catalyst

The backdrop to punk's rise in New York was a city in decline: unemployment, empty buildings, crime, and drugs. New York City was on the verge of bankruptcy in 1975. In October of that year, when President Gerald Ford made a speech to underline there would be no bail-out, the *New York Daily News* famously headlined: "FORD TO CITY: DROP DEAD."[22] This atmosphere surely impacted New York punk. However, in general punk in New York was "much less politicized," Sabin argues: "If we think of punk as an explosion [...] then the UK's economic recession during this period can be seen as the catalyst."[23] The already deeply rooted class struggle intensified in the mid 1970s: "While the rich became richer, the poor and the unemployed faced a daily battle to survive," John A. Walker writes.[24] In 1976, the devaluation of the pound, the IMF loan, and the subsequent heavy budget cuts to public spending, symbolically exposed the downfall of Britain.

The socio-economic situation in English cities like London and Manchester in the mid 1970s fueled the rise of punk. Indeed, punk as we understand the movement today, came into being through social struggle in the UK. In the UK, punk was more closely associated with resistance, and both the visual and musical expressions of British punk accentuated the fact. "Punk was a riot [...] intended to dramatize Britain's breakdown, if not actual apocalypse," Jon Savage writes.[25] Against this backdrop, London—as the capital, the seat of power, the symbolic head of the snake—assumed a special role, exemplified in the Clash's "London's Burning" (1977) and "London Calling" (1979).

The economic crisis turned into a much broader crisis of confidence: "The decline was seen as having diverse symptoms—not just military and territorial but moral, cultural, spiritual and physical. The centuries-old British empire was dismantled in a couple of decades," as Andy Beckett describes in his account of Britain in the 1970s:

> The population of Greater London dropped by 600,000 between 1961 and 1971. Many of the urban Britons who remained lived in landscapes spotted with

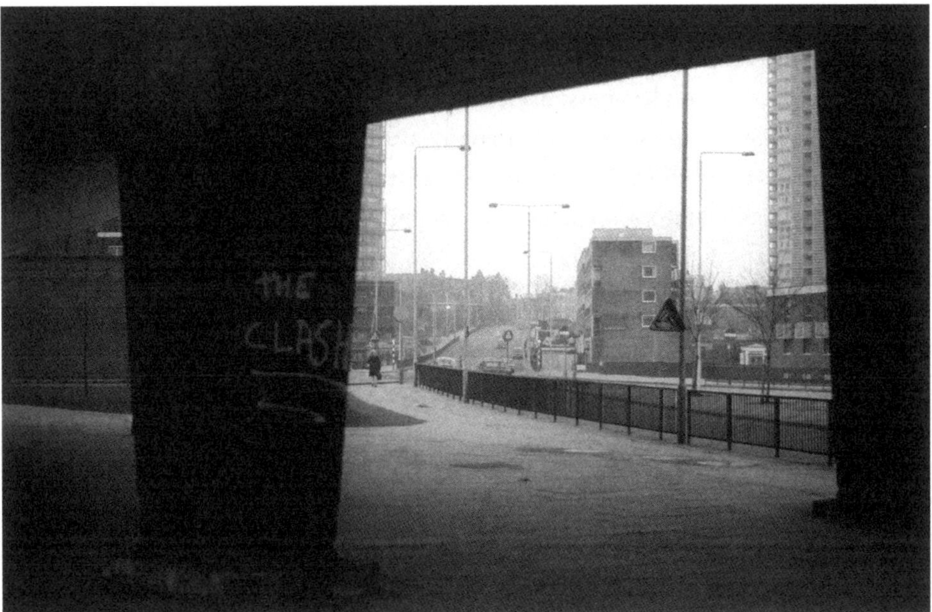

Figure 2.2: Jon Savage, Uninhabited London #35 *(London), January 1977. Courtesy Jon Savage.*

> decay: prematurely aged post-war housing estates, emptying docksides, bombsites unrepaired and lost to weeds, decades after the German air raids.[26]

An image series such as Jon Savage's *Uninhabited London* illustrates this atmosphere (Figure 2.2).

The empty buildings, however, also provided space for all sorts of self-organized actions. Squatting was already an important part of counterculture in the first half of the 1970s, and it became a defining element of punk. "The squats were the material basis and precondition for the emerge of political activism, art, and alternative life," Astrid Proll explains: "These houses, removed from the circulation of capitalist valorization, were open spaces for experimentations of all kinds of life lived without economic restraints."[27] Punk was closely entwined with this grassroots and extremist milieu, and many punks squatted—among them, Johnny Rotten, Sid Vicious, and the Clash's Joe Strummer. "There were streets and streets, a real community. There were certain areas that were being left to run down," Strummer remembers.[28] In the late 1970s, as the DIY sentiment of punk grew stronger, the squats became even more crucial.

DIY and activism became one of (at least) two different punk responses to the societal crisis. The first consisted of negation, nonsense, black humor, and dark poetry—an amoral, escapist liberation founded in the refrain "No Future." Johnny Rotten sang:

"When there's no future, how can there be sin / We're the flowers in the dustbin / We are the poison in your human machine."[29]

The other was no less pessimistic, but its protest was more concrete. In "White Riot," Joe Strummer expressed his admiration for the Notting Hill riots in August 1976, when the Black community had put up resistance against racism and police brutality. Strummer demanded the same courage from suppressed White groups:

> Black man gotta lot of problems but they don't mind throwing a brick / White people go to school where they teach you how to be thick / All the power's in the hands of the people rich enough to buy it / While we walk the street, too chicken to even try it / White riot, I wanna riot / White riot, a riot of my own.[30]

Punk's activist side also resulted in punk bands' participation in, for example, Rock Against Racism in 1978, which was established together with the Trotskyist Socialist Workers' Party, as well as a benefit show for anarchist prisoners in 1979, and concerts in solidarity with the strike organized by the National Union for Miners in 1984–85.

The Rock Against Racism movement in the UK, which had gained momentum after the Clash, the Ruts, X-Ray Spex, and Tom Robinson Band (TRB) participated in a joint concert in the spring of 1978, became reproduced in other European cities. In the autumn of 1978, for example, the first Rock Against Racism festival in the Netherlands took place in Paradiso. A large graffiti in the Amsterdam punk squat of the KoeCrandt group reproduced the Rock Against Racism slogan: "black & white, unite & fight." The rallying cry was an update of the 1930s US meatpacker union slogan "negro and white, unite and fight"[31] and its focus was interracial class solidarity. In the context of punk, class solidarity was complemented by outsider solidarity; the initiators of the Rock Against Racism events perceived alternative rock as having a true radical potential, and youth cultures, such as both punk and reggae, as lifestyles which would affect and change society (in contrast to the subjugating brainwashing of commercial mainstream pop).[32]

The slogan's intrinsic separation of Black people and White people as groups has been criticized—Stephen Duncombe, for example, mockingly reformulates Rudyard Kipling's famed sentence from *The Ballad of East and West* (1889) "Oh, East is East, and West is West, and never the twain shall meet" into "the twain may meet but they will never meld"—and he depicts both Black people in punk culture and White people in reggae culture as aliens, arguing that the punk movement essentially stayed White, just as reggae, in turn, essentially stayed Black, despite all interracial solidarity. "In order for Black and White to Unite and Fight, to stand shoulder to shoulder in solidarity, each category has to be discrete and assigned a dissimilar character proper only to itself," he argues.[33]

Although that is linguistically logical, Duncombe may underestimate both the closeness of punk and reggae culture (e.g. Don Letts, Bad Brains) as well as the de facto involvement of Black people in the punk movement (see bands such as Pure Hell, Death, Fishbone, National Wake, X-Ray Spex, and, in the beforementioned KoeCrandt squat, Lulu Zulu & The White Guys, the band of Ludwig Wisch. Wisch was Black and the band name was both a sarcastic arrogation of the ridiculing and racist connotations of the name "Lulu Zulu" and a reversal of the clichéd roles of dominance: "& The White Guys" referenced not the White front singer with Black musicians in the band, but the other way around). Not that there were no racists in punk, there were, no doubt—parts (not all) of both the Oi! and the skinhead scenes, as well as for example in Germany the so-called "Grauzone" scene were into neo-Nazism—the point here is rather that the depiction of punk as a predominantly White (or predominantly male, or predominantly hetero) culture, is misrepresenting what took place in the late 1970s and early 1980s. But we will return to this later on ...

Tearing open, tearing apart

Back in 1977, the Queen's Silver Jubilee was celebrated and the Sex Pistols' released their sarcastic single "God Save the Queen," with Johnny Rotten screaming about the "mad parade" and the "fascist regime."[34] One reason the song was so successful, despite being banned by BBC Radio, was the feeling among young people especially that no one else was saying the obvious: the Jubilee was "a state-reinforced lie: an attempt to pretend nothing was wrong in Rotten Britain," as Savage writes.[35] Punk's taboo-breaking was a way to draw attention to the double standards of the authorities, the tabloid press (especially Rupert Murdoch's papers and their scare campaigns), and the superficiality and injustice of capitalist society. When McLaren—with his usual flair for publicity—rented the *Queen Elizabeth River Boat* to enable the Sex Pistols to play the song while sailing on the Thames at the Jubilee (McLaren all the while shouting, "You fucking fascist bastards!"), reactions in the press were predictably hostile. The *Sunday Mirror* headlined "PUNISH THE PUNKS," which resulted in verbal and physical attacks on punks all over the UK.[36]

Especially for first-generation punks, it seems the need to avoid being defined was greater than the need to be acknowledged for a certain political opinion, but as the political climate hardened toward the end of the decade, many punks felt that their engagement must be less abstract, and the politically conscious, activist side of punk grew more important. In the UK, some saw the economic crisis and the many strikes, especially the so-called "Winter of Discontent" of 1978–79, as a national humiliation. The reaction was a neo-conservative backlash, as well as the rise of fascist factions. National Front had been on the rise since the mid 1970s; it was the same rightwing dissatisfaction that would lead to the rise of Margaret Thatcher some years later. Because of punk's refusal to explain itself and its antithetical gestures (such as wearing a swastika), it was immune neither to misunderstandings nor to the misuse of its strong visual language by far-right groups. At the same time, the initial protagonists of punk were worn out. "Punk was now tearing itself apart," Savage evaluates: "Theatrical violence became actual violence."[37] The media hype and the big record companies took their toll. The EP *Spiral Scratch* by Buzzcocks, released in 1977, was probably the first British punk record made independently of the mainstream music industry, but to many of the first-generation punks, DIY came too late. The Sex Pistols split up in an ugly way in January 1978. All too foreseeable was the overdose death of bassist Sid Vicious in February 1979, after he had presumably killed his girlfriend Nancy Spungen.[38]

"Punk is dead. Long live punk"

In the fall of 1979, at the end of the decade, anarcho-punk band Crass released their second album *Stations of Crass* with the track "Punk is Dead." Their frustration comes across in the lines:

> I see the velvet zippies in their bondage gear / The social elite with safety-pins in their ear / I watch and understand that it don't mean a thing / The scorpions might attack, but the systems stole the sting.[39]

Provocation had become an empty gesture, the style a cliché as well as a product. Under these circumstances, the pure negation that had been distinctive of punk's early years, was now untenable. Punks developed agendas. Feminist punk bands, such as the Raincoats, Poison Girls, and the Slits, all of whom released their debut albums in late 1979, gathered pace. In the song "Queer Riot" from 1988, the band Sluts from Outer Space demanded: "Dykes get a lot of trouble / cause we won't suck no pricks / why don't we get together / and throw some fucking bricks / Queer riot, we wanna riot of our own."[40] The hardcore punk band Minor Threat released *Straight Edge* in 1981, and with it coining the notion of living without any kind of alcohol, tobacco, or psychoactive drugs. Veganism, environmentalism, anti-consumerism, and animal rights became important themes in punk. The punk movement, however, in other versions (and in accordance with its contradictory nature) likewise incorporated both racist and misogynist elements.

The members of Crass, who lived together in the anarchist-pacifist open-house art collective Dial House in Essex, were advocates of a direct-action approach. "Our anathema was no future," Penny Rimbaud of Crass has explained: "We said: 'We're not going to have all these young kids thinking that there isn't. We'll go out and show that there is a future.'"[41] The autonomy of self-owned record labels, zines, and galleries became even more essential. In the late 1970s and early 1980s, under exactly that DIY motto, punk spread to the province as well as internationally, with very active scenes not only in continental Europe and on the West Coast of the United States, but also in Central and South America, Australia,[42] Asia, South Africa, etc.

To think of punk as a static position was always an illusion. "Punk was once an answer to years of crap," Steve Ignorant of Crass sang in 1979, "But the moment we saw a way to be free / They invented a dividing line, street credibility."[43] This "hipper-than-thou snobbery,"[44] as Sabin calls it, stands in opposition to the idea of punk as a self-empowering and individualistic culture-from-below, where those who were not part of the initial hub are reduced to the role of followers. Associated with this was an exclusive, even hierarchical, attitude in which the underlying concept of authenticity is defined by being close to the epicenter of action. This, as Huxley puts it, is the idea that "there is a central 'pure' core in any given field, which is then dissipated by a series of less authentic, and therefore 'lesser' practitioners."[45] We might identify two problems in this notion: First, the validity of an experience, or a work of art or a song, is judged on the basis of when and where, not on quality or content. Second, authenticity becomes the counter concept of progress, as it resembles cultural embalmment.

For many years, a graffiti slogan on the wall of the punk rock club Roxy in London read that "Punk is dead. Long live punk." In a way, this was true all along. Punk was something different in The Kitchen in New York in the mid 1970s than at SO36 in West Berlin in the mid 1980s, but to exclude any post-1979 actions and experiences would result in an undue and unrewarding narrowness in our understanding of punk culture. "The onus," as Sabin proposes, "is then on the historian to construct a narrative that is ideally led by empirical research rather than by theory."[46] Furthermore, rather than trying to smooth punk's inherent conflicts and paradoxes, it seems a much more promising approach to expose and explore them.

2.2 Art school vs. hard school

One central dichotomy, which does cover a lot of the bad blood in punk, was described by German writer Frank Apunkt Schneider as the art school vs. hard school conflict.[47] In *One Chord Wonders*, Dave Laing establishes that nearly a third of British punk rock musicians had been students, most of them in the field of art.[48] Among the most well-known art-student punks are of course Malcolm McLaren and Jamie Reid. Others include

Glen Matlock (Sex Pistols; St. Martins School of Art), Joe Strummer (the Clash; Central School of Art), Viv Albertine (the Slits) and Adam Ant (Adam and the Ants) at Hornsey College of Art, Richard Kirk (Cabaret Voltaire) at Sheffield Institute of Arts, and Budgie (Siouxsie and the Banshees; Liverpool School of Art).[49] Although less has been written about this, punk/art school links were similarly close in other countries.[50]

As authorized institutions, art schools per se did not represent what many of the punks stood for, and not all punks who were students became graduates. Art schools rather represented a place to spend time than a place to obtain a certain title or achievement. As Paul Burgess and Jon Savage both note, art schools in the late 1970s were less competitive, more laissez-faire places than now.[51] "It was the place where everybody went who did not fit anywhere else," McLaren said of his art school experience, "It was a brilliant hangout."[52] In the 1970s and 1980s, Central Saint Martins and Goldsmiths College especially, connoted an open-minded and non-hierarchical approach to art, whereas the Royal Academy was known to be more traditional.[53] In his private notebook, McLaren had a list of places he wanted to book for the Sex Pistols' shows: these were either in art schools (e.g. Royal College of Art) or gay clubs (e.g. Speakeasy). Next to this list, McLaren had written: "The Sex Pistols choose their situation."[54] The art school setting was thus chosen with the purpose of testing a situation that could be used either for experimentation or for provocation, depending on how progressive or conservative that setting turned out to be. The art school framework thus fitted two early punk propositions: *épater les bourgeois* and find the like-minded. The expression *Il faut épater le bourgeois* (Shock the middle classes) is attributed to Charles Baudelaire. It was used by the French Decadents in the second half of the nineteenth century and later in the 1960s students' revolt, as well as in punk. One recent example can be seen in the Italian hardcore punk band Epater Le Bourgeois (E.L.B.). When the Sex Pistols went on tour internationally, they often played in similar art school-like setups, such as the Art Centre in Rotterdam in the Netherlands or the Studenter Samfundet in Trondheim in Norway.[55]

Punk's informed integration of historical art avant-gardes' strategies and aesthetics can thus in part be attributed to the high number of art school students among punks, but above all else, the art school connection of punk reminds us that for many early punks, the movement was not solely about music. The knowledge about the history of art, which is present in the origins of punk, does seem connected to the fact that many early punks had an art school background. Nonetheless, this interest in art history also came from outside such institutions, as punk artist Hugo Kaagman explains:

> I studied Dada, collage techniques, but I never went to art school. The street was my school. Nobody was teaching what I wanted to learn: stencils, felt pen. The

art schools did not take that seriously, those were junk materials. I thought they were wrong.[56]

The same might be true for many of the provocative performances, the street slogans, and howling happenings of punk: the tradition here was one of *anti*-art and *anti*-school. On the following pages, we will make a quick and incomplete run-through of some of the key art historical precursors of punk, some of which belong just as much—to stay on topic—in a hard school history as an art school history.

2.3 Punk precursors: 1919, 1966, and 1968

There are many art-historical foretastes of what was to come with punk. Viewed globally, we could certainly find a true myriad. As art history traditionally goes, with its often too narrow focus on western art history, however, and with the focus of this book on Europe in particular—there are some highlights which set the tone. These are important punk precursors for two reasons: one, they emphasize historical moments that enabled an opening, particularly a creative opening between art and music. Two, they point to the countercultural tradition of subversion that would become so important in punk art. Without any attempt at being exhaustive (that would be futile!), some of the key art movement instants that preceded punk follow here.

Berlin 1919: "Shit and puke with me!!!!"

Punk has many intersections with Dada, Surrealism, and Futurism: collage and bricolage, excessive language, onomatopoetic expressions, sloganeering, proclamations, poetic radicalism, ephemeral materials, use of aliases, bodily transgressions, questioning of fixed gender identities, valuing of public scandal and shock, clashes with the audience and the self, and the conception of art as action.

In the 1910s and 1920s, Futurists, Dadaists, and Surrealists rethought music, art, and the relationship between the two. The Futurist Luigi Russolo's manifesto *L'Arte dei Rumori* (*The Art of Sounds*, written 1913, published 1916) established an understanding of noise as sound, integrating industrial sounds, mechanical sounds, urban sounds, and primal sounds—for example, explosions and hissing roars, screams, howls, death rattles—into the artistic and musical repertoire. The "bruitistic" music and poetry of both Futurists and Dadaists incited audience riots on several occasions.[57] Marcel Duchamp presented the *Erratum Musical* (Musical mistake, 1913, first performed at the *Manifestation of Dada*, 1920), a sort of readymade libretto with completely random notes, pulled from a hat. Such use of errors and coincidences in the process of creation and the defiance of customary composition would become key elements in neo-Dada and Noise Art, and later in punk.

Erwin Schulhoff, whose composition *In Futurum* (1919) consisted of nothing but pauses—a predecessor to John Cage's famous 4′33″ (1952)—dedicated his work to "the painter and Dadaist George Grosz:"

> Ich eigne Ihnen dies zu, weil dies reale Dinge enthält, die einer jeglichen ‚Kunst' im üblichen Sinne gänzlich ferne stehen, es ist nicht Pathos, bzw. dessen grosse Geste, es ist aus dem Bordell der Zeit herausgekommen und ist nichts mehr als ein Excrement, diesmal dem Gehirne entsprungen […]. Sie begreifen meines Erachtens nach, weil Sie sicher auch nichts anderes zu tun gedenken, in Ihrem Sinne geschieht das zwar optisch – im Grunde genommen: sagen Sie doch selber, ist es nicht einerlei, ob dies optisch oder akustisch […] geschieht. Scheissen und kotzen Sie mit mir!!!!
>
> Herzlichst immer Ihr Erwin Schulhoff.
>
> (I devote this to you, because it entails real things, that are far away from 'art' in the usual sense, it is not pathos […], it derives from the contemporary brothel and is nothing more than an excrement, this time arisen from the brain […] You will understand, I am sure, since you intend to do nothing else, admittedly in your sense it will happen optically—but essentially, say it yourself, is it not the same, if acoustically or optically […] Shit and puke with me!!!!
>
> Warm greetings, always yours, Erwin Schulhoff.)[58]

Schulhoff makes it clear that his and Grosz's radical artistic mission is the same, regardless of medium. Intrinsically, his whole letter radiates a punk attitude: opposition, reality, intensity, intelligence, shit, puke, and prostitution.

Furthermore, one might find a precursor to punk art/music zines in Dada, and especially Surrealist magazines and leaflets, which were also non-commercial, small-circulation, self-published, and self-distributed. Other common features of punk were Surrealist magazines' marginal themes (sex, violence), word/image juxtapositions, the propagation of radical thought, emphasis on collective activity, and the importance of network and autonomy. Though Dada is mentioned more often—due to Malcolm McLaren's self-labeling, Jamie Reid's collages, and Greil Marcus' analyses—the links to Surrealism seem equally significant: individual, personal, and substantial thematic ties from the Surrealists to CoBrA, the Letterist International, the Situationist International, and King Mob, through to punk, are apparent.[59]

The punk movement's interest in violence, (self-)abuse, sickness, and pain, its exploration of sex, guilt, and taboos, dominance and liberation, its instinct for corporeality and performativity—all this relates it to Surrealism. In his analysis of the

Surrealist movement, Walter Benjamin wrote that "the cult of evil as a political device, however romantic," has the ability "to disinfect and isolate."[60] To *disinfect* by *promoting evil*; that resounds also at the heart of the punk movement's aspirations. We will return to this connection between Surrealism and punk, throughout this book, as it has been much less scrutinized than the Dada link. Especially regarding questions of work vs. play (Chapter 7) as well as porn, pleasure, and pain (Chapters 8 and 9), the connections between these two movements crystallize.

1966: (Auto-)Destruction in art

The Viennese Actionists and their works of ritualism, bloodiness, and transgression could also be viewed as punk art progenitors; notions such as the aesthetic impact of pain and theatrical torture/self-torture align with punk art. The Viennese Actionists were among the participants in Gustav Metzger's *Destruction in Art Symposium* (*DIAS*) in London in 1966, which can be viewed as a key proto-punk event. In a press release, Gustav Metzger stated that "The main objective of *DIAS* was to focus attention on the element of destruction in Happenings and other art forms," and to relate this to destruction in society.[61] Such a perspective might be viewed as connected to the artistic and social effect of punk's destruction and self-destruction. "It was all about destruction, and the creative potential within that,"[62] stated Malcolm McLaren (who was at art school in London in the mid 1960s, and is likely to have known about, if not actually seen, *DIAS*). The *DIAS* symposium, which was accompanied by a series of events, manifested possibilities and means of subversive art.[63]

Metzger had coined the term "auto-destructive art" in his manifestos, published in London in the late 1950s and early 1960s. Pete Townsend of the Who states that

> When I was at art college I got fantastically interested in auto-destructive art. Gustav Metzger did a couple of lectures and was my big hero. He comes to see us occasionally and rubs his hands together and says "how are you?"[64]

The Who are frequently described as proto-punk, primarily because of their guitar-smashing, their connection to the mods, and songs like "The Punk and the Godfather" (1973). The Who's ritual of destruction was different from the Fluxus performances of a few years before (Nam June Paik's *One for Violin*, 1961; Phillip Corner's *Piano Activities*, 1962): the force, the physicality, and the anger—all in all, the destructive will—seem more blatant in Townsend's act. As Hannah Higgins notes, the Fluxus destructions were, at times, accompanied by "fine gestures: the careful rubbing of a brick over the strings, patient waiting for the right moment to use a hammer."[65] The settings were more

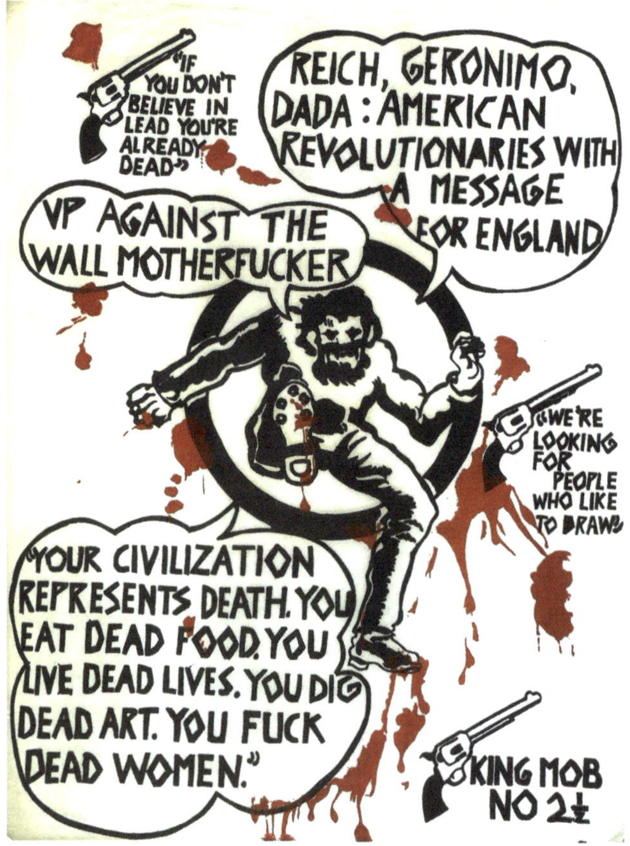

Figure 2.3: King Mob, Poster No. 2½ *(London), 1968. Courtesy of David Wise.*

intimate—the art club, not the rock festival, and it was violins and pianos, not electric guitars. The Who's performance of destruction was matched by now iconic band posters showing Townsend in the moment—"This guitar has seconds to live"—thus perfecting the message transfer from the world of art into the world of rock 'n' roll.

London 1968: "His Majesty, King Mob"

In the late 1960s, the topic of destruction was also reflected in the work of King Mob (the English Situationist International splinter group, with which both Jamie Reid and Malcolm McLaren were associated). One King Mob flyer prompted: "MUSICIANS—SMASH YOUR INSTRUMENTS."[66] The name King Mob derived from the (failed and disastrous) Gordon Riots of 1780 when inmates were freed from Newgate Prison, and the insurgents left behind graffiti on the destroyed prison wall—"His Majesty, King Mob"[67]—uttering an ideal of mobocracy.

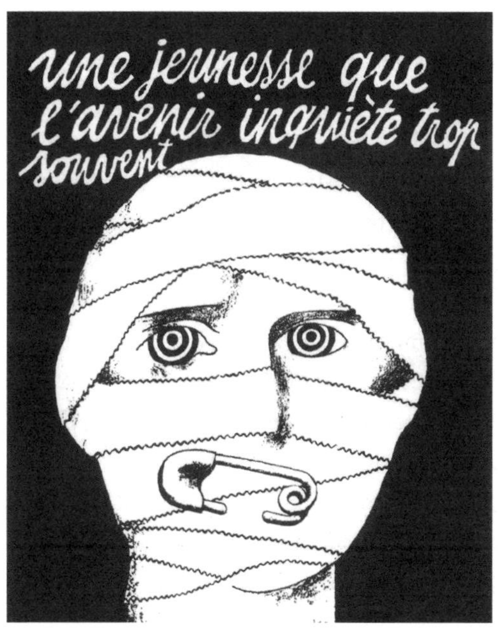

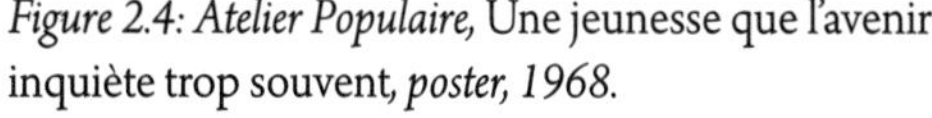
Figure 2.4: Atelier Populaire, Une jeunesse que l'avenir inquiète trop souvent, *poster, 1968.*

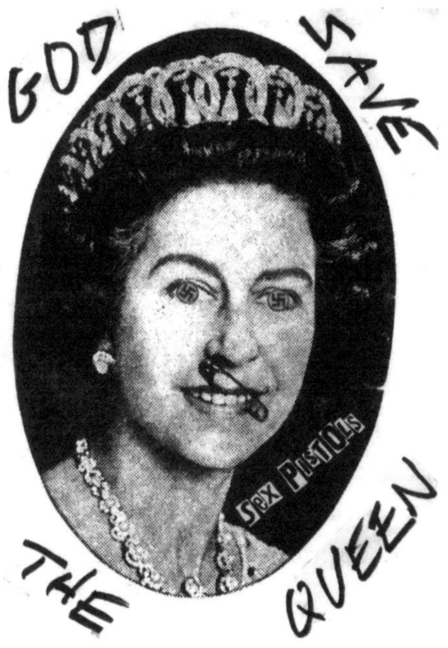

Figure 2.5: Jamie Reid, God Save The Queen (Swastika Eyes)*, 1977. Courtesy of Jamie Reid and John Marchant Gallery. © Sex Pistols Residuals.*

On the cover of the first *King Mob Echo* magazine in 1968 was a figure dressed in a black bomber jacket and ski mask with a Molotov cocktail, below a quote from Marx: "I am nothing but must be everything." On King Mob's black/white/red *Poster No. 2½* (Figure 2.3) a kicking and screaming figure drawn in graphic novel style is surrounded by guns and blood splats. The examples show the group's appropriation of divergent (anti-)cultural references—Comics! Crime! Communism!—and their superimposition of pop and mutiny. Herein lies the defining difference to the cultural negation practiced by the fraction of the Situationist International close to Guy Debord, as Sam Cooper observes: "King Mob's texts abound in symbols, icons, and images of transgression, of conflict, of rebellion. We might think of this switch from negation to affirmation as a move from an anti-spectacular Situationist practice to a hyper-spectacular one."[68] This switch to the hyper-spectacular was transferred into punk: in punk, the spectacle seems to be both *embraced* and consciously *operated.*

The backstory here is the split that occurred in the Situationist International in 1962. Following heated debate, almost all active artists were excluded from the Situationist International.[69] Together with other excluded artists, Jørgen Nash went on to create an alternative Situationist version, or vision. Nash, and his brother Asger Jorn, who had already left the Situationist International in 1960, both thought differently from

Guy Debord and Raoul Vaneigem about the role of art in society. Nash was skeptical of what he saw as Debord's Marxist understanding of the role of art (basically: art paralleled the capitalist society and thus must be abandoned). Instead, Nash wanted to mobilize the working classes through provoking public scandals. At the fifth Situationist conference in 1961, Vaneigem had argued that "the elements of the destruction of the spectacle must precisely *cease to be works of art*."[70] Nash in contrast thought that "the project was not to negate art but to realise it *as excess*"[71]—an understanding which relates to the practice of both King Mob and later punk art.

King Mob was closely linked with and inspired by the radical New York group Up Against the Wall Motherfucker! (Motherfuckers for short) led by Ben Morea. "We are the ultimate Horror Show," one of the Motherfuckers' statements read: "Hideous Hair & Dangerous Drugs."[72] To some extent, the actions, language, and aesthetics of King Mob, Motherfuckers, and other radical, often anarchistic, countercultural groups of the 1960s set a blueprint for punk groups. The synthesis of art, direct action, and self-publishing, as well as the integration of humor and rage, pop and politics, provided an intelligent way to express and process anger at the status quo.

Paris 1968: Atelier Populaire

In May of 1968—the same year that King Mob published its first magazine—their French Situationist counterparts played a significant role in the Paris student protests, including graffiti such as "The passion of destruction is creative joy," "Never Work," "Live without dead time," and Guy Debord's "Boredom is counter revolutionary": all these slogans were later re-used in punk culture.[73]

The silkscreen posters produced at the Atelier Populaire in the occupied space of the École des Beaux Arts reveal remarkable intersections with punk posters in form and content, as has been shown in Johan Kugelberg and Jon Savage's *Punk: An Aesthetic* (2012). One significant example is a white and purple Parisian student poster with the statement "Une jeunesse que l'avenir inquiète trop souvent" ("A youth disturbed too often by the future"; Figure 2.4). The title is echoed in punk's "No Future" and the image—a bandaged head, with eyes looking like targets and a large safety pin restraining the mouth—is mirrored in Jamie Reid's infamous Sex Pistols poster of the Queen with a safety pin across her lips and swastika eyes (Figure 2.5). For an even earlier example of a safety pin through lips, see the Surrealist photomontage by Leo Dohmen in Chapter 9.2 "'It hurts and looks cool!': Fetish fashion."

In 2016, the Punk Scholars Network's third annual conference on the theme of *The Art of Punk* (Figure 2.6) also took its key visual from a poster by Atelier Populaire (Figure

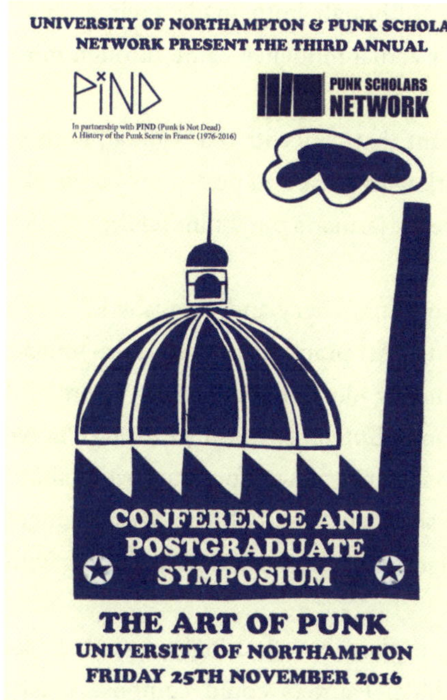

Figure 2.6: The Art of Punk Conference *poster, design by Russ Bestley, 2016. Courtesy of Russ Bestley and the Punk Scholars Network.*

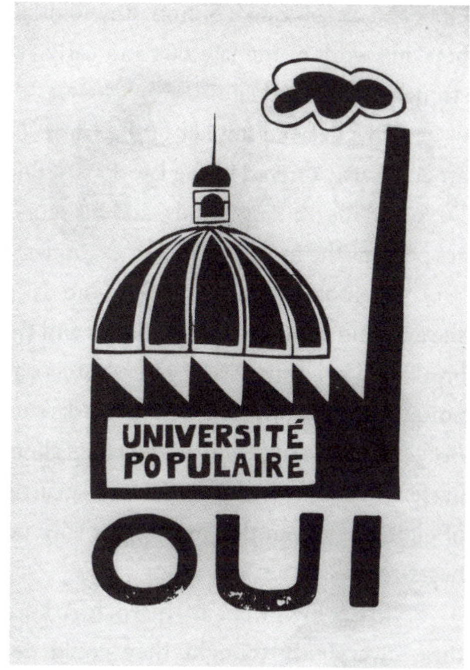

Figure 2.7: Atelier Populaire, Université Populaire Oui *poster, 1968.*

2.7). At that conference, Paul Hollins argued that "the ethos, visual aesthetic, and language of punk emerged from the streets of Paris in 1968 as much as west London in 1976."[74]

Interestingly, the Atelier Populaire used (American) Pop Art techniques, such as silkscreen and opaque projectors, thus, as Liam Considine points out, building a bridge between two versions of "popular" that were, at the time, often regarded as opposed. "The use of pop-derived graphics in the iconic posters of the Atelier Populaire to protest American-style capitalism and imperialism remains a salient, if under-examined paradox of the events of May 1968 in France," Considine notes.[75] With regard to punk, that heterogeneity corresponds with, on the one hand, the movement's sensitivity to the efficiency and the reach of pop, and, on the other hand, its political opposition to consumer society. In consequence—and with additional consideration of the themes of self-organization, art activism, détournement, and protest—it becomes clear that 1968 was a crystallizing moment for punk.

Ono/Eno: "Faced with a choice, do both"

"The first figures to bring art ideas right into the heart of their music-making were Yoko

Ono and Brian Eno," Simon Reynolds argues: "Although both made their groundbreaking work in the late 60s and early 70s, their actual influence came through most strongly in the […] late 70s."[76]

This delayed impact of the late 1960s meant that concepts that worked both in art and music thrived in the late 1970s. Eno's work with punk and post-punk bands like Devo and the Talking Heads, and his score for Derek Jarman's punk film *Jubilee* (1978), are perhaps the most prominent examples.

Reynolds describes Yoko Ono as "a proto-punk, angry and anguished."[77] Both she and Eno continued their Fluxus and Conceptual Art practices in their (non-)music, breaking down artistic and genre borders and pursuing ideas of dilettantism, errors, and noise. This attitude is reflected in works such as Ono's *Unfinished Music #1* (1968). In *No Bed for Beatle John* (1969), Ono chants lines from insulting newspaper quotations about herself and John Lennon. Such a sarcastic and somewhat masochistic détournement of quotations from the press aligns with punk's tactics of appropriation in dealing with negative press reactions.

Brian Eno went to Ipswich Art College, a place he admiringly describes like this: "Everybody thought they could do anything. Painters could compose music, bricklayers could do happenings, prostitutes could write operas."[78] In his depiction, Eno thus emphasizes not only an intersection between music and art but more pervasively a meltdown of all orthodox societal limitations of the lower and upper class, workers and intellectuals, outcasts and luminaries.

In his *Oblique Strategies* (1975–79), made together with artist Peter Schmidt, Eno offered small Fluxus-like instructions, such as: "Honour thy error as a hidden intention" or "Change instrument roles." Both revering the error and switching instruments would be made real by punk and post-punk artists and musicians in the late 1970s and early 1980s. Befriended artists also joined in with ideas for *Oblique Strategies*: "Faced with a choice, do both" (Dieter Roth), "Tape your mouth" (Ritva Saarikko) and "Try faking it" (Stewart Brand).[79] Both the form and the content of these messages—the sloganeering, the fakery, and the self-awareness—show an attitude that would become essential in punk.

Cut-ups and Xeroxes: "Gifts of non-art"

William S. Burroughs became another quintessential reference point in punk culture, so much so that Savage writes of punk as "a youth culture so saturated in Burroughs that it seemed as though the Wild Boys had come alive."[80] Burroughs was born in 1914 and had exhibited with Dada artists in 1935, before becoming part of the Beat Generation. He and Brion Gysin had developed their cut-up method based on Tristan Tzara's *To Make a Dadaist Poem* (1920), but it was especially their use of sound collage and feedback that influenced figures such as Lou Reed, Genesis P-Orridge, Thurston Moore, and Kurt Cobain. Gysin and Burroughs's *The Third Mind* was published in English in 1978, that is, coinciding with the eruption of punk.

The fragmented perception and dark ideas transported in Burroughs's cut-ups fit punk's worldview. Jon Savage describes how punk "injected Burroughs's ideas into the youth media" in montages and zines.[81] "[Burroughs's] overall concern was always to confront control systems and attack them," Barry Miles notes, "just take fairly ordinary situations and take them off on a weird, almost surreal angle and develop them."[82] This too, was highly punk.

Aligned with the rediscovery and expansion of cut-up techniques was the relatively new art form of Xerox art or copy art. Following the market rollout of the Xerox machine in 1959, Surrealist and Beat artists began using it to produce posters, collages, book art, and mail art. Among the first in the early 1960s was Wallace Berman, who self-published art and poetry in his looseleaf proto-zine *Semina*, copies of which were sent as gifts to collaborating artist-friends, such as Burroughs, Rachel Rosenthal, Bruce Conner, and Jay DeFeo.[83] It was not, however, until the late 1970s that Xerox Art was used more widely in the underground zine and mail art scenes. These scenes—whose protagonists were often punks—practiced a custom of exchanging letters and art gifts, or as COUM Transmissions put it in a letter to Anna Banana from the zine *VILE*, "gifts of non-art."[84]

2.4 DIY: The DNA of punk

Even bearing in mind these connections to the history of art and to the art school, there can nonetheless be no doubt that the primary impulse of punk was the *opposition* to authority and tradition. Even in the context of an anti-authoritarian and anti-institutional art forum, i.e. street art, the key was DIY. As Hugo Kaagman puts it: "On the streets, I met interesting people. [...] But still, it was: Don't follow a leader, lead yourself. Don't listen to the teacher, teach yourself. Do It Yourself."[85] The spirits of art, music, and DIY crossings and squatting were linked too, as Käthe Kruse describes:

> Did I know how to glaze a window or install a toilet bowl? Did I know how to make music or how to make art? No. I really did not know how to do anything, as my dad had told me often enough: You are nothing, you know nothing, and nothing will become of you. But when you enter into something, then you *do* know after all.[86]

DIY was applied in art and in life.

Perhaps more than any other single issue, DIY is regarded as punk's legacy. The

DIY method was used in production as well as distribution. Information on concerts, performances, and exhibitions was distributed via self-made zines and posters. Many of the concepts that were central in punk's DIY had first gained momentum in the late 1960s but were put into effect on a broader scale in the 1970s. In the mid 1970s, galleries and music companies alike were sustaining a style that punks criticized as elitist, distant, and over-produced. In music, this was incorporated by a band such as Pink Floyd, who ended up on punks' self-made "hate" T-shirts (Johnny Rotten for example wore a Pink Floyd T-shirt on which he had written "I HATE" above the band name). On the art scene, the egocentric, "genius" (White, male) artist had a comparable effect. Writing in his journal in 1976, COUM Transmissions' Genesis P-Orridge dismissed most contemporary art as "irrelevant in its lofty pretensions, requiring almost a degree in semantics."[87] As an alternative, punk's self-owned or squatted art/music spaces and communal clubs stood for accessibility and content over form. The pursuit of autonomy and the structural change of power relations, for example between performer and audience, was essential to the rise of punk. The prime example "This is a chord [...] this is another [...] this is a third. NOW FORM A BAND," accompanied by a rough black marker drawing of the guitar notes A, E, and G, appeared in the punk zine *Sideburns* no. 1 in 1977.

Mark P.'s *Sniffin' Glue*—among the first punk zines—likewise spread the DIY-credo. Robert Christgau argues, "it was from *Sniffin' Glue* that the whole issue of class authenticity in punk, the anti-poser ethic, really took off. I did it, Mark P. said, and now you should."[88] He is referring to the November 1976 issue of *Sniffin' Glue*, in which Mark P. wrote: "All you kids out there who read SG, don't be satisfied with what we write. Go out and start your own."[89] DIY indicated a democratization of art through a stronger focus on the importance of the reader, the listener, or the viewer. With the Xeroxed fanzines, the readers were often also the authors. The impetus of DIY was thus directness: the elimination of old power structures and the middlemen, the upheaval of established hierarchy.

DIY was perhaps also necessary as a counterweight to the negativity of the movement. In contrast to punk's negation, DIY thus emerges as creation. "This thing about doing it yourself, to me was the key characteristic of punk—the DNA of punk, so to speak," says musician and artist Martin Hall. At the same time,

> Several small impromptu galleries emerged momentarily in old storerooms or basements. Along the way, they became the galleries Deroute in Blågårdsgade or Kong in Store Kongensgade, but at the beginning, it was these short-lived conditions. You were at an opening in a cleared-out house, and the next time you passed by the same place, the whole building was leveled to the earth.[90]

In these DIY spaces, a new openness was possible. In Copenhagen, for example, one such place was the 13AB, named after the street number, where a 24-hour event took place in 1980. At the dilapidated (and potentially dangerous) building, there was art in each of the rooms (Super 8 films, drawings, installations, etc.), and graffiti on the walls. *13AB* was arranged by four visual artists: Michael Kirkegaard, Torben Voigt, Elmer, and Lillian Polack. The Sods and Billedstofteatret performed with a choir of twelve people in white shirts and seal-fur pants, and Henrik S. Holck read his poems out the window with a megaphone.

> We wanted to do something different from what was going on at the art scene at that time, where it was just one solo show after another, by some big artist running his show with whatever style he had come up with. Instead, we did three days and nights, each was really 24 hours, the whole building, all was art, all was action [...] There was an energy, there was a spirit among us.[91]

The *13AB* event was important because it joined punk makers and doers across disciplines. Furthermore, two historical occurrences in particular can be seen as paradigmatic for the merging of art and punk and how that merging was specifically connected to a DIY approach. One is the development of technical devices in the 1970s which augmented the development of the DIY approach. The other is the concurrent upheaval and energy of the graffiti scene, which especially at the outset was highly interconnected not only with hip hop, but also with punk. In the following, we will thus take a closer look at these two trends.

Xerox, Atari, Super 8: Punk media machines

From punk music to punk art to punk fashion to punk film, either brand-new or old and converted machines modified the possibilities. First and foremost, the Xerox machine played a key role in zines and Xerox art. Furthermore, the music business' investments in technically more advanced recording equipment also meant that the old gear could be acquired cheaply. Early DIY consoles, such as the Atari, enabled avant-garde electronic sounds, for example in a band such as the all-female Mania D. (later Malaria) of West Berlin. Gudrun Gut of Malaria used the same Atari device to program her music and her knitting machine(!). American punk singer Lydia Lunch had planned to release an Atari computer game along with her 1980 album *Atomic Bongos*. For women associated with the punk movement in the late 1970s and early 1980s, playing with machines and tech DIY signified an anti-hippie stance as well as a charge into an often male-dominated territory.

West Berlin underground fashion designer and musician Claudia Skoda for example also became known for her Atari and her technological approach to knitting.[92]

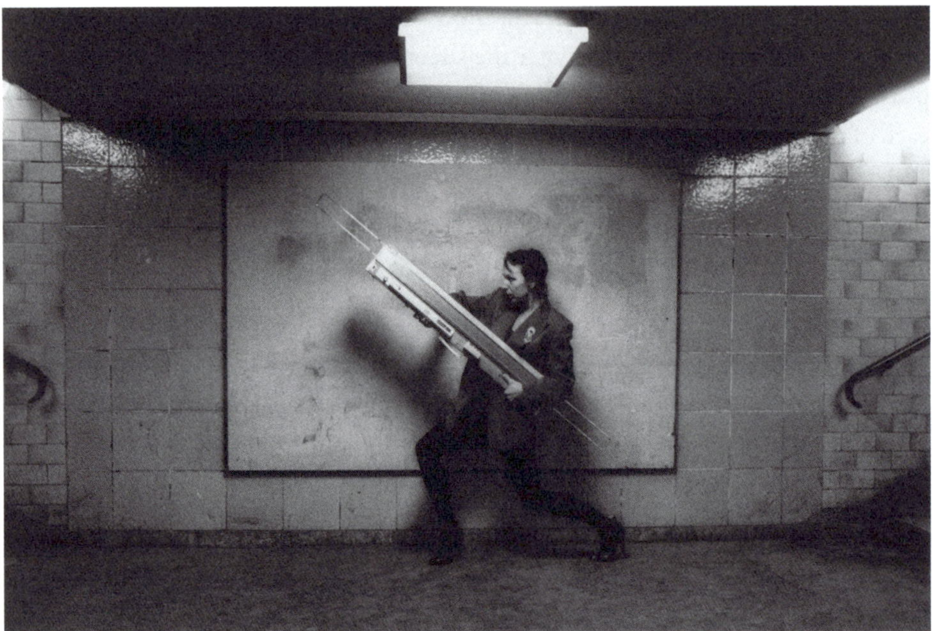

Figure 2.8: Martin Kippenberger, Claudia Skoda with her knitting machine in the Kottbusser Tor subway station, Berlin, *ca. 1976–77. Courtesy of the Estate of Martin Kippenberger, Galerie Gisela Capitain, Cologne.*

In defiance of the stereotypes of DIY knitting—the hippie handicraft homemaker—Skoda instead foregrounded the mechanical aspects, thus defying gender stereotypes in the process. In one prominent photo series by Martin Kippenberger, Claudia Skoda poses with her knitting machine in the subway station Kottbusser Tor in Kreuzberg. Skoda is dressed in lacquer high-heeled ankle boots, black tights, a men's jacket, and has her hair slicked backed. In one photo, she holds her knitting machine, as though it were an electric guitar (Figure 2.8); in another, it rather looks like a gun case (Figure 2.9). Punk DIY thus differed from hippie DIY in its mechanical, machine-based approach. No weaving, no tie-dye, no nature materials. Instead, Skoda knit with tape from discarded cassettes, among other things, and sold her designs at the West Berlin punk shop Eisengrau (see Section 10.2: "The Grand Downfall Show").

Like Xerox and Atari, Super 8 can be seen as an example of a punk media machine par excellence. "Super 8 became to film what the famous three chords were to music," as Martin Schmitz remarks.[93] Super 8 accommodated the intermediality of punk; it was used by performance groups for documentation, by bands for music videos, by art-school students for their projects.[94] The Super 8 format was introduced in 1965 by Kodak as a "home" medium. It became popular to use for family occasions, but was also used for alternative political cooperatives and amateur filmmakers, including Derek Jarman—the

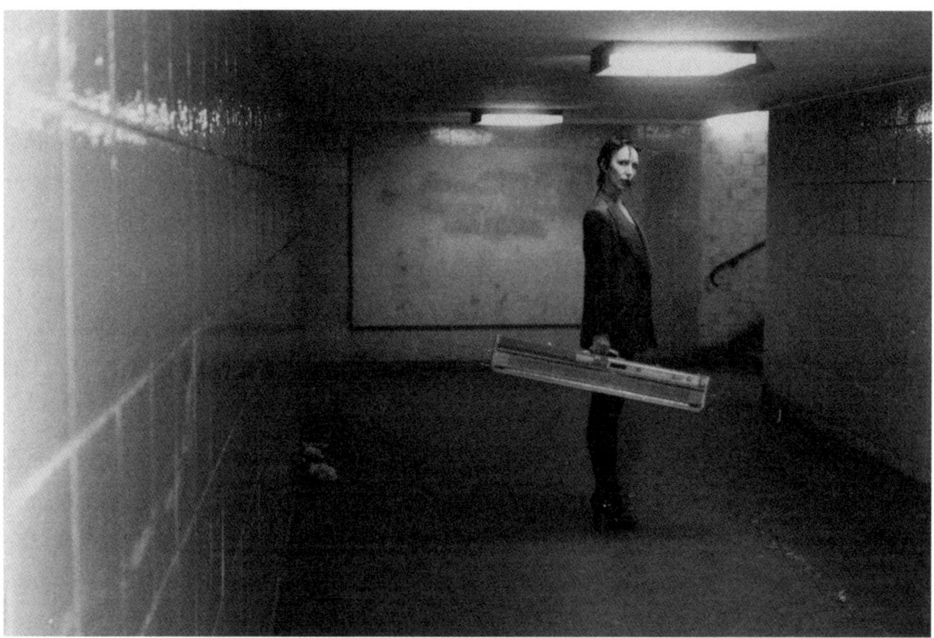

Figure 2.9: Martin Kippenberger, Claudia Skoda with her knitting machine in the Kottbusser Tor subway station, Berlin, *ca. 1976–77. Courtesy of the Estate of Martin Kippenberger, Galerie Gisela Capitain, Cologne.*

punk/gay filmmaker icon, who used Super 8 material for both *Sebastiane* (1976) and *Jubilee* (1978).[95] By the late 1970s and early 1980s, Super 8 was already outdated, but was still available everywhere. Nearly a fifth of all German households owned a Super 8 setup, but it was becoming apparent that the near future belonged to VHS, which made Super 8 very cheap. Cameras and film were bought at flea markets or were simply picked up in parents' basements. Apart from their cheapness and availability, the Super 8 cameras were also light, robust, and easy to operate, which likewise suited punk's DIY orientation. The ultra-short songs of punk even fitted with the Super 8 cameras; the 8 mm cassettes were only three minutes long anyway.

Super 8 signified independence, both because of its availability and because of the lack of distribution possibilities. Because of the reverse film process, the film strip was not a negative, but was made within the camera, so to speak, and this brought it closer to the artist's hand. Each Super 8 film was thus a unique copy. Since mass-produced copies were not possible, the films had no great commercial value. However, Super 8 films could be screened almost anywhere. In 1981, the group u.v.a. even painted a part of the Berlin Wall white and screened Super 8 onto it, upsetting authorities on both sides.

The technical limitations of Super 8 resulted in a distinct aesthetic; the images appear discolored, shaky, and grainy, with visible scratches and quick editing cuts mostly done ad hoc directly in the camera. "Super 8 is an incomparably direct, even corporeal medium of unusual vulnerability," Dirk Schaefer observes: "Every screening can be the last: indeed, every screen is the last in a certain sense, because a little bit is eroded from the original every time. We see and hear the film disintegrating."[96] This unique material quality was often reinforced by the artists, who urinated on the film strips or scratched or sewed into them. Typical punk themes, such as decay and destruction, were thus integrated into Super 8. Perhaps the most defining aspect was that the Super 8 filmmakers turned apparent weaknesses into strengths, faults into virtues, and this, as well, is quintessentially punk.

Punk and graffiti: "The Bastard Art of the Streets"

In punk, the city functioned concurrently as a stage and as a motif. Understanding punk as an everyday performance meant that places like clubs, bars, shops, and squats became exhibition spaces. The underground was often used as a metaphor: for example, in the line "London calling to the Underworld"[97] in the Clash's "London Calling" (1979) or in the Jam's "Going Underground" (1980). Streets and public transportation vehicles and stations were also used for communication through posters and painted slogans. "Graffiti was a much more authentic form of punk expression than most of the first wave bands," Jerry Goossens describes the scene in the Netherlands, "Arguably the most important Dutch punk group, the Ex, even started out as a graffiti tag."[98] The lyrics of punk songs and poems are replete with urban words; street, brick, wall, concrete, steel, city, subway, etc. Often, the *physical* and the *social* structure of the city were compared; both were depicted as decaying.

Consequently, different forms of street art—but graffiti in particular—were a quintessential part of punk in the late 1970s and early 1980s. The punk conception of the city as a place that must be claimed was interwoven with an ideal of art as something alert and immediate, which would help stake that claim. Punk graffiti was a rejection of the managed, faceless, controlled city. The nightmarish 1984 notion of control thus also plays into that rejection of regulation. "The best street art and graffiti are illegal," Cedar Lewisohn bluntly summarizes, "This is because the illegal works have political and ethical connotations that are lost in sanctioned works."[99] Graffiti was a means of resistance.

Furthermore, graffiti and street art were anti-bourgeois and anti-elite. Keith Haring wrote in a journal entry in 1978:

> The public has a right to art. The public needs art, and it is the responsibility of a 'self-proclaimed' [*sic*] artist to realize the public needs art, and not to make bourgeois art for the few and ignore the masses.[100]

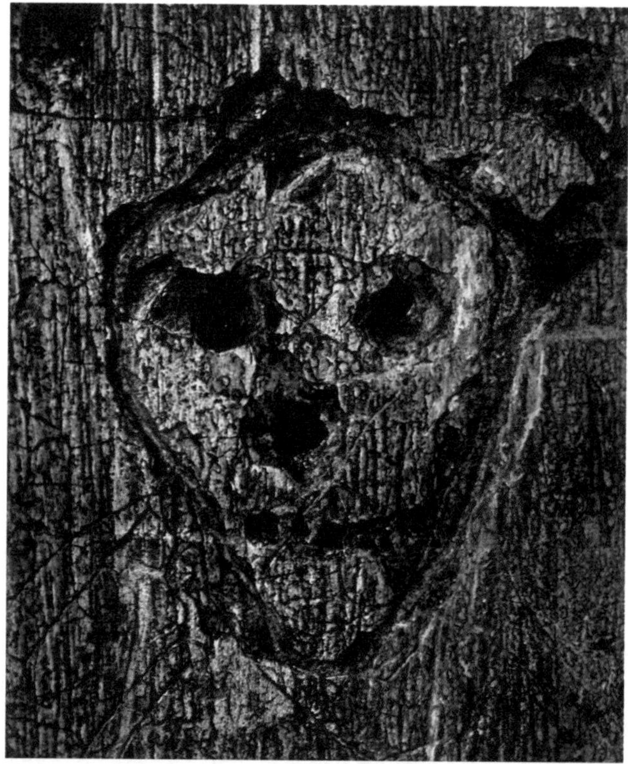

Figure 2.10: Brassaï, Graffiti Paris, *between 1935–50, Centre Pompidou, Paris. Courtesy of bpk / CNAC-MNAM / Estate Brassaï.*

"Street art in general was punk," Kenny Scharf notes, "The act of doing street art was punk. You were risking getting thrown in jail. I actually was thrown in jail."[101] The late 1970s and early 1980s works in New York all drew on the edginess of illegality. Aside from this criminal assertion, there is another—not unconnected—feature that graffiti and punk share: a sense of barbarism, tribalism, and archaism. Linking infantilism, anger, and graffiti, art critic Max Osborn wrote of Dadaist George Grosz' work: "Grosz has developed a style appropriate to his rage, in the manner of street urchins who deface walls and fences with graffiti. He swims in the tide of 'infantilism' [*sic*]."[102]

The Surrealists likewise saw street art as primitive and childlike, and attributed an anti-civilized insistence to it—but with more sensibility for the beauty and poetry of it all. Surrealist photographer Brassaï, for example, went searching for graffiti in the street of Paris, with an eye for their aesthetic (Figure 2.10). His photos are darkly compelling and visually satisfying. In 1933, in a feature about "the bastard art of the streets" in the Surrealist magazine *Minotaure,* Brassaï wrote about street art: "Its authority is absolute, overturning all the laboriously established canons of aesthetics."[103] Because graffiti

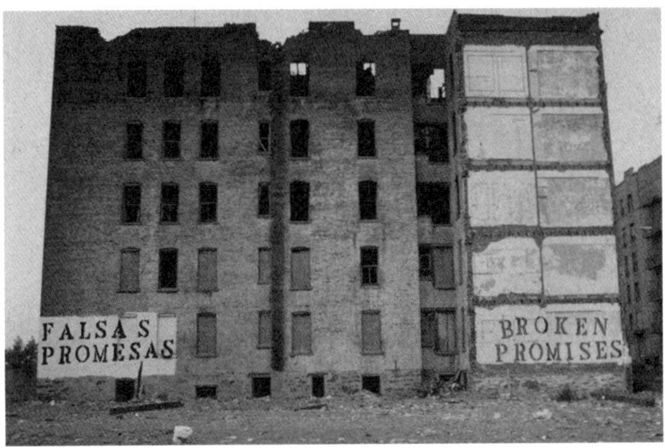

Figure 2.11: John Fekner, Broken Promises/Falsas Promesas *(Charlotte Street, South Bronx, New York), 1980. Photograph by John Fekner. Courtesy of the artist / Creative Commons.*

and street drawings are immediate, they evoke a sense of honesty. Brassaï's choice of the expression "bastard" furthermore gives his statement an air of social awareness; it alludes to bastards as unsanctioned children, innocent themselves yet punished, and at the bottom of society's hierarchy. Punks' identification as the enfants terribles of art and music corresponds to such a disposition.

There were other shared features between punk and graffiti in the late 1970s and early 1980s, such as their involvement with decay, dirtiness, ephemerality, and indeed their social criticism, as becomes palpable in a work like John Fekner's *BROKEN PROMISES/FALSAS PROMESAS*, executed in the Bronx, New York (1980, Figure 2.11). Punk and graffiti shared a no-nonsense approach that is also conveyed in the rapidness of their activity: Graffiti had to be executed as quickly as possible to avoid getting caught, and *speed* was a quintessential punk approach (more on this in the next chapter). Both sprayed and stenciled graffiti are, furthermore, associated with military and paramilitary messaging, in part due to the recognizable aesthetics of the stencils used by the US military, and the covertly famous "Kilroy was here" inscriptions by soldiers in World War II.[104] Graffiti worked as a recruiting method, too: "In order to get new people," Kaagman explains, "[we would] write our names and slogans on the street, so they would know punk is still alive."[105] Such clandestine comrade and guerrilla notions of graffiti thus likewise fit with punk's self-image as resistance. The goal of establishing an alternative way of communicating, outside the mainstream, is present both in the punk zine culture *and* in graffiti.

In the European punk movement, the graffiti connection was present in several countries, though perhaps most visibly so in the Netherlands: with punk, Amsterdam became the graffiti capital of Europe, Jonker argues in *NO Future NU*.[106] In Rotterdam, meanwhile, the Rondos were likewise engaged in street art, and were very outspoken about their reasons:

> We did have our own ideas about art. First and foremost, it had to be worthless. That is to say art should not represent any financial value. Rather a thousand bad stencils than one framed, unique but prohibitive pencil drawing with eternal value. To us, art was not a commodity, investment or status symbol. Art had to be reproducible, temporary, accessible to everyone and preferably exhibited in the streets.[107]

The band likewise expressed their view on the track "Black & White Statement": "No establishment's art / No dead man's heart / No bourgeois illustration / No ruling class frustrations / But art out on the street / A new heartbeat."[108]

One reason the interlink between punk and graffiti became especially pronounced in the Netherlands may again be a question of subcultural custom: "In Amsterdam, we had a tradition of graffiti, first and foremost the Provo movement. They wrote their name all around Amsterdam," Kaagman argues, "The hippies did some beautiful murals. [...] So, there was already a tradition of murals and graffiti."[109] Furthermore, Dr Rat aka Ivar Vičs incorporated both punk and graffiti and played a significant role in the development of the scene.[110] For a time, Dr Rat was in a relationship with Nina Hagen, who wrote the song "Dr Art" about him after his death, at the age of 21, from a heroin overdose in June 1981.[111] Vičs' pseudonym—Dr Rat—combined the ironic "Doctor" with the rat, a punk symbol par excellence. As Fanta Voogd notes, the punks adopted the rat as a mascot, with whom they shared the city as a biotope.[112] At the same time, the rat is an important symbol in street art, as can be seen, for example, in stencils by Blek le Rat and in Christy Rupp's *The Rat Patrol* (1979).

"Graffiti is the most direct form of art. It beautifies a city that is invariably becoming ever more impersonal," Gretchen Gestapo (aka Diana Ozon) stated in an article called "De Straat is ons museum" ("The street is our museum"), which was published in the summer of 1979 in *Het Parool*.[113] One year before, in the summer of 1978, John Fekner had curated the *Detective Show* in an outdoor park in Queens, New York, and written "Street Museum" on the invitation.[114] Both Fekner and Ozon thus play on the discrepancy between "street" and "museum." In 1978, the KoeCrandt group had also initiated the *Grand Prix du Graffiti*, which was awarded yearly from then on. The use of the French *Grand Prix* is comparable to COUM Transmissions' *Ecole de l'Art Infantile*—in both cases, the artists undermine the connotations of tradition

and institutionalism. In the title *Grand Prix du Graffiti*, the contrast between the art-historical implications of a *Grand Prix* (hierarchy, judgement, high/sanctioned art) and *Graffiti* (accessibility, equality, low/lawless art) crystallizes.

Notes

1. Torres, "Traces of a Punk Attitude," 45.

2. Sabin, "Introduction," 2.

3. Quoted in Kugelberg and Savage, *Punk: An Aesthetic*, 52.

4. Leo Margulies, ed., *The Young Punks* (New York: Pyramid Books, 1957).

5. See Dave Markey, director, *1991: The Year Punk Broke*, DVD (New York: Geffen Records, 2011) and Clinton Heylin, *Babylon's Burning: From Punk to Grunge* (London: Penguin, 2007).

6. Savage, *England's Dreaming*, 139.

7. See David Hopkins, "Oz Magazine and British Counterculture: A Case Study in the Reception of Surrealism," in *Radical Dreams. Surrealism, Counterculture, Resistance*, eds. Elliott King and Abigail Susik (University Park: The Pennsylvania State University Press, 2022).

8. Joe Madura and Dominic Molon, "A Timeline," in *Sympathy for the Devil*, 253.

9. Savage, *England's Dreaming*, 92.

10. See Jay Sanders, ed., *Rituals of Rented Island: Object Theater, Loft Performance, and the New Psychodrama: Manhattan 1970–1980* (New York: Whitney Museum of American Art, 2013).

11. Legs McNeil and Gillian McCain, *Please Kill Me: The Uncensored Oral History of Punk* (New York: Grove Press, 1996), 255.

12. Servando Rocha, "A Great Negative Work of Destruction to Be Accomplished," in *PUNK*, 290–291.

13. Savage, *England's Dreaming*, 93.

14. Malcolm McLaren quoted in Savage, *England's Dreaming*, 92.

15. Johnny Rotten quoted in Savage, *England's Dreaming*, 114.

16. Reynolds, "Ono, Eno, Arto," in *Sympathy for the Devil*, ed. Dominic Molon, 88.

17. Paul Burgess, "'Cut' – The Punk Use of Collage," paper, *The Art of Punk Conference*, University of Northampton, November 25, 2016. Burgess quotes from Malcolm McLaren's private notebooks, to which he gained access during his research.

18. "Malcolm McLaren im Gespräch mit Gerald Matt," in *Punk: No One Is Innocent*, 196.

19. Jon Savage, "The World's End: London Punk 1976–1977," in *Punk: No One Is Innocent*, 42.

20. Savage, "The World's End," 46.

21. Alan Palmer, *East End: Four Centuries of London Life* (London: Faber & Faber, 2011).

22. *New York Daily News*, October 29, 1975.

23. Sabin, "Introduction," 3.

24. John A. Walker, *Left Shift: Radical Art in 1970s Britain* (London: I.B. Tauris, 2002), 15.

25. Jon Savage, "London Subversive," in *Goodbye to London: Radical Art and Politics in the Seventies*, ed. Astrid Proll (Ostfildern: Hatje Cantz), 28.

26. Andy Beckett, *When the Lights Went Out: What Really Happened to Britain in the Seventies* (London: Faber & Faber, 2009), 15.

27. Astrid Proll, "Hello London," in *Goodbye to London: Radical Art and Politics in the Seventies*, ed. Astrid Proll (Cologne: Hatje Cantz, 2010), 11.

28. Savage, "London Subversive," 25, 28.

29. Sex Pistols, "God Save the Queen.".

30. The Clash, "White Riot" (Copenhagen: CBS, 1977).

31. Roger Horowitz, *A Social History of Industrial Unionism in Meatpacking, 1930–90* (Champaign: University of Illinois Press, 1997), xi.

32. Paul Gilroy, *There Ain't No Black in the Union Jack: The Cultural Politics of Race and Nation* (London: Routledge, 2002), 156.

33. Stephen Duncombe, "White Riot?" in *White Riot: Punk Rock and the Politics of Race*, eds. Stephen Duncombe and Maxwell Tremblay (Brooklyn: Verso 2011), 7.

34. Sex Pistols, "God Save the Queen" (UK: Virgin Records, 1977).

35. Savage, "London Subversive," 29.

36. Dave Laing, *One Chord Wonders: Power and Meaning in Punk Rock* (London: Open University Press, 1985), 137.

37. Savage, *England's Dreaming*, 479.

38. To this day, the case is disputed; because Vicious died before the case could be tried, there was no verdict.

39. Crass, "Punk is Dead" (Essex: Crass Records, 1979).

40. These lyrics were also put on the cover of the zine *Feminaxe*. See https://www.rebeldykeshistoryproject.com (accessed October 26, 2022).

41. Savage, *England's Dreaming*, 481.

42. Punk rock as a musical genre was present already in the mid 1970s in Australia, exemplified through such bands as the Saints and Radio Birdman, the latter of whom had close connections to the Detroit proto-punk scene.

43. Crass, "White Punks on Hope" (Essex: Crass Records, 1979).

44. Sabin, "Introduction," 7.

45. Huxley, "'Ever Get the Feeling You've Been Cheated?'" 82.

46. Sabin, "Introduction," 7.

47. Schneider, *Als die Welt noch unterging*, 180.

48. Laing, *One Chord Wonders*, 168.

49. Rocha, "Great Negative Work," 290.

50. In *Art Into Pop* (1987), Simon Frith and Howard Horne depict the art school/rock connection as a primarily British phenomenon, but (at least) in punk such connections were also strong in other countries, such as Germany, Holland, and the United States.

51. See Burgess, "'Cut' and Savage," in *England's Dreaming*, 23.

52. Malcolm McLaren quoted in Savage, *England's Dreaming*, 23.

53. Anna Coatman, "Watch These Spaces: The Future of Art Schools," in *RA Magazine*, Spring Issue 2016,

accessed December 8, 2017, https://www.royalacademy.org.uk/article/future-of-art-schools.

54. Malcolm McLaren's Notebook 1975–1976. Quoted by Burgess, "Cut."

55. As well as punk festivals and disco clubs, see "Gig Archive 1975–2008", accessed July 8, 2017, http://www.sexpistolsofficial.com/gig-archive-1975-2008.

56. Kaagman, interview, 2017.

57. See Hans Richter, "How Did Dada Begin?" in *Dada, Art and Anti-Art*, trans. David Britt (London: Thames and Hudson, 1997), 12–19.

58. Erwin Schulhoff (1919), quoted in Ralf Beil, ed., *A House Full of Music: Strategien in Musik und Kunst*, 29.

59. See Peter Wollen, "Bitter Victory: The Art and Politics of the Situationist International," in *On the Passage of a Few People through a Rather Brief Moment in Time: The Situationist International 1957–1972*, ed. Elisabeth Sussman (Cambridge: MIT Press, 1989) and David Wise, ed., *King Mob: A Critical Hidden History* (London: Bread and Circusses, 2014).

60. Walter Benjamin, "Surrealism: The Last Snapshot of the European Intelligentsia (1929)," in *Modernism: An Anthology*, ed. Lawrence Rainey (Malden: Blackwell Publishing, 2005), 1092.

61. Press release, *The Destruction in Art Symposium* (*DIAS*), Africa Centre, Covent Garden, London, September 9–11, 1966.

62. Malcolm McLaren, "This Much I Know," in *The Guardian*, November 16, 2008.

63. See Barry Miles, *London Calling: A Countercultural History of London Since 1945* (London: Atlantic Books, 2011).

64. Pete Townsend quoted in Miles, *London Calling*, n.p.

65. Hannah Higgins, *Fluxus Experience* (Berkeley: University of California Press, 2002), 51.

66. Undated, quoted in Savage, *England's Dreaming*, 27.

67. Wise, *King Mob*, n.p.

68. Sam Cooper, *The Situationist International in Britain: Modernism, Surrealism, and the Avant-Gardes* (New York: Routledge 2017), 136–37.

69. Mikkel Bolt Rasmussen, "Raping the Whole World in a Warm Embrace of Fascination: Drakabygget's Anti-Authoritarian Artistic Endeavors," in *A Cultural History of the Avant-Garde in the Nordic Countries 1950–1975*, eds. Tania Ørum and Jesper Olsson (Leiden: Brill Rodopi, 2016), 594.

70. Vaneigem quoted in Elisabeth Sussman, "Introduction," in *On the Passage of a Few People*, 9. Emphasis added.

71. Rasmussen, "Raping the Whole World in a Warm Embrace of Fascination," 594. Emphasis added. See also: Mikkel Bolt Rasmussen, "The Fantasy of a Powerful Myth; The Situationist International After Surrealism," in *Radical Dreams*.

72. Hari Kunzru, "The Mob Who Shouldn't Really Be Here," *Tate Etc.* 13 (Summer 2008), accessed January 23, 2018, http://www.tate.org.uk/context-comment/articles/mob-who-shouldnt-really-be-here.

73. See Paul Hollins, "Never Mind the Paradox; 'Situationists', the Sorbonne and Ongoing Influence of Atelier Populaire on Punk Art and Culture", paper, *The Art of Punk Conference*, University of Northampton, November 25, 2016 and Johan Kugelberg and Philippe Vermès, eds., *Beauty is in the Street: A Visual Record of the May '68 Uprising* (London: Four Corners Books, 2011).

74. Hollins, "Never Mind the Paradox" (manuscript obtained from Hollins).

75. Liam Considine, "Screen Politics: Pop Art and the Atelier Populaire," *Tate Papers*, no. 24 (Autumn 2015), accessed February 20, 2018, http://www.tate.org.uk/research/publications/tate-papers/24/screen-politics-pop-art-and-the-atelier-populaire.

76. Reynolds, "Ono, Eno, Arto," 81.

77. Reynolds, "Ono, Eno, Arto," 82.

78. Brian Eno quoted in Reynolds, "Ono, Eno, Arto," 83.

79. "The Oblique Strategies," accessed January 19, 2018, http://www.rtqe.net/ObliqueStrategies/OSintro.html.

80. Jon Savage, "Cut-Ups Go Pop: William S. Burroughs and a Mashed-up Future," in *Cut-Ups, Cut-Ins, Cut-Outs: The Art of William S. Burroughs*, eds. Kunsthalle Wien, Colin Fallows, and Synne Genzmer (Nuremberg: Verlag für Moderne Kunst, 2012), 42.

81. Savage, "Cut-Ups Go Pop," 42.

82. Barry Miles, "The Future Leaks Out: A Very Magical and Highly Charged Interlude," in *Cut-Ups, Cut-Ins, Cut-Outs*, 12.

83. See Michael Duncan and Kristine McKenna, *Semina Culture. Wallace Berman & His Circle* (Santa Monica: Santa Monica Museum of Art and New York: D.A.P., 2007).

84. Gretchen L. Wagner, "Riot on the Page: Thirty Years of Zines by Women," in *Modern Women: Women Artists at the Museum of Modern Art*, ed. Cornelia Butler and Alexandra Schwartz (New York: MoMA, 2010), 446.

85. Kaagman, interview, 2017.

86. Käthe Kruse, interview with the author, October 23, 2017.

87. Genesis P-Orridge quoted in Simon Ford, *Wreckers of Civilisation: The Story of COUM Transmissions & Throbbing Gristle* (London: Black Dog Publishing, 1999), 5.17.

88. Robert Christgau, "'We Have to Deal with It'. Punk England Report," in *Village Voice*, January 9, 1978, accessed January 5, 2018, https://www.robertchristgau.com/xg/rock/punk-78.php.

89. Mark P. in *Sniffin' Glue*, no. 5, November 1976, n.p.

90. Martin Hall quoted in Poulsen, *Something Rotten. Punk i Danmark: Maleri, Musik og Litteratur* (Copenhagen: Gyldendal, 2010), 217.

91. Elmer, interview with the author, May 24, 2018.

92. See Marie Arleth Skov, "Dominas & Paradisvögel. Sexyness, Spiel und Subkultur im Leben der Claudia Skoda," in *Claudia Skoda: Dressed to Thrill*, eds. Britta Bommert and Staatliche Museen zu Berlin (Dortmund: Verlag Kettler, 2020), 31–49.

93. Martin Schmitz, "The Medium Was the Message," in *Berlin Super 80: Music & Film Underground West Berlin 1978–1984* [DVD, CD, and booklet] (Berlin: Monitorpop, 2005), 7.

94. See Müller and Schmitz, *Die Tödliche Doris – Kino / The Deadly Doris – Cinema. Band* 4 (Berlin: Martin Schmitz Verlag, 2004).

95. Kulle, "Alle Macht der Super 8," 262.

96. Dirk Schaefer, "City of Projections: The West Berlin Super 8 Movement between Punk and Art School," in *Who Says Concrete Doesn't Burn, Have You Tried? West Berlin Film in the '80s*, eds. Stefanie Schulte Strathaus and Florian Wüst (Berlin: b books, 2008), 29.

97. The Clash, "London Calling" (Copenhagen: CBS, 1979).

98. Jerry Goossens, "A Black and White Statement," 201.

99. Cedar Lewisohn, *Street Art: The Graffiti Revolution* (London: Tate Publishing, 2008), 127.

100. Keith Haring quoted in Lewisohn, *Street Art*, n.p.

101. Kenny Scharf quoted in Lewisohn, *Street Art*, 76.

102. Max Osborn, 'Dada,' Vossische Zeitung, July 17, 1920. Quoted in Adamowicz, *Dada Bodies*, 138.

103. Brassaï in *Minotaure*, quoted in Lewisohn, *Street Art*, 29.

104. Lewisohn, *Street Art*, 70.

105. Kaagman, interview, 2017.

106. Jonker, *NO Future NU, Punk in Nederland 1977–2012* (Amsterdam: Lebowski Publishers, 2012), 155.

107. Rondos, "Biography," accessed May 8, 2018, http://rondos.nl/rondos_biografie/index.php?id=biography.

108. Rondos, "Black & White Statement" (King Kong Records, 1980).

109. Kaagman, interview, 2017.

110. See Martijn Haas, *Dr. Rat, godfather van de Nederlandse graffiti* (Amsterdam: Lebowski Publishers, 2011).

111. Nina Hagen, "Dr. Art" (CBS, 1982). See also Jerry Goossens and Jeroen Vedder, *Het Gejuich was massaal. Punk in Nederland 1976–1982* (Amsterdam: Schilt Publishing, 1996), 48.

112. Fanta Voogd, "Punk in Amsterdam," in *Ons Amsterdam*, no. 3, March 2013, accessed May 8, 2018, http://www.onsamsterdam.nl/tijdschrift/jaargang-2013.

113. Gretchen Gestapo, "De Straat is ons museum," in *Het Parool*, August 17, 1979.

114. Lewisohn, *Street Art*, 15.

3 Pop Multiples, Camp Affirmations

All that was fake, throw-away, and camp was celebrated in punk. In this chapter, we dive into that part of punk and punk art: the exaltation of trash. Trash in punk became a method, a way of showing reality, a way of distancing from High Art, and a way of attacking synthetic consumer culture. Punk as a movement had a double-sided relationship to the superficiality of pop and "unserious" entertainment: on the one hand, pop culture could be used to scare off the cultural snobs. By embracing the fake and cheap, punk distanced itself from the elite. On the other hand, pop culture was viewed critically, because it is born of a capitalist system that reduces culture to a product. Against this latter trait, two counter strategies formed in punk: either to draw away into a subcultural realm and attempt to avoid that mainstream pop culture altogether, *or* to engage with it and satirically overdo it, thus exposing its true nature. Groups such as the Sex Pistols in the UK and Die Tödliche Doris in West Germany, for example, worked with a kind of über-affirmation, the idea being to usurp the capitalist media scheme by excessively animating it. Either way—all that was camp, trash, pop, or fake was of interest.

It is not surprising then, that Andy Warhol, as Billy Klüver remarks, became the "hero of the punks."[1] In the first part of this chapter, we take a closer look at punk's relationship with and view of Warhol. There is the portrait of Andy Warhol, which was shown in the *Punk Art* exhibition in Washington and New York in 1978, and which Neke Carson painted with his butt. We also look at punk artworks that engage with a "Warholian" kind of strategy. One example is the *Art-o-Maat* in Amsterdam, which was an art vending machine, that is, art as a cheap commodity. Another example is Die Tödliche Doris' conceptual LP, which could only be played on a plastic play device: satirical pop pure.

The second part of the chapter, "Hedonism as attack," looks at the question of whether Pop Art can be subversive and if satirical über-affirmation of pop culture phenomenon can be used as an attack on commercialized consumer culture. The argument here is that punk as a movement in theory agreed with the critical thoughts voiced by the Situationist International, yet in praxis were closer to the ex-Situationists. We also take a look at how punk art positioned itself with regard to Peter Bürger's criticism of the neo-avant-garde.

The last part of this chapter is about "Trash and travesty": How was trash used in punk to traverse conservative ideas about art? This question touches on punk's concepts of history too. Punk art and punk music were often characterized by a sense of vicissitude and speed, for example in the cartoonish-dynamic style of a painting like *This Is Just a*

Temporary Place to Stay by Lars Nørgård (1982): art for the here and now. (Art/cultural) History, however, often plays a key role in punk art. How did Richard Hell put it in 1973? "Today's garbage is tomorrow's culture." In punk anno 1979, that also meant: yesterday's garbage is our culture today.

3.1 Andy Warhol: "Hero of the Punks"

Andy Warhol, with his subversive pop star status, factory entourage, and his play on surface, was admired among punk artists. The youth culture and trash culture aspects of Pop Art built a bridge to punk artists. Punk hit popular culture like no radical movement before. "It is art and pop that remain after the passing of the punk movement," Robert Garnett writes.[2] To him, punk was so effective because it opened a space between pop and art, and used both. We should not forget that at the time of the first punk generation, "pop" was widely considered vulgar and corrupt (and in the UK: "too American"[3]).

Pop Art like punk went against the fakery of sincerity in the artworld: P-Orridge thus, for example, produced a rubber stamp to use instead of the pathos-charged handwritten signature in the bottom right corner of the masterpiece.

> The repeated signatures [...] are actually a RUBBER STAMP ov [*sic*] my signature. So theoretically anyone could SIGN anything as me. Negating the ARTIST's signature confirming value of signed paintings etc. It was also inspired by DIVINE who we read had a rubber stamp that said "YOURS SINCERELY DIVINE" that she would use when asked to autograph records and photos etc. Thee [*sic*] negation of "sincerely" was so twisted and brilliant.[4]

The fact that P-Orridge got the idea from drag queen Divine (of the John Waters movies) just adds one more link between punk and the 1960s trash and pop scene in New York. John Waters and Divine might also be the perfect example of what Susan Sontag was getting at in her famed "Notes on Camp," when she observes the loving character of camp taste:

> It relishes, rather than judges, the little triuphs and awkward intensities of "character" [*sic*]. Camp taste identifies with what it is enjoying. People who share this sensibility are not laughing at the thing they label as "a camp," they're enjoying it. Camp is a tender feeling. (Here, one may compare Camp with much of Pop Art, which—when it is not just Camp—embodies an attitude that is related, but still very different. Pop Art is more flat and more dry, more serious, more detached, ultimately nihilistic.)[5]

It was that nihilist streak, which Sontag is getting at, and it was the lowness of pop that made it useful to punk. "Once the media gets in it's going to be slightly commercialized. But me personally [...] I love the commercialization of culture," Caroline Coon provoked.[6] Buzzcocks' debut album *Another Music in a Different Kitchen* (1978) was sold in a carrier bag with the word PRODUCT, and the catalog number printed bigger than the name of the band. After the wave of holier-than-thou moralistic and didactic-political artwork of the 1960s and 1970s, such a bluntness was a gulp of fresh air.

Asked by Bill Grundy in that infamous 1976 interview, if the 40,000 pounds they had earned were not "slightly opposed to their anti-materialistic view," the Sex Pistols laughed: "the more, the merrier [...] spent it didn't we, it is all gone down the boozer."[7] Filthy moneymaking and fame only added to their repertoire of shock tactics. The purpose, though, was to use the platform of pop to expose hypocrisy. Greil Marcus' analysis dissects the means by which this was achieved:

> Thus they made it clear that their attack on the vacuity of pop was merely an instinctive means to a far more disturbing attack on sex, as the mystification behind love, on love, as the mystification behind the family, on the family, as the mystification behind the class system, on the class system, as the mystification behind capitalism, and finally on the very notion of progress—as the ultimate mystification behind post-industrial Western society itself. Veterans of spontaneous student revolts would have been familiar with such an expansion of vision—but the world of pop had never seen anything like it before.[8]

Against Marcus's claim of an absolute lack of precedent, the one predecessor that must be invoked is exactly Andy Warhol: his *Exploding Plastic Inevitable*, his factory entourage, and his play on that same vacuity that Marcus targets. As we shall see, Warhol was a crucial figure in punk. Genesis P-Orridge and Malcolm McLaren were both fixated on Warhol, whose strategies are echoed in both their work. As for Westwood, according to Savage she "cultivated her own inner circle of performers [who] gave punk its Warholian edge." He observes "a similar carnival of the oppressed and the Bohemian, prostitutes and drug addicts, the brilliant and the publicity-seeking. These teenagers changed their lives in pop acts of transformation, using bizarre dress codes, cartoon pseudonyms and amphetamines."[9] Warhol's creation of a scene, a real-life tableau of performers and characters, staging their lives, was thus replicated in punk.

Portrait by an asshole

In 1978, Billy Klüver interviewed Andy Warhol and Victor Hugo for the catalog of

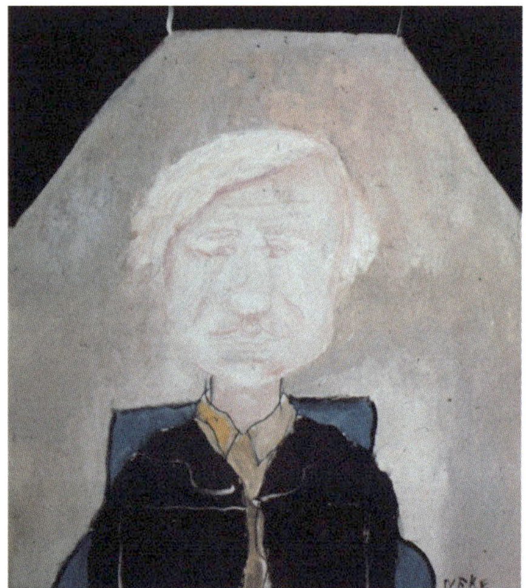

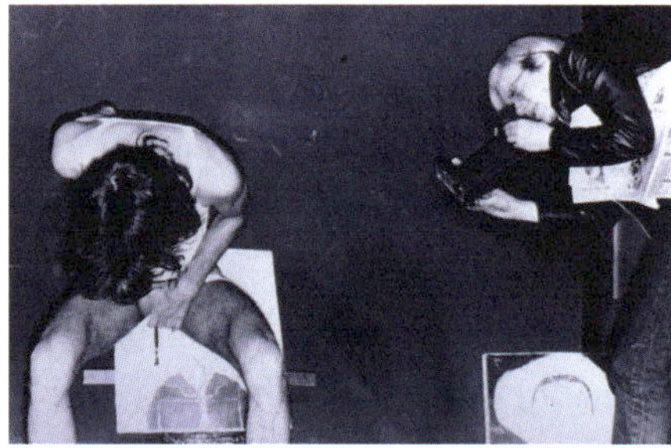

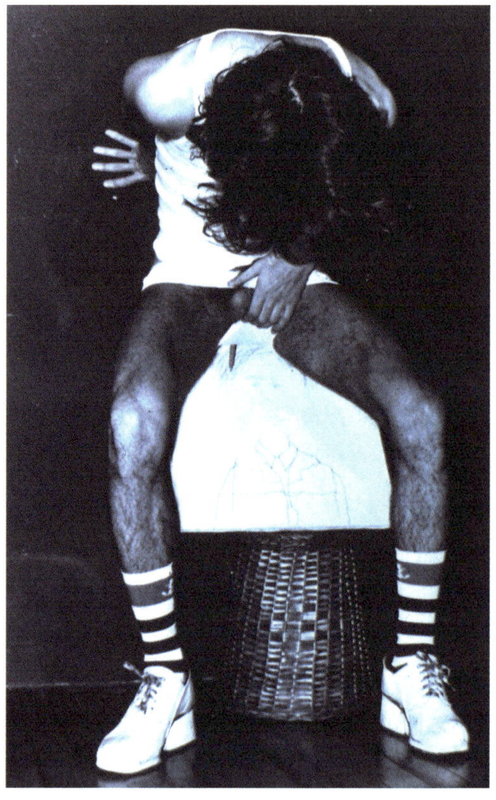

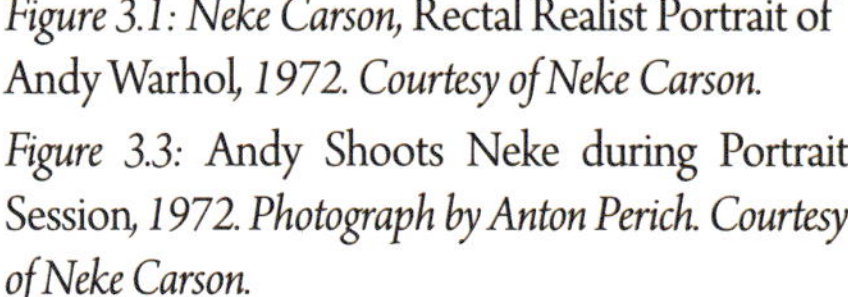

Figure 3.1: Neke Carson, Rectal Realist Portrait of Andy Warhol, *1972. Courtesy of Neke Carson.*

Figure 3.2: Neke Working on Andy's Hair, *1972. Photograph by Anton Perich. Courtesy of Neke Carson.*

Figure 3.3: Andy Shoots Neke during Portrait Session, *1972. Photograph by Anton Perich. Courtesy of Neke Carson.*

the *Punk Art Exhibition* (see Section 1.3: "Case in point: The first *Punk Art* exhibition, 1978"). Klüver remarks: "I was sitting in Max's [Kansas City] the other day and someone told me that you are the hero of the punks, Andy. Everyone is reading your books." The three of them discuss a punk girl who cut her wrists at Hugo's party. Hugo: "But that is too bad because she cannot sell that. She has impressed people but she doesn't get any money for it. Just a little publicity. Fame and no money." Warhol: "And a few cuts."[10] The short exchange shows the mutual fascination of the late Pop Art scene and punk, but also a certain incomprehension; perhaps fame, no money, and a few cuts were all the punks wanted, at least at the outset. "Andy seemed to think of punk as graffiti kids and drag queens," says Miller, adding, "And everybody loved Andy."[11]

Punk's fascination with Warhol stems from the intelligence of his provocation, his celebration of the low, his media diversity, and his dual existence as both mass media star and bohemian. Included in the *Punk Art Exhibition* was one special show of love for Andy Warhol: Neke Carson's "Rectal Realist" portrait (Figure 3.1). Carson stuck a paintbrush up his rectum, and thus ultimately painted Warhol with his asshole (Figure 3.2). Warhol—of course—sat for the séance, and very much enjoyed the idea, which he conversely documented with his own camera (Figure 3.3).[12] To paint Warhol—the master of ironic and iconic portraits—in this manner is not only very humorful but also quite precise in its adaption of a Warholian technique. The "realist" in Carson's description of his paintings alludes to Pop Art's own notion of the *base* and the *immediate* as what is "realist" in art. Realism in art, thus, is the everyday, including trash, commercials, and entertainment. Furthermore, Carson's work underlines how punk art often parodies both the self-importance of Body Art and the painterly genius gesture, and instead is oriented toward the lowbrow notions of Pop Art. Art historians thus might, one day, write about the painterly ductus of the piece, though not of the hand, but of the rectum. What a joke. Concurrently, in the performance and Body Art scene, some artists had at times a tendency to give themselves difficult little tasks and execute these with great pathos, sometimes bordering on biblical imagery. Carson is likewise mimicking such a pretend difficulty but undercutting the seriousness of it with his deadpan low humor.

The *Art-o-Maat*: Vending machine miniature artwork

Another example of Pop Art in punk is the series of so-called *Art-o-Maats* (1977–78) by the KoeCrandt artists group in Amsterdam. The *Art-o-Maats* were art vending machines, that is, art as a product, and a cheap one at that (Figure 3.4). The *Art-o-Maats* were converted from cigarette vending machines, with their original content removed and replaced by small boxes containing miniature artworks, tiny zines, and poem collections, or other small items fitting into the size of a cigarette pack, such as small-sized smoke bombs (smoke cakes). With a Pop Art-like use of punk symbols, the artists decorated the devices with nails, scissors, safety pins, and razor blades, but they were still recognizable as former cigarette vending machines. By inserting two guilders, it was possible to choose between five different options, matching the five cigarette brands before. Beneath the output compartment, the artists put an idea box for the buyers. In the first *Art-o-Maats*, the KoeCrandt group still used old cigarette packs, which they asked for or bought, but the packs of cigarettes were expensive compared to the rolled tobacco they usually smoked, and Ozon thus began making multiple boxes out of cardboard using a template.

The *Art-o-Maats* were placed all over Amsterdam, and sometimes moved around. One device was in the theater De Brakke Grond, one in Café Scheltema, one was in the

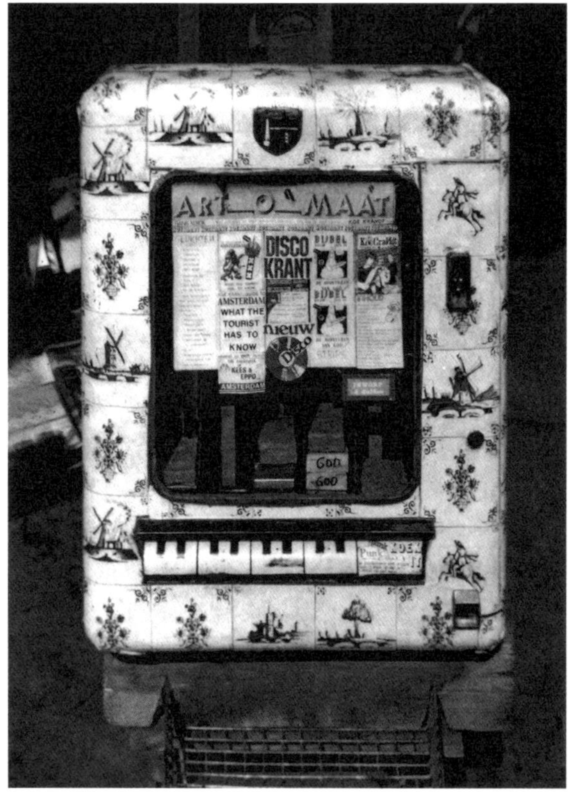

Figure 3.4: The KoeCrandt Group, Art-o-Maat, *Amsterdam, 1977–78. Courtesy of Hugo Kaagman.*

bookshop Athenaeum, and one in a supermarket. The chosen sites were thus a mixture of high and low. Ironically, one *Art-o-Maat* was placed on the Spui, where the illustrious anti-tobacco-company happenings of Robert Jasper Grootveld had taken place in the 1960s. According to the artists, the one that sold the most was placed in the Stedelijk Museum. Ozon says,

> The guards in the Stedelijk Museum were shocked that people were putting in money, so they were buying art in the museum. Doing something economical in the museum, perhaps even without the museum knowing? How disrespectful! Of course, we liked that.[13]

The equation of art and commodity was one of the points of the action. The artists played with the appropriation of commercial selling tactics and with the lowbrow connotations of merchandise, not unlike what Buzzcocks were doing at the same time in the UK with their PRODUCT imprint (see previously in this chapter).

"The shops complained about the smoke bombs, because people would open them inside the shop," Kaagman recounts, but overall, the response to the *Art-o-Maats* was positive, "Xerox even sponsored us! Because of the *Art-o-Maats*. We thought that was cool."[14] The sponsorship from Xerox shows both how the public perception of punk had not yet consolidated and how open the punk scene still was—a sponsorship was just a practical means, there was nothing to sell out. "[With the sponsorship from Xerox] it became possible to make huge amounts of photocopies. Xerox machines were still very rare. Hugo and Kristian went there and talked to them, said they were artists," Ozon says,

> Back then, it was so early, punk was still interesting, fashionable. The Xerox people had no idea. Punk was not yet connotated with squatting, graffiti. The magazines were writing: 'This is the new fashion, it is the new music, it is from London, it is from New York, Andy Warhol likes it!' So, the Xerox people did not know what punk really was, what we were doing. They did not know that it was really something coming from underneath, from kids.[15]

The *Art-o-Maats* combined several elements of punk art. With the *Art-o-Maats*, art was literally at street level. The art vending machines thus symbolized both *cheap* and *accessible* culture. The artists engaged with notions of the automatic and the Pop Art subject of the copy, rather than original, of art as a serial machine production. There was a playful element in this art-to-go, and perhaps also an element of the childish. The sensation of placing a coin in a machine is associated with colorful candy machines and the calculated small surprise of bulk vending. This childish ambiance is further enhanced through the miniature formats. There are Duchampian notions both of chance and of the miniature present in the *Art-o-Maats* (see Chapter 6: "Children Run Riot: The Art of the Infantile" on the childish elements of punk art too, specifically the doll record player used by Die Tödliche Doris for *Choirs and Solos*).

The collaborative concept of the *Art-o-Maats* is, furthermore, similar to that of George Maciunas' *Flux-Kits* (the first one was made in 1962), which variously contained works by Joe Jones, Mieko Shiomi, Alison Knowles, George Brecht, and others, as well as miniature editions of Fluxus newspapers, fitted into a converted attaché case.[16] In Europe, the *Flux-Kits* were distributed through the Amsterdam-based *European Mail-Order Warehouse/Fluxshop* of Willem de Ridder, incidentally also the founder of Paradiso. Both in the *Art-o-Maats* and the *Flux-Kits*, poetry and interaction were key factors. The *Flux-Kits* contained performance score cards and artworks to be touched and handled, for example, a noisemaker by Joe Jones, which thus had an effect comparable to the small smoke bombs in the *Art-o-Maats*. The main difference, however, was that the *Art-o-Maat* was placed on the street. Indirectly, the punk criticism of Fluxus as an art form for the privileged few art collectors is thus repeated in the format of the *Art-o-Maat* in comparison with the *Flux-Kits*. The Fluxus attaché cases were advertised at 100 USD—not a high price, we might argue—but nonetheless, more expensive than the punk artworks in the *Art-o-Maat* (two guilders). More important, however, was the means of dissemination: the *Art-o-Maat* concept emphasized street art notions of intervention in the flow of everyday life, the involvement of the passerby, and general accessibility; in opposition to the friends-of-friends trade of the Fluxus editions. On top of that, the *Art-o-Maats* and the sponsorship by Xerox was an open and candid play with the commercialization of culture.

Art and punk in little green boxes

In relation to the *Art-o-Maats*, the artists' group Die Tödliche Doris released their second LP *Chöre und Soli* (*Choirs and Solos*, 1983) on small doll records, colorful like candy (Figure 3.5). "The absolute wickedness of our first LP was followed by the opposite, the childish, the innocent, in *Choirs and Solos*," says Müller.[17] The LP was released in an edition of 1000. It consisted of eight children's toy mini-record discs in eight different colors, a matching battery-driven device for playing these discs, and a small booklet. All of this was packed in a green box.

The box was released by Ursula Block from the gallery Gelbe Musik (Yellow music) together with Carmen Knoebel from the Düsseldorf punk label Pure Freude (Pure happiness). Alongside Ingrid Kohlhöfer, Carmen Knoebel managed the Ratinger Hof in Düsseldorf, a venue where art and punk mixed. The co-label, Gelbe Musik, was a pioneer of the intersections between art and music, and one of the first galleries in Germany to devote itself to sound art. Die Tödliche Doris' move from their first label, the punk pioneers at ZickZack to Gelbe Musik/Pure Freude thus signifies a move toward a more obviously artsy concept. "We did that very strategically," says Müller,

> The *Choirs and Solos* box is green because of Duchamp's green box. We thought: Wouldn't it be great if the punks bought a piece of art, without knowing it, and then later the people of the art scene would have to buy it back from the punks for a whole lot of money [laughs]. You know, to counterbalance a bit![18]

Müller is referring to Marcel Duchamp's *The Green Box* from 1934, in which his alter ego Rrose Sélavy published his thoughts on *The Bride Stripped Bare by Her Bachelors, Even* or *The Large Glass* (1915–23). *The Green Box* includes items evidencing Duchamp's poetic incursions and abandoned paths, showing the openness of his process. The content is

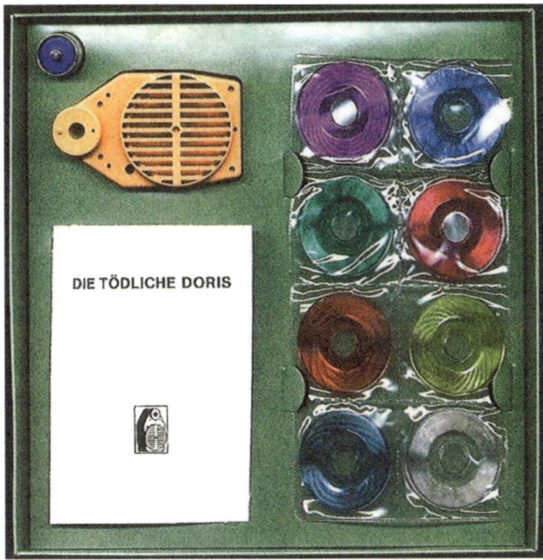

Figure 3.5: Die Tödliche Doris, Chöre und Soli (Choirs and Solos, *1983). Archiv der Tödlichen Doris. Courtesy of Wolfgang Müller.*

randomly sorted, and thus influenced by chance as well as the choices made by whoever opens the box: what to look at first? Duchamp's box was produced in an edition of 300, using collotype. The miniature increases the intimate relationship between viewer and artist. This effect of intimacy is reproduced with the miniature discs and special device in Die Tödliche Doris' box: the result is like a little mystery of intimate communication between the makers and their recipients. In both cases—*The Green Box* and the *Choirs and Solos* box—this intimacy is intensified through the physical task of opening the respective box, the unpacking, and the touching. The children's toybox connotation, which is already present in Duchamp's work, is even stronger in Tödliche Doris' box since it does indeed involve a children's toy, the doll record player (see Chapter 6: "Children Run Riot: The Art of the Infantile" on the topic of punk and infantilism).

The miniatures of both the KoeCrandt group's *Art-o-Maat* and Die Tödliche Doris' *Choirs and Solos* are attempts to break through the usual way of art distribution. Müller's musings on selling the artwork LP to punks, who would be able to sell them for a lot of money later on, point to his wish to circumvent the art market system or play with it at the least (the box is being sold for around 600 USD on various internet platforms, such as popsike.com, as of November 2021).

The aesthetics of Die Tödliche Doris' green box and its contents are in themselves very *pop*, indeed quite Warholian. There is the aspect of multiplication, the same product in various colors, like a Campbell's Soup Can, or a Marilyn Monroe. The small discs look like condoms or comfits, choose your favorite flavor. The music on the discs, however, is punk, moving in the direction of industrial. There are also the aspects of surface (smooth plastic) and of amusement (by consumption), both inherently pop. So, in the cases of the *Art-o-Maat* and the *Choirs and Solos* doll player record, we are looking at punk works of art, taking over and adapting Pop Art visual language and pop distribution (the automat, the product, the "fun" edition). As we shall see in the next chapter, "Hedonism as attack," these means of distribution were just one aspect of a full-on embrace of pop culture phenomena, but with the purpose to subvert.

3.2 Hedonism as attack

Andy Warhol's affirmation of cheap pop and trash culture, the overdone fakeness and fun of yellow press, blonde bombshells, and crazy comics was embraced and celebrated in punk. That above-mentioned play on surface and vacuity, the de-mystification of the artistic procedure, was key both in Pop Art and punk art. The critical question, however—which the punks were not the first to ask themselves—was if that kind of affirmation could indeed be subversive? Could consumer culture be undermined essentially by mirroring it? Demise by exaggeration? Hedonism as attack? There are several strands of argumentation on this entangled topic of fame, fortune, art, and opposition. Somewhat simplistically, the question of whether affirmation could be used to subvert has the Situationists and Peter Bürger united on one side, and the ex-Situationists and the punks on the other. Sam Cooper's argument, that the ex-Situationists tended toward *hyper*-spectacle rather than Debord's *anti*-spectacle (see Section 2.3: "Punk precursors") is thus continued in punk. While the Situationists proposed to disengage from and negate pop culture, punk instead accelerated it.

Let's break it down:

In the views of many punk art protagonists, the radicality of the original avant-garde, primarily Futurism, Dada, and Surrealism, had been lost in the dominant neo-avant-garde art (Pop Art, Nouveau Réalisme, Fluxus, etc.) in the post-war decades. Genesis P-Orridge, at that time of COUM Transmissions, called Fluxus a "self-congratulatory wank"[19] (see Section 3.3: "Trash and travesty") while Wolfgang Müller of Die Tödliche Doris criticized the "protestant cheerfulness"[20] of Fluxus artists (see also Section 5.1: "Originality and appropriation" and Section 7.2: "Ingenious Dilettantes"). Their criticism agrees with the argument of figures such as Situationist Guy Debord and Peter Bürger in his *Theorie der Avantgarde*. Essentially, the Situationists formulated much of Bürger's criticism of the neo-avant-garde around ten years before him. Debord describes in *Society of the Spectacle*—TV, advertising, celebrity culture, and so on as capitalism's vehicle for pacification and distraction. In *Theorie der Avantgarde*, Bürger specifically criticizes Warhol and more generally Pop Art, and he does not see how affirmation can be subversive. The core point of criticism both for Debord and for Bürger, however, was that the neo-avant-garde had become the avant-garde *gesture* without the content. That the international neo-avant-garde artists were working within the system and benefitting from it, while only pretending to be in opposition. The neo-avant-garde of the 1950s and 1960s was, in the eyes of the Situationists and Bürger, paper tigers of the art revolution.

Punk's Xerox copies, ephemeral art, violent Body Art, and street art, the dirty and the ugly, were all ways of countering the lightness of the neo-avant-garde and instead rather return to that radicality and anger of early twentieth-century avant-garde. Many artists involved with punk would furthermore agree with another line of reasoning, which Peter Bürger essentially picked up from Theodor Adorno: that the avant-garde always craving the new matches consumer society always craving the new. By refusing to become the next new thing on the art market, the next neo-neo-something, by rejecting pretend progress, punk as an art movement breaks through that craving for the new. The tale of a forward-moving linear art development was thus cut down by punk artists.

On the other hand, we have seen the admiration the punks had for Andy Warhol. His embrace of the low rather than the high was celebrated in punk and punk art. On this point, punks stand in contrast to Debord and Bürger's criticism of Warhol. The often-repeated link between Situationism and punk actually becomes clearer when we look at the dissidents from that movement. While the Situationists propose to disengage from and negate pop culture, punk accelerates spectacle, much like Sam Cooper has argued in relation to the ex-Situationists. Furthermore, ex-Situationist groups, such as King Mob in the UK or the Scandinavian Situationism-deserters who gathered at Drakabygget (The dragon's lair) tended toward action rather than theory. The Scandinavian ex-Situationists set up the Drakabygget, a farm in the south of Sweden, as an artistic commune, work collective, and platform for activities. Nash and his collaborator Thorsen carried out a range of activities with the idea of creating disruption, such as throwing cap bombs in the Royal Danish Theater, and releasing white mice in The Danish Academy. Nash's most famous action retrospectively seems like a proto-punk embezzlement: in 1964, he decapitated the Little Mermaid, the famous landmark of Copenhagen, and afterward claimed that it was not him, but that he knew who had done it.[21] Among this repertoire of actions was Jørgen Nash's habit of picking up different styles, stealing and quoting from others—another feature of punk art. Their project was, in the words of Nash, "not to negate art but to realise it as excess"[22]—in contrast to the theory-heavy ideas of Situationists like Guy Debord and Raoul Vaneigem. In both cases—ex-Situationists and punks—it is not Debord's anti-spectacle, but rather hyper-spectacle, not negation, but affirmation, the idea being to usurp the scheme by over-affirming it. Punk thus exposed fakeness and spectacle through exaggerated fakeness and exaggerated spectacle.

The ideas of the ex-Situationists were thus brought to (fake) life, like Frankenstein's monster. Christopher Gray of King Mob, for example, had had the idea of creating a crappy pop group, hyping them to the max, and then exposing the sham. Malcolm McLaren might have had such an idea in the back of his mind, as he casted the Sex Pistols—though the Pistols then indeed took on their own life. Mike Kelley describes how his proto-punk band Destroy All Monsters took the idea of a fake band from the world of music and implemented it in the artworld:

> It was all fake—programmatically fake. We were not a real band; we couldn't play music; we had no audience. But we knew what a band looked like. We knew how to package ourselves as a band […] And so we became art. It wasn't exactly ironic or parodistic; it was analytical.[23]

One punk group from Italy, HitlerSS, played a complete gig with cardboard instruments. The fake was also on the agenda of minimalist/punk group Gerry & The Holograms from Manchester, who released *The Emperor's New Music* on Absurd Records in 1979: the vinyl record was glued to the inside of the picture sleeve, impossible to take out and listen to.

The punk attack on late capitalist culture—whether it be music or art or something else—was, especially in the early years, executed by overdoing, exaggerating, and acting (in contrast to theorizing). The status of Andy Warhol as a "hero of the punks" matches this attitude, though surely Warhol was not at all vehemently attacking capitalist culture. He was, however, attacking High Art, Fine Art, and he was showing a way to bring trash and pop right into the heart of the bourgeois institutions.

With the growing importance of a punk DIY culture, however, it stands to be argued that a strategy of withdrawal later became more important, at least in large parts of the punk movement. While the Sex Pistols or COUM Transmissions were still working to shock and usurp the mainstream media, later groups rather avoided such a confrontation and preferred to work in a subculture, their own space, separated from the spectacle of TV, celebrity, and mass entertainment.

Pop multiples

There is one work of art that captures many of the concepts described above, plus a few more, and which at the same time points forward in art history—Gavin Turk's installation *Pop* from 1993 (Figure 3.6). Turk's sculpture is a wax figure standing on a pedestal, behind thick fiberglass with a golden framework. The figure's face resembles

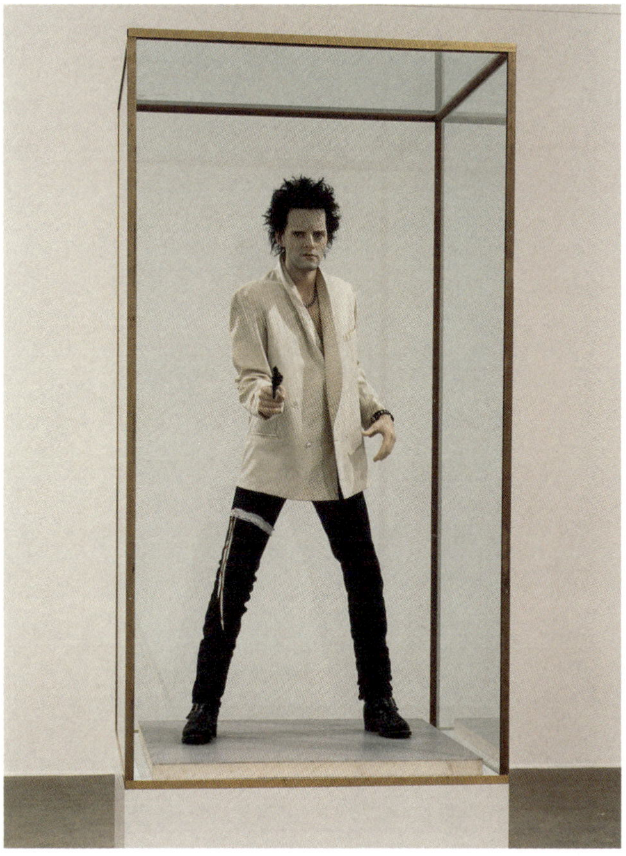

Figure 3.6: Gavin Turk, Pop, *1993. Courtesy of Gavin Turk/Live Stock Market.*

Turk himself but is wearing a white dinner jacket and punk accessories identical to the outfit Sid Vicious wore in a certain sequence in *The Great Rock 'n' Roll Swindle* (Julien Temple's 1980 mockumentary about the Sex Pistols). In his installation, Turk has positioned himself/Vicious just like Elvis Presley in Andy Warhol's 1960s silkscreen-on-canvas Elvis series, as a gunslinger at the point of the draw. Both figures, Turk's own-image Vicious and Warhol's Elvis are large, life-size, or slightly bigger, making it so that we as viewers must look from a distance.

Warhol, in his work, depicts the multiplication of Elvis (Figure 3.7). Like Marilyn or Mao, Elvis is an image of an image, multiplied by billions of posters and newspapers. The image is a still photo used for publicity for the western movie *Flaming Star* (1960), in which Elvis plays the son of a Kiowa mother and a white settler father, who gets caught between the fronts and dies at the end. A broken hero, thus, who in the picture seems rather to be gazing into the unknown than really aiming. Furthermore, Warhol amplifies

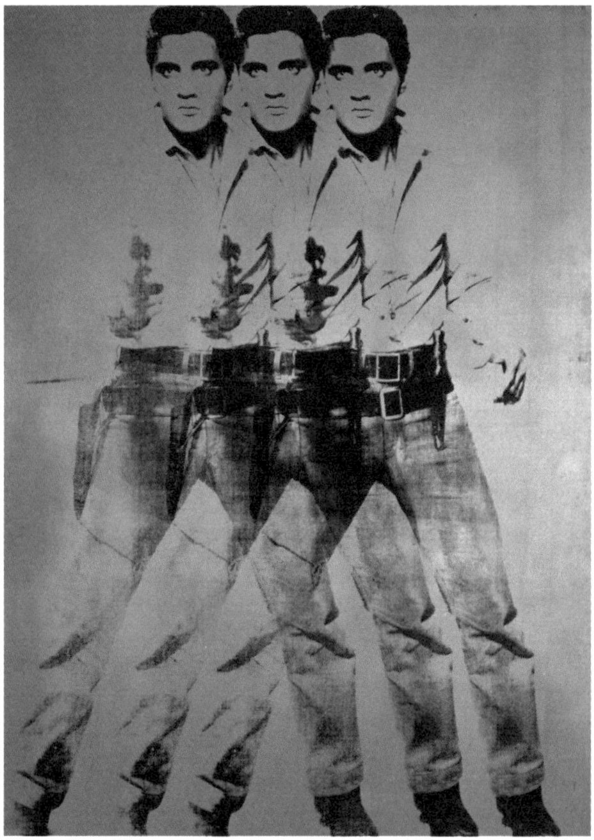

Figure 3.7: Andy Warhol, Triple Elvis, *1963. © 2022 The Andy Warhol Foundation for the Visual Arts, Inc. Licensed by ARS.*

that sense of vulnerability that is *always* present with Elvis by letting him fade away, each print a bit weaker.

Turk's Vicious holds what is obviously a plastic pistol, thus emphasizing fakeness, the mass-commodification of the spectacle. With this self-portrait as Sid Vicious, in the role of Elvis Presley, as depicted, multiply, by Andy Warhol, Turk opens a whole cabal of twentieth-century pop fame references. He links himself with the rock 'n' roll stardom of Elvis Presley, a stardom that Andy Warhol might have been the first to bring into art too. After Warhol, an artist could become famous like a movie star or a rock star. An important aspect of the work is the image of Vicious/the artist in a gilded cage: the threat of musealization. The title however—simply *Pop*—also links punk and Vicious in a matrix of fame and death, spectacle and representation, pop and art.

Connected to the punk idea of a hedonistic hyper-spectacle attack on pop culture is the thoughtful reflection of pop media phenomena, such as fame and celebrity culture.

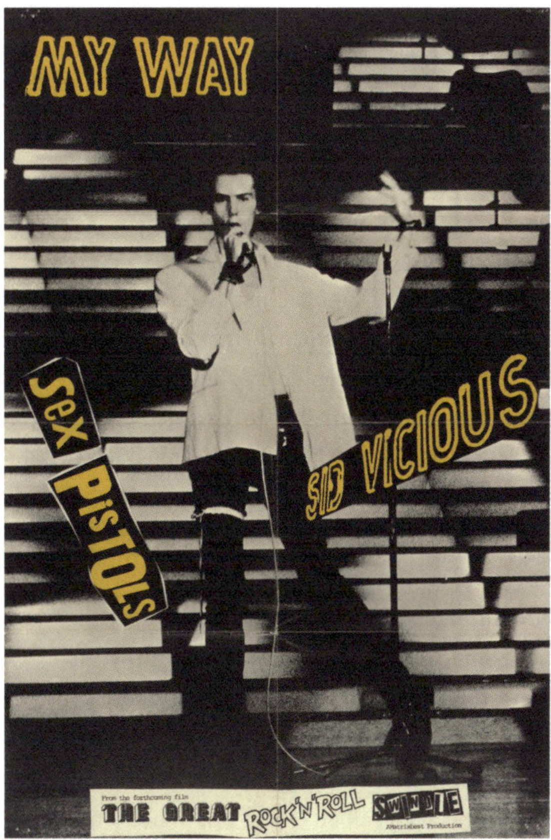

Figure 3.8: Unknown designer, Sex Pistols, Sid Vicious, "My Way," 1978.
© The Museum of Modern Art, New York/Scala, Florence, 2022.

"I got you in my camera / I got you in my camera / a second of your life / ruined for life," Johnny Rotten sang in 1977, such an early observance of the destructive force of paparazzi.[24] The story of Sid Vicious—his demise into drugs, the stabbing of Nancy Spungen, the stress of fame—is all too familiar. Elvis might only have shot at his TV, but the pills, the pressure, and the paranoia tell that same story: "Ruined for life." Neither of their stories fits into an idolized "live fast, die young" or "club-27" mythologization, Vicious too young, Elvis too old, both deaths too awkward, too real.

In the film scene from *The Great Rock 'n' Roll Swindle* which Turk is referring to with the outfit of the figure, Vicious sings his punk and very off-key version of Frank Sinatra's "My Way" (Figure 3.8). Vicious knee-jerk-dances like Elvis, and subsequently shoots into the ecstatic audience, which consists of mostly elderly, pearl, and tux-wearing conservatives. The scene ends with blood and screams and a middle finger from Vicious, as he escapes. This is an actual attack on the bourgeoisie, a fantasy of liberation from the false applause. (One imagines Kurt Cobain would, at some point, also have dreamt such a dream, of a violent backlash to the co-option.) With the triple reference of Elvis Presley and Sid Vicious and Gavin Turk himself, *Pop* could be read as a triple portrait of broken heroes in the twentieth century, of (failed) attempts to escape those "culture vultures forever circling in an ominous sky," which Bob Nickas described.[25] Whether dead or musealized, the triple, it seems, cannot break free.

Gavin Turk was part of the so-called Young British Artists (YBA) in the 1990s, like Tracey Emin, Angus Fairhurst, Damien Hirst, Sarah Lucas, and others. Interestingly, it was Simon Ford (writer of *Wreckers of Civilisation*), who coined the term YBA in an article for *Art Monthly* in 1996,[26] although he was highly critical. There are aspects in the work and in the self-concept of the YBAs that have earned them a reputation as the heirs to punk. There is the dirt and the sex in their imagery, plus the working-class vibe. There is also the notion of artists knowing how to work the market, not just being artists but actively promoting their own work, acting as cultural entrepreneurs, and using intelligent provocation. One direct link is the rejection of the romantic myth of the "pure" artist, untarnished by greed, untouched by, and unable to work the market. The misanthropic attitude of punk, exemplified also in the Sex Pistols' "filthy lucre" expression ("Filthy Lucre" is what the Sex Pistols called their reunification tour in 1996), repulses the attitude that only a poor artist or a poor musician can be an honest one.

Damien Hirst's work, for example, can readily be interpreted as another incarnation of the hyper-spectacle, albeit—and this is not a minor ramification—with a far more sleek, showy, and unpolitical posture than that evidenced by the artists connected with punk in the late 1970s. As one part of the Kipper Kid duo, Brian Routh, puts it in an interview with Dominic Johnson: "We were trying to cross over. We even tried to sell out. [...] But we never could, partly because we would always sabotage ourselves. It wasn't a strategy—we just couldn't help it."[27] This sense of an underlying urgency, a gut reaction against complacency, we see less in the YBAs.

3.3 Trash and travesty

"Punk is a prostitute, punk is a wretch, punk is a piece of shit, a pile of scraps, punk is below junk," David Torres states.[28] Punk (at least in one of its versions) was a trash culture. Though trash in punk is not congruent with Susan Sontag's description of "camp," there are pivotal overlaps: "It is the love of the exaggerated, the 'off,' of things-being-what-they-are-not."[29] Such a love of the exaggerated is the same which led Greil Marcus to comment that "the Sex Pistols did go too far; all the hue and cry and calculation aside, going too far was what they were about."[30] Sontag later in her text concludes, "The ultimate

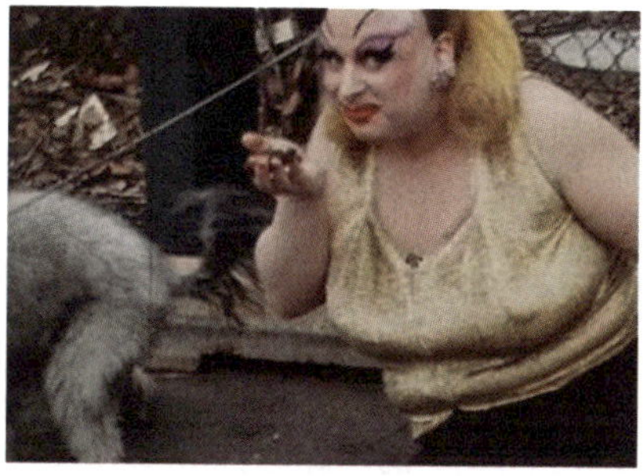

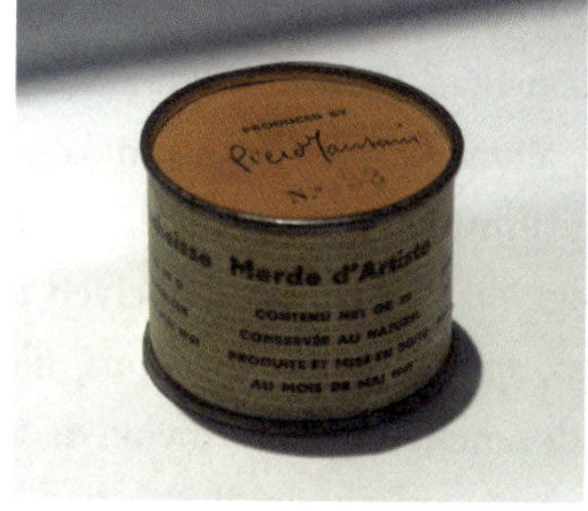

Figure 3.9: Divine eating dog feces in a screenshot from the film Pink Flamingos*, 1972, by John Waters. © Creative Commons.*
Figure 3.10: Piero Manzoni, Artist's Shit*, 1961. Photograph by Jens Cederskjold. © Creative Commons / © VG Bild-Kunst, Bonn 2022.*

Camp statement: it's good because it's awful."[31] *Good, because it's awful* is very punk indeed. Thus, next to the admiration of Andy Warhol, we also see many punk artists, punk filmmakers, and punk musicians being enamored with another figure of pop trash: Divine, as mentioned above by Genesis P-Orridge (see Section 3.1: "Andy Warhol: Hero of the punks"). The one infamous scene in John Waters' *Pink Flamingos* movie, in which Divine, playing Babs Johnson, eats fresh dog shit, is an intrinsic travesty (Figure 3.9).

We might here invoke the example of Piero Manzoni's 90 tin cans of *Artist's Shit* (1961, Figure 3.10) too, as this work also radiates a proto-punk attitude. The cans contained 30 grams, "freshly preserved, produced and tinned" of the artist's own excrement "with no added preservatives," which Manzoni sold for a price equal to its own weight in eighteen-carat gold. Apart from the obvious transgression of a taboo, other allusions in Manzoni's work seem even more precise in their connection to punk: ironizing the role of the artist and criticizing the (art) market's fetishism, for example. In a letter to Ben Vautier, Manzoni wrote: "if collectors want something intimate, really personal to the artist, there's the artist's own shit, that is really his."[32] John Miller reads the work as a critique of capitalism, by connecting Manzoni's shit to "Karl Marx's declaration that under capitalism even the greatest artwork is worth only so many tons of manure." He also notes how Manzoni relishes the delineation of art as a surrogate: "The technique of canning implies ersatz culture and ersatz cuisine, reflected in phrases such as canned laughter."[33] Such a salutation of the faux, the abject, and the camp in our culture likewise correspond to punk's disposition. Furthermore, the fact that Manzoni ridicules the art collector's wish to "own" the artist's personality likewise matches the punk's less exalted approach to the role of the artist: an artist, or a musician, in punk was not perceived as an otherworldly genius, not an idol, not an authority (for more on the concept of the artist in punk, see Chapter 7: "Work vs. Play").

Punk embraced everything that would be judged "bad taste" by the cultural elites or the holier-than-thou hippies, all that was considered fake and disposable—plastic, junk food, aluminum beer cans, make-up, all that was considered profane and vulgar—being unhealthy, being unnatural, advertising, and making money. Body functions and other things that would be perceived as repulsive or ugly re-emerge in punk culture: vomit, piss, spit, wounds, dirt, pus, filth, and rats. Related to this, subjects of decay and abandonment are also invoked: worms, maggots, skulls, cavity, ruins, rot, and rust. Referencing the puke-themed punk band names Rotzkotz (Snotpuke), Kotzübel (Nauseous), and Brechreiz (Urge to vomit), Wolfgang Müller of Die Tödliche Doris points out that "disgust" was used to point back to what the punks found to be *truly* repulsive: opportunism, phoniness, and self-righteousness.[34]

The expulsion of fluids from the body became a means of expression. In German, a specific way of uttering disgust is to say: *Ich kann gar nicht so viel fressen wie ich kotzen möchte*, that is, "I cannot even eat as much as I would like to puke" (allegedly uttered by Max Lieberman upon seeing Nazis marching through the Brandenburger Gate). Such an understanding of throwing up as an expression of disgust is conveyed in punk's repetition of puke songs, puke names, and puke artworks.

One example of a puke punk artwork is by Christian Lemmerz, who was a member of Værkstedet Værst, and later continued his work in the performance group VÆRST (WORST), together with Michael Kvium. Poignant examples of what was punk about their art can be found in the publication *Das Zeug* (*The Stuff*, 1986) which contains black-and-white photographs of performances and installations using bodily materials (hair, urine, and vomit) and mundane materials (dirt, chicken meat, and building foam). The images are accompanied by a booklet, which explains the materials with excessive directness, such as "schokolade: braun wie scheiße, sehr süß" (chocolate: brown like shit, very sweet).[35] The overt material fetishism seems like a combined caricature of and homage to Joseph Beuys and his symbolically charged use of—for example—felt, fat, or honey. The deadpan directness and humor in these works—*Kotzbild* (Puke picture; Figure 3.11), *Ekelrinne* (Gutter of disgust), or *Tote Hosen* (Dead Pants, referring to the German punk band)—are complemented by other works, which are much more ambivalent and critical, such as *Pornografisches Stück* (Pornographic piece) or *Pathologisches Stück* (Pathological piece; Figure 3.12), which convey a sense of grotesqueness and violence. There is thus more than one artistic strategy at work here: blank explication of the artwork, killing the illusion, spelling out the metaphor—but something else also: an expression of genuine horror, particularly in the performances by Michael Kvium, as can be seen in 3.12 *Pathologisches Stück*. Kvium's body is leaned

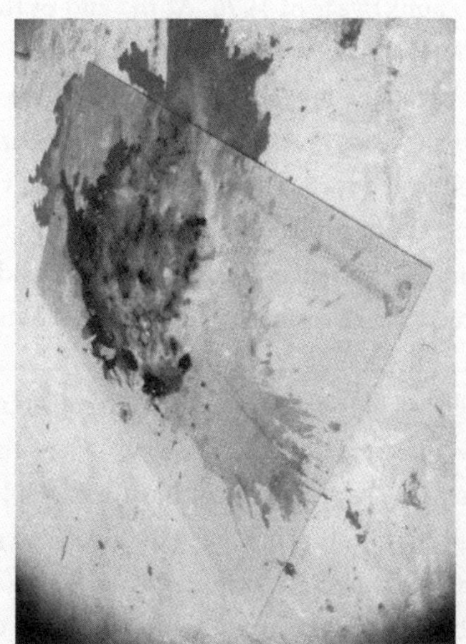

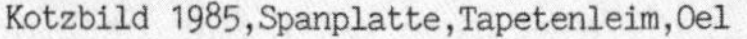

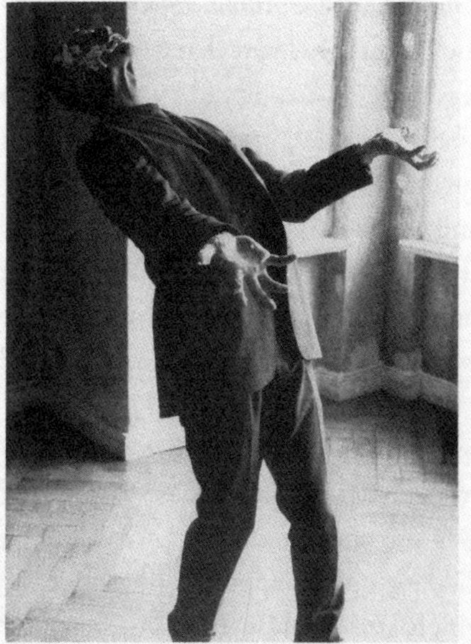

Figure 3.11: VÆRST (WORST), Kotzbild *(Puke picture), 1985, from* Das Zeug (The Stuff)*, 1986. Courtesy of Christian Lemmerz and Michael Kvium.*
Figure 3.12: VÆRST (WORST), Pathologisches Stück *(Pathological piece), 1985, from* Das Zeug (The Stuff)*, 1986. Courtesy of Christian Lemmerz and Michael Kvium.*

backwards in an awkward position, his hands stretched out before him, his face twisted, foam at his mouth. Expressive and excessive, he is looking mad like Klaus Kinski, like he is exploring his afflictions, in front of Lemmerz' camera.

Christian Lemmerz' raw and unapproachable attitude encompasses vulnerability, even agony. In 2010, in a speech at the opening of Lemmerz's exhibition *Genfærd* (*Ghost*) at AroS Art Museum in Arhus, the writer Carsten Jensen asked,

> Are you just here to antagonize? Or are you indeed yourself antagonized by what you see? […] Your work is a catalog of scandals, but not scandals which you have created or caused; they were here before you, our culture rests on them, you found them, and gave them disturbing forms. […] Some will find you to be raw, but you are not. You are vulnerable and exposed in a raw world.[36]

This description is highly punk, just as many features in Lemmerz's work are undeniably analogous to punk.

"I liked Herbert Achternbusch. He really had something punky: You don't have a chance, so use it!" Lemmerz states,[37] evoking the Achternbusch film *Die Atlantik-*

schwimmer (*The Atlantic Swimmers*) from the (punk) year of 1976. At the end of the movie, the two main characters stand at the shore, and want to go away, but no ship is leaving. Herbert, played by Achternbusch himself, tells his friend, "You don't have a chance, so use it!" and, fully dressed, jumps into the ocean and starts swimming (toward sure death). At this point the film ends. This offers a devastating assessment of reality, and ultimately a very angry comment on any positivistic motivation-spin on that reality. It is an Achternbusch version of "No Future" which Lemmerz makes his own. (On a side note, it is also a scene that is acutely relevant today, in reference to the "resilience" and working poor debate: you don't have a chance, so use it!).

Lemmerz uses staged scandals to highlight what is perceived as *truly* scandalous, much like Wolfgang Müller describes it above. In punk culture, showing where the true *scandal* lies is paralleled by showing where true *beauty* lies. Squatting, for example, was also about finding beauty where no one else saw it, making the rotting your own. "Taking up and appropriating the cast aside was part of this attitude," Dirk Schaefer emphasizes.[38] More than just romanticized beauty-of-decay, punk's appreciation of trash was linked with appreciation of, and indeed identification with, the discarded. It might seem counterintuitive to a movement that identified itself as disposable, that the artifacts of the first, small circles have now become fetishized. On the other hand, fetish was a part of punk culture from the start, and punk tends to be sentimental on its own terms. Trash was sometimes elevated and sometimes became linked with a personal agenda. Finding beauty where no one else could, being beautiful in a way that not anyone would understand. By making the trash their own, the punks changed its implication. In this sense, punk took a fresh look both at what was supposedly wrong, to redefine what that meant, and also what was supposedly right, to redefine what that meant that too.

Speed: Make it fast! Don't make it last!

Punk was a fast culture. That ranged from the shortness of the songs to quickly drawn artworks and zines photocopied at Xerox-speed, to the movement itself: it took no more than a few years before the first death announcements. Perhaps that fleetness is also one of the reasons that punk is returned to again and again; it all happened too fast. Punk was like a candle burning from both ends, as Thomas Mießgang notes,[39] or—for another metaphor—like the Youth Brigade song, was "Full Speed Ahead." Johnny Rotten sang, "I don't work / I just speed." The Prefects made a thirteen-second song called "I've got VD," and Lou Reed noted in the MMM album sleeve: "My week beats your year."[40] Most punk art exhibitions were on display for no longer than a week.

Even the drug of choice in punk was *speed* (in the form of amphetamine sulfate), which causes alertness, energy, teeth grinding, nervousness, restlessness, insomnia, aggression, and paranoia. It was the antidote to the hippie drugs, as speed was relentless and artificial. There was nothing psychedelic about it: no dreaming, no softness, nothing natural (unlike, for example, marijuana or psilocybin mushrooms). Amphetamine was given to pilots (on both sides) during World War II for them to stay alert and awake. It was also used in the milieu of 1950s mods. Andy Warhol insisted that "[t]he big social thrust behind the Factory from '64 to '67 was amphetamine."[41] He made the drug famous by showing Ondine and other so-called "fags on speed" from Greenwich Village shooting up powdered amphetamine on-screen in his collaborative work with Paul Morrissey, *Chelsea Girls* (1966).[42] *Speed* was also the title of William Burroughs Jr's amphetamine-addict, coming-of-age autobiography from 1970, with a tip of the hat to his father's semi-autobiographic debut *Junkie: Confessions of an Unredeemed Drug Addict* (1953). The mods, Warhol, and Burroughs were all seminal figures in punk. The cultural history and connotations of speed thus fit punk's disposition, as did its effects, as speed is a drug that keeps you on the edge. "Amphetamine doesn't give you peace of mind," Warhol noted.[43] And of course, "peace of mind" was not what the punks were looking for.

Both punk rock and punk art were thus, often: quick and dirty, fast and furious. The Sods, one of the first punk bands in Denmark, named their first album *Minutes to Go* (1979).[44] *Minutes to Go* channeled the energy and speed of the band. The title was both a reference to the fact that the album was only 26 minutes long and a reference to a collection of cut-up poems by William S. Burroughs, Sinclair Beiles, Brion Gysin, and Gregory Corso: *Minutes to Go* (1960). "The first time I heard the Sods play in Den Grå Hal [The Grey Hall, a music venue in Christiania], I was completely blown away," says artist Nina Sten-Knudsen, "It was like they played the whole set without a break. They stopped with one number and immediately began the next. [...] There was so much energy in it! It hit me full-on!"[45]

A few years later Lars Nørgård did a painting called *This Is Just a Temporary Place to Stay* (Figure 3.13).[46] According to Nørgård, it was painted in the summer of 1982, while he was staying alone at Værkstedet Værst. While painting the image, Nørgård listened to punk rock.

> I had my small mono cassette player [...]. To me, to listen to music created a special mental space to work within. Mostly I listened to Buzzcocks. At our parties, it was more Dead Kennedys, but when I was painting it was Buzzcocks and Siouxsie and the Banshees.[47]

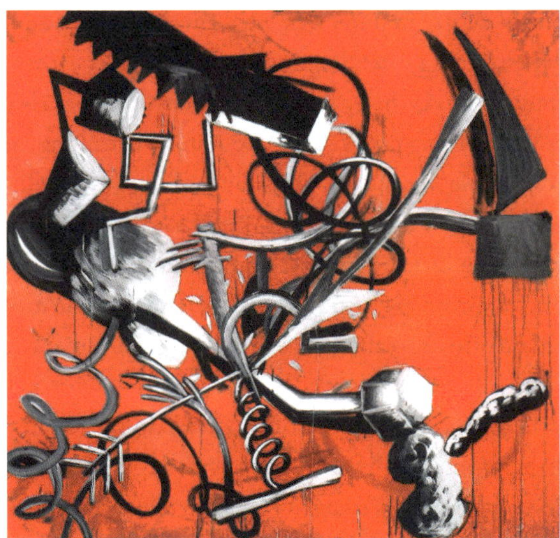

Figure 3.13: Lars Nørgård, This Is Just a Temporary Place to Stay, *1982. Horsens Kunstmuseum. Courtesy of Lars Nørgård.*

The painting's aesthetics insinuate punk: it is painted with industrial paint, not oil, and in a raw brushstroke, which looks unrefined and unfinished, with paint splattered on the lower half of the canvas. On a vivid red background, we see an explosion-like scattering of black, white, and gray tools emerging from the center of the surface and protruding outwards. Among the objects are a hammer, a corkscrew, a saw, an arrow, a rivet, and a chain. While the almost square canvas (180 × 190 cm) and the color scheme might remind us of Suprematism or Constructivism, the neo-Expressionistic traits and the large format size place the painting in a Bad Painting frame of reference. Its cartoonish style matches punk's inclination toward pop and teenage culture and (pretend/slapstick) violence.

Nørgård had been studying in California at the Academy of Art College in San Francisco, and in fact was planning to go back. At the time, Copenhagen too was to him *Just a Temporary Place to Stay*. By the late summer of 1982, however, Ronald Reagan, who had been inaugurated in January 1981, had tightened the visa rules (i.e. *The Immigration Reform and Control Act* of 1982). "I was no longer sure if they would let me back in," Nørgård says. He ended up staying at the Værksted (workshop). The painting, however, transports that sense of being in transit. But most of all *This Is Just a Temporary Place to Stay* conveys a Ramonesque "hey ho, let's go" attitude, a sense of both vigor and speed. Punk's self-definition as a fast culture was tied with art being, not for all eternity, but for the here and now. But we can also see (art) history in this painting: the instruments, tools, and machine parts convey a twentieth-century feel, which is only intensified by the schematic colors—

red, white, and black—used in propaganda posters both in fascism and communism. The aesthetics of propaganda and political posters were often invoked in punk designs. At the same time, these are utilitarian objects without any use, which might invoke the machine storming of the Luddites, a reference made so often by Malcolm McLaren (see Chapter 10.3: "Broken heroes, aces of failure"). All in all, thus, a twentieth-century punk painting par excellence: cartoons, politics, uselessness, energy, and explosion.

Merry pranksters, hippie trash

As is (hopefully) becoming apparent, punk was something completely new, but the movement's approach to art did not emerge out of nothing. Rather, the prior art movements and the culture, especially of the 1960s, provided the base. Something to lean on, but also something to distance from. And something to first do, then *over*-do.

For example, the first draft of COUM Transmissions was inspired by hippie communes. From late 1968 to early 1969, P-Orridge lived in Transmedia Explorations, the successor of the better-known Exploding Galaxy, which had been shut down after a police raid. "I basically set up COUM Transmissions which was a kind of extension of my interpretations of Transmedia and Exploding Galaxy, but pushing it [...] further," P-Orridge explained.[48] As noticed above, taking it further, going too far, taking concepts to the limit, and then over that limit—these tactics are key in punk culture, especially when it comes to the approach to (art) history precursors. Both Transmedia Explorations and Exploding Galaxy were involved in a total art/life experiment in which all routines and habits were to be erased: the members would eat breakfast in the evening, sleep in a different bed each night, and share all possessions. Many of these experimental practices were lived out in COUM too and intensified.

Early on, COUM like many other art and music groups at the time were finding their way forward by looking back too. The title of the very first COUM action, in Hull—where the group was based until 1973—gives an indication of their mindset at that time: *Clockwork Hot Spoiled Acid Test* (1969). The double reference to both Anthony Burgess' *A Clockwork Orange* (1962) and Tom Wolfe's *The Electric Kool-Aid Acid Test* (1968) retrospectively seems like a rough draft for the kind of group P-Orridge was setting up. From the Burgess novel (it was two years before Kubrick's film), P-Orridge took the construction of a language—in the book the fictional "Nadsat"—topics of youth gangs, revolt, violence, control, anti-conformity, drugs, dystopia, and a certain hooligan/ultra-aesthetic. Equally inspirational for COUM was the proto-hippie, experimental, communal, anti-authoritarian lifestyle of the Merry Pranksters in the early 1960s, as described by Wolfe in *The Electric Kool-Aid Acid Test*. The Merry Pranksters represented not only a link to the Beat Generation—after all, Neal Cassady drove the bus—but also an essential world view that would come to define COUM as well: "There was no goal of an improved moral order in the world or an improved social order [...] If there was ever a group devoted totally to the here and now it was the Pranksters," Wolfe writes.[49] This awareness of living in the moment would become an important notion in COUM's artwork, and more generally in punk art. The self-ironic "prankster" denotation likewise found an echo in the "swindle" of COUM in particular and in punk more generally. *Clockwork Hot Spoiled Acid Test* thus provides a strong indication of the importance of 1960s counterculture for COUM's work.

Furthermore, COUM Transmissions became very involved with mail art and Fluxus—though their tendency to travesty and exaggeration ended them up in a fight with one of the Fluxus initiators, Ken Friedman [...]. The 1972–73 traveling Fluxus exhibition *FLUXSHOE* (just a typing error away from "flux show") was organized by David Mayor, a close friend of Tutti and P-Orridge.[50] Fluxus had arrived late in the UK in comparison with continental Europe and the USA, and one of Mayor's goals with *FLUXSHOE* was to spread knowledge about the movement in the English province.[51] The actions of COUM Transmissions—who participated on three occasions—were characterized by absurdist humor. In Nottingham, COUM performed *Snail Trail* in which P-Orridge covered himself in plastic and left a trail of stickers while crawling through the streets. In Blackburn, COUM carried out *Blackmailing*—sending 50 postcards, spray-painted black, to 50 random citizens of Blackburn. During the *FLUXSHOE* summer, P-Orridge gave several interviews, among others to the *Lancashire Evening Telegraph*: "Genesis, Banana Expert is in Town" the headline ran.

> Mr P.Orridge [*sic*] says he gained his Bananology degree by joining two halves of a banana together so they revolved in any direction. This device, which he posted to the Centre for Banana Studies in Canada, was enough for the authorities to be convinced of his academic worth.[52]

There is a Fluxus-like lightness and playful humor in COUM's actions of those years, which is missing in later works. The first indication of COUM's, and especially P-Orridge's, growing skepticism toward Fluxus was his correspondence with Ken Friedman, during which he offered to destroy Friedman's archive: "In all honesty, it's becoum a bit of a self coumgratulationary wank. Let's now really FUCK it, once and for more." Friedman was at first amused and proposed a price of 20,000 USD. After further correspondence—in which P-Orridge declared: "E am a silly person [...] totally interested in the exploitation and prostitution of my friends in some ways. But as E have no illusions as to my corruption, it is bearable, just."—Friedman replied: "As far as I can tell at this point, you are playing a childish and petulant game of 'anti-art' [...] when you 'coum,' you better 'coum' with cash in hand. No dough, no go, as they say in the Western movies."[53] The correspondence shows how the disappointment with Fluxus, its artworld saturation, was beginning to manifest itself. By late 1973, COUM was moving on, toward punk and then industrial.

These early developments and endeavors of COUM Transmissions show where they were coming from. Fluxus played a key role, as it did to the members of the KoeCrandt group and Die Tödliche Doris too. In the transition from the 1960s to the 1970s, the effects of Fluxus made their way into punk through figures like Yoko Ono and Joseph Beuys, and punk art obviously adopted many Fluxus concepts (intermediality, material heterogeneity, anarchy, wit, inventiveness, poetic or absurd instructions, integration of mistakes, and the occasional smashing of an instrument). Despite these shared features, punk's break with Fluxus is nevertheless indicative of what artists involved in punk wanted to do differently. The criticism of Fluxus expressed by the artists involved with punk was that it was not radical enough! Too convenient, too artworldly. The artists of COUM, Die Tödliche Doris, and KoeCrandt were about the here-and-now, they were about pranksterism, trash, and travesty. And the means to deal with the baggage of the past was to exaggerate it. In the case of Fluxus and punk, it was a question of taking certain Fluxus ideas and appropriating and overdoing these, in punk style. In the case of other historical phenomenon (not art-historical paragons, but scars of history), exaggeration and parody were also invoked, as in the next case.

Coping with the past through trash

"In Berlin, the now always begins with the past," writes Wolfgang Müller in his book *Subkultur Westberlin*:[54] in the late 1970s and early 1980s, that past was visible all over the city. The violence of the twentieth century was omnipresent. Several buildings still showed scars and old insignia from World War II. Die Tödliche Doris played their debut concert in KuckKuck, a cultural venue in a squat house directly opposite where the documentation center Topographie des Terrors (Topography of Terror) lies today. Here is where the SS was based, here is where the heads of Nazi repression had worked. In August 1961, the Berlin Wall was built just next to it.

The Nazi past was not so far away as was officially pretended; the first neo-Nazis surfaced in the 1960s and the "*Alt-Nazis*" (old Nazis) were still present in all areas of society. "We sensed that all around were these ugly people, who somehow still carried the war within, and the whole Nazi-morass with it," Müller recounts.[55] Punk used trash and travesty to counter any revisionist mythologization. One example is Jörg Buttgereit's Super 8 splatter film *Blutige Exzesse im Führerbunker* (Bloody excesses in the Hitler bunker, 1982). The film begins with Hitler introducing himself to the audience: "Many of the younger ones among you may not know me anymore, but I am alive and am here to clean up." Later in the film, his wife Eva (Braun, later Hitler) and a "Germanic stud bull" (which is composed of dead bodies' remains) castrate and cut up Hitler. Buttgereit got the idea for the film after the punk Norbert Hähnel from the West Berlin Scheißladen [the shit(ty) store] brought a Hitler mask back from London.[56] Hähnel, a close friend of Käthe Kruse from Die Tödliche Doris, also performed as "der wahre Heino" ("the true Heino"), in a takeover of the identity of the super-blond German Schlager star Heino, who had been condemned at the time for performing in apartheid South Africa in spite of the UN embargo. Evidently, the "true Heino" doppelgänger is a fake, as is the carnivalesque rubber Hitler mask in the Super 8 film. Both Buttgereit and Hähnel satirize their enemies in punk propaganda "swindles": Their works are détournements of Germanic attributes. Furthermore, the past is used for effect, history plays a satirical role. We see this again and again: punk culture is steeped in history. There is no "historical amnesia," as diagnosed by Fredric Jameson with regard to the post-modern times; it is the opposite.[57]

Punk's taboo-breaking use of Nazi symbols thus worked differently in the UK and Germany. Some of the typical punk shock tactics, such as the swastika, were still used to provoke, but in a different way. In the UK, one of the manifold reasons these symbols provoked the older generation was that they were the enemy's. Apart from this anticipated shock effect (and a certain UK-specific morbid fascination with Nazi memorabilia), many young UK punks associated these symbols with the Weimar Republic and thus with decadent glamour.[58] In Germany, the shock effect worked in a different direction, because it was linked with a more inward fear. Common to both UK and German punk, however, was that these violations of taboos were also used to call attention to Nazi mindsets—such as racism, restriction, and rigidity—of the contemporary time. Again, travesty was used to point to point toward what was *truly* scandalous.

Notes

1. Victor Hugo, Billy Klüver, and Andy Warhol quoted in Marc Miller and Bettie Ringma, eds., *Punk Art Exhibition: The Catalogue* (Washington, DC: Washington Project for the Arts, 1978), n.p.

2. Robert Garnett, "Too Low to be Low: Art pop and the Sex Pistols," in *Punk Rock: So What?* (New York: Routledge), 17.

3. Sabin, "Introduction," 1.

4. GENESIS BREYER P-ORRIDGE, in an e-mail to the author, October 26, 2018.

5. Susan Sontag, "Notes on Camp," 291–92.

6. Speaking in the BBC documentary *Punk and the Pistols* (Arena, 1995). Quoted in Huxley, "Ever get the Feeling You've Been Cheated?," 96.

7. The Bill Grundy *Today* show, December 1, 1976, accessed October 26, 2022, https://www.youtube.com/watch?v=jRNOUz7uefA.

8. Greil Marcus, "Punk (1979)" [first published in *The Rolling Stone Illustrated History of Rock & Roll*, ed. Jim Miller, 1979], accessed December 17, 2017, https://greilmarcus.net/2014/09/08/punk-1979.

9. Savage, *England's Dreaming*, 183, 192.

10. Victor Hugo, Billy Klüver, and Andy Warhol quoted in *Punk Art Exhibition: The Catalogue*, n.p.

11. Miller, interview, 2018.

12. Tim Murphy, "'Rectal Realism' Artist Neke Carson on the Long-Lost Portrait of Warhol He Painted With His Butt," accessed July 17, 2018, http://www.vulture.com/2008/03/rectal_realism_artist_neke_car.html.

13. Ozon, interview, 2017.

14. Kaagman, interview, 2017.

15. Ozon, interview, 2017.

16. See Gretchen L. Wagner, "Fluxkit," in *Thing/Thought: Fluxus Editions 1962–1978*, Museum of Modern Art New York, September 21, 2011–January 16, 2012, accessed May 1, 2018, https://www.moma.org/interactives/exhibitions/2011/Fluxus_editions/category_works/fluxkit.

17. Wolfgang Müller, interview with the author, October 25, 2017.

18. Müller, interview, 2017.

19. Correspondence between Ken Friedman and Genesis P-Orridge quoted in Ford, *Wreckers of Civilisation*, 3.13–3.14.

20. Wolfgang Müller, "Die wahren Dilletanten," in *Geniale Dilletanten*, ed. Wolfgang Müller (Berlin: Merve, 1982), 12.

21. Rasmussen, "Raping the Whole World in a Warm Embrace of Fascination," 594.

22. Rasmussen, "Raping the Whole World in a Warm Embrace of Fascination," 594.

23. Mike Kelley, "I Rip You," in *Hungry for Death: Destroy All Monsters*, ed. Cary Lohen (Boston: Boston University Art Gallery, 2011), n.p.

24. Sex Pistols, "I Wanna Be Me" (UK: Virgin Records, 1977).

25. Nickas, "Komplaint Dept." See Section 1.4: "Forty-five Years of Trying to Capture the Art in Punk."

26. Simon Ford, "Myth Making," in *Art Monthly*, no. 194 (March 1996).

27. Brian Routh aka Harry Kipper, quoted in Dominic Johnson, *The Art of Living: An Oral History of Performance Art* (London: Palgrave, 2015), 74.

28. Torres, "Traces of a Punk Attitude in Contemporary Art," 44, 279.

29. Susan Sontag, "Notes On 'Camp' [first published in *Partisan Review*, 1964]," in Susan Sontag, *Against Interpretation and Other Essays* (London: Penguin Modern Classics, 2009), n.p.

30. Marcus, "Punk (1979)."

31. Sontag, "Notes on 'Camp,'" 292.

32. Letter reprinted in Freddy Battino and Luca Palazzoli, *Piero Manzoni: Catalogue Raisonné* (Milan: Vanni Scheiwiller, 1991), 144.

33. John Miller: "Excremental Value: Piero Manzoni's 'Merda d'artista,'" *Tate Etc.* 10 (Summer 2007), accessed January 5, 2018, http://www.tate.org.uk/context-comment/articles/excremental-value.

34. Müller, "Das Chaos reist mit dem Schönen Wochenende," 156.

35. Christian Lemmerz, *Das Zeug* (Copenhagen: Galleri Specta, 1986).

36. Carsten Jensen, "Christian Lemmerz og hans usømmelige omgang med verden," accessed June 29, 2018, https://www.information.dk/moti/2010/10/christian-lemmerz-usoemmelige-omgang-verden.

37. Lemmerz, interview, 2018.

38. Schaefer, "City of Projections," 28.

39. Thomas Mießgang, "No One Is Innocent," in *Punk. No One Is Innocent*, 13.

40. Sex Pistols, "Seventeen" (Hollywood, CA: Virgin, 1977) and Lou Reed, *Metal Machine Music* (New York: RCA Records, 1975). See also Nicholas Rombes, *A Cultural Dictionary of Punk: 1974-1982* (London: Bloomsbury, 2009).

41. Pat Hackett and Andy Warhol, *POPism: The Warhol Sixties* (Boston: Mariner Books, 1980), 80–81.

42. See Juan A. Suárez, "Warhol's 1960s' Films, Amphetamine, and Queer Materiality," in *Criticism* 56, no. 3 (Summer 2014).

43. Hackett and Warhol, *POPism: The Warhol Sixties*, 81.

44. Poulsen, *Under en Sort Sol: Fra Pisserenden til Statens Museum for Kunst* (Copenhagen: Aschehoug, 2002), 72.

45. Sten-Knudsen, interview, 2018.

46. See Signe Marie Ebbe Jacobsen, "Centrifugal Transformations: Looking at Lars Nørgård's Works," in Lars Nørgård. Luxury Visions, ed. Gitte Ørskou (Aalborg: KUNSTEN. Museum of Modern Art, 2011).

47. Lars Nørgård, interview with the author, March 28, 2018.

48. Genesis P-Orridge quoted in Julie Wilson, "As It Is," in *Painful But Fabulous: The Lives & Art of Genesis P-Orridge*, eds. Nick Mamatras, Maggie Balistreri, Ellen Moynihad, and Don Goede (Brooklyn: Soft Skull Press, 2002), 59.

49. Tom Wolfe, *The Electric Kool-aid Acid Test* [1968] (London: Picador, 2008), 126.

50. See The Fluxshoe Exhibition Correspondence 1972–74, David Mayor Collection, Tate Archive, London.

51. See Modern Art Oxford, "The Archive: FLUXSHOE, 1973", accessed February 10, 2018, https://www.modernartoxford.org.uk/the-archive-fluxshoe-1973/.

52. *Lancashire Evening Telegraph*, July 19, 1973, n.p.

53. Correspondence between Ken Friedman and Genesis P-Orridge quoted in Ford, *Wreckers of Civilisation*, 3.13–3.14.

54. Müller, *Subkultur Westberlin*, 24.

55. Wolfgang Müller, transcript of an interview with Jacek Slaski, in an e-mail to the author, October 10, 2017.

56. See Jörg Buttgereit, ed. *Nekromantik* (Berlin: Martin Schmitz Verlag, 2007).

57. See Fredric Jameson, *Postmodernism, or, the Cultural Logic of Late Capitalism* (Durham: Duke University Press, 1991).

58. See Nils and Ray Stevenson, *Vacant: A Diary of the Punk Years 1976–1979* (London: Thames & Hudson, 1999).

4 The Weapons of the Underdog

Punks spread their (anti-)messages with a high sense of humor, absurdity, and mission awareness: the weapons of the underdog. Language and dissemination play key roles in punk art: in aggressive, guerrilla art ways but also in more vulnerable, yet not less powerful ways. Punk art was very much about art reaching outside of the established artworld. On the contrary, the artworld was often only a means to get attention.

This chapter focuses first on Punk Propaganda, which was often, in the eyes of punks, factually counterpropaganda. The punk perception was that the media and the public sphere were dominated by a conservative and oppressive mindset (in the UK: Murdoch-media tyranny). Language thus became a means of resistance. Furthermore, the streetscape was used for posters, messages, and disruptions, in attempts to break through the omnipresence of conservative mass media.

In the second part of the chapter, "Punk Poetry," the importance of poetic images in punk is outlined. Punk was full of allegorical imaginations: flowers, poison, and machines. Patti Smith started out with poetry, opening for rock 'n' roll bands, with spoken words. Richard Hell (his alias an inspiration from Arthur Rimbaud's poem *A Season in Hell*, 1873) and Tom Verlaine (his alias comes from French fin-de-siècle symbolist poet Paul Verlaine) both followed a similar path from poetry to punk rock. Charles Baudelaire and Arthur Rimbaud were huge influences on punk rock (not only for Smith and Hell). In this aspect, too, punk was often close to the fantastical imagery of the Surrealists, who wanted to give poetry a revolutionary character. In the UK, poets such as Seething Wells, Mark Miwurdz, and Little Brother were aiming to bring punk into poetry, to wake up that genre just like the Sex Pistols had done in music. Here, we will focus on Michael Strunge in Denmark, Diana Ozon in the Netherlands, and Bert Papenfuß in East Germany as examples of punk poets.

In the third and final part of the chapter, we dive into the notion of not only *crime as art*, but also *scandal as art*—it is about transgressions, affronts, and insults. The focus here is on COUM Transmissions, whose members engaged in an exploration of the effects of extreme artwork. They also indeed understood their art as a kind of weapon, meant to disrupt and destabilize.

4.1 Punk propaganda

Greil Marcus writes,

> Punk was a carefully orchestrated media hype, the latest version of a tried-and-true scenario of pop outrageousness that elicited a hurricane of Establishment

> hysteria—a hysteria that was in many ways as cynical and self-serving as the provocation. Yet punk uncovered resentments, fears, hatreds and desires so fierce that their emergence threatened the legitimacy of the social order and revealed its tyranny.[1]

Punk provoked media reactions and then used them to expose double standards. Much like Dada—and Surrealism, too—punk was ready to subvert the contemporary media, create a scandal or a swindle or a court situation, and rattle the status quo.

"Punk's idea was to play the media's accelerated jumble of signals back at them, like one of William Burroughs' tape-recorder experiments in *Electronic Revolution*," Savage describes.[2] The conscious provocations led the media to "moral panic" responses. The term "moral panic" was first defined in 1972 in the seminal work of Stanley Cohen. It describes when "a condition, episode, person or group of persons emerges to become defined as a threat to societal values and interests," leading to a stereotyping and stigmatization of the group in question.[3] The media's reaction to punk thus demonstrated how a small group of dissidents was accused, while actual social injustices were not addressed.

The sensationalized interview with the Sex Pistols and their entourage on the Bill Grundy TV show *Thames Today* on December 1, 1976, is one example of punk's exploration of media responses. At the end of the aggravated exchange, Grundy salaciously suggests to Siouxsie Sioux that they can "meet afterwards," and is cut off by Steve Jones: "You dirty sod. You dirty old man." Grundy encourages Jones to "go on", and he repeats: "You dirty fucker." Grundy: "What a clever boy." Jones: "What a fucking rotter." Jones was indeed a clever boy; it is difficult to believe he did not—at least to some degree—anticipate the hypocritical consternation that would follow. In the wake of the scandal about the use of offensive language on TV, Bill Grundy was fired, the Sex Pistols' next concerts were canceled, and their music was banned. One caller to the overloaded complaints line claimed he had been so offended by Jones' swearing that he had "kicked in the screen of his new £380 television set."[4] The *Daily Mail* headlined: "THE FILTH AND THE FURY!", an expression that the band, as well as punk documentarist Julien Temple subsequently used for promotion on several occasions.[5]

Another infamous incident was the so-called "Thatchergate," a "forged recording of telephone conversation between Prime Minister and President Reagan during Falklands campaign," as it is labeled in PREM 19/1380 The National Archives in Kew, Richmond.[6] The cut-and-paste tape was put together from soundbites of actual speeches, mixed with telephone-line static, and distributed to the press a week prior to the British general elections in 1983 by Crass. On the recording, Thatcher can be heard saying she allowed the missile destroyer *HMS Sheffield* to be sunk to escalate the conflict with

Argentina. "Oh God!" Reagan exclaims, but himself later in the conversation threatens to bomb continental Europe to warn off the Soviet Union. "We wanted to come up with something which might get rid of Thatcher. It was just after the Falklands charade, when she was about to get re-elected," Penny Rimbaud asserts.[7] Though the majority of the contacted journalists detected the hoax, the affair was widely covered, and at first mistaken for KGB propaganda by both the US State Department and the British MI5. Crass argued that though the tape was fake, what it showed was true: cynicism, lies, war mongering, and abuse of power.

The Sex Pistols' Bill Grundy interview was pubescent and awkward, and cast in the realm of entertainment, whereas Crass' Thatchergate was political and constructed and in the realm of politics. Both affairs however were pure punk propaganda; they epitomize the attempt to call into question and to sabotage the cultural, social, political, and media status quo.

Punk's propaganda was inspired by the Situationists' idea of creating "situations" that could break the non-conscious monotony of work and consummation. McLaren and Reid were both involved with the English ex-Situationist group King Mob, whose methods they integrated into punk. Johnny Rotten, in his autobiography *Rotten: No Irish, No Blacks, No Dogs,* disagreed with the claim of a strong Situationist influence on punk: "Never mind the Situationists, this was situation comedy" reads the first chapter.[8] But perhaps—in consequence—the difference is not essential. Punk's "situation comedy" was targeting the stiff establishment and conservative culture, using humor and action to do so. As discussed above, the means of attack in punk were often close to those of the ex-Situationists, and the critical outlook substantially was close to that of Situationists and ex-Situationist both.

For years, one crudely painted graffiti attributed to King Mob could be seen on the Metropolitan Line in West London: "SAME THING DAY AFTER DAY TUBE-WORK-DINNER-WORK-TUBE-WORK-TUBE-ARMCHAIR-TV-SLEEP-HOW MUCH MORE CAN YOU TAKE ONE IN TEN GOES MAD ONE IN FIVE CRACKS UP!"[9] This sentiment resonates with the punk view of TV as "a conditioner of working-class acquiescence through its escapist mythology," as Dan Graham observes.[10] The Clash shouted that "everybody is drowning in a sea of television" (1977), Alternative TV's first album was called *The Image Has Cracked* (1978), and The Jam sang: "The braying sheep on my TV screen / Make this boy shout, make this boy scream!" (1980).[11] In punk, television was generally perceived as a pacifier, a way for big corporations and the elite to let rebellious thoughts lapse. So, either go on TV and do something that will make the viewer wake up—or avoid and boycott it.

WANTED: Poster action

As discussed again and again in this book (see, for example, Section 2.4: "DIY: The DNA of punk"), the streetscape, as well as street art and graffiti played a key role in punk art. The topic of street messages overlaps with the topic of punk posters. Punk propaganda here meant first and foremost: shaking things up. One example is the Danish artist Elmer who in the late 1970s was doing street posters, such as *Nu Også: Elmer* (*Now Also: Elmer*, 1977, Figure 4.1).

Elmer explains,

> We put the posters up overnight. People who walked by were supposed to see them: They were made for the people walking by on the street. They did not have to go into a gallery. That was really important. Today, it is different, everyone goes into a gallery, but back then, it was separated. Hardly anyone was using the streetscape. That was what I was trying to do.[12]

The poster action *Now Also: Elmer* shows a black-and-white frontal photo, apparently a snapshot, of the artist himself with pentagonal plastic sunglasses, an earring, greasy hair, and a silvery-white jacket. Above his head is a barcode. On the left side of the poster, "NOW ALSO: ELMER" is written vertically in big white capital letters on black. The posters were hung in series, so eight or more posters would hang directly next to each other, emphasizing the street poster as well as the serial character of the work. The poster mixes a kind of Kilroy-was-here notification with press sensationalism, product declaration, and "WANTED" call. "It was an introduction of myself as an artist and as a commodity," says Elmer,

> Maybe it was primitive and teenager-like, but it was also important, it was an opposition to all of the sameness. People did not know what to think, did not know how to decode it, what the hell was it? Advertising? Art? Music? *Now also with raspberry taste!*[13]

Thus the poster aimed to instigate and contradict the exclusiveness of high art, and instead played with the Warholian notions of fame, commotion, and multiplication. The poster likewise alludes to Marcel Duchamp's self-portrait *Wanted $2,000 Reward* (1923; Figure 4.2), in which Duchamp likewise engaged with his own image as an artist and set up a WANTED style poster for himself, including his various aliases.

In another poster action, Elmer put up posters that made the offer: *Lej en familie* (*Rent a Family*, 1979). The poster shows a happy smiling family above a text specifying that a family can be rented for a day, a weekend, or longer, and comes with "full equipment."

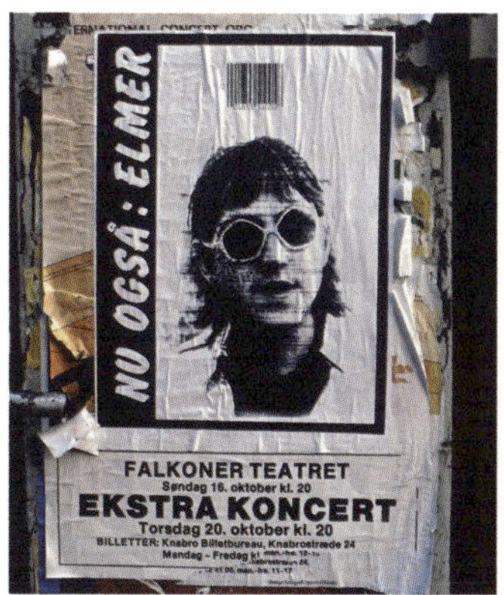

Figure 4.1: Elmer, Now Also: Elmer, *Copenhagen, 1977. Courtesy of Elmer.*

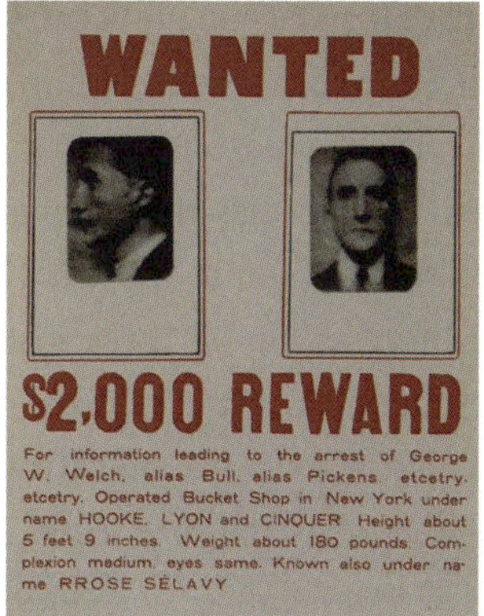

Figure 4.2: Marcel Duchamp, Wanted: $2,000 Reward, *1961 (replica of 1923 original). © VG Bild-Kunst, Bonn 2022.*

Elmer thus worked with appropriation and skepticism.

> It was a criticism of society, all of that family-orientated bullshit. I mean, you could not go to the supermarket or to the fair without a family, now could you? Well, now you could rent one, with video equipment, the newest on the market back then.[14]

The poster got many reactions, Elmer says, among others from the artist John Davidsen, who had himself engaged in ironic advertisement affirmations in the 1960s. For instance, he made a poster where he poses as Playmate's *Playboy of the Month* (1969). According to Elmer, Davidsen criticized there being no phone number on *Rent a Family*, but, as Elmer puts it, "That was the thinking of the Fluxus movement. I just wanted to provoke a chain of thought. It was about what was going on in the head. Would people stop and think: Can you really rent a family?" The different points of view thus echo the argument between Fluxus and punk art, which we have by now encountered several times: *Rent a Family* was not the playful interaction of Fluxus (or more generally of the 1960s), but rather was a simple one-way shove, a forceful gesture that did not seek dialogue. What the recipients did thereafter was up to them. "To me, punk has a lot to do with art," Elmer considers,

> because to be punk means to ask questions, or to say, no, we don't want it to be like this, does it have to be like this? All of the time. Be independent. Be on the watch. And to me, that is what being an artist is too.[15]

Punk alphabet

Besides the appropriation of radio, television, and commercials, punk propaganda was about *language*: Punk artists and musicians were very aware of the power of language.

The importance of language in punk can be seen in the often elaborate and sharp-witted titles of artworks, the collaborations with poets, and in the détournement of commercial and/or bureaucratic language. Punk art is often intermedial and often incorporates its own making and its own dissemination as part of the work, be it in the form of graffiti, zines, Super 8 films, or the more abstract forms of using controversy, spectacle, or crime as media in themselves. In all these instances, we can detect an interest not only in conveying a certain message but perhaps more profoundly, an interest in the very system of propagation. Ultimately, the objective was to understand and possibly subvert the most powerful weapon of the authorities and the establishment (i.e. the enemy).

COUM Transmissions, for example, saw language as a key means of subversion: Language, and more broadly communication, was understood as an instrument of oppression by the ruling class. Douglas Rushkoff reconstructs P-Orridge's line of thought as: "They own the land, the buildings, the money, the media and the sex. But maybe not the language."[16] P-Orridge thus engaged in a kind of reoccupation of the English language, using thee for the, E for I, butter for but, etc. These détournements became part of the "Coumalphabet" which was used in all statements made by the group. This method is akin to the Dadaists' tumultuous re-conquering of the language; indeed, as Elza Adamovicz puts it, the Dadaists used "language as action, subversion and performance."[17] The extra amount of attention, which was demanded by the listener or the reader, was a small power tool: Dada texts you often need to read twice, because of the chaotic grammar, the deliberate misspelling, and the fragmented structure of sentences. The incomprehensibility and the inconvenience were desired effects.

COUM Transmissions' interest in communication also becomes apparent in the name *transmissions* as well as *COUM* which could refer either to commune, communication, or come/cum, and is "pronounced coom or come."[18] The association with "cum" was enhanced by the COUM logo, featuring a hand-drawn, semi-erect penis ejaculating (Figure 4.3). COUM produced this logo as a black-on-black sticker, together with another sticker, which had the outline of a wax seal with ribbons, into which the text "COUM guarantee disappointment" was integrated (Figure 4.4). This was an inversion of advertising slogans, a commitment to failure.

Outside of the UK, young punks were faced with the decision of whether to use their own language (in our main cases: Dutch, German, and Danish). Both British English and American English had a touch of coolness. Not only did many song titles and refrains sound better in English, the cultural influence of the Anglo-Saxon countries throughout the 1960s and 1970s, especially with regard to fashion and music, was overwhelming. New York and London, as the two fire starter cities in punk, were

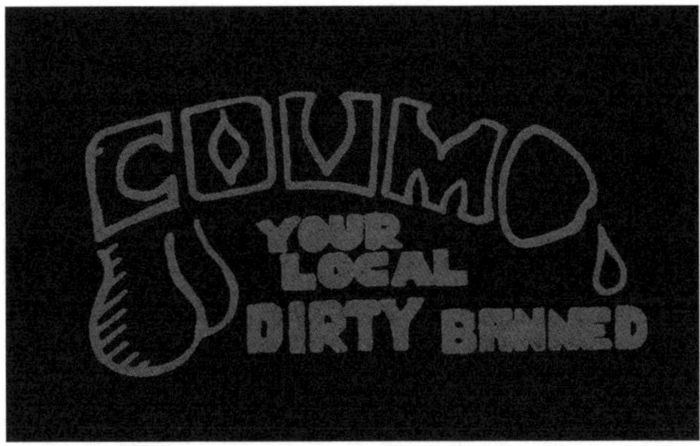

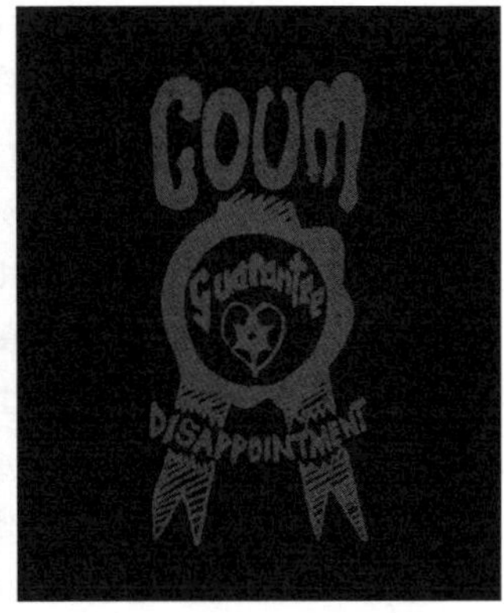

Figure 4.3: COUM Transmissions, "COUM Your Local Dirty Banned," 1969. Courtesy of the estate of Genesis BREYER P-ORRIDGE and New Discretions.

Figure 4.4: COUM Transmissions, "COUM Guarantee Disappointment," 1969. Courtesy of the estate of Genesis BREYER P-ORRIDGE and New Discretions.

English-speaking. Even punk itself was an English word, and it was not translated when punk spread to other countries.

The decision to use a different language than English was thus a conscious one. In West Germany, for example, punk bands, filmmakers, and artists often did choose to do their respective work in the un-relaxed and sometimes downright arduous German. The use of the German language was a countermeasure to the glamor of international English, a redirection of attention toward the here and now of West Germany, "whose low, trashy reality was in their [i.e. the punks'] view being given too little attention,"[19] Diedrich Diedrichsen asserts. Because punk was so much about appropriation and propaganda, the precision that most people only possess in their first language turned out to be of the essence. Thus, using German was not some kind of tribute to the mother tongue, but rather a reflection of a dull and quaint, but at times underlyingly aggressive reality. Punk's mocking affirmation of the desolation of the present circumstances was thus often best articulated in the native, uncool and awkward, but precise and harsh-sounding language. Punk's quest to show reality, as it were, could at times be done better in the actual language that the punks (often youths) spoke and knew. Punk in German was thus also a counter draft to something like ABBA, who in the punk view stood for Swedish slick emptiness, internationally consumable and full of banal love platitudes. In contrast, German punk band chose in-consumable names like Einstürzende Neubauten, Deutsch-Amerikanische Freundschaft, Kriminalitätsförderungsclub, or for a shorter one: Abwärts (Collapsing New Buildings, German-American Friendship [do view this one ironically], Criminiality-Furtherance-Club, and the short one:

Downwards). And named their punk zines *Hamburger Abschaum, Der Aktuelle Mülleimer, Willkürakt,* etc. (Hamburger Scum [Hamburg like the city, not the patty], the Latest Wastebin, Arbitrary Act).

Unlike Germany, most punk bands in the Netherlands also sang in English, whereas the punk poetry of the time was mostly in Dutch. The influence from the UK played a more defining role here than the influence from the USA, perhaps because the Netherlands was so close to the UK, both geographically and culturally, and because of the high level of English usage, as Kirsty Lohman suggests.[20] Some UK punk arguments were reproduced in the Netherlands: for example, at the Fuck the Queen Festival (1979)—which could not be done 1:1 in Germany, for obvious reasons (no queen).

Other punk circumstances reverberated: Just like the word "punk" itself was a demeaning expression, which the movement had made their own, punks used the same technique in other languages. In Denmark, for example, punks were criticized as being indifferent and lazy. In the newspaper *Politiken,* Poul Dines coined the expression "nå-generationen" ("nå," in this context, meaning a shrugging "whatever") and deemed punk "a desperate and random attempt" at formulating a youth revolt.[21] The "nå" label spread in the Danish press around 1980, underlining a view of punk as just teenage nihilism, with no sense of neither engagement nor participation. In the tabloid *Ekstra Bladet,* the 24-year-old unemployed Linda Wedel wrote a response,[22] and—together with her friend Synne Rifbjerg—began organizing *Nå!!80,* a punk art/music/poetry cross-over event, with the slogan "Brug medierne—ellers bliver de brugt imod dig" ("Use the media—or they will be used against you").[23] Calling the event "nå" was a typically punk way of taking possession of a bad reputation, of turning the meaning around. (Also typically punk, however, was that a row emerged, as some felt that punk was being misrepresented; this led to a protest action at the event.)[24]

Punk as a movement was thus highly aware of communication and mis-communication. Punks used all possible means, from zines to scandals to art to music to posters, to promote their cause, even if that cause at times was in itself conflicted. There was no unified coherent message or elaborate argumentation to be spread, but a stance to be taken, nonetheless. Punk propaganda meant a sharp observation, spreading chaos, salt in the wound. Punk propaganda meant agitation. To sum up, we might observe one version of punk, which attempted to subvert the mainstream popular media, and another version of punk, which was self-sustained and self-sufficient, working underground primarily with zines and—in the vocabulary of the 1970s—"agitprop" posters (i.e. communist agitation propaganda).

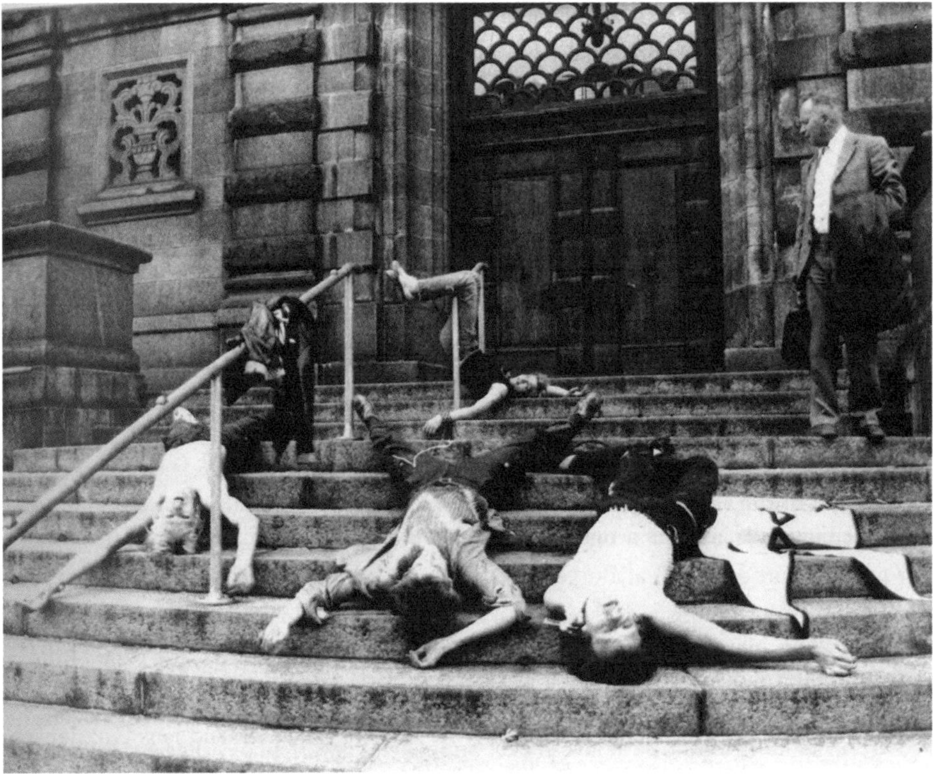

Figure 4.5: The Sods, D.o.A. (Dead on Arrival)*, 1978. Photograph by Per Katchetowa. Courtesy of Knud Odde and Per Katchetowa.*

4.2 Punk poetry

The weapons of the underdog are humor and insolence, nonsense, and poetry. And as Daniel Kane emphasizes, with the New York scene in mind: "Never poetry or punk—always poetry and punk."[25] Punks everywhere took their strength from being outsiders, not insiders, from being losers, not winners—and in doing so, they found a different kind of power. The fragility of punk takes shape in punk poems: as much as punk was about vigilant activism, it was likewise about melancholic *weltschmerz*. Poetry in relation to punk can mean vocalized poems, written verses, dirty limericks, sad requiems, poetic slogans spray-painted on a crumbling wall—but it can also mean the creation of an emblematic, evocative situation. In punk art, such suggestive situations became a kind of performative expression, the creation of a physical image. Punk poetry, art, and action went together: punks created subversive images, both in poetry and in reality. Punk was thus poetry in the sense of writing poetry and in the sense of living a poet's life—the outsider poet, that is, not the court poet, but the jester or the *poète maudit*.

The self-concept as the powerless fighting power can be seen for example in one black-and-white photo of the still very young and skinny boys from the Danish punk band the Sods, playing dead on the staircase in front of the Danish parliament. The Sods' first album was supposed to be called *Dead on Arrival* (*D.o.A.*) and this was the promotional photo (Figure 4.5), until the group found out that Throbbing Gristle had called their album *D.o.A.* (Sods thus changed their title to *Minutes to Go*, see Section 3.3: "Trash and travesty"). The image which should have been used on the cover shows the Danish seat of power, but the youth of the country is not attempting to take that house of power by storm. They are not knocking down the doors—they are lying motionless before them, dead on arrival, a man in a suit looking at them perplexedly. Such were the images created in punk: weakness turned weapon.

Armed with Wings

In Copenhagen, there was a tight-knit group of young poets many of whom debuted (or over-ground debuted) at Borgens Forlag in 1978: F. P. Jac with "Munden brænder på huden" ("The mouth burns on the skin"), Henrik S. Holck with "Vi må være alt" ("We must be all"), and Michael Strunge with "Livets Hastighed" ("The pace of life"). Jac, Strunge, Holck, and Søren Ulrik Thomsen became close friends, and all took part in the abovementioned event *Nå!!80*, along with Bo Green Jensen and Jens Fink-Jensen. Pia Tafdrup and Merete Torp were also part of this eruption of poetry. What jazz had been to the writers of the Beat Generation, punk rock was to this generation. Rhythm and themes overlapped. Punk's urban leitmotif was reproduced in magazine titles such as *Blitz*, *Graffiti*, and *Sidegaden* (The side street), and of course in Thomsen's *City Slang*. Punk topics such as alienation, negation, and failure were all themes in F. P. Jac's extended poem "Misfat" (1980), the title a reference to The Kinks' album *Misfits* (1978). F. P. Jac also wrote the poem "Jeg er fandme til" ("Damn, I am alive") in 1979, which with its ambiguity of affirmation and inherent doubt, formulates punk's mistrusting existentialism.

Perhaps the most famous of the punk poets was Michael Strunge. In 1980, he published the poem collection *SKRIGERNE* (*THE SCREAMERS*, quite obviously quoting the Los Angeles punk band The Screamers), with the subtitle *Punk Texts 1976–1979* (Figure 4.6). Many in the punk milieu, however, were skeptical of what they saw as Strunge's vanity, ambition, and punk pose, and they ridiculed him.[26] Thomsen says,

> The old punk underground was so damned snobbish and they did not like him [Michael Strunge] because he was known in the media. I think it was a huge source of sorrow for him, because he identified so much with that scene.[27]

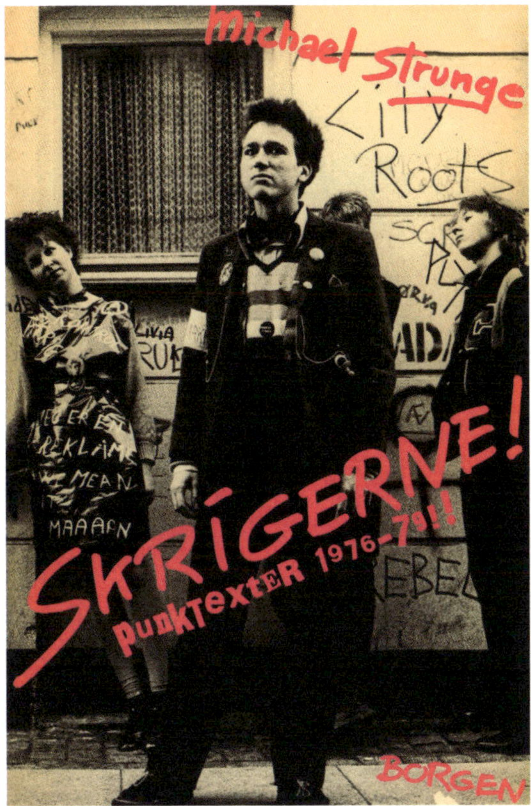

Figure 4.6: Cover of Michael Strunge SKRIGERNE! Punktexter 1976–79!! *Photograph by Peder Bundgaard. Publisher: Borgen, 1980. Courtesy of Gyldendal.*

Strunge effusively associated himself with the punk movement, citing the Sex Pistols' "WE MEAN IT, MAAAAAN" as an epigraph to *SKRIGERNE,* and writing one poem titled "London Calling" (in reference to the Clash) and another called "1 2 3 4! Akkorder —til the Sods" ("1 2 3 4! Chords for the Sods").[28] Strunge's short sentences often make use of abrupt staccato, monosyllables, and capital lettering for a forceful effect. The topoi in his poems—speed, urbanity, sex, revolution, symbols, myths, night—correspond to this inclination. Punk's romanticized version of childhood was also a returning theme in Strunge's poetry (see Chapter 6: "Children Run Riot: The Art of the Infantile"), as can be seen in the poster for his poetry recitation *Voxne er børn der er blevet sindsyge* (Grownups are children who have become crazy) in 1982 (Figure 4.7).

Strunge's writing style was in many ways characteristic of the young punk poets, their rejection of the 1970s social-realist, daily-routine themes, and their application

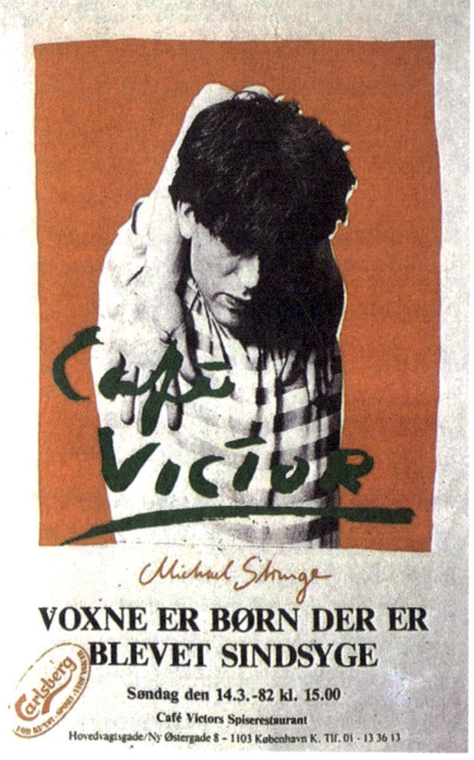

Figure 4.7: Unknown artist, poster for a poem reading with Michael Strunge with the title VOXNE ER BØRN DER ER BLEVET SINDSYGE *(Grownups are children who have become crazy), 1982. Image reproduced from Poulsen, Punk i Danmark, 237.*

of more fantastic and dramatic images instead. He often applied Surrealist topics and methods, such as automatic writing. As Marianne Ølholm points out:

> The focus on dreams and the unconscious is continuously present in Strunge's writing. The title of probably his best-known work is *VI FOLDER DRØMMENS FANER UD* (We Unfurl the Banners of the Dream), and the political potential of dreams and the subconscious is expressed in the connection between dream and rebellion throughout the book.[29]

In *We Unfurl the Banners of the Dream*, we find the poem "Revolt" (see Section 6.1: "Dead end kids") which combines dreamlike scenes with both the childish, the fantastic, and the revolutionary—that is, key Surrealist topoi. Ølholm also points to Strunge's book, *Fremtidsminder* (*Memories of the Future*, 1980) as clearly operating within a Surrealist tradition, deploying elements of visions and dreams, mental landscapes, and the eye as a recurring subject, as is often the case in Surrealist writing, film, and painting. Strunge was highly interested in visual art too. Before breaking off his studies, he had studied Art History at the University of Copenhagen, and he made drawings himself.

Strunge combines these Surrealist features with symbolism and science fiction, often taking the images to a max. Much like he often wrote his poems in all-caps, his metaphors seemed all-out. He explained:

> I wanted to see how far I could go, how much pressure could be withstood by a supersymbolist vision, using all the classical concepts of heaven and hell and queen and prince, before the embalmed world of beauty […] is smashed to pieces in depression and suicide poems.[30]

Strunge suffered from manic-depression, and in 1986, at the age of 27, he died after jumping out his window, while temporarily visiting home after a stay at the psychiatric hospital. It remains unknown if he was consciously committing suicide or was suffering from a delusion that he would fly. For his last collection of poems under his own name[31] which was called *Væbnet med vinger* (*Armed with Wings*, 1984), he asked Lars Nørgård to paint an image for the cover. The poem "Væbnet med Vinger" has only four lines:

> Jeg ruger i mørket—
> Ruger mig ud
> Og breder vipperne, flyver på syn
> Ind i mit næste liv.
>
> (I brood in darkness—
> Hatch myself out
> And spread my lashes, fly on visions
> Into my next life.)[32]

Nørgård recounts:

> I was with Dorte Dahlin back then, and she introduced us. We all met at a café, and he [Strunge] says, "I am putting out a book called *Armed with Wings*. Would you like to do the cover?" […] I just said yes. He told me to come by next Saturday, he already had an idea. I had a reflex camera, few did back then. I went to his place at Østerbro, it was still early in the morning. He undressed. He had shaved himself, completely, his head, his whole body. He got up on a table and I started photographing. Then he put his clothes back on and said to me: "Paint me with wings, like I am taking

> off." So, I did. […] We saw each other more often after that. Until he opened the window and jumped.[33]

The cover is a juxtaposition of photography and semi-abstract painting. The background is an assembly of different shapes and forms painted with thick, wavy strokes in saturated colors. At the center, the black-and-white photo of Strunge's naked, shaved body is inserted. The face is turned away, as though he is in motion. Nørgård has painted breasts onto Strunge's skinny, androgynous body, reinforcing the already statuesque quality of his figure in the image. Behind Strunge's neck is an orange, vertical figure-eight-shaped curve, which might, as Trine Ross writes, be interpreted as wings.[34] Toward the bottom edge is written STRUNGE, with a downward pointing arrow in the S (something that Strunge did himself when signing his name).

Around 1980, the collaboration between punk artists, musicians, and poets was close in Copenhagen. Before Strunge had worked with Nørgård for the cover of *Armed with Wings*, the poet Søren Ulrik Thomsen had worked with Nina Sten-Knudsen for the cover of his poems collection *City Slang* (1981, Figure 4.8). Thomsen got the idea for the title from Patti Smith, whom he saw perform at Daddy's Dance Hall on May 12, 1976, wearing a badge with the words: City Slang.[35]

Sten-Knudsen and Thomsen started their friendship off with a big argument against one another: following *Nå!!80*, Rifbjerg and Wendel, together with Thomsen, edited the anthology *Platform* with punk images and texts, and a dispute between Thomsen and artists from the academy arose. The group of artists from the academy demanded that all ten of them be included or none at all. The ultimatum made Thomsen furious, and the upshot was no academy artists being included. In the course of the heated debate nevertheless, Søren Ulrik Thomsen had an hour-long telephone discussion with one of these academy artists, Nina Sten-Knudsen, about a series of photos of violent Body Art she had made. Both describe the dispute as the beginning of a close friendship: "I mean, it was all about pushing each other," says Sten-Knudsen, "at the concerts too."[36] The collaboration between the poet Thomsen and the artist Sten-Knudsen once again indicates the shared mindset across disciplines at the time. And that a little tension and dispute can be good, in friendship and in art.

PROVO poetics

The poetic streak of punk manifested in different ways. In Amsterdam, the KoeCrandt group moved between sloganeering and poetry, graffiti, and the creation of new words. "IEDEREEN met ideën is WELKOM!" (EVERYONE with ideas is WELCOME) it says on one collaged flyer, next to further slogans such as "PUNK ART" and "Amsterdamned

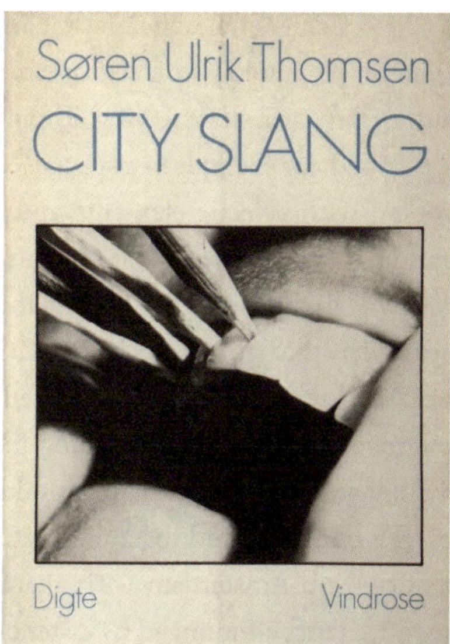

Figure 4.8: Cover of Søren Ulrik Thomsen, City Slang. *Publisher: Vindrose, 1981. Image by Nina Sten-Knudsen, 1980. Courtesy of the artist.*

BABYLON." The effect of the chaotic and overloaded aesthetics of the flyer is further enhanced by spelling errors and disruptive changes between lower- and upper-case characters. The creative crossover between art, music, poetry, theater, activism, and fashion, which is so intrinsic to punk, was lived out in the KoeCrandt group too. The group's mouthpiece and house bulletin, the *KoeCrandt*—sometimes spelled *Koekrant, Koekkrant, KoeCrandt, Koekrand, Coekrant, Coeqrand, Coekrandt, Quekrant*—referred to the stained inner edge of a toilet seat. "We changed our own names all the time, we changed the name of the magazine to be impalpable," says Ozon, "We did not want to be managed."[37] The first issue came out on August 1, 1977 and was inspired by punk zines, which Kanstadt had brought back from London. The zines were either photocopied or mimeographed, and contained announcements about happenings, demonstrations, and concerts as well as drawings, comics, and collages by Ivar Vičs aka Dr Rat and Hugo Kaagman aka Amarillo, reviews by Ludwig Wisch aka Rocky Rat aka Lulu Zulu, poems by Kristian Kanstadt and Gretchen Gestapo aka Diana Ozon aka Douglas Groezel, among other things. Some of the punk poems by Diana Ozon and Kristian Kanstadt published in KoeCrandt were later painted onto streetscapes and walls, such as Kristian Kanstadt's *Wibautotisme* (1982) on the bottom of the M. S. Vaz Dias Bridge.

The content of the zine oscillated between the political and the nonsensical, the practical and the poetic. In one unified message in a *KoeCrandt* montage, the group stated:

"Punk is not a fashion. It is a lifestyle. It is the only relevant art form today."[38] *KoeCrandt* was a quintessential punk zine in its emphasis on self-organization, directness, art and social transformation, co-authorship, and sloganeering. Topics that would be perceived as disgusting or trashy were pursued, for example in a special "Sperma Songbook" edition in 1979. The aesthetics worked with eclectic elements and culture jamming (i.e. the subversion of corporate branding by appropriation). On some occasions, for example, the artists drew the title *KoeCrandt* in the distinctive style of the Coca Cola brand (such a parodying imitation was also used by the Italian punk band CCCP Fedeli alla linea [CCCP is the Italian abbreviation of USSR] who likewise appropriated the Coca Cola font).

Punk poetry in Amsterdam can also be understood in a more abstract way: the creation of poetic ephemeral images through protesting. Building on the creation of the anarchist group The Provos, the punks around the zine KoeCrandt thus used action to create images. The Provos stirred up Amsterdam with anarchic humor, with slogans, happenings, and sit-ins. Provo was first announced by a stenciled leaflet, dated May 25, 1965. The text proclaimed the PROVOcative method to effect change in society. In one action, the members of the group distributed raisins and were arrested for disorderly conduct. In another, they carried banners demanding democracy (against the monarchy in the Netherlands) and when these were confiscated, they carried blank banners, demanding nothing; these were confiscated too.[39]

Twelve years later, before the opening of the metro line in 1977, the KoeCrandt artists had decorated the area with black flags, banners with slogans, empty milk cartons, and rotten tomatoes, and in their zine, they announced a "happening/performance" at eleven o'clock on the day of the opening, during which the artists threw fake banknotes and orange paint at the inauguration guests, among them Princess Beatrix, Prince Claus von Amsberg, and the Minister of Traffic and Transportation Tjerk Westerterp.[40] The orange paint and the fake money can be seen as symbols of anti-monarchism (orange as the color of the Oranje-Nassau Dynasty and the national color of the Netherlands) and anti-capitalism (the metro plan as a monopoly game with real lives). It was poetic imagery carried out in real action, manifested symbols.

The close link between the Provos—known for their stencils and wall slogans—and the punks shows how the punk movement in Amsterdam was affected by a cultural tradition running through the twentieth century, and the artists group that formed around the *KoeCrandt* zine especially, invoked and positioned itself in relation to that tradition. "The punks wanted to be as important as Provo," Hugo Kaagman remembers, "They were our example, you know? We also went to some of the Provos to ask for advice! And they gave us lots of advice."[41] Furthermore, both the Provos and the punks were highly involved with the massive kraakbeweging—the squatter movement—of the 1970s and 1980s in Amsterdam. The onomatopoeic "kraak" was originally used for break-ins and burglaries (based on the sound it makes when you break open a door). During World War II, resistance groups used the term for sabotage against the Nazis.[42] The squatters placed great value on these implications of "kraak" as resistance: squatting, too, was a way of underground fighting.

A dog named Margot

As we focus in this chapter on the weapons of the underdog, on ways of being subversive, when you do not—as argued above—own neither the land, the buildings, the money, the media, nor the sex, a glance on the other side of the Wall in Berlin proves especially prolific. East Berlin had a punk scene too, beautifully portrayed in the melancholic photo series by Ilse Ruppert taken in Prenzlauer Berg (1982; Figure 4.9). Here poetry played an especially important role, as most of the expressions of opinion that were, after all, still possible in West Germany, were fought with a different rigor in East Germany.

The barriers between art and music were traversed in East German punk also, but with more severe consequences, since intermediality in itself was a breach of official East German cultural politics. The strategies and anti-strategies of punk in East Germany were much like those in the West, but attained a different potency and explosiveness, because of the decidedly harsher repression of the East German authorities. The Ministerium für Staatssicherheit ("StaSi") monitored and infiltrated the punk scene, which was closely linked with other resistance groups in East Germany and shared the same alternative spaces—often churches, such as the Kirche von Unten (Church from below) in East Berlin. The punk technique of demasking through absurd humor was applied by one punk who went by the name of Speichel (Saliva), who named his dog "Margot" after the East German Education Minister (and wife of Erich) Margot Honecker, and subsequently ran around yelling: "Komm, Margot, Platz! Brav, gib Pfötchen!" (Come on, Margot, down! Good doggie. Shake!).[43] Pure poetry in action.

"The rigidity of the East German system gave punk a human face,"[44] writes poet Bert Papenfuß, who was a central figure in East Berlin's Prenzlauer Berg punk milieu. Papenfuß often performed his poems at punk rock concerts, also because what he wrote could not be published (would have been censored) in the GDR. The view of punk, as Papenfuß recounts, as something human, vulnerable, and flawed, is often mentioned by East German punk artists and musicians. The artist Cornelia Schleime, for example, stresses the fact that in East Germany, everything was made to sound definite, whereas punk was obscure, blurred, and contradictory. "To me, punk was the breaking of patterns,"

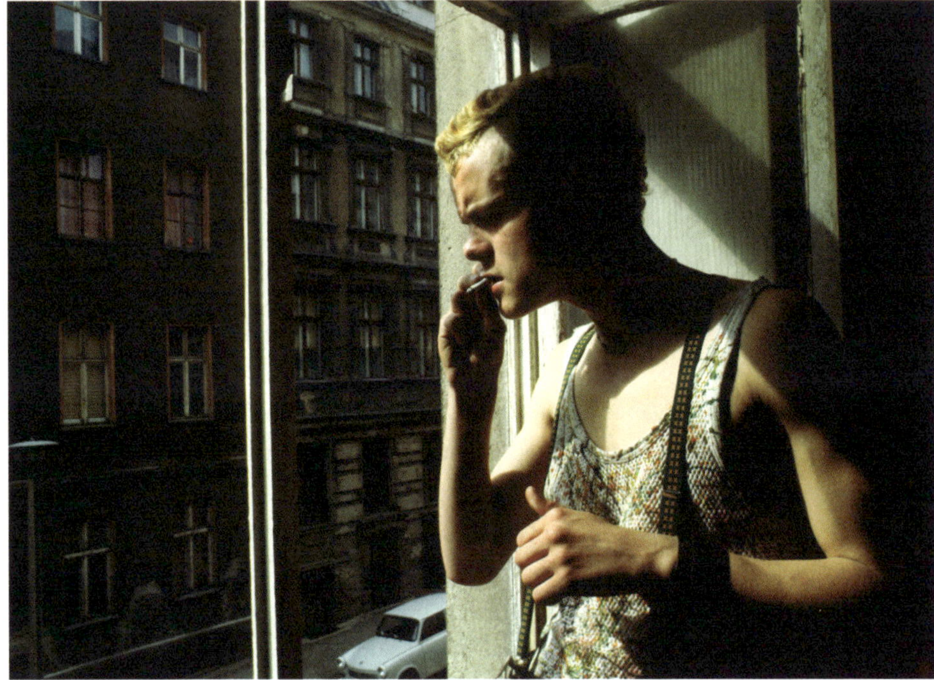

Figure 4.9: Ilse Ruppert, Punk in East Berlin, *1982. Courtesy of Ilse Ruppert.*

she says,[44] and patterns were abundant in East Germany. The "No Future" sentiment in the punk movement in western Europe finds its inverted equivalent in the "Too Much Future" watchword of East German punk.[46] The prescribed, inescapable "socialistic" future was perceived as a threat, an unavoidable prospect arranged to eradicate all subjectivity.

Punks on both sides of the Wall were unified in their reproach of conformist systems and in their attempts to unmask oppressive structures. The names of the punk bands in East Germany bear witness to their closeness to those in West Germany: trash was one topic (Schleimkeim, Totalschaden, Zerfall, Müllstation, i.e. Slime Germ, Total Loss, Decay, Garbage Station), others were destruction, anger, mania (Paranoia, Wutanfall, Die Besessenen, i.e. Paranoia, Tantrum, the Obsessed), and hopelessness (Planlos, Namenlos, Zwecklos, i.e. No Plan, No Name, No Purpose).[47] One equivalent to punk art in the West might be seen in the Auto-Perforations-Artisten (auto-perforation-artists) in the East. In 1984, a small group of punks and artists succeeded in organizing the exhibition *NO ART* in Erfurt (among others with the work of abovementioned Cornelia Schleime, as well as Gabriele Stötzer, Mita Schamal, Christian Duschek "Spinne," Jens "Tuckie" and Matthias Schneider KULT). Punks in Erfurt regularly met in that house, until 1986, when the StaSi orders police to clear the building.[48]

In Berlin especially, an exchange between East and West punks was possible, to a limited degree. Punk author Frank Willmann recounts how Palestinian diplomats' sons, who were into punk, carried Stranglers and Dead Kennedys LPs to the other side of the Wall.[49] Käthe Kruse smuggled a Tödliche Doris audio cassette across the border into East Berlin by hiding it in her beehive dreadlocks.[50] East German playwright and author Heiner Müller succeeded in carrying twenty *Brilliant Dilletantes* books across the border in his diplomatic pouch. One book found its way to Bert Papenfuß.[51] In the eastern parts of the city, it was possible to receive radio broadcasts from Sender Freies Berlin (SFB), the American RIAS (Rundfunk Im Amerikanischen Sektor) and the especially well-liked program of John Peel on the British Forces Broadcasting Service (BFBS). Unsurprisingly, there was less flow in the other direction.

In both systems, however, punks were fighting power with ludicrousness and laughter. Punk as a movement was illogical, its poetic attacks unpredictable. The self-identification of punks as outsiders meant finding strength in weakness. Seeing themselves as the outsiders also meant that punks would often identify with the criminal—and crime and insubordination likewise belong to the weapons of the underdog. This brings us to the last part of this chapter and the topic of crime as art (or: transgression as art, scandal as art).

4.3 Crime as art, scandal as art

Of the artists' groups examined in this book, COUM Transmissions was the most extreme. COUM intertwined performance with pain, sex with greed, and entertainment with violence to maximize the effect of their work. They explored whether crime could be art, and whether art could be a crime. COUM tested out scandal-as-art, pornography-as-art, and in that very ex-Situationist way: art-as-excess (see Section 3.2: "Hedonism as attack"). And then—as though taken from the playbook of Warhol's Factory ensemble—they used controversy, press agitation, and transmission feedback as media in themselves.[52]

Two COUM cases specifically stand out as examples of this approach. In the first case, P-Orridge was charged with sending five postcards of "indecent, offensive, and obscene character," thereby violating the Post Office Act of 1953.[53] The artists of COUM documented the related trial at Highbury Magistrates Court in London in the publication *G.P.O. vs. G.P.-O.*—the letters stand for General Post Office versus Genesis P-Orridge—and used the trial as an art material. The second case, the *PROSTITUTION* exhibition and scandal, is perhaps the most punk art event of the 1970s, at least in the UK, and likewise a prime example of COUM's talent for provocation and subversion.

G.P.O. vs. G. P.-O.: The courtroom as a stage

P-Orridge sent several postcards to a network of actual as well as fictitious artists and friends during the 1970s. One postcard shows an image of Buckingham Palace and Queen Elizabeth II next to naked male buttocks on the front, and on the back side features a hand-written note: "The lady on the front has her mouth shut because her teeth are filed to points." The vampire analogy brings to mind Johnny Rotten's "God save the queen. She ain't no human being."[54] The "blue blood" aristocratic un-realness of the queen is put in the context of shadowy gothic horror. Like the Sex Pistols, COUM Transmissions were attacking the monarchy as such, deeming it corrupted to the core. "As we all know," P-Orridge told Dominic Johnson, "the most perverted, debauched, and unpleasant people, sexually, are usually the aristocrats who can be untouchable."[55] Furthermore, the collage mixed the cheap glossy imagery of pornography with the cheap glossy touristy imagery of the royals, both vulgarly for sale.

Another postcard had at the front a reproduction of René Magritte's painting *Time Transfixed* (1938) but superimposed on top of it was an image of a couple having intercourse, which P-Orridge had cut out of a pornographic magazine. The replicated Magritte painting on the postcard shows a steam train exiting a marble fireplace, on top of which are placed two empty candlesticks and a large mirror. The train inside the fireplace could be interpreted as a metaphor for penetration. In his work, Genesis P-Orridge thus made the hidden sexual symbolism of Magritte's arrangement manifest. There is a meanness—but also wittiness— in the way Magritte's painting is exposed to the tastelessness and crudity of both the overlaid image and the cut-out pornography magazine text: "We bucked and heaved, our mingled juices soaking our groins and also the quilt beneath us," it reads.

COUM Transmissions made an event—a fun show! a spectacle!—out of the trial. Tutti photographed P-Orridge as he received the court summons. In the *G.P.O. vs. G.P.-O.* publication, this photo was included in the first pages, with an ironic caption specifying the date and time (10:00 a.m. on Saturday morning, January 17, 1976), the name and rank of the police detective, and the artists' address in Hackney, as well as the observation: "Genesis had just been woken up and as can be seen, was not looking his best."[56] COUM sent out wedding-style formal invitations to all their associates, resulting in an illustrious crowd being present at court. The press was notified and P-Orridge gave several interviews, among others to the *Observer* and *National News*. At the trial, he wore an elaborate outfit, resulting in a visual clash ready for the stage, as noted by *Time Out*'s Duncan Campbell:

> There was the defendant, P-Orridge, resplendent in lurex suit, red socks, silver fingernails and with his hair just growing back on the crown of his head from where

> he had but recently shaved it. Facing him was the doughty magistrate, Mrs. Colwell, in a twin set that matched her blue eye-shadow.[57]

The scene is highly vivid.

The key witnesses consisted of a string of personalities from the art establishment as well as the radical avant-garde, and ranged from the director of the Tate Gallery, Sir Norman Reid, to the director of the Fine Arts Department at the British Council, Gerald Forty, and William S. Burroughs. There is a certain irony of history in the fact that Burroughs—whose book *Naked Lunch* was once banned under the accusation of obscenity—was the one to write in his testimony: "Genesis P.-Orridge is an artist and not a pornographer."[58] Ted Little, Director of the ICA, noted in his court statement that he was planning a show with the accused at the ICA later that year (which would then become the scandalous *PROSTITUTION* exhibition). In spite of these explanations, the main line of defense by P-Orridge's lawyers—artistic merit—was judged "irrelevant," and P-Orridge was fined 100 British pounds plus all court costs. After the trial, he stated, "I don't find it the be-all and end-all to use nude ladies on postcards, but I resent the fact I can't do it," and added New Scotland Yard to the list of exhibitions on his résumé.[59]

High Crime Is Like High Art

After the trial, COUM Transmissions engaged in a series of performances held at the AIR Gallery in London entitled *Crime Affirms Existence—High Crime Is Like High Art*, in July 1976. In the accompanying article "Annihilating Reality," in the prominent art magazine *Studio International*, co-written by P-Orridge and Christopherson,[60] they pose the question of murder as a performative act, thereby drawing on the infamous text *On Murder, Considered as One of the Fine Arts* by Thomas De Quincey (1827), a text which incidentally takes its starting point in London East-End's Ratcliffe Highway murders. In "Annihilating Reality," P-Orridge and Christopherson identify with artists and writers who had been on the verge of criminality or who had been convicted of crimes, including Marquis de Sade, Hugo Ball, and Vito Acconci. The article is fragmentary and sensationalist, but some core arguments nonetheless can be ascertained. Among other arguments, P-Orridge and Christopherson assert that in how we perceive art, as well as crime, the values of a society might be revealed. Art and crime can both be seen as foils against which to test social (dis)order and inconsistencies between public perceptions and reality.

This argument was also made by the Surrealists. Jonathan P. Eburne has shown that the Surrealists were deeply fascinated by De Quincey's *On Murder, Considered as One of the Fine Arts*. They thought that—through exaggeration—he pointed to a core of truth. According to Eburne, "Recognizing the popular and clinical impact of crime to be an admixture of fiction and fact, the Surrealists viewed crime as a phenomenon of the marvelous, an event characterized by the discrepancies and excesses it brought to light."[61] Crime scenes and accounts of violence thus were also used as inspiration in Surrealist magazines. The Surrealists found heroes in murderers, for example Germaine Berton, the young anarchist who assassinated the publishing secretary of the extreme right nationalist party L'Action Française. The Surrealists demonstrated their solidarity by arranging headshot photographs of themselves in a photomontage centered around a police mug shot of Berton in *La Révolution Surréaliste* no. 1 (1924).

The associated notion that the societal role of the artist can be the same as the outlaw was also reflected in punk. In both punk and Surrealism, there was a view of the criminal as the ethical one who fought against an immoral system, and who had only been pushed to his or her actions because of that injustice, that is, the weapons of the underdog. The idea reflected in this argumentation was akin to Breton's "pistol in hand": the outlaw/artist incorporating a conscious alternative to the "system of debasement and cretinization."[62] COUM Transmissions thus inscribe themselves in a double-sided crime-as-art and art-as-crime tradition. The figure of the persecuted artist fighting for the liberty of art and/or for sexual expression in court had been spurred by several prominent international cases in the 1960s and 1970s, such as the cases against the Vienna Actionists (1968) in Austria, against the group SPUR (1975) in West Germany, and Miller v. California (1973) in the USA.

In the performance and live art scenes especially, there was a heightened interest in the taunting of the institutional frame. Positioned somewhere between moral testing and daring contest, art actions in the 1970s, much like punk actions in the 1970s, drew on the mixture of tabloid scandal, conservative outcry, genuine ethical and political examination of societal rule sets, situation comic, and a joke on the cost of the establishment. When German performer Ulay stole Carl Spitzweg's painting *The Poor Poet* (1839) from the Neue Nationalgalerie in 1976, he tellingly called the act There Is a Criminal Touch to Art, and landed in court.[63]

The comparison between art and crime in "Annihilating Reality" led P-Orridge and Christopherson to the argument that art and crime can both emerge from a heightened alertness or consciousness that is concentrated into one moment of action: "Art is perception of the moment. Action. Conscious."[64] This notion of art-as-awareness was the background behind the title of the article, "Annihilating Reality," which is taken from British poet Arthur Symons' words on the Symbolist movement: "Allowing ourselves, for the most part, to be but vaguely conscious of the great suspense in which we live, we find our escape from its sterile, annihilating reality in many dreams, in religion, passion, art."[65] In COUM's view, art and crime were both means to become aware of that "great suspense" of living. Thus, they repeated the argument of their performance series *Crime Affirms Existence*: Art, just like crime, can make you feel alive.

Art = Prostitution

In a further exploration of the nature of art, COUM organized *PROSTITUTION* at the ICA in London in 1976. Again, the group probed the possibility of using controversy as an artistic medium in itself. The controversy around the opening night was willfully staged. COUM's quasi-Situationist setup of the opening night of *PROSTITUTION* was intended to expose double standards and taboos within the artworld, and to exploit predictable media reactions. P-Orridge recounts:

> I'd secretly assembled, then surreptitiously utilized, a list of 'yellow' journals and journalists—around fifty or so names and addresses. I'd done this before and nothing had happened. I was thinking very much in terms of Dada and Surrealism. Sending out flyers to titillate and arouse.[66]

Not unlike the Sex Pistols' TV interview with Grundy, COUM might not have anticipated the *extent* of the scandal, but the affront in itself was calculated. The exhibition coincided not only with the emergence of punk, but with the social rupture and rightwing backlash that resulted from the economic crisis of the 1970s. The provocations of *PROSTITUTION* were thus fueled by the neoconservative moral climate and the insecurity of a country that was deeply divided.

It was "the only artworld event equivalent to the impact made by the Sex Pistols shortly afterwards," writes John A. Walker.[67] "The Prostitution furore rivalled the December 1976 folk-devil panic about the Sex Pistols swearing on TV," Reynolds remarks.[68]

PROSTITUTION has later been named "a highly 'punk' event" by Mark Sladen, "the first punk exhibition" and "the confluence point of English punk" by David G. Torres.[69] The exhibition and its contents are directly or indirectly referred to as punk art by Gerald Matt in *No One Is Innocent*, by Dick Hebdige in "Contemporizing 'Subculture'," and by Ian Lowey and Suzy Prince in *The Graphic Art of the Underground.*[70] When the exhibition opened on October 18, 1976, however, "punk" was not yet a familiar term in the UK—a circumstance that would change explosively within the following two months. Unconnected to the exhibition, the Clash and Subway Sect played their set called *A NIGHT OF PURE ENERGY* at the ICA Theatre on October 23, 1976:[71] that is, four days after the opening of *PROSTITUTION*. This event resulted in the Clash's "first significant press coverage."[72] Six weeks later the Sex Pistols appeared in that infamous Bill Grundy interview, and the *Daily Mirror* asked on their front page: "WHO ARE THESE PUNKS?"[73]

COUM Transmissions, meanwhile, were already moving on: at the opening of *PROSTITUTION*, the group proclaimed that from now on, they would be Throbbing Gristle (which is, apparently, Yorkshire slang for an erection), with the same cast as before, plus Chris Carter. COUM had chosen a most official setting for their swan song. The ICA is situated in the center of London, close not only to Buckingham Palace—as P-Orridge remarked in an interview with Richard Metzger: "we were almost within *spitting distance* of Buckingham Palace"[74]—but also to the House of Commons and the National Gallery. As an institution, the ICA represented "the place where art's radical fringe collided with high culture," as Simon Reynolds puts it,[75] and its location represented the heart of the capital's political and traditional power.

The exhibition contained framed pages from pornographic magazines featuring Tutti as well as photos of past performances and used props, such as bloody tampons, meat cleavers, rectal syringes, chains, knives, Vaseline, and a double-ended dildo with spikes. Among the artworks were also an old Art Deco clock filled with 28 used tampons called *It's That Time of the Month*, a plywood frame with a used tampon emerging out of a hairpiece called *Pupae* or *Larvae*,[76] and a box of maggots turning into flies. In an art-institutional setting like the ICA, with an audience presumably well-informed about art, the *memento mori* association was assured: the clock, the metamorphosis, and subsequent decomposition of the maggots, as well as the transient subjects of rotting materials, blood, and flies all pointed in this direction. The ephemerality of the materials was countered by the series title *TAMPAX ROMANA*—which might be seen as a hint at the decay and downfall of empires, as the *Pax Romana* is used to describe the time right before the Roman imperial crisis in the third century AD. The *TAMPAX ROMANA* series thus expressed the artists' derisive view of the contemporary state of the former British Empire anno 1976.

COUM performed as Throbbing Gristle on the opening night, that is, as an opening act to their own art show. Dorothy Max Prior, who at the time worked at the ICA as an art assistant, anticipated the show:

> COUM Transmissions are going to commit artistic suicide and simultaneously rise from the ashes […] There's an electric guitar sitting there that Cosey is going to play. She doesn't play guitar. Gen is going to sing, or perhaps howl or chant or declaim […] Gen makes a fine frontman. He shares with Johnny Rotten an ability to stare out anyone giving him the evil eye, with a similar we-don't-care air of lunacy that suggests that it is best not to mess with him.[77]

October 19th-26th 1976

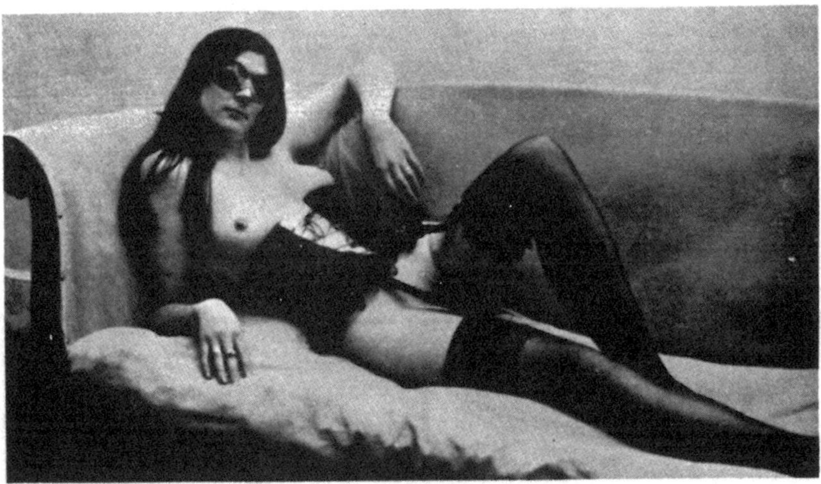

SEXUAL TRANSGRESSIONS NO. 5

PROSTITUTION

COUM Transmissions:- Founded 1969. Members (active) Oct 76 - P. Christopherson, Cosey Fanni Tutti, Genesis P-Orridge. Studio in London. Had a kind of manifesto in July/August Studio International 1976. Performed their works in Palais des Beaux Arts, Brussels; Musee d'Art Moderne, Paris; Galleria Borgogna, Milan; A.I.R. Gallery, London; and took part in Arte Inglese Oggi, Milan survey of British Art in 1976. November/December 1976 they perform in Los Angeles Institute of Contemporary Art; Deson Gallery, Chicago; N.A.M.E. Gallery, Chicago and in Canada. This exhibition was prompted as a comment on survival in Britain, and themselves.

2 years have passed since the above photo of Cosey in a magazine inspired this exhibition. Cosey has appeared in 40 magazines now as a deliberate policy. All of these framed form the core of this exhibition. Different ways of seeing and using Cosey with her consent, produced by people unaware of her reasons, as a woman and an artist, for participating. In that sense, pure views. In line with this all the photo documentation shown was taken, unbidden by COUM by people who decided on their own to photograph our actions. How other people saw and recorded us as information. Then there are xeroxes of our press cuttings, media write ups. COUM as raw material. All of them, who are they about and for? The only things here made by COUM are our objects. Things used in actions, intimate (previously private) assemblages made just for us. Everything in the show is for sale at a price, even the people. For us the party on the opening night is the key to our stance, the most important performance. We shall also do a few actions as counterpoint later in the week.

PERFORMANCES: Wed 20th 1pm - Fri 22nd 7pm
Sat 23rd 1pm - Sun 24th 7pm

INSTITUTE OF CONTEMPORARY ARTS LIMITED
NASH HOUSE THE MALL LONDON S.W.I. BOX OFFICE Telephone 01-930-6393

Figure 4.10: COUM Transmissions, press release for the exhibition PROSTITUTION *at ICA, London, 1976. Tate Archives. Courtesy of Cosey Fanni Tutti and the estate of Genesis BREYER P-ORRIDGE and New Discretions.*

As TG went on stage, P-Orridge announced:

> We'd like to thank you all for coming tonight. It's nice to know there are so many pop fans in London. Tonight we're going to do a one-hour set called *Music from the Death Factory*. It's basically about the post-breakdown of civilization. You know, you walk down the street and there's a lot of ruined factories and bits of old newspaper with stories about pornography and page three pin-ups, blowing down the street, and you turn the corner past the dead dog and you see old dustbins. And then over the ruined factory there's a funny noise.[78]

This narrative of urban decay was followed by improvised noise, and mantras on murder, hate, and dead ends. Together with the exhibited artworks, this dystopian introduction and the following performance elucidate COUM/TG's version of the "No Future" mantra. The Sex Pistols, incidentally, were in the studio in October 1976, recording "God Save the Queen" with that infamous line, "No Future in England's Dreaming."

P-Orridge's opening sentence, labeling the audience as "pop fans" was clearly meant to taunt. The whole show was determinedly orchestrated "to annoy everyone."[79] The art establishment—by the mid 1970s increasingly tolerant toward bodily matters and suggested violence in performances—was unsettled by the notion of art as prostitution. COUM aimed to disclose hypocrisy in the artworld too, specifically what the artists saw as the art institution's hollow self-appraisal as a place of emancipation. Punk band Chelsea—who also played at the vernissage—was announced as "LSD," the worst hippie name that COUM could come up with. "It was a really, really crazy night," Cosey Fanni Tutti remembers, "It was absolutely packed out. There were fights involving all of us and the audience."[80] She recounts how Ted Little, the director of the ICA, wound up in a fight (which also involved Kipper Kid Brian Routh and absurdist performer Ian Hinchliffe) and "got kicked in his balls so hard that he had to be taken to the hospital."[81] To the artists, the vernissage of *PROSTITUTION* and its after-effects were the most revealing part of the exhibition, as they stated in their press release (Figure 4.10): "Everything in the show is for sale at a price, even the people. For us the party on the opening night is the key to our stance, the most important performance."[82]

The next day, the reaction of Tory MP Nicholas Fairbairn to the exhibition was quoted on the cover of the *Daily Mail*: "A sickening outrage. Sadistic. Obscene. Evil. These people are the wreckers of civilisation. They want to advance decadence."[83] The critique was accompanied by a photo of the then still unknown punks Debbie Juvenile, Siouxsie Sioux, and Steve Severin on the opening night. The show was a scandal: over 100 newspaper and magazine articles were published, questions were

THROBBING GRISTLE AT I.C.A. OCT 76 SELECTED PRESS CUTTINGS © 1976 T.G.

—— 'These people are the wreckers of civilisation' ——

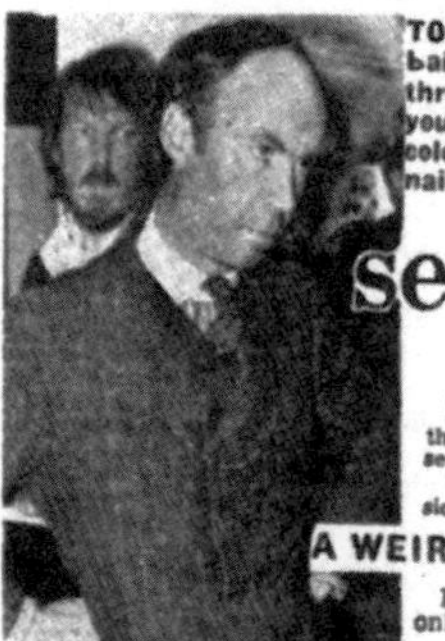

Nicholas Fairbairn . . . outraged.

TORY MP Nicholas Fairbairn fought his way through Hell's Angels and young men with multi-coloured hair, lipstick and nail varnish last night — AND SAW

sex-show

A STRIPPER, accompanied by a rock group called "Throbbing Gristle." far, far worse than anything I have ever seen. I was appalled.

"They must be very sick people indeed."

A WEIRD porn-and-pop show,

Its filth is exceeded only by its banality.

their pornography can only destroy the values of our society.

And the MP's critical appraisal was: 'It's a sickening outrage. Sadistic. Obscene. Evil.' money is being wasted here to destroy the morality of our society. These people are the wreckers of civilisation. They want to advance decadence.

'I came here to look, and I am horrified,' said the MP.

THROBBING GRISTLE

ARE attemptiong "to destroy the difference between good and bad, and right and wrong

"I'm sickened

"This show is an excuse for exhibitionism by every crank, queer, squint and ass in the business."

Mr. Fairbairn said he saw:

SADISM with sticks and flails.

WEIRD music from what exhibition organisers called the Death Factory, by a rock group called "Throbbing Gristle." allowing people to promote every swill-bin attitude they can to degrade language, meaning and thought"

CEASE TO EXIST

Stripper

The show includes a stripper accompanied by masochistic performances by a rock group called Throbbing Gristle; They are devoid of any sense of proportion and respect for the decencies of life.

MASOCHISTIC performances by a rock group. may be a scabrous symbol of one facet of Britain today; but not yet, thank heavens, of the whole. And the underlying impulse is not one of survival but of destruction and the death-wish–

GENETIC FEAR

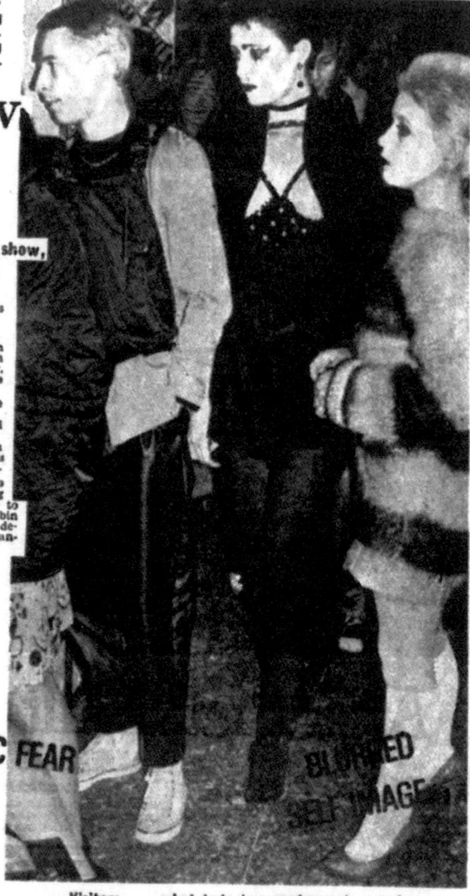

BLURRED SELF IMAGE

Visitors . . . what today's connoisseur is wearing.

SECONDARY ORGASMIC DISFUNCTION

controversial pop-and-porn show

A rock group called Death Rock ← T.G. will be taking part at the opening. They will be singing songs about mass murder and about the child murderer Ian Brady. "They offer reflections on the way TV programmes and the other media work."

"spooks with soft-belt intellectual arrogance . . . anxious to promote every swill-bin attitude they can to degrade language, meaning and thought."

"The organisers must be very sick people. I wish I'd never got involved." it was an excuse for exhibitionism by every crank, queer, squint and ass in the business."

'We're only just getting a look at the maggots in the nest. By the time the current controversy dies down their scrapbook will be fat enough to ensure gigs a plenty here and abroad for them, their rock band Throbbing Gristle and any professional striptease artiste they care to take along with them.

—PARANOIA CLUB—

'We are presenting information. Without people, information is dead. People give it life.

But for me, it was like a scene one of a real-life horror show last night.

As I walked in, a drunken young woman was being carried out. She had green hair.

At the bar, a girl in trousers and bright orange hair was embracing a blonde in a gold lame dress.

Next to them was a 6ft. 5in. tall West Indian transvestite in a red off-the-shoulder gown.

There was also a very noisy rock group called Throbbing Gristle, dressed in more black lurex.

My main concern is that it has become the phenomenon of the age in music for non-creative people to make up for their inability and lack of imagination by being obscene, vulgar and depraved." Such filthy rubbish has always been available in holes and corners for those willing to pay for it; and there have always been people ready to make a living by purveying it.

A red-and-white crewcut nearby wiggled its black lurex trousers and shouted: "God there are so many straights around."

Scotland Yard said today: "A report is being sent to the Director of Public Prosecutions."

"This all sounds rather menacing, but these are always the things which attract publicity."

Figure 4.11: COUM Transmissions, collage of press clippings, 1976. Courtesy of Cosey Fanni Tutti and the estate of Genesis BREYER P-ORRIDGE and New Discretions.

asked in Parliament, and the Arts Council publicly rescinded its funding of COUM Transmissions.

Six years later the same Nicholas Fairbairn once again made his stance on prostitution known when he chose not to press charges against a group of men who had mutilated a sex worker with razor blades during a gang rape in Glasgow.[84] He was subsequently forced to resign from his position as Margaret Thatcher's Solicitor General for Scotland. Back in 1976, he had complained of the *PROSTITUTION* exhibition in the *Daily Telegraph*: "Every social evil is celebrated [...] there were a few photographs which attempted to make prostitutes look like victims instead of the vultures which they are."[85] Fairbairn's outrage over COUM's work, as opposed to his indifference toward the victim of a crime, highlights the irreconcilable conflict of perceptions (keeping in mind, as noted earlier, that one of the meanings of "punk" is "prostitute.")

COUM appropriated the media response by integrating photocopied press articles into the exhibition and collaging outraged quotations together for distribution material, such as flyers (Figure 4.11). When the artists found verbal death threats on their answering machine following the exhibition, they used these in the song "Death Threats" on the album *D.o.A.* (*Dead on Arrival*) in 1978. Later, Simon Ford took the "wreckers of civilisation" quote by Nicholas Fairbairn as the title of his book about the group, much as Julien Temple did with the *Daily Mail* headline "THE FILTH AND THE FURY!" about the Sex Pistols. *PROSTITUTION* thus entered a media feedback loop between art and life. It was a way to spectacularize. The argument that the ex-Situationists (in the UK, primarily King Mob) changed from anti-spectacular theory to hyper-spectacular practice, and the continuation of that argument—that punk pushed even further into a hyper-spectacular practice—is thus explicitly visible in the work of COUM Transmissions.

"Today, this might seem like [...] deliberate shock tactics, but then it seemed like reportage, front line dispatches from a convulsed country," Savage recalls.[86] COUM's press release read: "This exhibition was prompted as a comment on survival in Britain." COUM/TG saw their work as a kind of counterpropaganda. The artists created and exploited a disruptive situation. At the center of the opening night, scandal was thus a very punk sort of détournement. In both cases discussed here, the postcard trial and the ICA exhibition, COUM Transmissions used the "scandal" as an artistic medium in itself, and willfully staged the repercussions—courtroom hearings, press frenzies—to highlight hypocrisy in 1970s Britain.

Notes

1. Marcus, "Punk (1979)."

2. Savage, *England's Dreaming,* 231.

3. Stanley Cohen, *Folk Devils and Moral Panics* [1972] (London: Routledge Classics, 2002), 9.

4. *The Guardian,* December 3, 1976, n.p.

5. *Daily Mail,* December 2, 1976. See Julien Temple, *The Filth and the Fury,* DVD, FilmFour UK, 2000.

6. The National Archives, accessed January 7, 2018, http://discovery.nationalarchives.gov.uk/details/r/C14134421.

7. Penny Rimbaud, "You're Not Punk," accessed January 7, 2018, https://www.vice.com/en_uk/article/fuck-v12n3.

8. John Lydon, Keith Zimmerman, and Kent Zimmerman, *Rotten: No Irish, No Blacks, No Dogs* (London: Picador, 1994).

9. Savage, "London Subversive," 14.

10. Graham, "Punk as Propaganda," 130.

11. The Clash, "London's Burning" (UK: CBS, 1977) and the Jam, "Going Underground" (London: Polydor, 1980).

12. Elmer, interview, 2018.

13. Elmer, interview, 2018. Emphasis in orginal.

14. Elmer, interview, 2018.

15. Elmer, interview, 2018.

16. Douglas Rushkoff, "Good Trip or Bad Trip? The Art and Heart of Genesis P-Orridge," in *Painful But Fabulous* (New York: Soft Skull Press), 20.

17. Adamowicz, *Dada Bodies,* 125.

18. COUM Transmissions, *G.P.O. vs. G.P.-O. – A Chronicle of Mail Art on Trial Coumpiled by Genesis P-Orridge and COUM* [1976]. No. 76 of edition of 500. MoMA Archive: MoMA Queens Artists' Books.

19. Diedrich Diedrichsen, "Geniuses and Their Noise," in *Brilliant Dilletantes: Subculture in Germany in the 1980s,* ed. Leonhard Emmerling, Mathilde Weh, and Goethe Institut e.V. (Ostfildern: Hatje Cantz, 2015), 19.

20. Kirsty Lohman, *The Connected Lives of Dutch Punks. Contesting Subcultural Boundaries* (London: Palgrave Macmillan, 2017), 5.

21. Poul Dines, "Nå-generationen og et svar på den," in *Politiken,* January 28, 1979.

22. Linda Wedel, "Generationen, der bare siger nå," in *Ekstra Bladet,* October 12, 1979.

23. Poulsen, *Under en Sort Sol,* 115.

24. Poulsen, *Something Rotten,* 117.

25. Daniel Kane, *Do You Have a Band? Poetry and Punk Rock in New York City* (New York: Columbia University Press, 2017), 120. See also Gerfried Ambrosch, *The Poetry of Punk: The Meaning Behind Punk Rock and Hardcore Lyrics* (London: Routledge, 2018).

26. See Poulsen, *Something Rotten,* 236–38.

27. Poulsen, *Under en Sort Sol,* 108.

28. Michael Strunge, *SAMLEDE STRUNGE. Digte 1978–85* (Copenhagen: Borgen 1995), 254, 448, 948.

29. Marianne Ølholm, "Traces of Avant-Garde Strategies in Danish Poetry of the 1980s," in *A Cultural History of the Avant-Garde in the Nordic Countries 1975–2000*, eds. Benedikt Hjartarson, Camilla Paldam, Laura Schultz, and Tania Ørum (Leiden and Boston: Brill Rodopi, 2022), 835.

30. Michael Strunge, in "Information," November 29, 1985. Quoted in: In Strunge, *A Virgin from a Chilly Decade* (Todmoren, Lancs: Arc Publications, 2000), 15.

31. He subsequently published *Verdenssøn* (Son of the world, 1985) under the pseudonym Simon Lack.

32. Strunge, *A Virgin from a Chilly Decade*, 68–69.

33. Nørgård, interview, 2018.

34. Trine Ross, *Lars Nørgård. Maleri* (Copenhagen: Aschehoug, 2004), 21.

35. Søren Ulrik Thomsen, "Om forsiden til City Slang," accessed June 27, 2018, https://www.soerenulrikthomsen.dk/sut/boeger/city-slang/city-slang-om-forsiden.html.

36. Sten-Knudsen, interview, 2018.

37. Ozon, interview, 2017.

38. Gallery ANUS flyer in the archive of Diana Ozon.

39. See Goossens, "A Black and White Statement," 200.

40. Jonker, "Introduction," in *Punk in Holland*, n.p.

41. Kaagman, interview, 2017.

42. Bart van der Steen, Ask Katzeff and Leendert van Hoogenhuijze, "Introduction," in *The City Is Ours: Squatting and Autonomous Movements in Europe from the 1970s to the Present*, eds. Bart van der Steen, Ask Katzeff, and Leendert van Hoogenhuijze (Oakland: PM Press 2014), 3.

43. Müller, "Das Chaos reist mit dem Schönen Wochenende," 156.

44. Bert Papenfuß, "Kunsterziehung durch Punk" in *Lieber zu viel als zu wenig*, 62.

45. Cornelia Schleime, quoted in Hans-Christian Dany, "Im Kohlenkeller eines neuen Dekadenzbewußtseins," in *Lieber zu viel als zu wenig*, 50.

46. See Michael Boehlke and Henryk Gericke, eds., *Too Much Future. Punk in der DDR* (Berlin: Verbrecher Verlag, 2007).

47. See Melani Schröter and Steffen Pappert, "Der Punk-Diskurs in der DDR," in *Politische Wechsel, Sprachliche Umbrüche*, eds. Bettina Bock, Ulla Fix, and Steffen Pappert (Berlin: Frank & Timme, 2011).

48. Angelika Richter, *Das Gesetz der Szene. Genderkritik, Performance Art und Zweite Öffentlichkeit in der späten DDR* (Bielefeld: transcript, 2019), 245.

49. Frank Willmann, *Leck mich am Leben: Punk im Osten* (Berlin: Neues Leben, 2012).

50. Schmitz, "Reunification through Dematerialization," in *Die Tödliche Doris – Kunst*, 7 and Käthe Kruse, interview with the author, October 23, 2017.

51. Kito Nedo, "Ornament & Verbrechen – eine Band als Phantom" (January 2015), accessed April 5, 2018, https://www.goethe.de/de/kul/bku/20495364.html

52. See Simon Reynolds, *Rip It Up and Start Again: Postpunk 1978–1984* (London: Faber & Faber, 2005), 127.

53. COUM Transmissions, *G.P.O. vs. G.P.-O.*, n.p.

54. Sex Pistols, "God Save the Queen" (Copenhagen: Virgin Records, 1977).

55. P-Orridge quoted in Dominic Johnson, *Unlimited Action: The Performance of Extremity in the 1970s*

(Manchester: Manchester University Press, 2019), 101.

56. COUM Transmissions, *G.P.O. vs. G.P.-O.*, n.p.

57. Duncan Campell in *Time Out*, April 16, 1976, quoted in Ford, *Wreckers of Civilisation*, 6.13.

58. Burroughs, quoted in COUM Transmissions, *G.P.O. vs. G.P.-O.*, n.p.

59. *The Observer*, April 11, 1976, reproduced in COUM Transmissions, *G.P.O. vs. G.P.-O.*, n.p.

60. Genesis P-Orridge and Peter Christopherson, "Annihilating Reality," in *Studio International* 192, no. 982 (July/August 1976): 44–48.

61. Jonathan P. Eburne, *Surrealism and the Art of Crime* (Ithaca: Cornell University Press, 2008), 1–2. See also Simon Baker, "Crime," in *Undercover Surrealism: Georges Bataille and DOCUMENTS*, eds. Dawn Ades and Simon Baker (Cambridge: MIT Press, 2006), 102–05.

62. André Breton, "Second Manifesto of Surrealism [1930]," 125.

63. For more on this case, see the interview with Ulay in Johnson, *The Art of Living*, 16–40.

64. P-Orridge and Christopherson, "Annihilating Reality," 44.

65. Arthur Symons, *Selected Writings*, ed. Roger Holdsworth (New York: Routledge, 2003), 84.

66. Richard Metzger, "Nothing Short of a Total War" [first printed in *World Art Magazine*], in *Painful But Fabulous*, 44.

67. John A. Walker, "Panic Attack!" in *The Art Book* 15, no. 1 (2008): 14.

68. Reynolds, *Rip It Up and Start Again*, 230.

69. Mark Sladen, "Introduction," in *Panic Attack!*, 10 and Torres, *PUNK* and wall text in the exhibition *PUNK: Its Traces in Contemporary Art* at MACBA in 2016.

70. Kunsthalle Wien, Matt and Mießgang, eds., *Punk: No One is Innocent* and Dick Hebdige, "Contemporizing 'Subculture': 30 years to life," in *European Journal of Cultural Studies* 15, no. 3 (2012): 409, and Ian Lowey and Suzy Prince, *The Graphic Art of the Underground: A Countercultural History* (London: Bloomsbury Visual Arts, 2014), 98–159.

71. See Savage, *England's Dreaming*, 240 and Martin Schneider, "Shane MacGowan Perpetrates 'Cannibalism at Clash Gig,' 1976," posted January 2, 2016, accessed March 4, 2018, http://dangerousminds.net/comments/shane_macgowan_perpetrates_cannibalism_at_clash_gig_1976.

72. Bob Gruen, *The Clash* (London: Omnibus Press, 2001), n.p.

73. *Daily Mirror*, December 2, 1976, front page.

74. Metzger, "Nothing Short of a Total War," 43. Emphasis added.

75. Reynolds, *Rip It Up and Start Again*, 228–29.

76. The title differs between the Tate Archive Main Collection (*Larvae*) and the exhibition *Punk: No One Is Innocent* at Kunsthalle Wien (Pupae).

77. Dorothy Max Prior in *Showboat: Punk/Sex/Bodies*, ed. Toby Mott (New York: Dashwood Books, 2016), 158–59.

78. Ford, *Wreckers of Civilisation*, 6.28.

79. Savage, *England's Dreaming*, 252.

80. Cosey Fanni Tutti quoted in Tom Doyle "Throbbing Gristle 'Hamburger Lady,'" accessed March 28, 2018, http://www.soundonsound.com/people/throbbing-gristle-hamburger-lady.

81. Cosey Fanni Tutti, *Art Sex Music* (London: Faber & Faber, 2017), 205.

82. Press release by COUM Transmissions, in Tate Archive.

83. Nicholas Fairbairn quoted in *Daily Mail*, October 19, 1976, n.p.

84. In 2014, around 20 years after Fairbairn's death, multiple accusations of child sexual abuse were also advanced against him. Guy Adams and Andrew Malone, "Revealed: The Full Horrifying Truth About Sir Nicholas Fairbairn, the Other Pedophile at Margaret Thatcher's Side," accessed March 29, 2018, http://www.dailymail.co.uk/news/article-2732234/Revealed-The-Full-horrifying-truth-Sir-Nicholas-Fairbairn-paedophile-Margaret-Thatcher-s-side.html.

85. Nicholas Fairbairn quoted in *Daily Telegraph*, October 19, 1976, n.p.

86. Savage, "Foreword," in *Wreckers of Civilisation*, 0.8.

5 Art with No Future?

As a movement, punk rejected the perception of progress; the notion that society was moving forward toward something better—socially, economically, and culturally. No Future. In punk art specifically, it was the denial of an evolutionarily tinted, advancing understanding of art history as well as the refusal to just become the next new ism, the next artworld hype. How could a NO FUTURE movement possibly embody an "avant-garde" notion of, literally, "leading the way"? It could not, as we shall see…

In the first part of this chapter, we deal with the notions of "Originality and appropriation" in punk.

Punk's concept of originality is not compromised by appropriation. Artists associated with the punk movement leaned heavily on past art movements, appropriating formats, ideas, and motifs. Quotations are seen as inspiration; the past is reinterpreted, even actively extended. Punk art was thus both like an echo of past times and the epitome of its own time. Through their reworking of art-historical precursors, the artists change our perception of the past, too.

Often, punk artworks are a sort of mannerist exaggeration of modern art concepts. This notion is discussed in the second part of this chapter: "Modernity in extremis." What was only hinted at, for example in Surrealism or Fluxus, was exaggerated or taken to (brutal) reality in punk, which resulted in a double effect of seemingly both admiring and mocking the paragons. Metaphors are materialized, motifs are physicalized, and fantasies are acted out. This strategy also underlines punk's sense of mannerism, the fin-de-siècle dark overdoing of what had once been a bright modernism. The punk movement thus borrowed from and détoured the historic avant-garde, while often positioning themselves either in lineage with or in opposition to (anti-)art history. Either way, punk art is very invested in history.

In the last part of this chapter, "Avant-garde vs. rear-guard," this sense of history becomes clear: punk artists reached back through the twentieth century to find kindred and un-kindred spirits. These stories of the past, however, seemed to all end (unwillingly) with a contribution to that very understanding of art-historical development, which was incongruous with their lived experience. It was for this reason, that punk as art, punk as a movement, and punk as a lifestyle refuted being "avant-garde."

5.1 Originality and appropriation

Punk appropriated concepts, styles, and strategies from the most diverse sources: the historical avant-gardes, student revolts, pop, guerrilla combat, fin-de-siècle ambiance, cartoon universes, and many more. Toby Mott describes Westwood and McLaren's SEX shop as a "gleeful appropriation of authentic S&M subculture."[1] In *Lipstick Traces,* Greil Marcus traces the teeth grinding of Johnny Rotten back to Kurt Schwitters' *Ursonate* (1923–32).[2] Style-wise, "objects borrowed from the most sordid of contexts found a place in the punks' ensembles,"[3] Dick Hebdige remarks: lavatory chains from a domestic context, kinky raincoats and fake leopard prints from sexual fetishism, and bloody school uniforms from horror movies. The pseudonyms chosen by punks were often cultural references: "Sid Vicious" came from Lou Reed's song "Vicious" (1972), "Cosey Fanni Tutti" from Wolfgang Amadeus Mozart's "Così fan tutte" (1790) and Little Richard's "Tutti-Frutti" (1957), "Blixa Bargeld" from the Dadaist alias Johannes Baargeld and from Johnny Cash (Bargeld means cash in German).

Punk appropriated totalitarian, nationalistic, and military symbols, subverting their original meaning—for example, Jamie Reid's arrogation of the Union Jack in his designs for the Sex Pistols. Punk's appropriation thus often manifested itself as a kind of détournement (French: diversion, hijacking). This term originated with the Lettrists and became a key concept for the Situationists as well. "Détournement proposes a violent excision of elements [...] from their original contexts, and a consequent destabilization and recontextualization through rupture and alignment,"[4] Elisabeth Sussman writes, thereby stressing the violent aspect, the hostile takeover. Malcolm McLaren too brought in what he had learned in the ex-Situationist group King Mob. As Nils Stevenson remarks:

> Christopher Gray [of King Mob] said that Malcolm was 'just another wide-eyed art student—he wasn't very involved.' Nevertheless, many of the achievements and ideas of King Mob were to recur as Malcolm's own in ways that echoed Karl Marx's dictum that 'events and personages occur twice, the first time as tragedy, the second as farce.'[5]

Like Reid, McLaren took his King Mob training to a new maximum, appropriating the appropriation.

Collage and bricolages, which were so important in punk art and design—see Linder Sterling, Jamie Reid, Winston Smith, and Gee Vaucher—are the ultimate appropriation media. In punk rock, cover versions of loved as well as hated songs were common: Sid Vicious singing Sinatra's "My Way," the Slits altering Marvin Gaye's "I Heard It Through the Grapevine," Dead Kennedys' take on Doc Pomus' "Viva Las Vegas." The attitude toward the appropriated material is difficult to detect. Skepticism is oftentimes paradoxically blended with true admiration. The level of self-consciousness varies, but generally the use of appropriation was a deliberate tactic. The unabashed eclecticism demonstrates both an *anti-authoritarian* and *anti-authorial* point of view on art and culture, which was further reinforced by the highbrow–lowbrow juxtapositions.

With a view to art history, punk art is not only connected with Dada, as emphasized almost exclusively by previous studies: Surrealism is just as crucial, and there are substantial ties between punk art and Fluxus, Pop Art, and post-Surrealism (especially CoBrA and ex-Situationist groups). As we have seen in the several examples throughout this book (and there are more to come ...), punk art is very often copied and stolen from the past. Tellingly, COUM Transmissions wrote in their manifesto: "COUM enable all kinds of people to discover their abilities to express ideas through different media. COUM believes that you don't NEED special training to produce and/or enjoy worthwhile significant and unique works [...]. It has NOT all been done before, and that which has can still bear valid re-interpretation."[6] *A valid re-interpretation*: oscillating between critique and admiration, artists involved with punk used (art) history to reflect on and affect both the perception of the past and the perception of the contemporaneous.

"I learnt all my politics and understanding of the world through the history of art," said Malcolm McLaren, "Plagiarism is what the world's about. If you didn't start seeing things and stealing because you were so inspired by them, you'd be stupid."[7] Punk's perception of originality was thus not compromised by appropriation. This was not necessarily something completely new. Bertolt Brecht (admired by punks for his Weimar republic-time plays) worked with the motto: no revolution without tradition.[8] When Brecht was accused of plagiarizing—he had used pieces of fifteenth-century French poet and criminal François Villon's texts in the *Dreigroschenoper* (*The Threepenny Opera,* 1928) without citing his source—he wrote a sonnet: "Nehm' jeder sich heraus, was er grad braucht! Ich selber hab mir was herausgenommen" ("Take each man what he needs just then! I myself did").[9] Each from their own end of the twentieth century, Brecht and McLaren thus make the same proposition: an understanding of art in which quotations are inspirations. Stealing, copying, or appropriating as one sees fit does not undermine their concept of originality.

We could see this attitude in connection with what Rosalind Krauss calls "the ever-present reality of the copy as the underlying condition of the original."[10] In her seminal text on "The Originality of the Avant-Garde," she proposes "to void the basic propositions of modernism, to liquidate them by exposing their fictitious condition." Her main argument is that the originality of the modern avant-garde is a myth: "we look back on the modernist origin and watch it splintering into endless replication."[11]

Surely, there are different ways of replicating or quoting. In their *User's Guide to Détournement* from 1956, Guy Debord and Gil J. Wolman had written:

> Since the negation of the bourgeois conception of art and artistic genius has become pretty much old hat, [Duchamp's] drawing of a mustache on the Mona Lisa is no more interesting than the original version of that painting. We now must push this process to the point of negating the negation.[12]

Incidentally, in the same text, Debord and Wolman praise Brecht's way of plagiarizing, deeming it "the revolutionary orientation we are calling for."

The idea of "negating the negation" was present in punk too, but it was much more ambiguous. Likewise referring to Duchamp, COUM Transmissions did a piece called *Marcel Duchamp's Next Work*: in the accompanying essay, the artists wrote it was "both a homage to Marcel Duchamp plus an extension of his work."[13] It is an appropriation of art history, a reuse of the past to affect—and this is essential—*both* the past *and* the present. To this extent, the artists reinterpret, recycle, and redo art history, thus not only creating new works but also altering our perception of the old works. The artists are conscious enough of history to know that the past is always how we *look at* the past, at a given moment in time.

As Mieke Bal writes in *Quoting Caravaggio: Contemporary Art, Preposterous History*: "Art is an active reworking [...] the work performed by later images obliterates the older images as they were before the intervention."[14] Her argument is that for us, as viewers today, having seen the reimaginations of Caravaggio's works by contemporary artists forever changes the way we look at the originals also. "Paradoxical history," James Elkins calls it, but explains:

> That apparently paradoxical result is really only an image of the way that history builds meanings: as I look past Picasso to see Rubens, Rubens begins to seem clunkier, more extravagant, and more unintentionally humorous than he could possibly have in his own time.[15]

With regard to punk, Bal's expression "active" is significant; punk artworks are no passive copies, they are infiltrations of the older works. In a sense, punk takes art's ability to tint our perception of older artworks and turns it into an active artistic strategy. As we shall see, the artists involved with punk find different ways of reworking art history, and their attitude toward the tradition in which they insert themselves varies. In punk art, the handling of precursors oscillates between admiration and criticism, expansion and destruction. What they all have in common is a very intense awareness of history and the making of history.

One effect of Krauss' dismantling of originality and repetition within the early avant-garde is that the—already muddy—discussion of opposition, and of transition, between "modernism" and "post-modernism" becomes even muddier. As a movement of the late twentieth century that is perpetually quoting, copying, and appropriating, punk would fall into that category of the post-modern. But this perspective works only to a certain extent. Punk art takes positions of modernism, anti-modernism, and post-modernism to extremes, but all in a distinctly punk manner. In some ways, the originality of punk art *is* its extremity, in the sense that punk art takes positions from the past and the present and pushes them to their limits. As a movement, punk thus transcends and challenges a strictly linear or evolutionary perception of art history.

Countercultural family tree: From CoBrA to ZEBRA

One example shows particularly clearly, how "no revolution without tradition" was interpreted in punk art, namely a drawing by Hugo Kaagman published in *KoeCrandt* around 1979 (Figure 5.1). Kaagman made manifest his ideas about a punk art genealogy, or what he calls "carrying the torch."[16] Under the caption *Dialektiek* (Dialectic), he sets up two lines leading from 1900 to 1984, in which one represents "counter culture" and the other "big brother culture." The black-and-white aesthetics of the outline emphasize the clearness of the message. This is a statement, written black on white, without too many nuances. The image emphasizes an us-against-them reading. The dialectical process does not bring forward any sort of common thread, but rather illustrates progress as attack and counter-attack. The black-and-white aesthetics furthermore indicate that this is a photocopy, meant for reproduction and distribution, thus emphasizing its pamphleteering character.

For each new epoch, Kaagman composes an interdependent development between the two sides. Dada stands at the beginning of the countercultural chain and is bestowed with the Raoul Hausmann quote, "Der Dadaist hasst die Dummheit und liebt [den] Unsinn" ("The Dadaist hates stupidity and loves nonsense"). This is followed by "Snobisten kopen Dada-kunst" ("Snobs buy Dada art") on the other side. This inversion of each step of progress on the countercultural side by a commercial replica on the counter side continues over the decades. Pop Art accordingly becomes nothing more than Warhol in the museum. The hippie movement with its sexual revolution turns into long hair and Jesus-people. On the countercultural side, the succession briefly reads as follows: Dada to neo-Dada and Pop Art to Fluxus and Provo to hippie and Kabouter to punk and reggae to hardcore and squatting. On the other side paintings of "huuisje, boompje, beestje" ("cottage, tree, little animal")—that is, idyllic depictions—

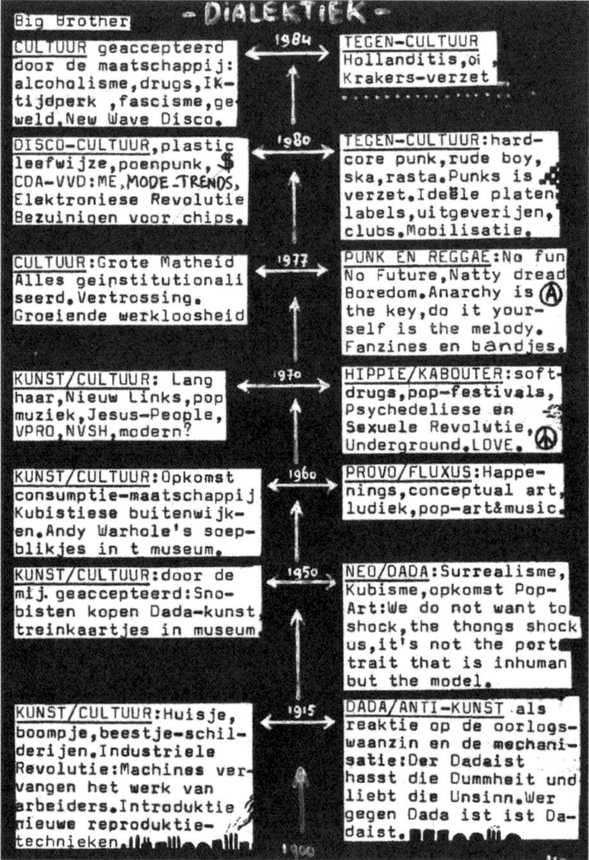

Figure 5.1: Hugo Kaagman, drawing published in KoeCrandt, *ca. 1979. Courtesy of Hugo Kaagman.*

are grouped together with the menaces of industrial capitalism, followed by consumer society, electronic revolution, fascism, violence, etc.

Kaagman's dichotomy displays his pride in the attempt to change culture through counter-cultural activities. Recognition of the tradition in which he places the KoeCrandt artists, and indeed the whole punk movement, once more shows punk's (art) historical awareness. The schema also shows the difference between the KoeCrandt group and the much more skeptical attitude of Die Tödliche Doris and, especially, COUM Transmissions, to historical predecessors. In comparison to P-Orridge's message to Friedman, "let's now really FUCK it, once and for more," and Müller's criticism of Fluxus' "protestant cheerfulness" (see Section 3.2: "Hedonism as attack"), Kaagman's view is not that the neo-avant-garde movements were too tame. One reason for this viewpoint might be that CoBrA

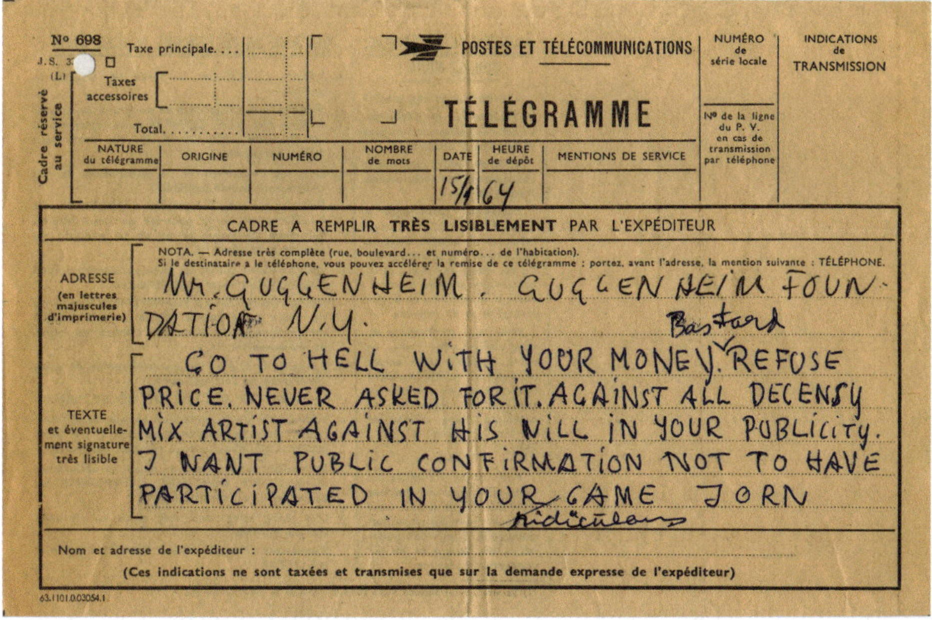
N° 698
Taxe principale. . . .
Taxes accessoires
Total. . . . .
Cadre réservé au service
POSTES ET TÉLÉCOMMUNICATIONS
TÉLÉGRAMME
NUMÉRO de série locale
INDICATIONS de TRANSMISSION
N° de la ligne du P. V. en cas de transmission par téléphone

NATURE du télégramme	ORIGINE	NUMÉRO	NOMBRE de mots	DATE	HEURE de dépôt	MENTIONS DE SERVICE
				15/4	64	

CADRE A REMPLIR **TRÈS LISIBLEMENT** PAR L'EXPÉDITEUR

NOTA. — Adresse très complète (rue, boulevard... et numéro... de l'habitation).
Si le destinataire a le téléphone, vous pouvez accélérer la remise de ce télégramme : portez, avant l'adresse, la mention suivante : TÉLÉPHONE.

ADRESSE (en lettres majuscules d'imprimerie)
MR. GUGGENHEIM. GUGGENHEIM FOUNDATION N.Y.

TEXTE et éventuellement signature très lisible
GO TO HELL WITH YOUR MONEY Bastard. REFUSE PRICE. NEVER ASKED FOR IT. AGAINST ALL DECENSY MIX ARTIST AGAINST HIS WILL IN YOUR PUBLICITY. I WANT PUBLIC CONFIRMATION NOT TO HAVE PARTICIPATED IN YOUR ridiculous GAME JORN

Nom et adresse de l'expéditeur :
(Ces indications ne sont taxées et transmises que sur la demande expresse de l'expéditeur)

Figure 5.2: Asger Jorn's telegram to the Guggenheim foundation, 1964. Courtesy of Museum Jorn © VG Bild-Kunst, Bonn 2022.

did indeed keep the radical edge: Just think of Asger Jorn's (now famous) angry rebuttal of the Guggenheim's prize money (Figure 5.2)—"Go to hell, with your money, bastard. Refuse prize. Never asked for it."[17]

The question is thus, always: *which* art history? Kaagman's drawing fits into the heated debate about the legacy of Dada and Surrealism: when the exhibition *Dada, Surrealism and their Heritage* opened at the Museum of Modern Art in New York in March 1968, it was met with protest from around 300 people, among others Ben Morea and the Motherfuckers. The protesters criticized the exhibition as the embodiment of "a formalist and evolutionary narrative of art history," which omitted the radical facets of Dada/Surrealism.[18] In the dialectic drawing by Hugo Kaagman, we find the same criticism. The perceived institutional embezzlement of the legacy of Dada/Surrealism is thus a key element in understanding the arguments of late 1960s radical artistic groups, and it plays a significant role in punk art as well (more on the MoMA exhibition in the last part of this Section 5.3: "Avant-garde vs. rear-guard").

When the KoeCrandt Group painted black-and-white Zebra-stripes on their squat houses in Sarphatistraat in 1981, it was not without a nod to another art historical animal symbol: "The 'zebra' in 'zebra' house was an allusion to CoBrA," says Kaagman, referencing the neo-Dada art group that had been founded in 1948, the group's name put together from Copenhagen, Brussels, and Amsterdam, the home cities of the group's initiators, including Asger Jorn, Constant, Karel Appel, and Christian Dotremont.

> They were important. They still are. To us, CoBrA meant: If you want to be strong, you need to stay together. So, we were a group. It was a sort of follow-up to CoBrA. We liked how they took inspiration from the imbecile, outsider art, and we liked their energy, and how they were smashing things, smashing painting, provocation, it was a kind of punky movement.[19]

With "smashing paining" Kaagman references how for example Asger Jorn in *Le canard inquiétant* (*The Disquieting Duckling*, 1959), modified—or respectively: vandalized—older paintings, which he bought on flea markets and while leaving some of the older painting visible, painted over in strong expressive ductus: it is destruction leading to new creation, détournement par excellence. For the Danish punk group the Sods (later: Sort Sol, i.e. black sun), who had previously borrowed Burroughs' title, *Minutes to Go* (see Section 3.3: "Trash and travesty"), CoBrA likewise played a key role, the title of their 1983 album, which they recorded in collaboration with Lydia Lunch, referenced CoBrA artist Asger Jorn's first book, *Held og hazard: Dolk og guitar* (*Luck and Chance: Dagger and Guitar*; 1952).

In the post-war culture of the Netherlands, CoBrA played a central role in its inquiry into how to move forward in art and society after the catastrophe of World War II. The KoeCrandt artists' admiration for CoBrA underlines their very conscious historical positioning. After all, the CoBrA artists were, in the words of Carter Ratcliff, the "sons of the Surrealists"[20] and, in the words of Richard Kempton, "the spiritual grandfather[s] of the Provo movement."[21] The group structure and collaborative approach are key elements in all of these movements, as is the social element of art. Furthermore, the descriptions as spiritual "sons" and "grandfathers"—apart from the obvious maleness of both terms—make clear how both artists and art historians often think about historical relationships. The succession from the radical-revolutionary side of Surrealism and the socially conscious Berlin Dada fraction to 1960s activism as envisioned by the Provos, King Mob, the Motherfuckers, and others, to the punk movement, draws up such a countercultural family tree.

5.2 Modernity in extremis

Michael Bracewell calls punk "modernity *in extremis*."[22] Modernity on the verge of death. This notion of a dying modernity both fits the fin-de-siècle sentiment in punk, and it underlines the extremity of maturity: the ripe apple smells the most, the old man exaggerates his ways, a passé style is taken to its limits, before being abandoned. We might then consider punk a mannerism, the dying of the twentieth century. In art history the story of progress was coming to an end, too, as Arthur C. Danto made clear in his two most famous essays "The Death of Art" and "The End of Art." The punk movement was an early sign of what was to come; punk art embodied the death of art, at least the death of the idea of an advancing, progressing art.

The artists involved with punk often took up modern art motifs, but exaggerated them or made the implicit *explicit*, as we saw for example in the case of P-Orridge spelling out the hidden sexual innuendo of Magritte's painting (see Section 4.3: "Crime as art, scandal as art"). One tendency in punk art was to take up past avant-garde techniques and transfer them from a classic-modern artistic medium (sculpture, painting, and collage) to gritty reality (a real body, a real site), thus (ironically very avant-garde-like) breaking down the barriers between art and life. Punk art thus emerges as a hyperbole of modernity and a mannerism of the waning twentieth century—but also as a street-level incarnation and concretization of modern art ideas.

Let us look at how two of the artists' groups transferred avant-garde art concepts to 1970s realness: first, COUM Transmissions; second, Die Tödliche Doris.

Venus, mutilated

The statement in the Manifesto by COUM Transmissions, as mentioned above—"It has NOT all been done before, and that which has can still bear valid re-interpretation"[23]—leaves the question, what is meant by "valid reinterpretation." In their most essential exhibition, *PROSTITUTION*, COUM Transmissions emerge as highly conscious of and critically interested in art history. The artists use art-historical references both to place themselves within a certain tradition and, at the same time, to challenge other aspects of that tradition. The artists reflect on themselves in their precursors and—as we shall see—put these precursors to the test by reengaging with their artwork.

The assemblage *Venus Mount* or *Venus Mound*[24] by P-Orridge (part of the *TAMPAX ROMANA* series) depicts a shattered, blackened female torso (Figure 5.3). The breasts and head are partly broken off. A dark wire holds two of Cosey Fanni Tutti's used tampons on each side of the bust, which is placed centrally in a traditional exhibition display case. The title is an appropriation of the classic art historical figure of *Venus*, the Roman goddess of love, desire, sex, and beauty. Combined with *Mount*, which may be understood here in the sense of *staged*, *installed*, or *encased*, this could imply a critique of fixed or enforced roles of women. We may also read it as a critical, even satirical comment on the wholeness and harmony of the classical sculpture, and its implication of perfection. As Elza Adamowicz points out, Dada artists had been at the forefront of such attacks on ideal bodies since

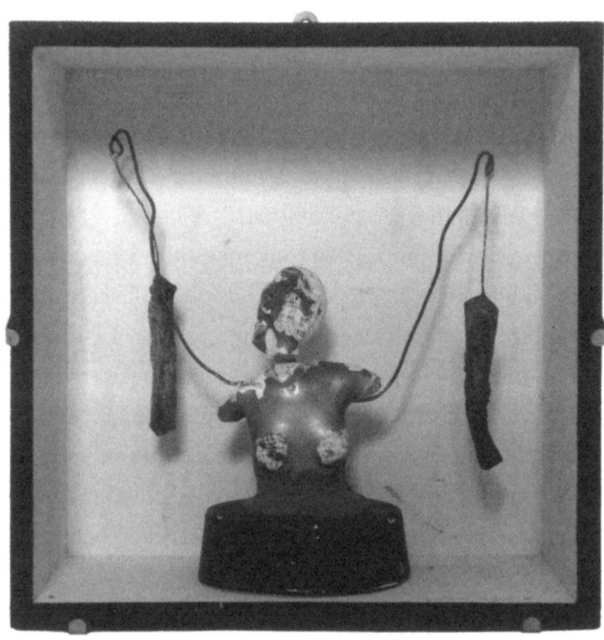

Figure 5.3: Genesis P-Orridge, Venus Mount/Venus Mound*, 1976.*
Courtesy of the estate of Genesis BREYER P-ORRIDGE and New Discretions.

the 1910s: "The Dadaist rebellion is exemplary of this shift, exploding classical aesthetic norms by parodying the (neo-)classical body as contained or framed."[25] That is much alike what P-Orridge does to the classic goddess Venus here. Furthermore, the term "Venus mound" is used to describe the pubic mound: that is, the mons veneris. With the overall theme of the exhibition—prostitution and art—in mind, the title thus evokes Gustave Courbet's *L'Origine du monde* (The origin of the world, 1866) as well as Marcel Duchamp's *Étant Donnés* (1946–66) which was in turn inspired by Courbet's work.

The composition of *Venus Mount/Mound* furthermore mirrors Salvador Dalí's *Retrospective Bust* (1933, see Figure 5.4) which is also a female bust, centered between two corncobs held together by a necklace of straw. On her head a loaf of bread is balanced, and on her face, Dalí has painted little ants. Both *Venus Mount/Mound* and *Retrospective Bust* make use of unusual juxtapositions of ephemeral materials and classical busts, and both are assembled out of found objects. Dalí's surprising use of bread and corn, however, is exaggerated in P-Orridge's use of Tutti's old tampons. Dalí's bust is made of white porcelain—fragile, beautiful—and the woman is presented in a context of consummation. P-Orridge counteracts this with a rough setting: the bust is made of plaster and is ruggedly attached to her black plinth. Both artists thus seem to comment on the female body, but in contrast to the lush sexuality of Dalí's work, P-Orridge

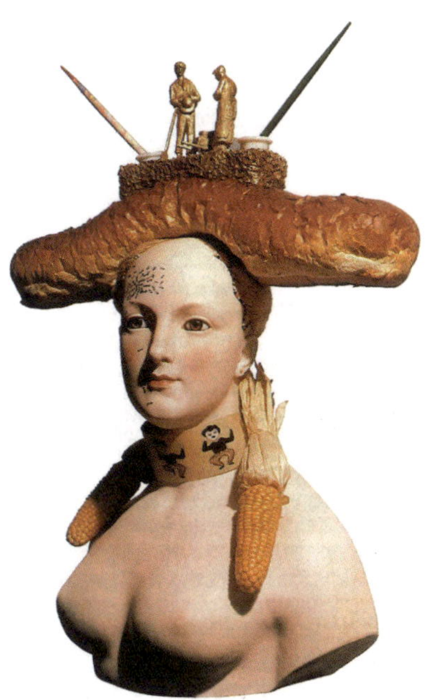

Figure 5.4: Salvador Dalí, Retrospective Bust of a Woman*, 1933, Museum of Modern Art, New York. © VG Bild-Kunst, Bonn 2022.*

shows a bloody everyday version of what the female body does. The metal wire and the brokenness of the figure allude to violence against women. The face of Dalí's bust is idealized and neutral, with a small smile, an empty gaze, and rosy cheeks, but P-Orridge's bust has no face, the features have been smashed. The involvement with fetishism, physicality, and sexuality in both sculptures thus results in two very different depictions of female corporeality. In COUM's work, there is no aestheticization, there is mutilation. The string could thus also evoke fantasies of strangulation or hanging. These violent and sexual connotations of P-Orridge's *Venus* furthermore allude both to Hans Bellmer's destruction of dolls and mannequins (1932–45) and classical statues in bondage by Man Ray, such as *Venus Restored* (1936), as well as Danish Surrealist Wilhelm Freddie's *Sex-paralyseappeal* (1936), which likewise shows a classical female bust with a rope around her neck (and a red, glistening, and erect penis painted onto her cheek, pointing towards her mouth). The hints to S&M in Surrealist art are matched by anti-aesthetics in punk. The casing of Venus creates yet another layer: she is literally boxed in. This small black sculpture reeks of reality check.

P-Orridge's concept of love and desire was not Venus in a box: it was both more raw and more romantic. Many years later, in the 1990s and 2000s, P-Orridge and h/er wife, Jackie Breyer, undertook a year-long process in an endeavor to become one another,

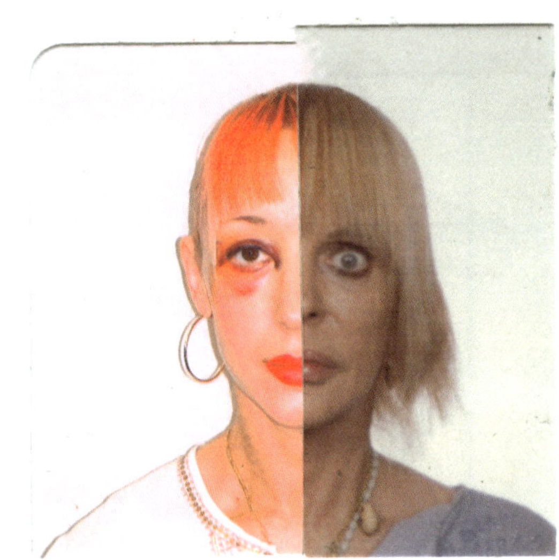

Figure 5.5: BREYER P-ORRIDGE, You are my other half, *2003. Courtesy of the estate of GENESIS BREYER P-ORRIDGE and New Discretions.*

each changing gender and identity through hormones, implants, costumes, gold crowns, and surgical operations. Breyer and P-Orridge strived to create a third gender out of love and subsequently used the personal pronoun *they*. The result was a two-person-cut-up, a real-life exquisite corpse, or the collage technique transferred to actual bodies. Less extreme, but related, is Linder's *SheShe* photo series (1981; photos by Christina Birrer), in which she poses as a live collage, holding cut-out magazine snippets in front of her face, in a quasi-photomontage of her own image.

The process of Breyer P-Orridge was documented in an exhibition entitled *Painful, but Fabulous,* shown at Künstlerhaus Bethanien in Berlin in 2004. On view were blown-up photographic details of the operations, healing process, and results. Among the bloodiness and suffering, there is a touching vulnerability and almost naïve outsider beauty to the work, as the romantic idea of consuming or becoming one's lover is made real. The morbidity of cutting-up (which, darkly, might be associated with autopsies) is countered and transcended with the creation of a new body, of two new bodies. The process was against all odds, against biology itself, in defiance of the idea of a divine mastery of the body. Instead, the masters of BREYER P-ORRIDGE's bodies are themselves. The photo collage *You are My Other Half* (2003, Figure 5.5) specifically uses the idea of a cut-up personality, too. The fragmented faces of Breyer and P-Orridge allude to the Surrealists' use of poetic automatism as well as their use of photo booth images in *La Révolution surréaliste* in 1929, for example. Breyer P-Orridge thus literally takes Surrealist concepts to reality.

Exquisite corpse of the punk scene

The notion of an assembled person is present too in the art/music group Die Tödliche Doris. The name Deadly Doris was created by Nikolaus Utermöhlen and Wolfgang Müller. Utermöhlen thought of a girl from his school class called Doris, who had always been mocked by their classmates.[26] (A mocked school girl who turns deadly might call to mind Stephen King's *Carrie*, which was published in the USA in 1974 and in Germany in 1977.) At that time, Doris was a very common German name, which gave the figure a certain anonymity. The two then added the "deadly" to give death an unexpected and unspectacular form. Even today—but even more so in West Berlin of the 1980s—the name also sounds like, even immediately associates to "die tödliche Dosis," the deadly (over)dose. "You think, is that a Freudian slip, is it a mistake?", Müller explains, "In one book in East Germany the name was then indeed misspelled: Die Tödliche *Dosis* [The Deadly *Dose*], of course we found that terrific. 1987. Great."[27]

Die Tödliche Doris worked with installations, photography, video, painting, performance, and mail art; they also performed and recorded music. The participants came from various backgrounds: Wolfgang Müller, Nikolaus Utermöhlen, and Chris Dreier were all students at the Hochschule der Künste (today: Universität der Künste) in West Berlin. Dagmar Dimitroff had been in art school in Dresden; she was imprisoned for ten months, among others for selling her paintings without a permit at a flea market in East Berlin's Pankow, and had been bought free in 1979 and released to West Berlin, where she joined Die Tödliche Doris.[28] Tabea Blumenschein was an actress and costume designer, Käthe Kruse was a squatter and a doctor's assistant, and Max Müller was a musician. Wolfgang Müller and Utermöhlen started the group and then integrated the others. Müller noticed Blumenschein's featured fashion drawings in the German version of Warhol's magazine *Interview*. She had drawn models outside of the norm (one with only one leg, one with a mohawk haircut, for example), which interested Müller, and the next time he saw Blumenschein in Das andere Ufer he convinced her to work with Die Tödliche Doris. Utermöhlen and Müller approached Käthe Kruse after they had seen her perform in SO36 on Christmas Eve (together with "the true Heino"). She was dressed as a black angel and was breathing fire, a trick she had learned at a hippie festival in Vlotho.[29] All these members and collaborators worked together, with a strong sense of conceptualization, where every contribution was attributed to the ominous "Doris." PR was handled by the fictive secretary "Monika Reich" (behind which pseudonym resided the artists of the group).

As a result of these diverse creative inputs, the artwork of "Doris" varied vastly, which only made the figure seem all the more impenetrable. Müller says,

> To us, the thought was: Deadly Doris is the deconstruction of the pop star. The absolute deconstruction, but at the same time, with the knowledge that you cannot dissolve anything to the extent that nothing new comes out of it, something else always emerges after all.
>
> The aesthetics of the Sex Pistols, to me, was very important. They cut out the letters, like a ransom letter, different fonts and sizes, so the personality is not identifiable. But the result is, this aesthetic is distinctly identifiable as punk.[30]

One evening in 1981, this concept was carried to an extreme. Alfred Hilsberg, the Hamburg "punk-pope"[31] who had released the first recordings by the group, had put Die Tödliche Doris' name on the poster of the Berlin Atonal Festival at SO36 without asking first.[32] As a reaction, the members of Die Tödliche Doris let themselves be replaced by Matthias Roeingh (later known as techno DJ Dr Motte), the podiatrist Hermoine Zittlau, and the transsexual Vivian Wilms on stage.[33] "Doris" thus actually did perform, but was incorporated in unfamiliar and novel components. The usual Tödliche Doris members, meanwhile, were in the audience, distributing flyers.

The collage-construction of the group distinctly reminisces the *Cadavre Exquis* game, a collaborative and intuitive drawing technique first used by the Surrealists in the 1920s. Each player draws his or her part and folds the paper, so the next participant continues the drawing without seeing what is already on it. With reference to the exquisite corpse notion, this stranger incarnation can be viewed as a real life, meta-level conveying of Surrealist concepts and ideas. Die Tödliche Doris simultaneously concretizes and expands Surrealist techniques. The creation of a novel formation, assembled out of essentially dissimilar components, partly unaware of each other, could be regarded as a sort of reinterpretation of the Surrealists' exquisite corpse, but with real bodies creating a stage phantom.

Furthermore, the tendency of viewers to search for a personality or identity for "Doris," though none is to be found, could be interpreted as a construction leaning toward pareidolia, which is "the imagined perception of a pattern or meaning where it does not actually exist, as in considering the moon to have human features."[34] Whereas Surrealist painters often used pareidolia effects to create unnerving juxtapositions and deceptive mirages, the artists of Die Tödliche Doris redirected the phenomenon to deal with questions of projection. "In the punk scene, there was an openness which was good for developing this kind of conceptual and performative ideas," says Müller, "We thought: Can we create a figure that only amounts to a sum of projections? That is composed of singularities and at the same time forms a unified whole?"[35]

Such a distortion of perception corresponds with the notion of punk (art) as the fin-de-siècle mannerism of the twentieth century. In mannerist art, scale and perspective are exaggerated, something is *off*. This sense of something being off, of something being strange is quintessential to the artwork of Die Tödliche Doris. The deflection of expectations appealed to the artists of the group. We will dive further into this aspect in Section 7.2: "Ingenious Dilettantes"—for the argument in this chapter, two aspects are of relevance: one, that oddness of reality; two, the rejection of progress. The second aspect, rejection of progress, was a criticism of the perception of cultural history as a process of improvement. This brings us to the next and last part of this chapter: the refusal of punk to become the next avant-garde.

5.3 Avant-garde vs. rear-guard

There is one story that took place in Copenhagen in 1981, and which epitomizes punk's relationship with the avant-garde term: some punks participated in a series of nine evening events with music, dance, poetry, and visual art, which was called *Fortropper* (avant-gardes). The event series was organized by Poul Borum, an older critic, a writer, and the editor of the influential literary magazine *Hvedekorn* (Grains of wheat), in which he published the young punk poets (see Section 4.2: "Punk poetry"). Borum became part of the scene, often attending punk concerts and defending punk against conservative attacks in the daily newspapers. The punk poets met at Borum's home, often the punk musicians from the Sods would be there too. With *Fortropper*, however, he angered a fraction of the punk movement, who saw it as a kind of over-sophistication of punk. In response to the event, the *Bagtropper* countermovement emerged, meaning the "rear-guards" (as opposed to the avant-gardes). Bagtropperne was led by Camilla Høiby and Sickie, two of the earliest, youngest, and most street-level punk girls, who were closer to the underground community. The *Fortropper* vs. *Bagtropper* incident is yet another example of the art schools vs. hard school conflict in punk. The rear-guards events sought to move against the pretentiousness of the avant-garde name and its connotations of cultural elitism. Many punks preferred to identify themselves as losers, not winners, and opposed the idea of "leading the way" for a culture they saw as doomed. American punk band Devo for example took their name from *De-Evolution*; their understanding was that mankind was regressing, not progressing.[36]

With this attitude, both the art school *and* the hard school fractions of the punk movement leaned into a phase at the end of the twentieth century that was characterized by a feeling of ending. The closing stages of modern culture, perhaps? The end of the world? In art history, the late 1970s and early 1980s have been identified as a turning point. Significantly, 1984 (that Orwellian year) was the year in which Arthur C. Danto published "The Death of Art." Danto emphasizes how the reassuring narrative of a kind of evolutionary progress, with appropriate next stages, had come to an end—and, notably, not that art had died. Danto pointedly distanced himself from the title "The Death of Art," which his name had come to signify, writing that:

> That title was not mine, for I was writing about a certain narrative that had, I thought, been objectively realized in the history of art, and it was that narrative, it seemed to me, that had come to an end. A story was over. It was not my view that there would be no more art, which "death" certainly implies, but that whatever art there was to be, would be made without benefit of a reassuring sort of narrative in which it was seen as the appropriate next stage in the story. What had come to an end was that narrative but not the subject of the narrative.[37]

That sense of post-history was inherent in punk culture: NO reassuring narrative, NO appropriate next step, and NO future for linear art history. In the sense of Arthur C. Danto, punk art can thus be understood as *posthistorical* (rather than *postmodern*). While the term postmodernism still inherently suggests a sequence, a straightforward chronology (in the succession: modernism, antimodernism, postmodernism), punk, as a movement, questions such a linear and progressing understanding of culture and of history. These doubts are not uttered in the sense of a postmodern all-signs-are-equal cliché, not Jean Baudrillard's notion of empty "simulacra" nor Fredric Jameson's conception of "historical deafness"[38]—on the contrary, the punks were highly historically alert—but rather in the sense of not contributing to a forward-moving history of progress. It is in this sense that the punk movement is more rear-guard than avant-garde.

Incidentally, the one other art movement of the twentieth century that had caused an art-historical fight-to-the-teeth, because of its unfitness to match an evolutionary understanding of art's progress, was Surrealism. The Surrealists had a beef with the canon: like punk, Surrealism did not fit into the linearly progressing story of modern art, exasperating critics such as Clement Greenberg, who notably struggled to fit the Surrealist artists, with all their kitsch and jumble, their figurative painting and political radicality, into the modern art canon. The Surrealists themselves were aiming to overthrow the canonized version of art, but nonetheless ended up partaking in that ritual of avant-gardism defined by a logic of: each new art revolution leads to the new ism. One of the first and most influential steps toward institutionalization and canonization of the Surrealist movement had been made by the founding director of the Museum of Modern Art in New York, Alfred Barr, who curated the exhibition *Fantastic Art, Dada, Surrealism* in 1936. In the show, Barr included Mickey Mouse cartoons and advertisements and specifically named Surrealism "a way of life."[39] In doing so, he expressed an understanding of the hybrid quality of the Surrealist movement that later formalist art historians, such as the just mentioned influential essayist and Abstract Expressionist campaigner, Clement Greenberg, or his younger colleague Michael Fried, condemned. Greenberg especially saw Surrealism as a deviation that messed up modernism's pursuit of art-immanent abstraction.

Come the 1960s, however, it became increasingly clear that Dada and Surrealism had a major impact on then-contemporaneous art, such as Pop Art, neo-Dada, as well as Abstract Expressionism. This realization led to the much-debated exhibition *Dada, Surrealism, and Their Heritage* in 1968 (yes, the one where the Motherfuckers protested outside, see Section 5.1: "Originality and appropriation"). The criticism was that the curator of that show, William Rubin, in essence, attempted to reduce Dada and Surrealism to pure art movements, that he was pressing them into an aesthetic lineage and excluding their radical and subversive aspects. The expanded field of artistic production, which both Dada and Surrealism had opened, as well as their political implications were omitted—which is even more striking when we consider that *Dada, Surrealism, and Their Heritage* took place in 1968, a year that was the pinnacle of social, political, and artistic activism.

One question, evidently, is how well *any* musealization of radical art can work. At any rate, the *Dada, Surrealism, and Their Heritage* display at MoMA seemed to further underline the perception of a sterilization, the artworks behind glass as though behind bars. If we think of P-Orridge placing Venus in a wooden case (Figure 5.3 in Section 5.2: "Modernity in extremis") or Gavin Turk's Sid Vicious captured in a golden frame (3.6 in Section 3.2: "Hedonism as attack"), these works are both readable as a thematization of exactly that question. Of course, the punks were not the first to fight institutionalization. Regarding CoBrA, which—as we have seen—played such an important role for punk artists, Carter Ratcliff writes:

> The trouble is that the moment revolutionary art achieves recognition, it becomes part of the culture it wants to subvert. In the view of the COBRA artists, this is what happened to the Surrealists and to every other avant-garde group with utopian impulses, from Dada to de Stijl. To avoid that fate, COBRA committed suicide.[40]

It could be argued that punk art likewise avoided its own assimilation into the cultural establishment and the annals of art history, because the artists were aware of the fate of prior movements, and that this is a part of the reason why the term "punk art" never did become established. Then again, the difference between punk art and CoBrA is that punk art was not really that "utopian," as Ratcliff calls the impulse of CoBrA. Punk was dystopian. The CoBrA artists still moved within a Hegelian-Marxist framework and believed in a historical dynamic that would abolish capitalist society and set art free. Artists involved in punk did not buy into this historical–philosophical idea. Instead, punk art stood for a post-utopian sense of rejection.

As a movement and as a way of life, punk was too conflicted to be dealing with the way forward. Rather, punks would be found, figuratively speaking, at the end of the line, at the bottom, taking care of and identifying with those left behind.

Notes

1. Mott, *Showboat*, n.p.

2. Greil Marcus, *Lipstick Traces: A Secret History of the Twentieth Century* (Cambridge: Harvard University Press, 1989), 23–141.

3. Dick Hebdige, *Subculture: The Meaning of Style* (London: Routledge, 1979), 107.

4. Sussman, "Introduction," 8.

5. Stevenson, *Vacant*, 9.

6. COUM Transmissions Manifesto 1974, quoted in Ford, *Wreckers of Civilisation*, 4.11.

7. Savage, *England's Dreaming*, 24.

8. See Alexander Karschnia, "OUT OF JOINT: The 'New Spirit of Capitalism', Creative Class Struggle and the Ghosts from the Future," keynote talk, *Impossibility of Novelty? (Re)Creating the Old and Consuming the New*, Freie Universität Berlin, November 7, 2013, accessed February 5, 2018, https://alextext.wordpress.com/2013/11/11/out-of-joint/.

9. Marcel Reich-Ranicki, "Bertolt Brecht, Hans Mayer und die Sklavensprache," in *Die Zeit*, no. 25, June 16, 1961.

10. Rosalind Krauss, "The Originality of the Avant-Garde [1981]," in Krauss, *The Originality of the Avant-Garde and Other Modernist Myths* (Boston: MIT Press, 1986), 11.

11. Krauss, "The Originality of the Avant-Garde," 19.

12. Guy Debord and Gil Wolman, "Methods de Détournement," in *Les Lèvres Nues*, no. 8 (May 1956). Quoted in *The Cambridge Companion to Brecht*, eds. Peter Thomson and Glendyr Sacks (Cambridge: Cambridge University Press, 2006), 311.

13. Essay by COUM written 1974, published 1979.

14. Mieke Bal, *Quoting Caravaggio: Contemporary Art, Preposterous History* (Chicago: University of Chicago Press, 1999), 1.

15. James Elkins, *Stories of Art* (London: Routledge, 2002), 33–34.

16. Kaagman, interview, 2017.

17. Telegram from Asger Jorn to Harry Guggenheim, January 15, 1964. See Gingeras, *The Avant-Garde Won't Give Up: Cobra and Its Legacy* (Los Angeles: Blum & Poe, 2015), 13.

18. Gavin Grindon, "Poetry Written in Gasoline: Black Mask and Up Against the Wall Motherfucker," in *Art History* 38, no. 1 (February 2015): 170–209.

19. Kaagman, interview, 2017.

20. Carter Ratcliff, "Snakes & Ladders: The COBRA Group, Sons of the Surrealists," in *Tate Etc.*, no. 4 (April 2003), accessed May 1, 2018, http://www.tate.org.uk/context-comment/articles/snakes-and-ladders-the-cobra-group.

21. Kempton, *The Provos*, 9.

22. Bracewell, "Some Notes for the Exhibition," 13. Emphasis in original.

23. COUM Transmissions Manifesto 1974, quoted in Ford, *Wreckers of Civilisation*, 4.11.

24. Again, different titles exist; see Tate Archive Main Collection and Kunsthalle Wien.

25. Elza Adamowicz, *Dada Bodies: Between Battlefield and Fairground* (Manchester: Manchester University Press, 2019), 10.

26. Thomas Groetz, *Doris als Musikerin: Die Tödliche Doris, Band 2* (Berlin: Martin Schmitz Verlag, 1999), 10.

27. Müller, interview, 2017. Emphasis in orginal.

28. Stiftung zur Aufarbeitung der SED-Diktatur, Berlin. Quoted in Müller, "Das Chaos reist mit dem Schönen Wochenende," 157.

29. Kruse, interview, 2017.

30. Müller, interview, 2013. He is referring to Jamie Reid's collages for the Sex Pistols.

31. Julian Weber, "Biografie über Alfred Hilsberg. Er ist Punk-Papst" (April 5, 2016), accessed April 4, 2018, http://www.taz.de/!5291759.

32. Groetz, *Doris als Musikerin*, 63.

33. Wolfgang Müller, "No Future now! Das SO36: Beitrag zum Experiment der Selbstmumifizierung (Sokushinbutsu)," in *SO36: 1978 bis heute*, 69.

34. Quoted from "Pareidolia," in *Collins English Dictionary*, accessed April 5, 2018, https://www.collinsdictionary.com.

35. Müller, interview, 2013.

36. Devo, "Bio," accessed January 3, 2018, http://www.clubdevo.com/devo-bio.

37. Arthur C. Danto, *After the End of Art: Contemporary Art and the Pale of History* (Princeton: Princeton University Press, 2014), 4.

38. See Jean Baudrillard, *Simulacra and Simulation*, trans. Sheila Faria Glaser (Ann Arbor: University of Michigan Press, 1994) and Fredric Jameson, *Postmodernism, or, the Cultural Logic of Late Capitalism* (Durham: Duke University Press, 1991).

39. Alfred Barr, "Preface," in *Fantastic Art, Dada, Surrealism*, 8.

40. Ratcliff, "Snakes & Ladders," n.p.

6 Children Run Riot: The Art of the infantile

"I try as well as I can not to grow up," punk poet Michael Strunge said, "To grow up is to stiffen and to have your visions suffocated."[1] This is indeed a very punk view. Unwillingness to grow up was a key punk theme. The standard definition of infantilism is the "retention of childish physical, mental, or emotional qualities in adult life."[2] The term stems from Latin *infantilis*, meaning childish, and was first introduced as a psychiatric diagnosis by Ernest-Charles Lasègue in 1864.[3] Punk's perception of the childish oscillates between Sigmund Freud's version of the child's anal-sadistic phase vs. Jean-Jacques Rousseau's version of the Romantic child. Whereas Rousseau believed that children were pure and innocent, until ruined by their environment (i.e. adult society), Freud (not unlike Thomas Hobbes some centuries before) unsentimentally saw children as wicked and egoistic. In punk music, poetry, and art, we see allusions to both these conceptualizations of the childish. The child might be egoistic, might even be evil, or it can be innocent, playful, and full of fantasy, but in either case, the childish is the *free*. In punk culture, this sentiment of freedom is what makes the childish attractive.

In the following pages, we focus on the punk movement's relationship with the infantile. In the first part of the chapter: "Dead end kids," we look at examples of how the child was conceptualized in punk rock lyrics and poetry, while also zooming in on Peter Christopherson's photos of young punks and his store decoration for BOY in London. Second, the Super 8 movie *The Life of Sid Vicious* (1981; Figure 6.1) by Die Tödliche Doris is analyzed. In the last part of the chapter, called "*Infancy conforms to nobody*"—an Emerson quote used by P-Orridge—we examine the collage *L'ecole de l'art infantile* (1974) which is a joint work by COUM Transmissions and Robin Klassnik.

6.1 Dead end kids

"Can't go on, drag along / can't go wrong, sing along / Pied Piper will lead you to the water," John Lydon (by this time with Public Image Ltd.) sang in 1980.[4] In the fable, the people of Hammelin hire the Pied Piper to get rid of the rats and he does so by leading them with his pipe to the water to drown. But the people of Hammelin refuse to pay him as agreed. The Pied Piper returns in disguise, and this time plays a tune that makes all children follow him: they are never seen again. Abandoned children were a leitmotif in punk, and punks themselves were often very young. The punk community saw itself as a safe haven for children who lashed out because they alone could see the greed and hollowness of adult society.

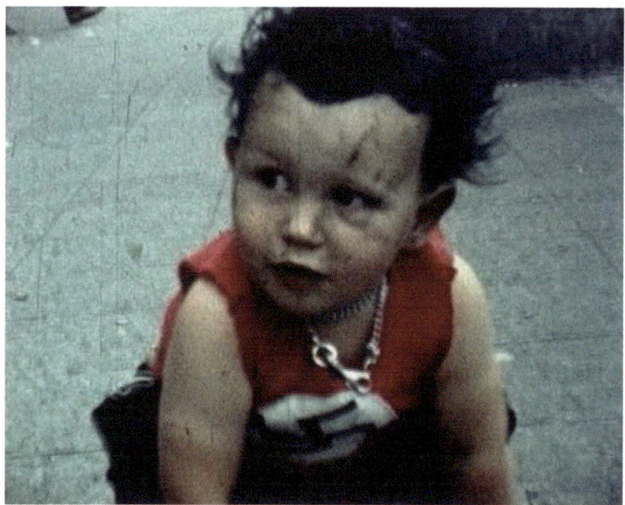

Figure 6.1: Die Tödliche Doris, Das Leben des Sid Vicious (The Life of Sid Vicious), *1981, Super 8 film still. Archiv der Tödlichen Doris. Courtesy of Wolfgang Müller.*

In the poem "Revolte" ("Revolt"),[5] Danish punk poet Michael Strunge writes:

> Og børnene folder sig rigtigt ud
> Som blomsterne i lyset,
> Legen erobrer de kedelige huse
> Med uanstændige frisurer og dragter.
>
> (And the children run riot
> like flowers in the light,
> their game captures the boring houses
> with indecent hair styles and costumes.)

This is a revolution through play, but an agonizingly vulnerable one. "In a world gone crazy," sings Iggy Pop, "I am a real wild child."[6] The infantile sentiment of isolation is an oft-repeated motif in punk. The lyrics "Now I wanna be a good boy / I don't wanna be bad / Now I wanna run away from home / Now I wanna be on my own / Now I wanna be sad alone,"[7] from the Ramones' album *Leave Home* can also be interpreted in this light: youth represents both innocence and sadness, whereas malevolence is caused by a reaction to neglect and injustice. The figure onto whom these fantasies were projected most prominently was Sid Vicious. Ironically, heroin—to which Vicious and Nancy Spungen were heavily addicted—actually does "embalm the user's body and emotions. Sid and Nancy were locked into permanent adolescence," Savage points out.[8]

The punk movement's identification as a pronounced movement of the *youth* shows in its preoccupation with the childish. In punk art, the infantile is interpreted as honest, free, and real. In art as in life, punk had an eye for vice and vulnerability, for the ugly sides of society. The child's unfiltered, non-conformist, non-normative truthfulness was perceived as an ideal in punk and, simultaneously, infantilism—meaning the retention of childish qualities—was an often-applied mode: punk denounces the cruelty of (grown-up) society and seeks a fragile escape in childishness.

Punk's understanding of youth relates to the understanding of art-historical movements, primarily Dada and Surrealism. In Dada, youth was likewise conceptualized as innocent opposition to the corruption of adult society. The term *Dada* itself was a reference to the childish. In 1916, Hugo Ball wrote:

> Childhood as a new world, and everything childlike and phantastic, everything childlike and direct, everything childlike and symbolical in opposition to the sensibilities of the world of grown-ups. The child will be the accuser on Judgement Day, the Crucified One will judge, the Resurrected One will pardon.[9]

The childlike is thus associated both with directness and with fantasy, and the child becomes a symbol of justice in an unjust world. "Dada proclaimed the return of the stuttered articulations of childhood as a defense mechanism in defiance of an idealistically holistic concept of art that glosses over reality," as Heinz Schütz points out—a vocation that he links to the punk movement in Germany in the early 1980s.[10] Schütz' point that Dada's infantilism was a way to oppose empty art pour l'art certainly echoes in punk.

The Surrealists, too, had an idealistic understanding of the integrity of a child's artistic expression and artists such as Max Ernst, Yves Tanguy, and Joan Miró sought to reconnect with the vividness, magic, and imagination of their own infancy. Leaning on Freud's theories, however, the Surrealists were also interested in that "evil" side of childhood—which we will return to later in Section 6.3: "Infancy conforms to nobody." Later, the Situationists identified themselves as enfants perdus, or "lost children." This is an old military term, which describes soldiers on a dangerous post or mission.[11] Guy Debord used it at the end of his film *Hurlements en faveur de Sade* (Howls for Sade, 1952) in which the line "Nous vivons en enfants perdus nos aventures incompletes"—"We live our incomplete adventures as lost children"—is followed by 24 minutes of darkness.

For many in the punk movement, however, "infantility" was not a question of reconnecting with the child, of living *as* lost children; they *were* lost children. Punk was a quintessentially youthful movement. Punk's relationship with the childish was thus

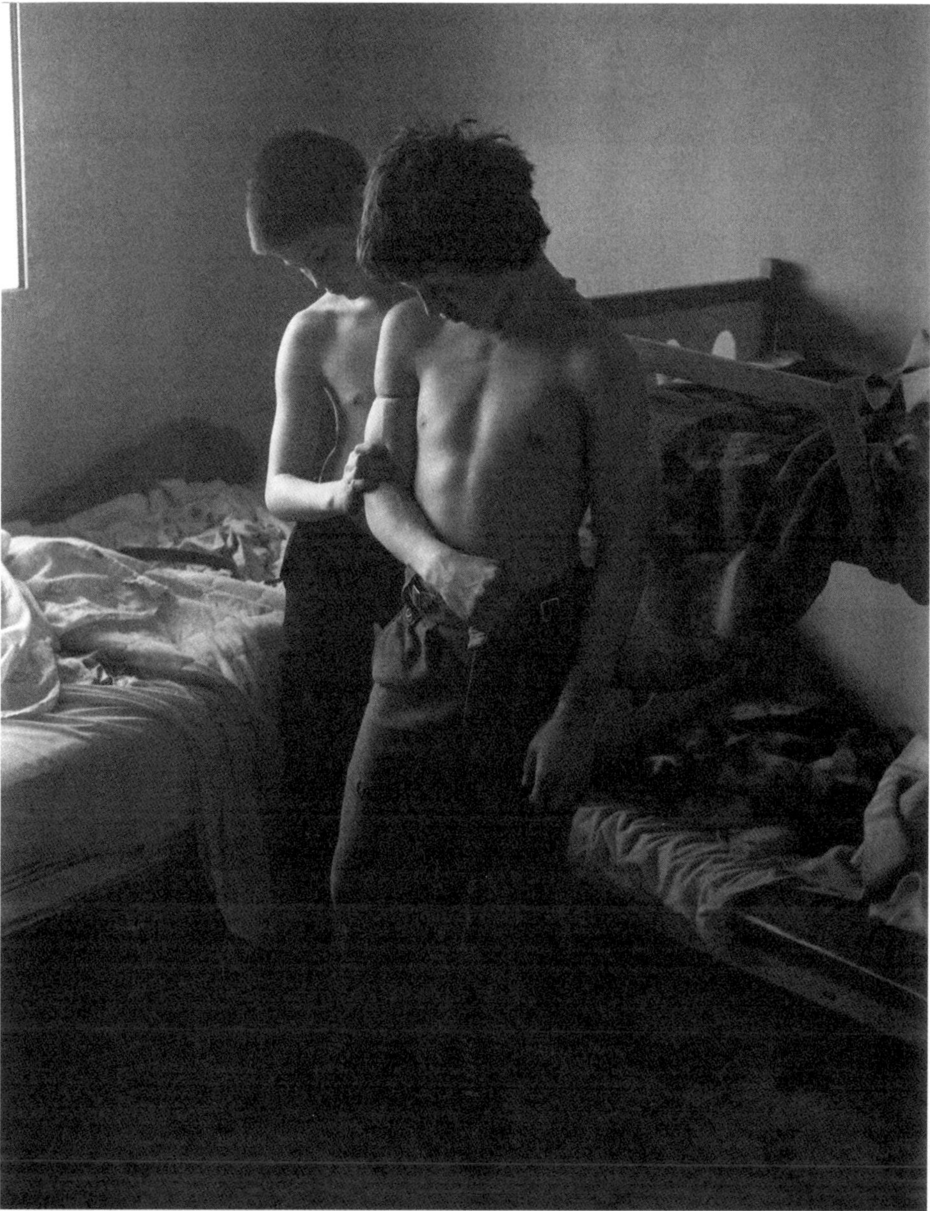

Figure 6.2: Peter Christopherson, Untitled, *ca. 1976. Courtesy of Timeless Editions, timelessedition.com*

less artistic philosophy and more rooted in experience. Punk's aggressive language and imagery conveyed nothing other than an assessment of actual reality, and the child's perception of that reality was viewed as significant and true. But, as Savage notes, "[a] proper reading of the 20th century history tells us that youth is not inherently progressive: it can be authoritarian, cruel, indeed fascistic."[12] Like the Futurists, punks could be youthfully ruthless and raving. The radical, even fanatical, disposition of punk, however, was linked with an underlying doubt. Punk engaged not only in sloganeering, but in a process of questioning, as well. In punk, ruthlessness and tenderness were not necessarily conceived as mutually exclusive.

Peter Christopherson (shortly before joining COUM) took a series of photographs of young punks around 1976 that underline this raw connection between ruthlessness and tenderness. In one image, we see two young boys standing close together, in a dorm-like room, in the background are a messy bunk bed and bare walls (Figure 6.2). The image is of almost classical beauty, the soft light accentuates their faces and their bodies, as they stand in contrapposto, half-profile, looking down. One boy is pressing his fingers against the vein of the other boy's arm, which has been tied with a thin strap. Their torsos are bare, their pants old-fashioned and threadbare, their hair short. The boy in front wears black jump boots with white laces. The photo has a sense of stillness and intimacy. The two boys stand in harmony, their bodies linked in parallel motionlessness. Yet all things concrete around them evoke a tough reality, possibilities of misuse, violence, and abandonment.

In contrast to the calm of that image, Christopherson shot two other photos of a street fight scene, which convey brutal physical turmoil. The two images complement each other: one shows the victim, it is taken from above (Figure 6.3); the other shows the violator, it is taken slightly from below (Figure 6.4). Adjourned, the two images thus almost give us the perspective, which the two boys must have of each other. The characteristic of Christopherson's photography is the sense of directness. The realness of the emotion in the boys' faces. The asphalt, the sports jacket, the leather jacket, the black hole of the sleeve, where the fist will shoot out in the next second. The blurry streetscape in the background, which gives just enough indication to make out, is not the pretty side of town. A jeans leg and a hand giving us a clue of the on-lookers, the helpers. The chaos of tipped viewpoints, the expectance of the next blow, the inescapability of the situation, the fear. As viewers, we are transported into their world, which is stripped of pretense. We are uncomfortably close to the hurt caused and the hurt felt. Christopherson's image series is reminiscent of Larry Clark's image series of kids in *Tulsa* (1971): the images are moving and hardcore, and the kids are very, very young. Marcia Resnick's *Bad Boys* (1977–82) series, which was shown in the *Punk Art* exhibition in 1978, is likewise related to Christopherson's photographic work with young boys.

Christopherson also did the store decoration for the punk fetish and fashion store BOY on 153 King's Road in 1977. In the window lay the fake burnt leg of a boy, and the walls were pasted with newspaper clippings of all sorts with BOY in the headline, such as

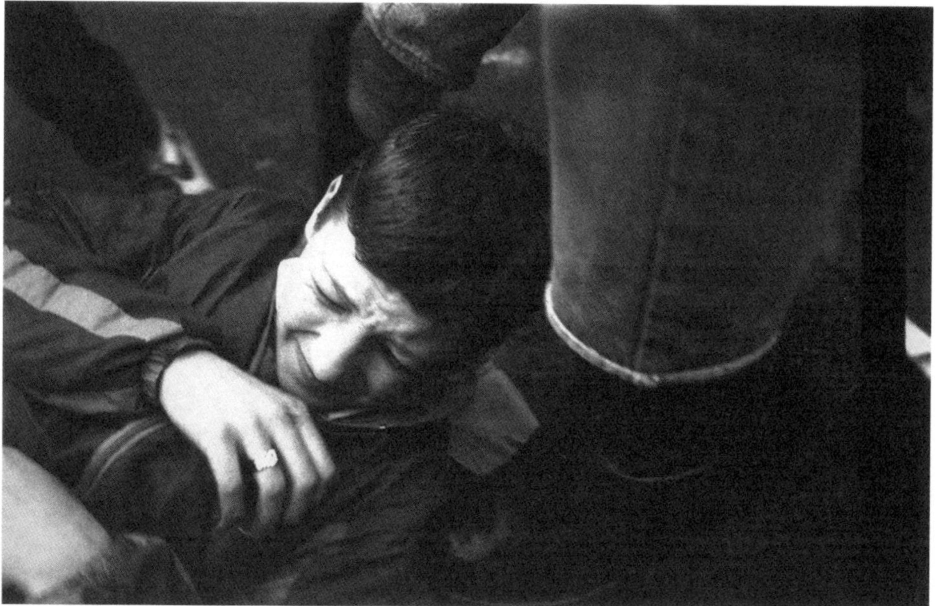

Figure 6.3: Peter Christopherson, Untitled*, ca. 1976. Courtesy of Timeless Editions, timelessedition.com*

"Boy of 12 on Murder Charge." One poster shows a battered and bleeding boy lying on the ground, with BOY written at the top and, at the bottom, in all caps and quotation marks, as though being screamed out: "THE STRENGTH OF THE COUNTRY LIES IN ITS YOUTH!"[13] This is a nationalistic ("country") and potentially militaristic ("strength") message that points to a view of the youth as an instrument in a closed, traditionalist scheme (and considering the times: a very toxic masculinity). The focus on young boys thus both implicitly introduces an aspect of sexuality as well as a military aspect. Especially for boys, not for all, but for too many, at that point in time, and as it were in hundreds of years before, coming of age also meant a shift from being victim (at school, at home) to being perpetrator. The dread of this shift is inherent in Peter Christopherson's work. In his poster, the strength of the country quote is juxtaposed with the image of an aching and destructive youth: boys as victims, boys as offenders. Not the strength, but the weakness of the country likewise lies in its youth, Christopherson's image suggests. The violence implicit in the quote is thus turned around: this country's immorality ruins its youth. The traditionalist expectancy of heroic military violence is met with a chaotic violence on the street. Because violence is violence is violence.

What is so punk about Christopherson's photos from the mid 1970s is how they visualize the strong bond of being friends and being outsiders, of giving and receiving small tokens of understanding, in a bleak, violent, and hostile world. Accordingly, the

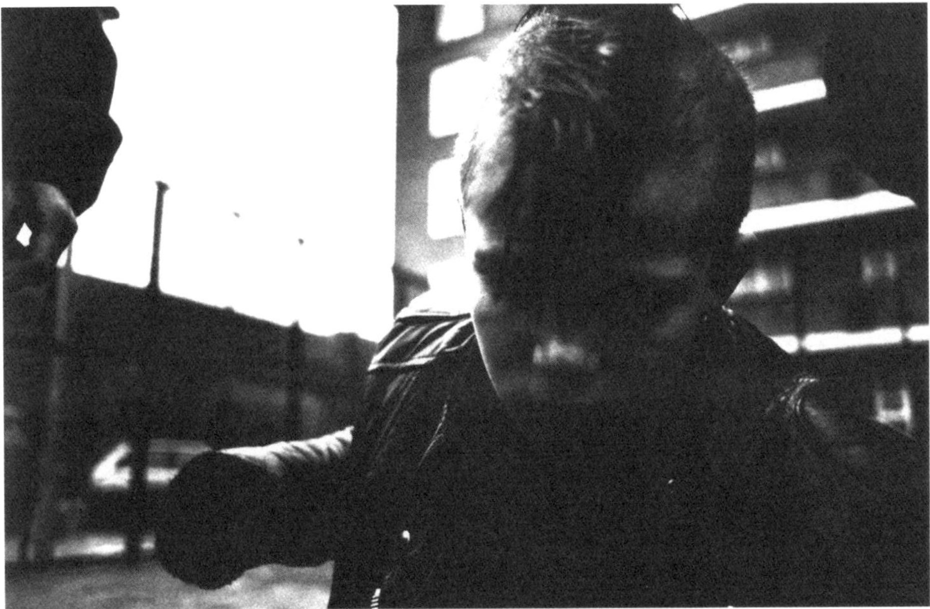

Figure 6.4: Peter Christopherson, Untitled, *ca. 1976. Courtesy of Timeless Editions, timelessedition.com*

concept of the youth gang was strong in punk. "Steve Jones [of the Sex Pistols] was a perfect Artful Dodger to McLaren's Fagin," Savage notes, referring to the pickpocket gang in Charles Dickens' *Oliver Twist*, an analogy also used by McLaren himself.[14] "We're not just a band, we're a gang. Like the *Dead End Kids* of today," drummer Jerry Nolan of the New York Dolls said, quoting the stage play about a group of youths growing up on the streets of New York during the Great Depression.[15] The violent boys' gangs in William S. Burroughs' *The Wild Boys: A Book of the Dead* (1971) and in Stanley Kubrick's film version of *A Clockwork Orange* (1971)—both set in dystopian societies—were similar points of reference.

The Lost Boys—a Swansea-based punk band formed in early 1980[16]—named themselves after J. M. Barrie's novel *Peter Pan, or the Boy Who Wouldn't Grow Up* (1911) and his band of outcast boys—all mischievous, yet pure at heart. They are the boys "who fall out of their prams when the nurse is looking the other way and if they are not claimed in seven days, they are sent far away to the Neverland. I'm Captain," as Peter Pan explains in Barrie's play. When Wendy asks why there are no girls, Peter tells her they are much too clever to fall out of their prams.[17] Without having the space to go into depth with this question here, it does become clear that between societal expectations, traditional upbringing, and perhaps also a trace of biological predicament, there are more boys than girls among these *Dead End Kids*. Peter Pan's lost boys, in any case, are the forgotten children, who flee the real world to join together in an alternative one. "If the kids are united / then we'll never be divided," the English punk band Sham 69 sang.[18] Punk invokes the vicious style of the violent teenage gang in *A Clockwork Orange*, but often enough in combination with the sadness, playfulness, and pure-heartedness of the Lost Boys.

The punk community saw itself as a safe haven for children who lashed out, because they alone could see the greed and hollowness of adult society. The escapism into childhood, thus, was no Disneyfication: it was a bare minimum protection. In the next example, a film by Die Tödliche Doris, that clash between the childish and the menacing is driven to the max.

6.2 *The Life of Sid Vicious:* The sad, dead boy

In Die Tödliche Doris' Super 8 film *The Life of Sid Vicious*, which premiered in the alternative Arsenal movie theater in West Berlin in 1981, the bass player of the Sex Pistols is played by a 2-year-old boy.[19] The film reenacts some of the key stages of Vicious' life; his performance in Julien Temple's mockumentary about the Sex Pistols, *The Great Rock 'n' Roll Swindle* (1980, see also Section 3.2: "Hedonism as attack"), his self-destructive love–hate relationship with Nancy Spungen, Vicious allegedly stabbing Spungen to death at the Chelsea Hotel in New York in October 1978, and his death not long afterwards from a heroin overdose. Die Tödliche Doris begin the film with the weirdly conventional biographical title "The Life of…". The title is put together from cut-out letters, recalling the seminal album cover designed by Jamie Reid for *Never Mind the Bollocks, Here's the Sex Pistols*. The dryness of the title is soon counteracted by the appearance of the Surrealistic image of a toddler wearing a swastika T-shirt, chains, studded-leather bracelet, and black spiked hair.

In the background, the French version of "Anarchy in the UK" plays in a slightly distorted version. However, instead of the streets of Paris (as in Temple's movie), it is recognizably the streets of West Berlin. The child crawls, stumbles, finds some loose paving stones, and throws them about. He is filmed from above, from the position of an adult. Die Tödliche Doris' film is a swindle version of an existing swindle: the reenacted scenes are mainly taken from Julien Temple, the title screen copies Jamie Reid, and the camera following "Sid" in the street could refer to paparazzi.

In the next scene, "Sid" is with "Nancy" (played by a 7-year-old blonde girl in black mascara and fishnet suspender stockings, Figure 6.5) in a dark and chaotic room, filled with cigarette butts and empty liquor bottles. The two get into a pillow fight, play with a knife, and "Sid" stabs the girl to death in a whirl of ketchup (or blood). In the final

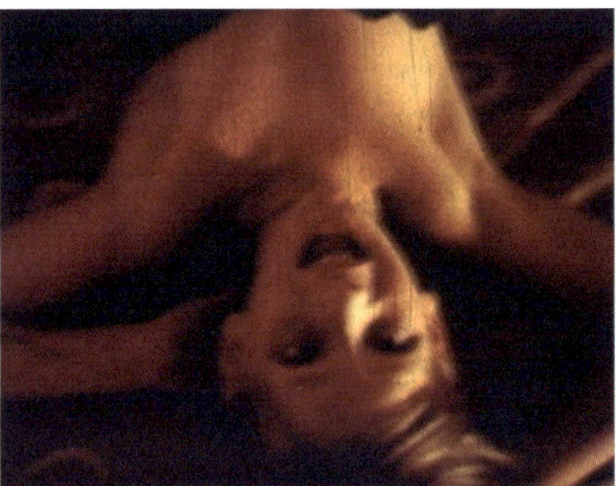

Figure 6.5: Die Tödliche Doris, Das Leben des Sid Vicious (The Life of Sid Vicious)*, 1981, Super 8 film still. Archiv der Tödlichen Doris. Courtesy of Wolfgang Müller.*

sequences, the camera shows a syringe, then the child appears to give himself a fix. He looks about, disoriented, cries (Figure 6.6), then falls asleep (or dies). "L'anarchie pour le U.K." sets in again.

Perhaps the most forceful effect of the film derives from the way it circumvents expected perceptions. The violence emerges as banal, the perpetrator as innocent, and the surreal as the real. The "childhood" moment is reinforced by the use of Super 8, an effect that would have been even stronger in the early 1980s when this medium was associated with family recordings. At the same time, the specific Super 8 aesthetic imbues the scenes with a paradoxical sense of trashiness, truth, and trauma (for more on Super 8 and punk, see Section 2.4: "DIY: The DNA of punk"). All crying and screams, both "Sid's" and "Nancy's," were done by Wolfgang Müller. In Super 8 films, sound and image were recorded separately, resulting in a certain alienation effect (not unlike the one in Rainer Werner Fassbinder's films). The actions and people on the screen appear both real and unreal.

Even with the distance of an alienation effect, *The Life of Sid Vicious* is nonetheless extremely difficult to watch. The innocence of the child, playing, crying, is at times heartbreaking. As a viewer, one looks at the child—"Sid"—from above, and, as one understands the context better than he does, one assumes that he is being instructed what to do. The viewer is thus made into an accomplice, an effect which is reinforced in the moments when the boy looks straight at the camera (thus breaking whatever small remnant of filmic illusion was still there).

The naïveté of Sid Vicious is often described by his contemporaries. "We'd go to the shop and Vivienne [Westwood] would just put a pair of trousers on him. He was like a toy almost [...] he was [...] so idealistic and so clever," Viv Albertine remembers.[20]

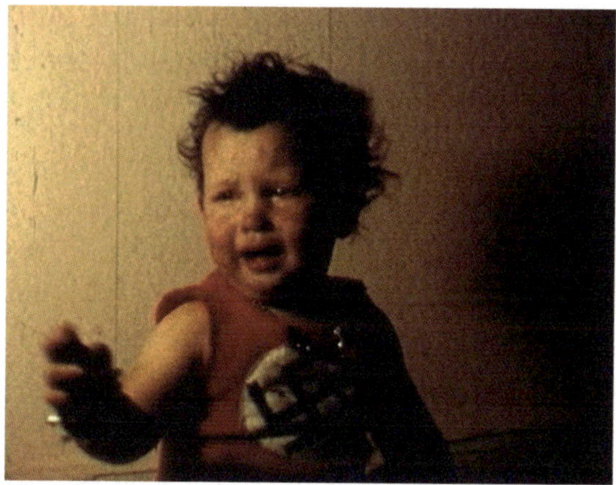

Figure 6.6: Die Tödliche Doris, Das Leben des Sid Vicious (The Life of Sid Vicious)*, 1981, Super 8 film still. Archiv der Tödlichen Doris. Courtesy of Wolfgang Müller.*

Vicious' role in the media, especially in the English tabloids, was the opposite. After Nancy Spungen's death, "Sid had finally turned in to a fully-blown scapegoat: a media monster from the id," Jon Savage notes.[21] With a single move, Tödliche Doris turns that image around: vicious becomes an abandoned child. *The Life of Sid Vicious* thus displays punk's sentimental ideal of the sad and true child who is ruined by the corrupted society of grown-ups, and who ultimately is faced with either adaptation or escape (into death). Sid Vicious became a strong identification figure for such perceptions; "Sid ist unschuldig (ich auch)!" ("Sid is innocent (so am I)!") read one graffiti of the punk scene.[22] The sweetness of both children—we are looking at a "Sid" as vivid as Caravaggio's *Cupid* (*Amor Vincit Omnia,* 1601–02) and a Lolita-like "Nancy"—complicates matters. There are sentiments not only of innocence here but also of sex.

Reactions to the film were mixed: its method and moral were questioned, but in the punk-rock press, one assertion often resurfaced: it was shocking and (thus) true to its subject. "*The Life of Sid Vicious* short portrays the punk idiom better than the thousands of disposable artefacts that have appeared since its beginning," wrote *SOUNDS* magazine. The *East Village Eye* found: "The pure shock value of Die Tödliche Doris' *The Life of Sid Vicious* would make Malcolm McLaren turn green." The *New Musical Express* wrote: "Once the shock wears off, one is left with the devastatingly simple metaphor for a childmind playing with things beyond his control."[23]

Die Tödliche Doris' *The Life of Sid Vicious* ambiguously implements both punk's romantic and its cynical sentiments. The short film amalgamates punk's tragic child-hero with the multiplied and mediated pop phenomenon, and does so in a setting that is both pure swindle and oddly social-realistic. The feeling in Die Tödliche Doris' film, however, is raw. Its contemporaneousness is felt (it was shot only one year after Sid Vicious died). Furthermore, the immediacy and openness of the child bleeds into the sensation of the film as a whole.

6.3 "Infancy conforms to nobody"

Whereas the film by Die Tödliche Doris thus seems like an echo of Jean-Jacques Rousseau and the Romantic child—that is, a contrasting of infantile immediacy and naturalness vs. adult materiality and corruption—the next example, a collaboration between COUM and Robin Klassnik, seems much closer to Sigmund Freud's understanding of the candid evil in the child: it is a black-and-white collage spread from *VILE*, no. 1, 1974 (dated 1985) called *L'ecole de l'art infantile* (Figure 6.7). *VILE* aimed "to reflect the negative, anti-social aspects of humanity," according to the zine's founder, Canadian artist Anna Banana.[24] The name and logo of *VILE* was an allusion to the art magazine *FILE*, which Banana criticized for its increasingly exclusionary understanding of what qualified as mail art. The first *FILE* "megazine" had been published in 1972 by the art collective General Idea. Up until 1973, *FILE* had furthermore been the main international forum for mail artists, but the editors condemned the new "quick-kopy krap."[25] Banana in contrast had no problem with "quick crap." In *VILE*, there was thus more Xeroxing, more violence, more trash, and more "up-yours type messages," in the words of Banana.[26] That included works like Pauline Smith's punkish and offensive *Adolf Hitler Fan Club* (in which COUM also participated).[27] In several issues, Banana displayed the Dada influences on *VILE*, for example through cooperation with the Bay Area Dadaists and the London Dada Services. The small-circulation zine was done at Speedprint, an instant-print shop in San Francisco, which made it evident to Banana "that anyone could be a publisher."[28] COUM Transmissions sent their collage *L'ecole de l'art infantile* to Anna Banana, because *VILE* gave them "carte blanche to be more tasteless and provocative," as P-Orridge formulated it.[29]

COUM Transmissions' two-page spread shows photocopied clippings from advertisements featuring picture-perfect blonde mothers and their babies next to photographs of male genitals, a baby with an open hole in its back, and crude misspelled statements put together using cut-out letters, such as "thEse ahh famUZ Peepholes SLUGS / FRee SUbscriptiön" and repeatedly the title *L'ecole de l'art infantile*. One picture shows four toddlers on their potty-chairs, with the caption "Photograph of the Artist's Studio" and repeated signatures by Genesis P-Orridge, as though he were an adolescent practicing or developing it. Another image shows a baby with the cut-out letters "art" written on her dress, placed next to cut-outs of commercial templates and grown-up

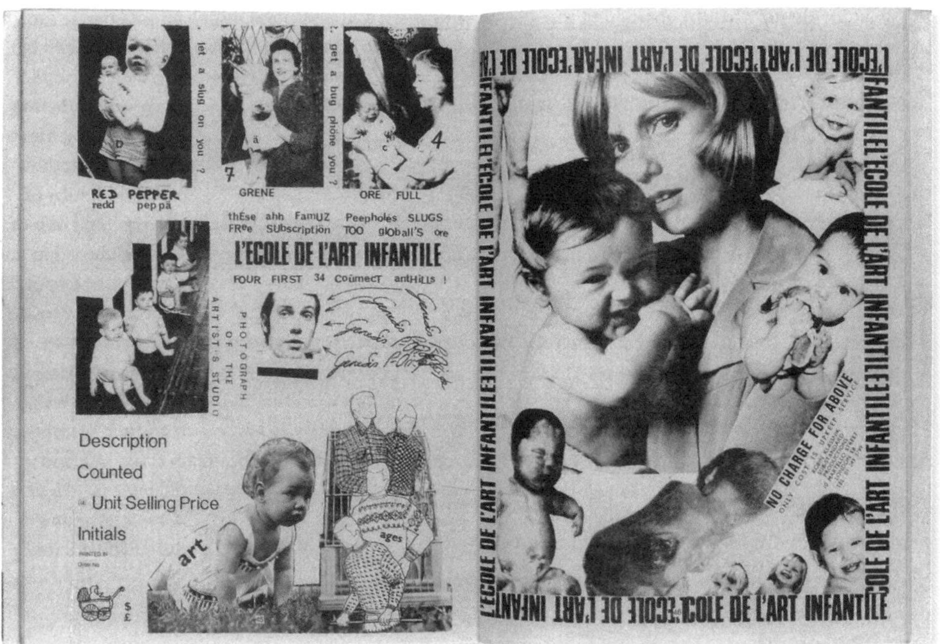

Figure 6.7: COUM Transmissions and Robin Klassnik, L'ecole de l'art infantile*, 1974. Courtesy of the estate of GENESIS BREYER P-ORRIDGE and New Discretions.*

figures with empty faces. Toward the right bottom corner, where the artist's signature would traditionally be, there is a "no charge for above" notification, with the address of the artists at Martello Street in London. The overall composition is irregular, with uneven spacing and rough edges, sometimes chopping off parts of images, such as the top of a head. The collage thus conveys the impression of an amateurish approach. The act of defecating, the weirdly out-of-context penis, and the deliberately abrasive spelling errors are all also used for their humor and shock value, thus highlighting the punkish-infantile aspects of the presentation.

In *L'ecole de l'art infantile*, the infantile is represented in both a negative and a positive way. On the one hand, childishness is used to ridicule what P-Orridge calls "shamelessly self-promoting and success oriented" artists.[30] This disdain shows in the caricatured image of toddlers on the potty coupled with the "Artist's Studio" caption; the image links the pride of the pooing infant—"look what I did, Mommy!"—to the posing of self-important artists (and thus peripherally also compares art to excrement, though with less irony than, for example, Piero Manzoni in his 1961 work *Artist's Shit*, see Section 3.3: "Trash and travesty"). In P-Orridge's words, COUM engaged in the "raw celebration of the inexpert" rather than "careerism."[31] This stance is underscored through the "no charge for above" notification, a sideswipe at the commercial art system. The line-up of infants, who are being trained in social convention by learning to defecate at the same time, furthermore raises questions of obedience and restriction. In the equation of that image, the artists are thus disciplined to do as told by the (art) authorities.

This latter notion becomes even stronger if we invoke Sigmund Freud's theory of "psychosexual development" (1905), which was widely known in the mid 1970s. Briefly, Freud's concept of sexual infantilism was determined by his description of five sexual stages in young childhood—the oral, anal, phallic, latency, and genital stages—which, if suppressed, could result in a variety of mental disorders. The defecating children in the collage would accordingly be in the so-called anal or anal-sadistic stage. In this stage, Freud saw sadism, aggression, and mastery in the child as connected to the progressive development of autonomy. He wrote that children's narcissistic focus on obtaining independence often makes them cruel. Freud thus explains later dreams of cruelty as originating in this stage: "The evil impulses of the dream are merely infantilism."[32] The childish represents the candid, the egocentric, indeed the evil, that has not yet been tamed. Psychologically, in the theory of Freud, the infantile stands for the *id*: "Thus it becomes more certain that *the unconscious in our psychic life is the infantile*," he asserts.[33] What is more: Freud understands art as the play of grown-ups, a creative situation where the adult artist again becomes omnipotent, because he/she can create a world according to the dictates of their own desire. By implication, the artist, like the child, is unfiltered in his/her desires. "Art, Freud asserted, is merely an acceptable, sublimated form of play for adults," as Susan Laxton summarizes.[34] Both in contrast and agreement, we see a figure such as the psychologist Kazimierz Dąbrowski, who in the 1960s coined the expression "positive infantilism" or "positive immaturity" and found this quality in "highly gifted and creative individuals, especially artists," who, even as adults, maintain childish qualities of wonder, imagination, and sensitivity.[35] In both cases, art is linked with childhood—only, the understanding of childhood differs vastly.

COUM Transmissions perceive the infantile as an outsider position in a positive sense: defiant, limitless, free. The image of the baby with the short assertion "art" might thus be read as an open symbol of the creative potential of children. The ideal of curiosity toward art as well as music remained an ideal for the group. After the artists transformed from COUM to Throbbing Gristle, P-Orridge stated: "You should approach any instrument the way a child will."[36] What they desire is thus an approach that is in no way bound by normativity. This absolute lack of normativity is at the core of COUM's concept of the infantile: the search for an unfiltered mindset. Critically, this also means not respecting the rules of conservative adult society.

Furthermore, the collage targets the superficiality of advertisements in a double attack on what the artists saw as fake "ideal world" family values and the capitalistic exploitation of the same. This criticism is further emphasized in the choice of media: the collage per se transports a worldview that leaves room for fragmentation, disarray, and confusion. The glossy pretense of advertising's perfection is thus counteracted, both through the chosen medium and through the subject matter. COUM Transmissions point to abusive structures hidden behind traditional norms. The group exposes society's heteronormative imperative and mocks the gender stereotypes (e.g. the collage's triple repetition of mother–toddler images) conveyed through it. The genre in religious paintings, Maria with baby Jesus, is just one more association which COUM and Robin Klassnik mock in this collage.

The artists did not only engage with infantilism in this collage. By the mid 1970s, the infantile had become a central theme in COUM's work. In 1974, the same year they created *L'ecole de l'art infantile*, the group wrote a detailed explanation of their actions at an art festival in Rottweil, Germany. In the thirteen-page report, called *COUM Decoumposition: "Schlimm"* they wrote: "In a way thee themes were, disturbance, thee similarities between mental stress and infancy. Infancy conforms to nobody said Emerson."[37] The topic of childishness was thus linked with both non-conformity and estrangement. Given P-Orridge's interest in the Beat Generation, one might wonder if he picked up Ralph Waldo Emerson's assertion—"infancy conforms to nobody"—from Jack Kerouac, who cites Emerson on infancy in *Big Sur* (1962).[38]

The *decomposition* in the title points to the themes of decay, rottenness, and breakdown: all central topics in punk art. The German word "*schlimm*" can be translated as bad, nasty, or wicked, and it is a term used to scold a child. The title alone implies both the iniquity of grown-up society and children's defiance against it. Infantility was also linked to COUM's egalitarian and autodidactic approach to art, as stated in their art manifesto (see Section 5.1: "Originality and appropriation"). Despite the apparent optimism in a statement like "COUM enable all kinds of people to discover their abilities," COUM Transmissions made it clear that the option of free creation will have to be a fight. "You don't NEED special training" alludes to: "Don't let nobody tell you that ..." In this context, childhood is perceived as a unique position of freedom—Emerson's "infancy conforms to nobody"—and by extension, infantility emerges as an act of defiance.

The "School of Infantile Art" concept epitomizes COUM's attack on all institutions and all inherited systems. Tutti and P-Orridge made several works that incorporated a School of Infantile Art in one way or another, mostly in collaboration with Klassnik and the mail artist and Surrealist publisher Opal L. Nations from Strange Faeces Press.[39] The use of French in the title might be read as an ironic allusion to art history and art schools, particularly the most influential of the nineteenth century, such as the École des Beaux-Arts in Paris. At the made-up *Ecole de l'art infantile*, "everyone was the director/principal and there were no students."[40] The exclusivity and hierarchy of the traditional academy are thus replaced by an autodidactic ideal. It is worth noting that the egalitarianism of the school results not in everyone being a student, but in everyone being a director (which perhaps conveys punk's anarchistic ideal, too). And with this autodidactic ideal we are right set for the next chapter: "Work vs. Play."

Notes

1. Michael Strunge quoted in Nielsen, *Ung i 80erne*, 8.
2. See "Infantilism", in Merriam Webster, accessed December 11, 2017, https://www.merriam-webster.com/dictionary/infantilism.
3. Christian Müller, ed., *Lexikon der Psychiatrie: Gesammelte Abhandlungen der gebräuchlichsten psychiatrischen Begriffe*, 2nd ed. (Berlin: Springer Heidelberg, 1986), 354–56.
4. Public Image Ltd, "Pied Piper" (UK: Virgin Records, 1980).
5. Michael Strunge, "Revolt" [1981], in Strunge, *A Virgin from a Chilly Decade*, 41.
6. Iggy Pop, "Wild Child" (A&M Records, 1986). Original song, called "The Wild One," by Johnny O'Keefe, 1958.
7. Ramones, "Now I Wanna Be a Good Boy" (USA: Sire Records, 1977).
8. Savage, *England's Dreaming*, 502.
9. Hugo Ball, "Dada Fragments 1916–1917," in *The Dada Painters and Poets: An anthology*, ed. Robert Motherwell (Cambridge: Harvard University Press, 1981), 52.
10. Heinz Schütz, "Excess of Ruins, Cult of Catastrophe: Jencks, Einstürzende Neubauten and Punk and Tödliche Doris and", in *Brilliant Dilletantes*, 136.
11. "Enfants Perdus," Merriam-Webster, accessed December 11, 2017, https://www.merriam-webster.com/dictionary/enfants%20perdus.
12. Savage, "Don't Just Watch," in *Europunk*, 193.
13. Peter Christopherson, *Photography* (Cugnaux: Timeless, 2016), n.p.
14. Savage, *England's Dreaming*, 71. See also Kugelberg and Savage, *Punk: An Aesthetic*, n.p.
15. Jerry Nolan, quoted in *Beaver County Times*, February 20, 1974, 14.
16. "The Lost Boys," Punkhouse Record Shop, accessed December 18, 2017, http://punkhouserecordshop.com/the-lost-boys-history.
17. See J. M. Barrie, *Peter Pan*, Act I, Scene 1 (London: Hodder & Stoughton, 1928).
18. Sham 69, "If the Kids Are United" (London: Polydor 1978).
19. Oskar, the son of Tödliche Doris member Dagmar Dimitroff. See Wolfgang Müller, "Das Leben des Sid Vicious," in *Die Tödliche Doris – Kino*, 29.
20. Viv Albertine quoted in Savage, *England's Dreaming*, 194–95.

21. Savage, *England's Dreaming*, 509.

22. Kunsthalle Düsseldorf, *Zurück zum Beton*, 80.

23. Dave Henderson in *Sounds*, London, July 1983, the *New Musical Express*, London, October 1983, *East Village Eye*, New York, 1984, all quoted from *Die Tödliche Doris – Kino*, 32.

24. Banana, *About VILE*, 1.

25. *FILE* 2, no. 3 (September 1973). Quoted in Banana, *About Vile*, 2.

26. Banana, *About Vile*, 2.

27. See Collection of Pauline Smith at Tate Archive, London and Pauline Smith, "Corpse Club [1977]," in Banana, *About Vile*, 59–60.

28. Banana, *About Vile*, 2.

29. P-Orridge, e-mail to Wagner, "Riot on the Page," 446.

30. Genesis P-Orridge, "To Be Ex-Dream: Photographic Sources of COUM Actions," in *Painful But Fabulous*, 155–57.

31. Genesis P-Orridge, "To Be Ex-Dream," 155–57.

32. Sigmund Freud, *A General Introduction to Psychoanalysis*, trans. G. Stanley Hall (New York: Boni and Liveright, 1920), 19.

33. Sigmund Freud, *A General Introduction*, 19. Emphasis in original.

34. Susan Laxton, *Surrealism at Play* (Durham: Duke University Press Books, 2019), 13.

35. Elizabeth Mika, "Dabrowski's View on Authentic Mental Health", in *Dabrowski's Theory of Positive Disintegration*, ed. Sal Mendaglio (Scottsdale: Great Potential Press, 2008), 142.

36. Reynolds, *Rip It Up and Start Again*, 230.

37. COUM Transmissions, *COUM Decoumposition: Schlimm* [Rottweil 1974]. MoMA Archive: MoMA Queens Artists' Books.

38. Bradley J. Stiles, *Emerson's Contemporaries and Kerouac's Crowd: A Problem of Self-location* (London: Associated University Press, 2003), 83.

39. Tutti, *Art Sex Music*, 127.

40. P-Orridge, e-mail to Wagner, "Riot on the Page," 448.

7 Work vs. Play

As Gerald Matt notes, punk manifested "differently yet consistently"[1] in different cultural spheres. In this chapter, then, we have three different, but consistent versions of the conceptual pair work vs. play, in three different cities. Across the boarders, it is about free time and free space, about youth unemployment and squatting, do-it-yourself (DIY) and dilettantism, yes, all of that, but also about a specific concept of art and life as something that is full of failures and mishaps, and that is all the more interesting, because of it.

First, we approach Amsterdam and look at how Constant Nieuwenhuys adapts Johan Huizinga's *Homo Ludens* theories to a utopian ideal of the after-war city—and the Provos act it out in small interventions. The punk movement engaged with Huizinga's notions, too, in a more dystopian version of *Punk's Homo Ludens*. Second, we consider the Ingenious Dilettantes in West Berlin, and how work vs. play integrates into their understanding of the role of the artists as well as their concept of dilettantism (and here, we make a short detour to explain the historical origin of that term). Finally, in the third part of the chapter, we deal with the experimental attitude at the Værkstedet Værst and with their "Baby Wagner Lullaby," a quite mischievous persiflage of Wagner's *Ring of the Nibelungs*.

7.1 Punk's *homo ludens*

Before we turn to punk, let us take a step back. To *play* rather than *work* had been an essential idea in the Surrealist movement[2] and later in post-Surrealist groups, such as CoBrA and the Situationist International.[3] In both Surrealism and Dada, the attack on the "sacred" status of work was combined with the idea of art-as-autonomy, meaning that aesthetic play was set up as the alternative to capitalist work, politicizing the independence of art, as Gavin Grindon argues: "The sovereignty of art, expressed in autonomy-as-a-value's ideal of free play, could be imagined as allied with attacks on other forms of sovereignty, such as that of capital or the state."[4] The Surrealists, and later the Situationists, were influenced by Johan Huizinga's seminal study *Homo Ludens* (1938). In that study, Huizinga counters the notion of *homo faber* (Latin, the working human) with *homo ludens* (Latin, the playing human) and essentially presents the thesis that the greatest achievements are reached through play, not work.

Among the artists who engaged with that idea was artist Constant Nieuwenhuys. Constant was among the founders of CoBrA, a close friend of Asger Jorn, and he also worked with Guy Debord, with whom he wrote "The Amsterdam Declaration" in 1958, which was published in *Internationale Situationiste,* expressing Situationist views on the utopian city.[5] Constant Nieuwenhuys' *New Babylon* (1952–72) was a project consisting of three-dimensional models, drawings, and declarations, all envisioning a utopian city of the future in which people could do things at their own pace, and free. Constant's *New Babylon* consisted of ideas like the collective use of space, constant mobility, no time keeping, and a complete automatization enabling creativity instead of utility. "Every reason for aggressivity [sic] has been eliminated in New Babylon," he wrote in 1974, "The conditions of life favor sublimation, and activity becomes creation."[6] Constant imagined that New Babylon would be inhabited by the *homo ludens.*

The art activist group Provos (see Section 4.2: "Punk poetry") took Constant's "New Babylon!" as a battle cry. Though Situationist International and Provo were not directly connected, they used the same vocabulary and had many of the same ideas. *New Babylon* thus provided the Provos with a "perspective for a radical socio-economic critique of society on a utopian plane," as Kempton notes.[7] Constant in turn viewed the happenings of the Provo collective as brief enactments of his ideas, and he published a detailed description of his vision in the underground pamphlet by the group *Provo* #4 (1965), in which he equates "Provo = New Babylonian."[8]

The utopianism in Constant's work was subversively linked with a dark assessment of the alternative, should that vision not come true, as becomes clear in the title of a 1971 compilation of texts in German: *Spielen oder töten: Der Aufstand des Homo Ludens* (Play or kill: The revolt of homo ludens). It was New Babylon, or violence. In his article in *Provo,* Constant emphasized the lack of understanding for the youth masses—"hipsters, teddy-boys, rockers, mods, halb-starken, blouson noirs, beatniks, nozems, stiljagi"—who were all frustrated and thirsty for action. By using the derogatory English, German, French, Dutch, and Russian expressions for the rebellious youth, he emphasized both the international nature of youthful unrest and the utter incomprehension with which it was met by authorities (and parents) in *all* countries. The many different languages are of course also a hint at the Babylon myth.

From the political Dada and Surrealist fractions to the Lettrists around Isidore Isou, the interconnectedness between youth culture, music, phonetic sound poetry, film, and visual art was not a creative byproduct, but an essential feature; this interconnectedness enabled cohesion of radical likeminded beyond national borders. Lettrist poems often sounded like scat in jazz, atonal rhythmic music, transnationally understandable. The destruction of conventional semantics, the disregard for the rules of language, was empowerment (akin to the Coumalphabet, see Section 4.1: "Punk propaganda").

In the late 1970s and early 1980s, the punk movement in Amsterdam linked itself with Provo, CoBrA, and Situationist International. Andrew Hussey describes how the slogans of Situationist International were all over the squats in Amsterdam in the early 1980s.[9] Punks in Amsterdam likewise related to the ideas expressed in Constant's *New Babylon.* Diana Ozon of the KoeCrandt group wrote a poem called *WERKLOZEN ALLER LANDEN* (*JOBLESS OF THE WORLD,* 1982), in which she proclaimed:

> Werklozen aller landen
> amuseert u!
> Mevrouw en meneer
> profiteer en recreëer
> werk is uit den boze
> leef en geniet
> als een werkloze.[10]

A rough translation would be:

> Jobless of the world
> keep amused!
> men and women
> benefit and recreate
> work is impossible
> enjoy
> be unemployed.

["Recreation" here is meant in the sense of "leisure," not "re-creation" in the sense of "recreating something."] The poem overlaps with Constant's vision in terms of international solidarity, (re)creation, and no work. The title alludes both to the famous slogan of Karl Marx's *Communist Manifesto* (1848), in Dutch "Proletariërs aller landen, verenigt u!" ("Workers of the world, unite!"), and to the situation in the Netherlands at the time, with massive youth unemployment. The unemployment rate for people between 15 and 25 years of age had jumped from 2.0 percent in 1970 to 17.3 percent in 1983.[11] Ozon's poem reverses the pessimism of that situation. Punk is thus perceived as a playground, the realization of free space and free time (and thus a free mind).

In *En Avant Dada: A History of Dadaism* (1920), Richard Huelsenbeck and Raoul Hausmann had presented a similar vision. Under the heading "What is Dadaism and what does it want in Germany?" Huelsenbeck and Hausmann respond: "The introduction of progressive unemployment through comprehensive mechanization of every field of activity. Only by unemployment does it become possible for the individual to achieve certainty as to the truth of life and finally become accustomed to experience."

For this purpose, the Dadaists demanded "[d]aily meals at public expense for all creative and intellectual men and women on the Potsdamer Platz [Berlin]."[12] Huelsenbeck and Hausmann's call echoes both in the *New Babylon* and in punk ideas of unemployment. In all three versions (Dada, Constant, punk), it was the complete automatization and respective mechanization that would enable this recreative unemployment.

"We had two views," Kaagman explains, "One was 1984, apocalypse, everything is going to be over. Babylon is falling. On the other hand, we had a vision of the robots coming to do all the work and we can recreate."[13] Both visions are connected with a sense of being on the verge of something, a fin-de-siècle sentiment transferred to the late 1970s.

> We thought, either the world is going down, or paradise is coming. In a way I think now, both are happening at the same time. The computers are taking over a lot of stupid work. In the punk time, we did not know it was going to be like that.

Kaagman reminisces,

> Now, google knows everything! In the punk time, we were even against post codes. Fuck it! That is control! We were against credit cards, we were against administration, we associated it with fascism, with the Second World War.

"Babylon shall fall […] that is a realistic vision," Kaagman wrote in *Het Parool* in August 1979.[14] The equivocation of the Babylon notion in Amsterdam's punk culture becomes clear in the connotations of such a statement. There is a drawing back from Constant's *New Babylon* vision, which is replaced by the anticipation of a doomed future. There is also an allusion to the biblical myth of Babylon's downfall in Kaagman's choice of words, in the scriptural expression "shall fall" (Jeremiah 51:49), which fits in with the apocalyptic instinct of the punk community. And then there is the fact that Kaagman wrote this sentence just two months after the punk/reggae band the Ruts had released "Babylon's Burning" in June 1979, with Malcolm Owen, forcefully singing over sirens: "Babylon's burning, baby can't you see? / Babylon is burning with anxiety / It's positively smoldering / With ignorance and hate."[15] In reggae music, Babylon is referenced as a symbol of oppression and discrimination. There was more common ground between reggae and punk than is often superficially assumed,[16] and in Amsterdam punk, this bond was particularly strong. The KoeCrandt zine thus made several special issues on reggae and Rastafarian culture in the late 1970s and early 1980s.

The second vision of Babylon in the post-war cultural history of Amsterdam was thus the punk *Burning Babylon*. This concept echoed Constant's *New Babylon*, but in the paradoxical manner that was so characteristic of the punk movement. The connotations of rebellion and insubordination in the myth of Babylon—particularly the Tower of Babylon—were nurtured and mixed with the Provo's and Constant's imaginings about the New Babylonians as *homo ludens*. At the same time, however, Babylon was associated with a tyrannical and repressive system, and its fall was urged on and celebrated. Two visions of the city and its future thus collide and mirror each other in the postwar cultural history of Amsterdam; interestingly, both use Babylon as a symbol. The negative biblical connotations of Babylon—Babylon, the city of rebellion against God; Babylon, the city of sin and pride—reverberate, but in both visions are turned around. Punk's conflicting visions of gloom and rapture were thus mixed into this one potent urban symbol, *New Babylon, Burning Babylon*. Likewise, Punk's *homo ludens* was a dystopian version of Huizinga and Constant's utopian vision. Constant's "hipsters, teddy-boys, rockers, mods, halb-starken, blouson noirs, beatniks, nozems, stiljagi" were now the punks, and yes, they were thirsty for action, but they were also desperados, not actually expecting to change the circumstances for the better, not envisioning a brighter future, but rather responding to the imminent cultural crisis and de facto mass unemployment.

7.2 Ingenious Dilettantes

Dilettantism is a key concept in punk. Dilettantism equals to DIY and likewise fits with the punk notion of free time and free space (mostly enabled through unemployment and squatting). Artists who associated themselves with punk had a specific idea about dilettantism not only as practice but as a philosophy. Fractions such as the Ingenious Dilettantes in West Berlin (we will return to them in a few sentences) thus very consciously positioned themselves in an old discussion of work vs. play, genius vs. idiocy, and sense vs. nonsense. Again, we see an alignment of punk artists with figures of the radical fractions of Dada and Surrealism in particular.

The origin of the term dilettantism is the Latin word *delectare*, meaning to delight in something.[17] In the seventeenth and eighteenth centuries, dilettantism was used in opposition to professionalism, that is, to describe both musicians and visual artists for whom their creation was not a means of subsistence, but pleasure (and who thus mostly belonged to the upper or middle classes). Johann Wolfgang von Goethe and Friedrich Schiller slandered the mediocrity and lack of genius in the "dilettante" in their text *Über den Dilettantismus* (*About Dilettantism*, 1799), which they wrote together. Especially the tendency of the dilettante to always plagiarize was criticized by Goethe and Schiller (which might call to mind the discussion on Section 5.1: "Originality and appropriation"). Whereas "dilettante" is generally used derogatorily, decadent authors, such as Charles

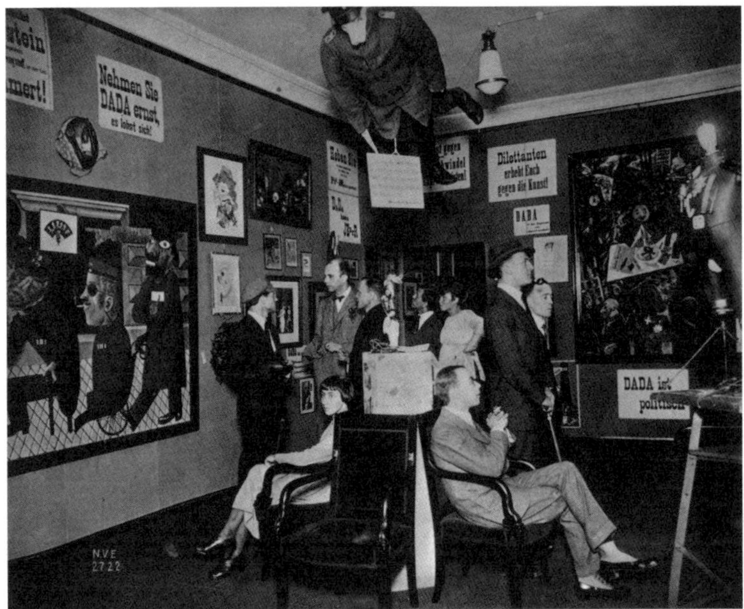

Figure 7.1: Opening of the First International Dada Fair in Berlin, July 1920. On the back wall, the sign "Dilettanten erhebt Euch gegen die Kunst!" © VG Bild-Kunst, Bonn 2022.

Baudelaire, and later the artistic reform movement in the late nineteenth and early twentieth century embraced the idea, linking it with enthusiasm, the processual, and a critical distance toward predefined objectives. The Dadaists drew on these positions, and furthermore linked dilettantism with an attack on artworld structures. The message on the sign that hung over the entrance at the First International Dada Fair in Berlin in 1920—"Dilettanten erhebt Euch gegen die Kunst!" (Dilettantes, rise up against art! Figure 7.1)—was a slogan both for independence and rebellion.

Dilettantism in Dada became linked both with anti-art and anti-work: anti-art against art as a commodity, anti-work against the capitalist system. As Gavin Grindon summarizes, in Dada: "Th[e] rupture with the idea of art was bound up with a rupture with the idea of *work*."[18] Art should neither be bourgeois amusement, nor should the artist be defined by his or her centimeter cost at the latest art sale. Instead, Dadaists argued that one's mode of living in itself could be considered art. Dadaists admired figures such as the hedonistic poet, artist, bartender, and boxer "Arthur Cravan," aka Fabian Avenarius Lloyd, whose oeuvre chiefly consisted of the course of his life.[19] Ten years after the "Dilettantes, rise up against art!" slogan, the Parisian Dada group had merged into Surrealists and were being accused of careerism, of slipping into a commodity. Bréton, in an attempt to rebut this, wrote in the *Second Manifesto of Surrealism*:

> There are still today, in the lycées, even in the workshops, in the street, the seminaries and military barracks, pure young people who refuse to knuckle down. It is to them and them alone that I address myself, it is for them alone that I am trying to defend Surrealism against the accusation that it is, after all, no more than an intellectual pastime like any other.[20]

The refusal "to knuckle down" was exactly that: refusal of work. Punk's conception of lifestyle-as-art, the *homo ludens* of punk, agreed with this idea of merging art and life. In West Berlin in the late 1970s and early 1980s, a movement came out of it: the *Geniale Dilletanten* (Ingenious Dilettantes), at the forefront of which were the members of Die Tödliche Doris.

In West Berlin in the late 1970s and early 1980s, many punks were "artists without works,"[21] as Müller describes: their life was their performance. They looked to Warhol's superstars who had likewise incorporated the idea of living art, even if in a highly mediated way. Parallel to punk, in the 1970–80s, photographers such as Nan Goldin, Larry Clark, and Robert Mapplethorpe documented the private spheres, abuse, parties, drugs, and sexual acts of and between themselves and their friends, and their community. Performances and actions took place in small venues, clubs and bars, such as the joint performance *Wassermusik* (Watermusic) by Einstürzende Neubauten and Die Tödliche Doris in the club RISIKO in West Berlin in 1982 (Figure 7.2). These artists' identity and lifestyle became integral to the work as artists; their photographs were like subcultural family albums. Between 1982 and 1984, Nan Goldin also lived and worked for shorter periods of time in West Berlin, where she photographed the scene and stayed in Kreuzberg in the squat house of Die Tödliche Doris member Käthe Kruse.

Since many artists at this time were squatting, they were living cheap. Not having to pay rent liberated the artists from the worst monetary pressures and thus meant artistic freedom. In West Berlin, most of them used this freedom for leisure, as Wolfgang Müller describes in *Subkultur Westberlin,* which is subtitled *Freizeit* (Free time). This way of life was connected to an anti-authoritarian, anti-capitalistic ideal of not pursuing a career: not just nothing "respectable," but not even a career as an artist. In the late 1970s and early 1980s, the commercial artworld structures (galleries, collectors, art fairs) were indeed insignificant in West Berlin in comparison to Cologne, Düsseldorf, and Munich. It was, as Müller puts it, "the time before the big-game hunters arrived."[22] Artists, who did pursue a career, were accordingly not inclined to seek it in West Berlin. The conformists' advice on how not to waste one's youth was reversed into a proud affirmation on how to do just that: "Waste your youth!"[23]

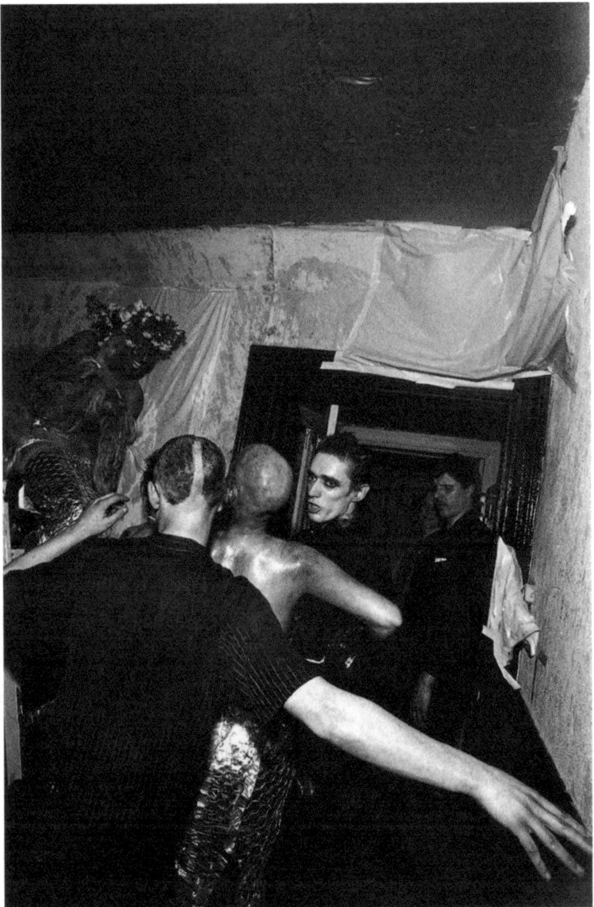

Figure 7.2: Joint performance Wassermusik *(Watermusic) by Einstürzende Neubauten and Die Tödliche Doris in the club RISIKO in West Berlin, 1982. Photograph by Anno Dittmer. Courtesy of Anno Dittmer.*

The term *Geniale Dilletanten* was coined by Blixa Bargeld (of the band Einstürzende Neubauten) after the avant-garde art historian Carl Einstein's 1912 novel *Bebuquin oder die Dilettanten des Wunders* (*Bebuquin or the Dilettantes of the Miracle*).[24] On a flyer advertising the first joint event, the Festival Genialer Dilletanten in 1981, dilettante was misspelled with a double "l" and single "t": Dilletante (in German *Dilettant* is correct; for more on the festival, see Section 10.2: "The Grand Downfall Show"). For the publication, the editors, among others Die Tödliche Doris, decided to keep it: Erring fitted the artistic concept. As inspiration for integrating the mistake, Müller refers to two Dada sources: Marcel Duchamp's magazine *RONGWRONG* and the poem "fmsbwtzäu," which Raoul Hausmann took from a misprint on a Czech poster.[25]

The "ingenious" or "brilliant" before "dilettantes" was a way of ridiculing the pseudo-mystical talent of the artist-genius. "The serious musician or artist is a victim of his own inbreeding," Müller writes, and further: "Where actual emptiness is visible, dilettantism can evoke a provocative shock by attacking this 'progress,' which is most antiquated, with noise and racket."[26] The line of reasoning then, was that the process of refinement, whether in art or music, only covers up emptiness. Here, "mistakes"—stuttering, forgetting, mispronouncing, wasting, and losing—are understood to be productive.[27] In art, the Ingenious Dilettantes argued, nonsense was often more stimulating than sense, a fail more interesting than perfection.

In the *Geniale Dilletanten* publication, the movement also connected dilettantism with a view of art as a process instead of a finished object, a criticism of originality as an absolute term, and a skeptical attitude toward moralistic or pretentious declarations in art. In the view of the Ingenious Dilettantes, silliness was better than seriousness, and yes, play better than work. "Those who have understood the idea of Dilettantism properly will never be able to become serious musicians," writes Müller, "That would be the end, death itself."[28] Lack of skill was conceived in terms of openness, playfulness, and was cast as the opposite of the stubbornness, tenseness, of the "serious" artist or musician. Through the publication and its reception, the Brilliant Dilettantes came to be understood as a movement, the West Berlin artists version of punk. Diedrich Diedrichsen makes the claim that "Rather than the first generation of dilettantes, they were the second generation of Fluxus."[29] Wolfgang Müller, however, though acknowledging a certain kinship, also distances punk from Fluxus: "There was a protestant cheerfulness to Fluxus, which we disliked [...] Fluxus, if you want to be a bit mean, or critical, never addressed its own limits."[30] The artists of the Brilliant Dilettantes wanted to be grittier, more real, and perhaps also less (or inversely) successful.

In this sense, punk was engaged in a double rupture: "It was not only about not being *able* to do something, but not being *willing*," said Thomas Meinecke, the singer and guitarist of F. S. K.[31] He is playing on a conservative bon mot in Germany—"Kunst kommt vom Können, nicht vom Wollen, sonst hieße es Wunst" (art comes from *a*bility, not *i*ntention, otherwise it would be called irt)—which had been in use since the nineteenth century, was popular with the Nazis,[32] and was restated every so often as a critique of modern art. It has been countered with other versions over the years. With a certain degree of pathos, Arnold Schönberg stated "Kunst kommt vom Müssen,"[33] that is, art comes from necessity. The version "Kunst kommt vom Künden," that is, art comes from announcing, is attributed to Joseph Beuys.[34] Meinecke's claim—not able and not willing—thus also makes clear punk's difference to the omnipresent Joseph

Beuys. What is distinctive in Meinecke's assertion, is that he refuses to engage in *any* sort of justification.

Beuys did however play a central role in German punk, as Thomas Groetz has disclosed.[35] Whereas the connections were much closer in Beuys' hometown of Düsseldorf, there were encounters in West Berlin, too, where Beuys assumed sponsorship of a squat house in Bülowstraße, and donated drawings for a "Soli" (solidarity) exhibition for the squatted Villa Schilla in Schillerstraße.[36] At the same time, some punks were critical of Beuys' propensity to taking a kind of anthroposophic savior pose as well as his entanglement with rich collectors, such as Erich Marx, who, as a property investor, was on the opposite side of the squatting conflict. As a motif, punk's "not able and not willing" relates to both: the artist does not have the solution and he/she rejects cooption. The artists and musicians who were involved with punk did not want to belong: no professionalism, but also no explanation, no pronouncement, no edifying mission.

7.3 "The Baby Wagner Lullaby," or Brilliance blackout

At the Værkstedet Værst in Copenhagen, meanwhile, some of the same ideas were taken up. The group's signature workshop was to be a former tea warehouse at Rosenørns Allé 29, but this was not where they actually began. They started in 1981 in the summer cottage of artist Per Kirkeby, who liked the group and offered them a space until they got their own.[37] Then, from January 1, 1982 until the place was torn down in the winter of 1983/84, the artists rented (very cheaply) the large tea factory and depot that had been slated for demolition, and which was situated above the printing shop of Eks-skolen ("the Ex-School").

The Ex-School had been an anti-academy, process-oriented, and open art school situated on Nørrebro from 1961 to 1969. Among many others, Per Kirkeby, the provocateur Bjørn Nørgaard, John Davidsen (who had criticized Elmer's poster, see Section 4.1: "Punk propaganda"), and Fluxus artist Eric Andersen attended the Ex-School.[38] Two of the Ex-School initiators, Poul Gernes and Peter Louis-Jensen, actually worked at Værkstedet Værst for a short time.[39] The link between Værkstedet Værst and the Ex-School was significant, especially if we consider the Ex-School's earlier years of absurd provocation. The "ex" in "Ex-School" could simultaneously stand for the abbreviation of "experimenting," but also for "not" or "out of," that is: not a school, out of school. The artists involved with the Ex-School criticized hierarchy and egoism in art, and instead pursued an anti-academic, egalitarian, and autodidactic ideal. (If that ideal was always met, or if not a palpable trace of the myth of the [White, male] genius remained is a different story.)

In a direct reference to their neighbor downstairs, the initial members of Værkstedet Værst put up posters promoting "Den eksperimenterende kunstskole" (The experimental art school). The experimental art school of Værkstedet Værst, however, was half-fictional. The artists cashed in money from the authorities for offering a course in art, but after a month the only "student" left was Lars Nørgård. From then on, the artists put up two signs on each side of the large building, in case someone should come by checking on their course activities. On the one side, the sign said "Er på Louisiana" ("We're at Louisiana [Art Museum]") on the other "Er på Glyptoteket" ("We're at the glyptotheque").[40]

The experiment played a key role in the working process of Værkstedet Værst, and the group's sense of self was closely connected to that working process, and thus, indeed, to its purpose as a workshop. Several works from this period were destroyed, canvases were re-used, overpainted, installations were lost. At the same time, the artworks were done at high speed, resulting in a high frequency of exhibitions: ten to fifteen alone in the first year of the Workshop.[41]

Værkstedet Værst was simultaneously shared atelier, half-fake art school, exhibition and performance space, and (at times) a place to sleep. "On an average, Christian [Lemmerz] and me slept there—as far as I remember—around four nights a week," Nørgård recounts.[42] The artists worked in different media; painting, sculpture, installation, actions, and performance. The artistic process was often spontaneous and collective. The space itself became part of the art:

> The tea factory was huge […] One day, we were walking through the ground level, which was just one big space. We found some deep holes in the floor, it was sort of dangerous. So, we went to the grocery shop and bought ten kilos of flour to fill into each of the holes. Then Christian [Lemmerz] said, 'We will call them The Elephant's Dead Footprints.' It was very poetic.[43]

That sense of the poetic is likewise mirrored in the title *Græsset malker koens ben* (*The Grass Milks the Leg of the Cow*), an exhibition that took place at Værkstedet Værst in 1983. The catalog, which was printed in-house at the Eks-Skolen Forlag, was kept simple: no text, no explanation, only nineteen drawings, and an index by Lars Nørgård (Figure 7.3), all in black and white. The imagery of the index matches Nørgård's poster and invitation: capital letters, some of them reversed, simple signs (skull and bones, daggers, spiked maces, and rockets), and a chaotic, thrown-together Xeroxed look. The title of the exhibition was taken from a line in a poem by a schizophrenic Austrian named Herbert, Lemmerz recounts: "Das Gras Melcht der Kuh ein Bein."[44] At the same time,

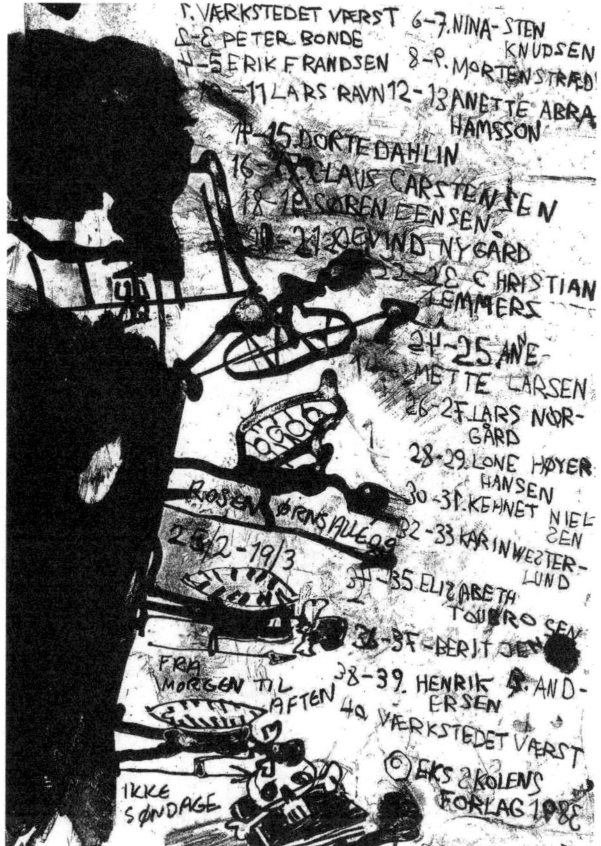

Figure 7.3: Lars Nørgård, index of the catalogue The Grass Milks the Leg of the Cow, *1983. Courtesy of Lars Nørgård.*

long sentences or parts of poems were often used as titles of artworks or exhibitions, a feature which underlines the cross-conceptual and intermedia aspects of the scene. As an exhibition title, *The Grass Milks the Leg of the Cow* furthermore transports a sense of the upside-down; in the context of the frenzied visuals of the featured works, the nonsensical (or Surrealistic) becomes programmatic. At the same time, the rural imagery of the title (grass, milk, cow) starkly contrasts with the urbanity, both in the exhibition's location and in the subjects of the artworks.

At the opening of *The Grass Milks the Leg of the Cow* (Figure 7.4), the punk band Tapehead played: a loose constellation of musicians from Sods and No Knox; whoever had time on the night of the concert would play. Søren Ulrik Thomsen read his poems. According to both contemporary witnesses and photos from the evening, the space was crowded, perhaps also as a result of a large number of artists participating: the catalogue

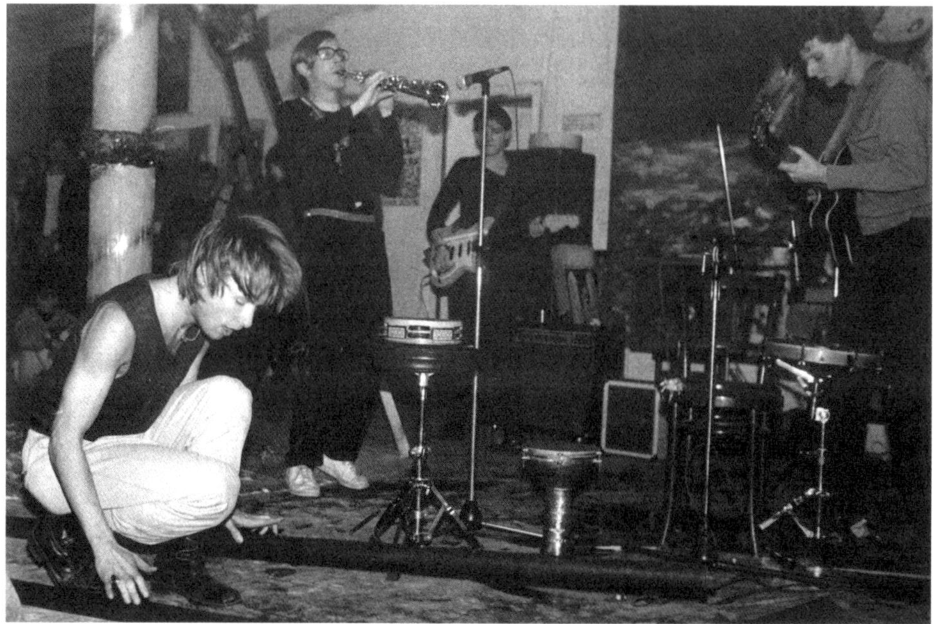

Figure 7.4: Tapehead performs at Værkstedet Værst (The workshop called worst), 1983. Photograph by Steen Møller Rasmussen. Courtesy of Steen Møller Rasmussen and Lars Nørgård.

features nineteen artists, whereas on the poster 23 names are listed; Nørgård remembers "over thirty."[45] The number of participants may very well have changed during the course of events; this was not a curated, conceptually tight-knit exhibition, but an open space. "People just brought whatever they wanted," says Nørgård.

A year earlier, in September of 1982, a performance that took place at Værkstedet Værst, stretching over three consecutive days, united humor, anarchy, and anti-genius: *Der Ring der Nibelungen* (Richard Wagner's *Ring of the Nibelungs* premiered at the Bayreuth Festival in 1876, and likewise stretched over three days). The Værkstedet Værst rendering was, in the words of Stjernfeldt and Tøjner, "conducted in a collective furor against academism."[46] Wagner furthermore incorporates the ultimate "genius" myth, the successor in spirit of Goethe and Schiller's criticism of dilettantism.

Apart from the members of Værkstedet Værst, several international performers made guest appearances, among others, the German Norbert Tefelskij, the Belgian Jacques Calonne, and the Englishman Ian Hinchliffe—the very same Hinchliffe who had been involved in a fight with the Director of the ICA, Ted Little, and one of the Kipper Kids, Brian Routh, at COUM Transmissions' *PROSTITUTION* opening in 1976 (see Section 4.3: "Crime as art, scandal as art"). Jacques Calonne had in turn been part of CoBrA as well as Fluxus and Movemente Arte Nucleare activities in the 1940s and

1950s. As Kamma Overgaard Hansen remarks, Værkstedet Værst thus "took the role of a catalyst for the art scenes of different times and places."[47]

The performance was not a faithful rendering of the ultra-complex *Ring of the Nibelungs*, but a rather ludicrous and cacophonic composition of visual and musical elements, fragments from Wagner's opera, enactments of half-true or entirely made up of details from Wagner's life story, unrelated fragments from other sources, and a fifth scene being added to the fourth act that does not exist in the original *Ring of the Nibelungs*, and in which Wagner "eventually dies whilst freaking out," followed first by a "grotesque procession," and then "blackout."[48]

There are two sources of information about this performance: one is the script and the other a series of black-and-white photos from the event, some of which were published in *CRAS*; these two sources do not always accord, underlining that the rendering was characterized by improvisation. The play revolves around Wagner himself: he is introduced with the "Baby Wagner Lullaby," sung to the tunes of "Rockabye Baby" and accompanied by flutes and the sound of breaking glass.

> Rock a bye Wagner in the House top
> Shitting his nappy ploppety plop
> When the shit stops the pissing will start
> Oh no my God, he's starting to fart.

So the text goes in a Dadaistic and infantile dismantling of the genius. According to the manuscript, the musicians improvise, but are urged to maintain a "Wagnerian heroic style." Following the "Baby Wagner Lullaby," a narrator—according to the script, the pregnant Marlene Dietrich wearing a cage on her head—praises Wagner's brilliance:

> Percy Wagner was not only a child prodege [*sic*] in music, but his talents amounted to winning the long jump event at the Stuttgart Olympics whilst still in his pram. He made an exact replica of the Concord before he was one year old. This worked perfectly and transported 30 mice from Berlin to Albertslund in 4 minutes, 12 seconds flat.

The description breathes anarchistic humor, exaggeration, childishness, and sensationalism. Pure swindle. The artists travesty the notion of genius, and they themselves act in the most banal way, undercutting the Gesamtkunstwerk notion of brilliance with fart jokes and dilettante manners. Nonetheless, themes from the original play, such as death, greed, and destruction are also absorbed, and—after all—blended into the remix. The hyper-referencing from all categories of low and high culture, reality and fantasy, and from diverse epochs (Marlene Dietrich, the Concord, the lullaby, etc.) furthermore emphasizes the notion of fragmentation in opposition to Wagner's artistic synthesis. As in the cases of the KoeCrandt group and the Ingenious Dilettantes, Værkstedet Værst likewise ridicules the old-fashioned, serious genius.

Both the infantilism, which we examined in Chapter 6: "Children Run Riot: The Art of the Infantile," as well as the dilettantism encountered in this chapter represent an understanding of art, which is more about failure than success, which emphasizes free time over career, and which watches the world through absurdity, not holism. Dilettantism in punk art is connected to the search for autonomy (DIY!) and anti-authority Punk art's "not able and not willing" refusal to engage in the justification and explanation of itself is a refusal to contribute to any progress. "The rationale of progress is obsolete", as Wolfgang Müller wrote in *Geniale Dilletanten*.[49] This negation was expressed as a critique of careerism and pretentiousness, but also in a manifest distance toward moralism in art. Furthermore, the anti-academism stand runs through both chapters, as do notions such as the integration of coincidence and error, the fragmentation of process, and the substitution of play for work.

To Arthur Cravan, the quote is attributed: "Perhaps I am the king of failures, for I am surely the king of something." (A quote that is not verified, but not much is when it comes to the life of Arthur Cravan.) The "Arthur Cravans" of punk made it clear that punk was as much a way of living as it was a way of making art or music. It was about everyday performance. With that notion in mind, we turn in the following two chapters to: performance, appearance, lifestyle, sexuality, Sadism, Masochism, black sheep, bad girls, bad boys, and Jordan, "Queen of the punk rock style" (and quite surely the queen of something!) who stated: "I wanted to be a living work of art."[50] But first we turn to: SEX.

Notes

1. Gerald Matt, "Vorwort," 7.

2. See Abigail Susik, *Surrealist Sabotage and the War on Work* (Manchester: Manchester University Press, 2021) as well as Laxton, *Surrealism at Play.*

3. See Libero Andreotti, "Architecture and Play," in *Guy Debord and the Situationist International: Texts and Documents,* ed. Tom McDonough (Cambridge: MIT Press, 2002), 213–40.

4. Gavin Grindon, "Surrealism, Dada, and the Refusal of Work: Autonomy, Activism, and Social Participation in the Radical Avant-Garde," *Oxford Art Journal* 34 (2011), 83–84. Emphasis in original.

5. Andrew Hussey, "Mapping Utopia: Debord and Constant between Amsterdam and Paris," in *Paris-Amsterdam Underground,* 39.

6. Constant Nieuwenhuys quoted in Mark Wigley, "New Babylon: Outline of a Culture [1974]," in *Constant's New Babylon: The Hyper-architecture of Desire* (Rotterdam: Witte de With Center for Contemporary Art/010 Publishers, 1998), 163.

7. Kempton, *The Provos*, 86.

8. Constant Nieuwenhuys, "NEW BABYLON," in *Provo #4* (October 28, 1965).

9. Hussey, "Mapping Utopia," 37.

10. Diana Ozon, *Laag Bij De Gronds* (Amsterdam: Guus Bauer, 1982).

11. Voogd, "Punk in Amsterdam," n.p.

12. Richard Huelsenbeck, "En Avant Dada: A History of Dadaism (1920)," in *The Dada Painters and Poets*, 41.

13. Kaagman, interview, 2017.

14. Hugo Kaagman, August 17, 1979, quoted in Jonker, *NO Future NU*, 57.

15. The Ruts, "Babylon's Burning" (London: Virgin, 1979).

16. See Don Letts and David Nobakht, *Culture Clash: Dread Meets Punk Rockers* (London: SAF Publishing, 2008) and Clinton Heylin, *Babylon's Burning: From Punk to Grunge* (London: Penguin, 2007).

17. Harald Olbrich et al., eds., *Lexikon der Kunst*, vol. 2 (Leipzig: Seemann Henschel, 2004), 163.

18. Grindon, "Surrealism, Dada, and the Refusal of Work," 84. Emphasis in original.

19. Gabrielle Buffet-Picabia, "Arthur Cravan and American Dada [1938]," in *The Dada Painters and Poets* (Cambridge, MA: Harvard University Press, 1981).

20. André Breton, "Second Manifesto of Surrealism (1930)," in *Manifestoes of Surrealism*, eds. Seaver and Lane (Ann Arbor: University of Michigan Press, 1969), 134.

21. Müller, *Subkultur Westberlin*, 262.

22. Wolfgang Müller, "Produktion West 1980: Punk, Kunst, Aura: Die wilden Jahre, bevor die Großwildjäger kamen," in *Lettre International*, no. 86 (Fall 2009), 115.

23. See Jürgen Teipel, *Verschwende Deine Jugend: Ein Doku-Roman über den deutschen Punk und New Wave* (Frankfurt am Main: Suhrkamp, 2001) and Detlef Diederichsen, "Wie ich mal meine Jugend verschwendete," in *Zurück zum Beton*.

24. Müller and Schmitz, *Die Tödliche Doris – Kunst*, 50.

25. Müller, interview, 2017.

26. Müller, "Die wahren Dilletanten," 12.

27. Müller and Schmitz, *Die Tödliche Doris – Kunst*, 52.

28. Müller, "Die wahren Dilletanten," 12.

29. Diedrich Diedrichsen, interview with Ulrich Gutmair in "Geniale Dilletanten: Als das Nichtkönnen produktiv wurde," accessed April 5, 2018, https://www.goethe.de/de/kul/bku/20488988.html.

30. Müller, interview, 2013.

31. Staatliche Kunstsammlungen Dresden, "Geniale Dilletanten: Subkultur der 1980er Jahre in Deutschland," YouTube video, accessed December 18, 2017, https://www.youtube.com/watch?v=-MSN2P5VIs4.

32. Katrin Engelhardt, "Die Ausstellung , Entartete Kunst in Berlin 1938: Rekonstruktion und Analyse," in *Angriff auf die Avantgarde: Kunst und Kunstpolitik im Nationalsozialismus*, ed. Uwe Fleckner (Berlin: Akademie Verlag, 2007), 104.

33. Arnold Schönberg, "Probleme des Kunstunterrichts [1911]," in Arnold Schönberg, *Stil und Gedanke: Aufsätze zur Musik 1909–1950* (Frankfurt am Main: S. Fischer, 1976).

34. Günther Uecker, "Die Kunst des Kündens," in *Die Zeit* 6 (1986), accessed December 18, 2017, https://www.zeit.de/1986/06/die-kunst-des-kuendens.

35. See Thomas Groetz, *Kunst–Musik: Deutscher Punk und New Wave in der Nachbarschaft von Joseph Beuys* (Berlin: Martin Schmitz Verlag, 2002).

36. See Marius Babias, "Die Décollage des Kapitalistischen Realismus," in *Jungle World*, no. 1, 1999.

37. Frederik Stjernfeldt and Poul Erik Tøjner, *Billedstorm: Om dansk kunst og kultur på det seneste* (Copenhagen: Amadeus, 1989), 14.

38. For more on the Ex-School, see Lars Morell, *Broderskabet: Den Eksperimenterende Kunstskole 1961–69* (Copenhagen: Thaning & Appel, 2009) and Tania Ørum, *De eksperimenterende tressere: kunst i en opbrudstid* (Copenhagen: Gyldendal, 2009).

39. Ross, *Lars Nørgård*, 20.

40. Stjernfeldt and Tøjner, *Billedstorm*, 60.

41. Ross, *Lars Nørgård*, 20.

42. Nørgård, interview, 2018.

43. Nørgård, interview, 2018.

44. Lemmerz, interview, 2018.

45. Lemmerz, interview, 2018.

46. Stjernfeldt and Tøjner, *Billedstorm*, 60.

47. Kamma Overgaard Hansen, "Vi har ikke noget at sige, men vi gør det så koncentreret som muligt," *De Unge Vilde i dansk kunst*, PhD dissertation (Aarhus: Universitet, 2017), 264.

48. Original score reproduced in Hansen, "Vi har ikke noget at sige," Appendix.

49. Müller, "Die wahren Dilletanten," 12.

50. Lauren Cochrane, "'I Wanted to be a Living Work of Art': Why Jordan Is the Queen of Punk Rock Style," in *The Guardian*, accessed April 7, 2021, https://www.theguardian.com/fashion/2021/apr/06/i-wanted-to-be-a-living-work-of-art-why-jordan-is-the-queen-of-punk-rock-style.

8 SEX

As punk was challenging society's confines, sex was bound to be a central theme. "The whole thing was about looking at things with a fresh eye," Viv Albertine of the Slits told Jon Savage, "and sexuality had to be looked at."[1] In an interview with Len Richmond in the soft porn magazine *Forum* in June 1976, Vivienne Westwood stated about her famous shop on King's Road:

> The whole point of SEX is that we want to inspire other people with the confidence to live out their fantasies and to change. We really are making a political statement with this shop by attempting to attack the system.[2]

Punk addressed the darker aspects of sex, those associated with money, violence, and power relations. The way sex was depicted, it became a counter-concept both to the traditional heteronormative family structure and to the hippie delusion of an alternative "free love" which had generally turned out not to be so free after all. Correspondingly, love was a damaged word, over-used, out of touch, and meaningless to punks. "Why would I want to fall in love?" sang Talking Heads in 1978, "Do people really fall in love?"[3] David Bowie said, "I am not at ease with the word love."[4] In the *Village Voice*, Christgau cited Rotten: "Love is what you feel for a dog or a pussy cat. It doesn't apply to humans."[5] Punk demystified and made fun of romantic clichés. On the cover of Radio Star's "Songs for Swinging Lovers" (1977; referencing the eponymous Frank Sinatra album) was, quite wickedly, a picture of a young couple hanging (i.e. swinging) from a tree, in front of a romantic sundown. With a great deal of irony, punk dismantled the nostalgic myth of love, at least the standard superficial version, "as seen on TV." Punks perceived the romantic and family clichés, as they were being pushed by conservative society, as tools to promote both a reactionary concept of femininity as well as consumerism. Dismantling these clichés thus became especially essential for punk women. The overt sexuality displayed in punk art and fashion, like Westwood's T-shirts with cocks and tits, served as a vehicle for affecting liberation, but so did the androgynous style of many young punks. Either perceived as overtly sexual or anti-sexual, the punk movement questioned conformist gender formulae.

Matthew Worley writes,

> The showing of Kenneth Anger's *Scorpio Rising* (1963) at the Sex Pistols' seminal Screen on the Green gig of 29 August 1976, replete with interconnecting scenes of leather, sex, swastikas, and gay bikers on acid, revealed all too clearly McLaren's homology of subversion.[6]

Especially in the early days of punk, there was an overlap between the queer and the punk scenes, and a sense of community, reinforced by a shared sense of exclusion as well as a shared interest in performativity and gender fluidity, as we shall see in the first part of this chapter: "Queer Punks and Dykes in High Heels." In the following two sections, "Defiant prostitutes, porn artists and well-dressed whores" as well as "Sadism and submission," we dive deeper into punk's relationship with deviant sexuality. Again, the link to the Surrealists becomes especially clear: opposition to patriarchal structures, overt sexuality (also female desire!) as a channel to revolution, as well as an outspoken interest in S&M all underline this link. In the final part of this chapter—"Punk feminism: Vamp up!"—we look at how punk women positioned themselves with regard to feminism in the late 1970s and early 1980s, by staging themselves as sexy femmes fatales, warriors with machine guns, and as black sheep feminists.

8.1 Queer punks and dykes in high heels

"Before it got a label, it was a club for misfits," Siouxsie Sioux told Jon Savage, "Waifs, male gays, female gays, bisexuals, non-sexuals, everything."[7] This is how early punk is most often described: a community for all those who opposed the conventional way of life; it was about personal empowerment. Punks denounced the hegemonic society, which they saw as oppressive and dishonest. Queerness was also a model counter to rock's macho impulse. "The New York Dolls cross-dressed in their platform heels, wigs, and satin suits. This context opens the door to the entrance of sexuality into rock that is not just hetero or masculine," David Torres writes.[8] There is thus a connection reaching from 1960s and 1970s New York transvestite visibility—Lou Reed, New York Dolls, Divine—to queerness in punk: for example, the *Queerpunk Manifesto*[9]—and continuing into the emerging queercore subculture of the 1980s.[10]

Tellingly, Dick Hebdige begins his seminal book *Subculture: The Meaning of Style* (1979), with a long and poignant quote by the French poet, writer, vagabond, and petty criminal Jean Genet, who describes the laughter and humiliation he must endure when police find Vaseline in his possession, and they, "strong in their moral assurance" as Genet writes, make hostile jokes about his homosexuality.

> I have chosen to begin with these extracts from Genet because he more than most has explored in both his life and his art the subversive implications of style. I shall be returning again and again to Genet's major themes: the status and meaning of revolt, the idea of style as a form of Refusal, the elevation of crime into art.[11]

Genet was influential in punk culture, as was Oscar Wilde. The Irish punk rock band Virgin Prunes, for example incorporated lines from Wilde's poem "The Ballad of Reading Gaol" (1898) in their song "Theme for Thought" (1982). Wilde wrote the poem about his experiences in the Reading Gaol prison, after being sentenced to two years of hard labor for "gross indecency" with another man. Not only that decadent look, the dandiness of Oscar Wilde, was attractive to punks, but his flamboyance and nonconformity, his combination of clear-eyed cynicism and touching outsider sentiment: "We are all in the gutter, but some of us are looking at the stars."[12]

One of the reasons that many of the first punk events took place in queer clubs was that here, the punks would not get beat up; there was a sense of shared exclusion.[13] Early punk for a large part was played out in queer clubs, in London as well as in New York. The very first punks simply drew on the already existing alternative spaces. In Copenhagen, for example, that was the gay venues Pan and Cozy, because, as Per Buhl Ács explains, "there, we were not assaulted."[14] On their LP *Power in the Darkness* (1978), British punk band TRB (Tom Robinson Band) established the common enemy of a violent police force. On the track, "Glad To Be Gay," Robinson sarcastically sings:

> The British police are the best in the world
> I don't believe one of those stories I heard
> 'Bout them raiding our pubs for no reason at all
> Lining the customers up by the wall
> Picking out people and knocking them down
> Resisting arrest as they're kicked on the ground
> Searching their houses and calling them queer
> I don't believe that sort of thing happens here.[15]

Punks leaned on the experience of other socially alienated groups and minorities to learn from their struggles and adapt their strategies. One was to adopt and invert hostility, akin to how the Gay Liberation Front had shifted "gay" from a word of offense to a word of pride, as exemplified in Carl Wittman's "A Gay Manifesto" (1970). The triangle which had been used by the Nazis to stigmatize different groups—yellow for Jews, red for communists, pink for homosexuals—was an often-applied symbol in punk art and fashion. To overtake—to *détour*—the stigma, had been a trait in the overlapping youth culture and underground music scenes for decades, so again punks leaned on a subculture tradition, if you will: in 1940s Paris, for example, non-Jewish artists and musicians began wearing the yellow stars, which Jewish people were forced to wear during the Nazi occupation. In DIY manner, young people sew their own yellow stars

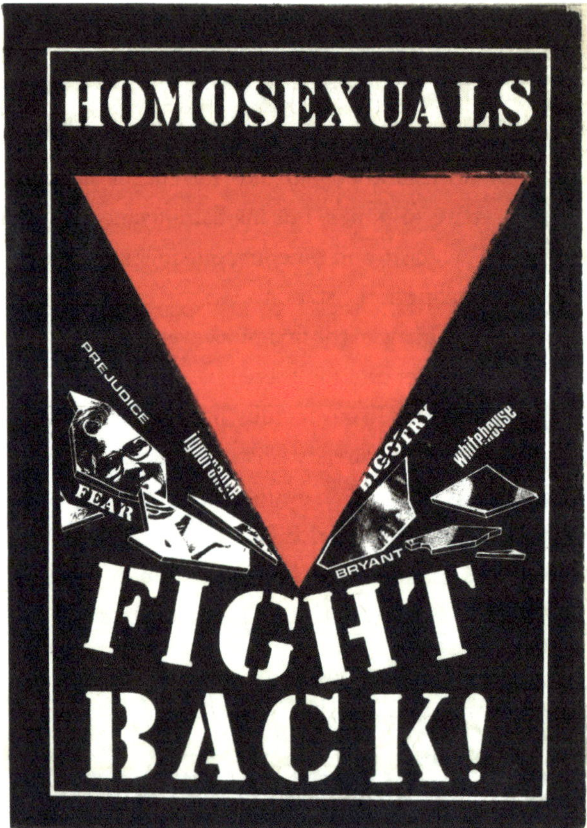

Figure 8.1: Ian Townson, "Homosexuals Fight Back," poster, 1978. Courtesy of Ian Townson Archive, Bishopsgate Institute.

and wrote upon them "Goi," "Buddhist," or in reference to music "Swing" or "Zazou" (slang for jazz and bebop fans).[16] Such political gestures of resistance overlapped with questions of identity and style.

In punk culture, we see, for example, how the Rotterdam punk art/music group Rondos appropriated the red triangle in their graphics; around the same time, in West Berlin, the artist Salomé wore the pink triangle used by the Nazis to stigmatize homosexuals. On the cover of the live single version of "Stand Together / Glad to Be Gay" (recorded 1979, released 1982), we likewise see the pink triangle. In his poster "Homosexuals Fight Back" (Figure 8.1) which was used at protests against discriminating bars and pubs, Ian Townson, who was part of the early punk and squatting scenes, actually uses the *red* (i.e. communist) triangle, which shows the overlapping of struggles.[17] In the poster, the triangle smashes "prejudice, fear, ignorance, bigotry, Whitehouse, and Bryant"—Whitehouse being Mary Whitehouse, a British conservative teacher and

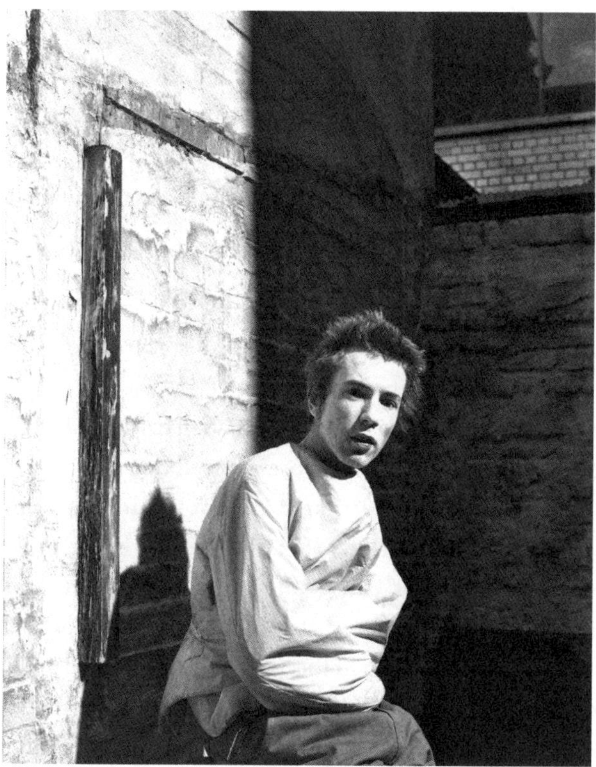

Figure 8.2: Peter Christopherson, Untitled *(Johnny Rotten), 1976. Courtesy of Timeless Editions, timelessedition.com.*

campaigner against LGBTQ rights as well as against sex and drugs education in schools, and her American counterpart, Anita Bryant.

This is not to state there was no homophobia at all in punk, alas and of course—this was the 1970s and 1980s, a time when society was steeped in homophobic, sexist, racist sentiments. Especially over time, as the movement grew bigger, some of the initial queer-punk solidarity was not transferred into mainstream. Furthermore, the political stance of punk was often ambiguous: the urge to provoke and negate would sometimes torpedo a stand just taken. For example, at Ramones concerts, Leee Black Childers remarked, "gay people made up most of the audience,"[18] and the band copied the style of the young boy hustlers on "53rd and 3rd" and wrote the eponymous song about Dee Dee Ramone's experiences on that strip. But then the band would engage in homophobic sentiments, even if partly just to annoy the liberal hippies.

In early 1976, Peter Christopherson (later of COUM Transmissions) took a series of pictures of the Sex Pistols in the toilets of the local YMCA (the pictures are quite reminiscent of his "hopeless boys" see Section 6.1: "Dead end kids"). Sex Pistols manager McLaren never used them, and these images are still relatively little known. In the words of P-Orridge, they were

> too real […]. The photographs were a bit harder and suggested sexual perversions, suggested they were gay, and I guess McLaren realized that this was potentially too threatening. It was probably the right business decision. I think Sleazy [Christopherson] saw so clearly what it all meant that he was ahead of them in their imagery. He got it right.[19]

In one of the images, Johnny Rotten is photographed in a straitjacket, looking directly at the viewer, with a wild and hurt expression (Figure 8.2).

In essence, Christopherson's imagery was perhaps less about showing the Sex Pistols as homosexual, as P-Orridge proposes, but about showing them as outcasts, as deviants, as mad men (see also Section 10.3: "Broken heroes, aces of failure"). For the traditionalist, conservative part of society in the UK in the mid 1970s, however, one would have been deemed as bad as the other. Concerning McLaren's decision not to use the images, we might note that there is less fashion, less of the show that McLaren and Westwood were selling, in this photo. Instead, there is a kind of clear-eyed psychosis, a demand to look. What Christopherson "got right" might have been just that: Rotten's earnestness behind the commotion, the realness of youthful pain—much like Christopherson's other images of "hopeless boys."

Venus in fur, Adonis in leather

In punk art, there are interrelations between identity and sexuality, everyday performance and signal imagery, the amplifying of a club visit to an act of resistance, refusal, and revolt. In West Berlin, for example, this link was very vibrant. In West Germany, consensual sex between two adult males could be punished with imprisonment up until 1969.[20] In the 1970s, all sexuality that was not heterosexual was still widely condemned socially. West Berlin became one of the centers of political resistance and a refuge for those who wanted to live differently. Founded in 1971, the organization Homosexuelle Aktion Westberlin (HAW) was the first in Germany. Many artists and musicians were members, and HAW was closely linked with the squatter scene as well, including the first *Tuntenhaus* (queer house), located in the Schöneberg district. In West Berlin, the punk and queer scenes overlapped.[21]

Many of the key protagonists of West Berlin punk identified as queer, a circumstance that also became visible in the art/music venues. RISIKO, for example, was "extremely creative and the most important meeting place for queer punks."[22] In

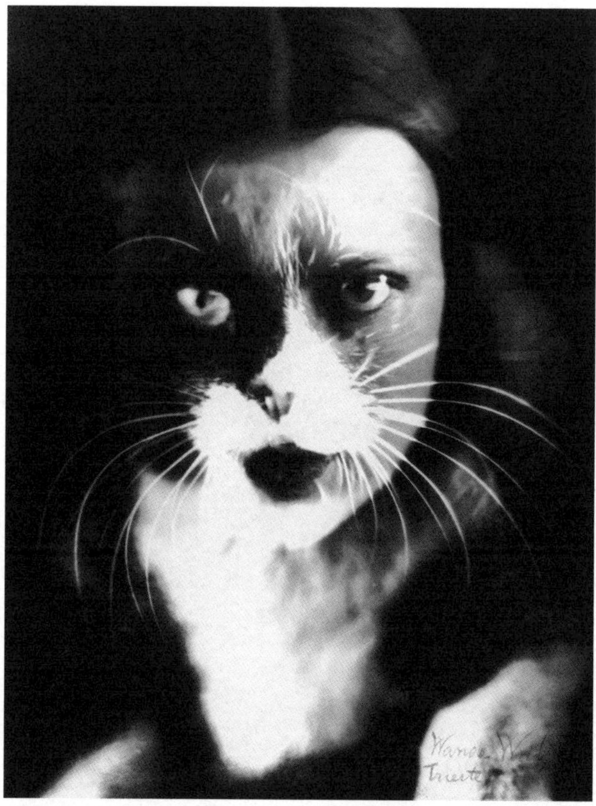

Figure 8.3: Wanda Wulz, Io + Gatto*, 1932, Alinari Archives, Zannier Collection, Florence. Courtesy of Alinari Archives.*

Das andere Ufer (The other shore), Wolfgang Müller (who worked there) met Tabea Blumenschein and she joined Die Tödliche Doris.[23] Blumenschein was an ultra-feminine *femme*, a lesbian who defied the widespread prejudice (at least back then) that all lesbians were *butch*. She was also the incorporation of lifestyle-as-art, a translucent queer figure of music, art, theater, fashion, film. The action space *Pelze* (Furs) was a squatted women's commune, and a meeting place for sex workers, lesbians, punks, and artists. At Pelze, they had a darkroom for women as well as an art exhibition space showing Polaroid, Super 8, and copy art. The name Pelze originates from the fact that the space had indeed been a fur shop, before it was taken over by artists. The name also evokes a certain corporeal tangibility. In the context of 1970s and 1980s body shaving discussions, "fur" might be associated with female body hair.

Art historically, "fur" in combination with "female" has often been used to pin animalistic projections onto women, from Wanda Wulz's *Io + Gatto* (*Me and Cat*, 1932;

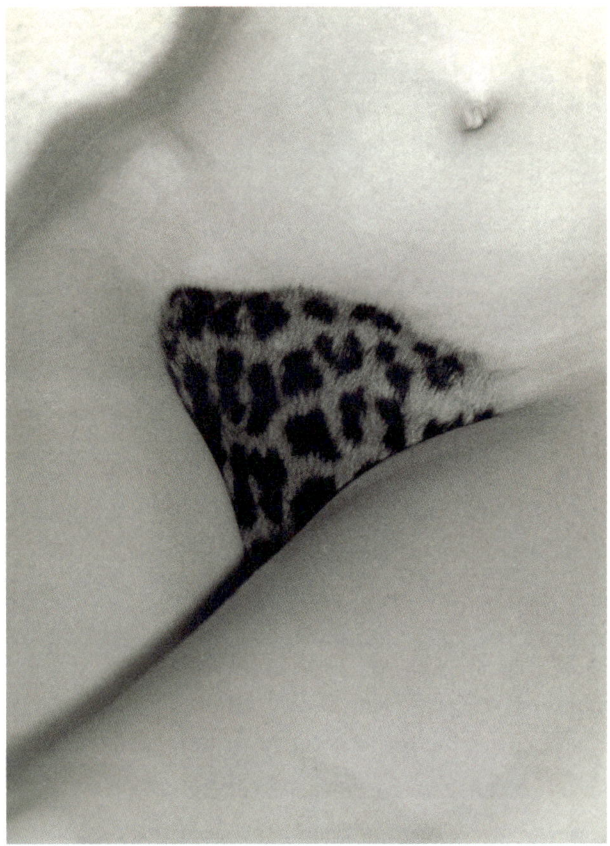

Figure 8.4: Leo Dohmen, L'Ambitieuse, *1958. Courtesy of the estate of Leo Dohmen, Antwerp.*

Figure 8.3) to Leo Dohmen's 1950s collages (Figure 8.4) to Birgit Jürgenssen's *Untitled* (*Olga*, 1979; Figure 8.5), which all feature double exposures of images of felines and women.[24] Such juxtapositions of felines and female bodies play on the visual concept of the cat-woman (much like, e.g. Soo Catwoman did with her cat styling, see Section 8.3: "Sadism and submission"). Felines here associate the feral, the ferocious, the fierce; and fur stands for fetish. Meret Oppenheim's fur-covered teacup (*Object*, 1936) juxtaposes an item associated with feminine politesse (the tea cup) with an animalistic material (fur). Further, *Venus in Furs* is a Velvet Underground and Nico song (1967) that took its name from Leopold von Sacher-Masoch's 1870 novella *Venus im Pelz* (*Venus in Furs*) and its dominant female protagonist. (On a sidenote, Steven Severin took his name from a character in Sacher-Masoch's *Venus in Furs*). The key to all these examples is how Pelze relates to a wider narrative of female empowerment and sexuality, which was highly present in the queer punk scene in West Berlin.

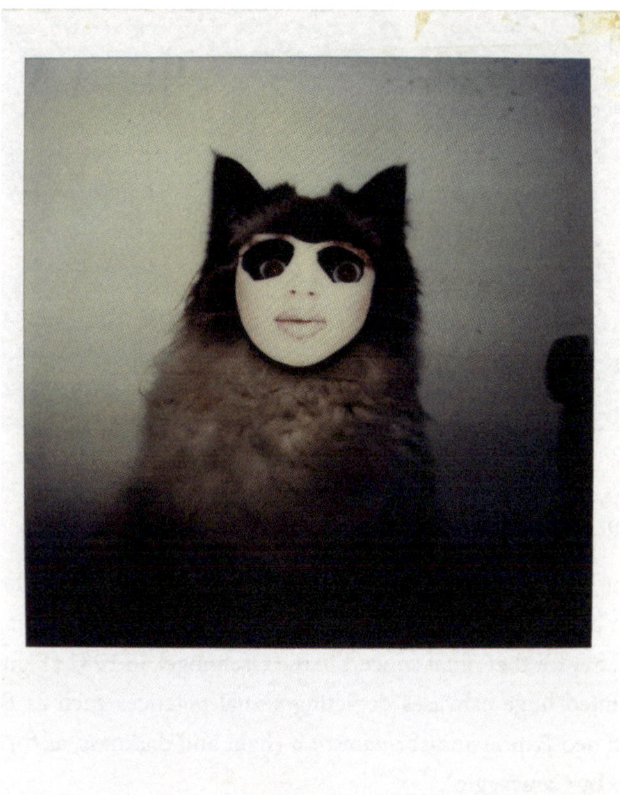

Figure 8.5: Birgit Jürgenssen, Untitled (*Olga*)*, 1979. The Verbund Collection. Photograph by Wolfgang Woessner. Courtesy of Galerie Hubert Winter. © Birgit Jürgenssen, Estate Birgit Jürgenssen. © VG Bild-Kunst, Bonn 2022.*

Both the queer scene and the punk scene were important points of orientation for the Neue Wilde too, many of whom were active both as musicians and painters: for example, Salomé (who was also an active member of HAW) and Swiss artist Luciano Castelli both painted, and played in the punk band *Geile Tiere* (Horny animals). At the night club *Dschungel* (Jungle), Salomé performed with Luciano Castelli as a "bitch" on all fours and in a dog collar. This is a scene that calls to mind VALIE EXPORT's dog walk with Peter Weibel in 1969, as well as proto-punk band the Stooges' song "I Wanna be Your Dog," also from the year 1969. Legendarily, Siouxsie Sioux in high heels and her friend Berlin (aka Bertie Marshall) in a dog collar went into a bar, where she ordered a vodka for her and water for the dog.[25] The performativity and symbolism of such club and bar and everyday performances were mirrored in art works.

"If you do a show," Salomé explained, "then you think about something crazy that you can use afterwards in your painting."[26] A photo from one of Geile Tiere's performances,

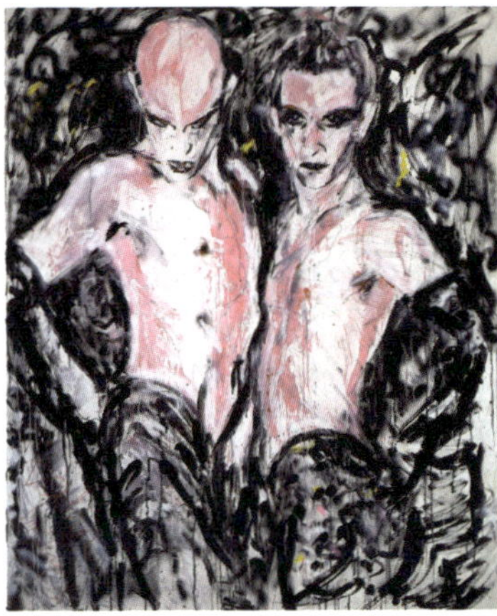

Figure 8.6: Luciano Castelli, Berlin Nite, *1979. Courtesy of Luciano Castelli. © VG Bild-Kunst, Bonn 2022.*

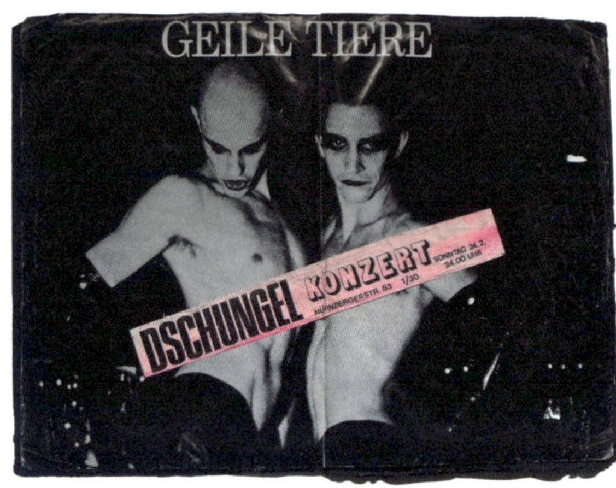

Figure 8.7: Salomé and Luciano Castelli, poster of the band Geile Tiere, 1982. Courtesy of Luciano Castelli. © VG Bild-Kunst, Bonn 2022.

showing Salomé and Castelli dressed up and posing in black latex and leather, was used as the template both for Castelli's 240 × 200 cm (!) painting *Berlin Nite* (1979; Figure 8.6) and as a poster for their final concert in the Dschungel, in 1982 (Figure 8.7). Salomé on his part painted huge canvases depicting sexual practices such as *Blutsturz* (1979, hemorrhage) in neo-Expressionist *chiaroscuro* (light and darkness, as for example in the dramatic effects by Caravaggio).

In West Berlin, in the late 1970s and early 1980s, we thus see a closely woven net of inter-connectedness between expressions of sexuality and art, in which playful storytelling and strong imagery are important. The name Salomé is typical of the scene: both a play with art history, with gender roles, with madness and with violence (Salomé, daughter of Herod, demands and indeed receives the severed head of John the Baptist on a silver tray. She also touches everything she desires and goads every person around her with her limitlessness—see Oscar Wilde's French version of the story, which he wrote in a play for the scandal magnet Sarah Bernhardt).

The punk/queer scene was full of symbols, codes, and fantasy. Cross-dressing with attributes, like corsets, laces, garnet, and stockings; or alternatively with the monocle, cylinder, mustache. Role playing with Lolita, Venus, the vamp, the diva, the mermaid, the female sphinx, the femme fatale. Or with Adonis, Elvis, and bikers.

8.2 Defiant prostitutes, porn artists and well-dressed whores

In the introduction to his large punk/sex archive documentation *Showboat,* Toby Mott notes that in the sixteenth century, William Shakespeare used the expression "taffety punk"

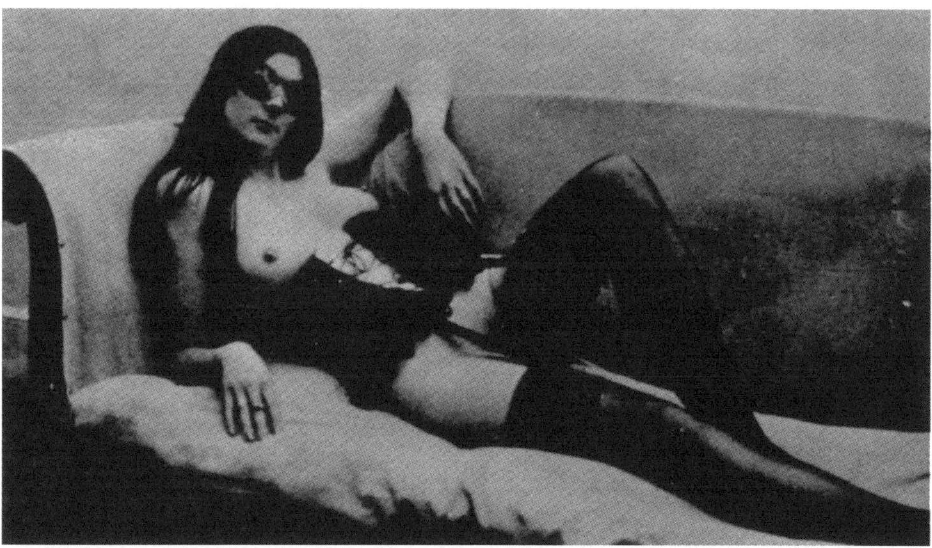

Figure 8.8: Cosey Fanni Tutti, Sexual Transgression No. 5. *Courtesy of Cosey Fanni Tutti.*

in the sense of "well-dressed whore."[27] This image of unapologetically flaunted sexuality and an over-the-top style still shines through in punk in the late twentieth century.

As said Westwood: "If you want change, the best thing to do is to attack sex, because there is so much hypocrisy about sex in Britain."[28] In the process of attacking the status quo, of skipping the charade, punk tauntingly delineated that (in late capitalist society) art is like sex: it is always about dominance and dependency, and it always comes with a price tag.

That is what they all do

The reference of Cosey Fanni Tutti's name, Mozart's *Così Fan Tutte* is the lustrous story about how all women wander and betray; *that is what they all do*, as the title suggests. Cosey Fanni Tutti took the name and exploded its connotations: prostitution is what we all do, admittingly or not.

The key visual of the *PROSTITUTION* exhibition at the Institute of Contemporary Arts (see Section 4.3: "Crime as art, scandal as art") was Cosey Fanni Tutti's *Sexual Transgression No. 5* (1976; Figure 8.8). The photo shows a woman (Tutti) lying on a divan, her arm draped casually over its backrest, her left leg propped up to reveal her genitalia. She is wearing a black corset, garters, and a black eye mask. The image is a clear reference to Édouard Manet's *Olympia* (1863, Figure 8.9), which provoked a scandal when it was presented at the *Salon de Paris* in 1865. *Olympia* in turn references other historic nudes such as Titian's *Venus of Urbino* (1534) and Jean-Auguste-Dominique

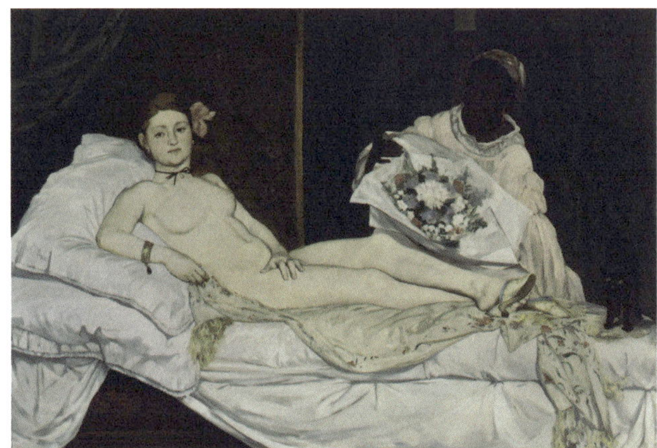

Figure 8.9: Édouard Manet, Olympia*, 1863, Musée d'Orsay, Paris.*

Ingres' *Grande Odalisque* (1814), but Manet makes no secret of the fact that the model is a prostitute, and perhaps even a defiant one. Not only did Manet thus break the traditional academic illusion of a higher allegory to explain and justify the nudity, but the viewer is unsettled by the directness of her pose and glare: "Show me the money," as Michael Kimmelman interprets her.[29]

Tutti both augments and twists the image: she stares down (at) the viewer, but her own face remains disguised. Her legs are open (as opposed to Manet's *Olympia*, who holds her hand over her crotch), but her appearance is aggressive. The reference to Manet—again—is loaded: Manet, the father of modernism and Manet, painter of the controversial *Déjeuner sur l'herbe* (Luncheon on the grass, 1863) with all its connotations of the ownership of art and the ownership of women, its construction of both transgression (the naked woman turning to look at the viewer) and impenetrability (the lack of interaction). Tutti's vagina-exposing outfit and her confrontational stare furthermore recall Peter Hassmann's photos of VALIE EXPORT's *Action Pants: Genital Panic* (1969; Figure 8.10).

In Tutti's case, the duality of her open crotch and hidden face carries these motifs of transgression and impenetrability to an extreme. The sarcasm of Tutti's set-up later found an echo in Tracey Emin's *I've got it all* (2000, Figure 8.11). Here, Emin sits on a red linoleum floor, wearing a pulled-up Vivienne Westwood dress, naked legs spread wide out, and clutching bundles of bills and coins at her crotch. The travesty here is about more than Tracey Emin's go-to shocker about sex (as in her work *Everyone I Have Ever Slept With*, 1963–95); it is also about that societal no-go of a women artist making money. As the rich upper class saying goes: "Money is not something you talk about, it is something you have." Emin refuses the role of poor and misunderstood, but actually brilliant artist

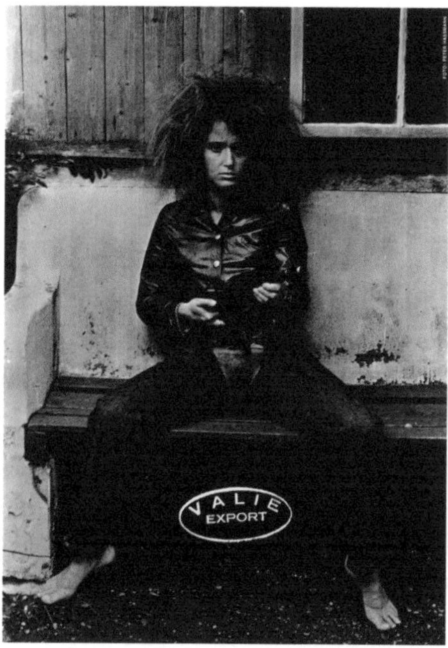

Figure 8.10: VALIE EXPORT with Peter Hassmann, Action Pants: Genital Panic, *1969. © VG Bild-Kunst, Bonn 2022.*

(the genius to be discovered after one's death), interested only in pure art, art for art's sake. Instead, she deliberately poses like a dirty art whore, sitting in an expensive dress on a cheap linoleum floor, at the end of a night in the strip club, counting her coins.

"We called the show Prostitution for obvious reasons, because art is prostitution," P-Orridge told Savage.[30] Beneath the layers of references and comments on the interrelations of art and money, aggression and emancipation, greed and lust, there is thus an analysis of the artworld that amounts to a condemnation. The artists felt they were selling their most intimate, their most vulnerable selves. Other artists had pursued the topic of art and prostitution, too. Only a few years before COUM's *PROSTITUTION*, Stuart Brisley in his work *Artist as Whore* (1972) dressed in dirty clothes and makeup and lay on a bed in a seemingly bloodstained room in an un-renovated house in London for one week. Whereas, however, Brisley's work had a strong social component and engaged with topics of presence and exploitation, COUM communicated neither affection nor moral positioning. Their perspective was linked to a cynical assessment of a society in which we are all prostituting ourselves. As P-Orridge stated in a letter to *VILE*: "Thee Arts Council have stopped our grant midway [...] finance is harder, *we survive by prostitution in every form*. Butter that's integral to our way of death anyway."[31]

There is a Marxist echo in that: "prostitution is only a specific expression of the general prostitution of the laborer" in the capitalist system.[32] The "*as*" in Brisley's *Artist as Whore* thus implicitly conveys a categorical separation; it is an identification with and solidarity with someone different from yourself, but in the end, it is the preliminary division that makes the comparison meaningful. In COUM's argument, conversely, prostitution was not a theme, but the essence of art: Artist *is* whore.

With *PROSTITUTION*, COUM Transmissions thus not only sided with the outcast but also identified themselves as such. This position is even more outspoken in what the artists themselves called the "core of the exhibition,"[33] the *Magazine Actions*, which were a photo series of Tutti from commercial sex magazines such as *Fiesta* and *Playbirds*. This work is interesting for a number of reasons: It shows how Tutti worked, and how connected her work was to other behavior artists and undercover journalists in the late 1970s, who worked covertly for the purpose of gleaning insights. However, it also shows how she fully identified with the other models who posed for these publications, thus breaking the illusion of only being there for the documentation.

Tutti's cooption of pornography was intended to reveal its objectifying mechanisms. Staging the photos in an art institutional setting—as a second step—aimed at exposing the double standards of how the nude (created by a man) was considered in contrast to a naked woman (in a work by a female artist). The images were framed and signed, and COUM at first wanted to hang them openly and as a series. However, the directness of the sexual content prompted the ICA to exhibit the pictures covered, and apart, thus—inadvertently—confirming COUM's critique.

When reframed within an unexpected context, the pretense in the sex magazines becomes palpable, and the ridiculousness of its language is made manifest. This also desexualizes the images, an effect which, ironically, was reduced, or even effaced entirely through the mystifying concealment at the Institute of Contemporary Arts. Furthermore, the social critique of *Magazine Actions* (1973–80) is sharper when viewed serially: it is almost tiring going through the repetition of clichéd poses and roles: Cosey as secretary, Cosey as flower girl, Cosey as biker chick, Cosey as vamp. Each time with a new wig and as a new type: Tessa from behind, Susie spreading legs, then as herself: Cosey bending forward, looking over her shoulder, with the corny subtitle: "Feeling Cosey?." To borrow from Susan Sontag: A deadpan, burlesque theatre of types (rather than individuals). She notes: "The personages in pornography, like those of comedy, are seen only from the outside, behaviouristically."[34] Thus, Tutti's series calls to mind Cindy Sherman's *Untitled Film Stills* (1977–80) of 1950s Hollywood female stereotypes, but the *Magazine Actions* are less subtle, less beautiful, and less mediated. Tutti explained,

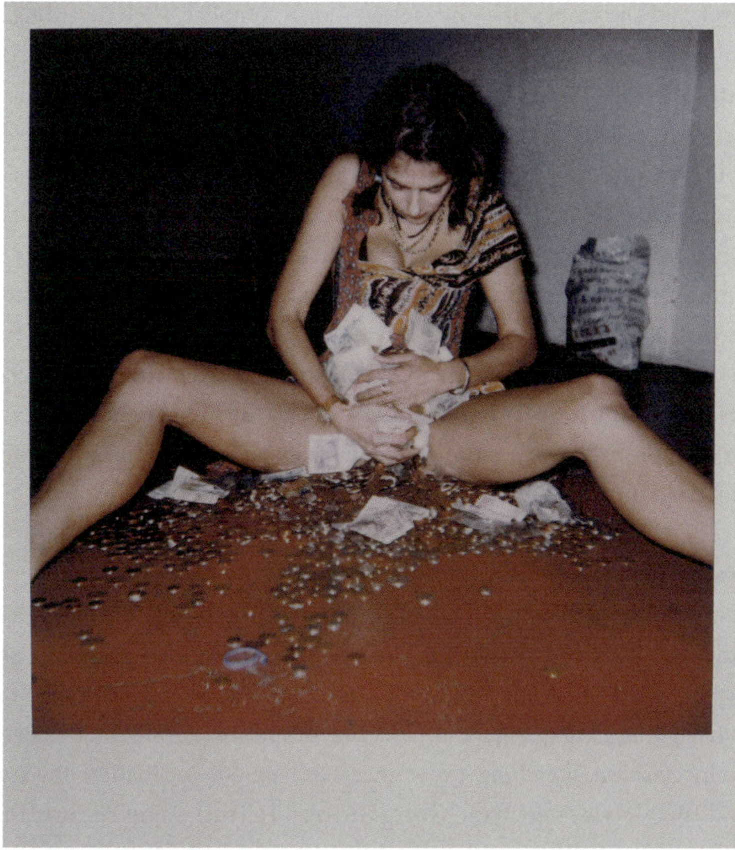

Figure 8.11: Tracey Emin, I've got it all, *2000 © Tracey Emin. All rights reserved, DACS/ Artimage 2022. Courtesy of White Cube. © VG Bild-Kunst, Bonn 2022.*

> My express intention with the project was to both infiltrate the sex market to create (and purchase) my own image for use as collage material in my work and to gain firsthand experience of being a genuine active participant in the genre.[35]

Tutti adopted an undercover-researcher approach:

> I surrendered myself into that industry to be used as they use any other girl, but I didn't let them know who I was or anything or why I was doing it, otherwise it would be pointless, because I wouldn't be treated the same way.[36]

Like other COUM works, the *Magazine Actions* examined power abuse, sexual exploitation, and voyeurism, but there was no open moral indignation in the works. In addition to this exposé of the sex industry, Tutti also explored her *own* fascination with losing control, and she makes us—the viewer—an accomplice, both regarding her own sense of allure and its effect on the (male) voyeur. For the viewer in an art-institutional setting, Tutti's method thus might have a touch of psychological manipulation.

"Cosey Fanni Tutti not only transgresses what we think certain surfaces of woman represent but also critiques any default belief that liberation can be found simply by reversing those perceptions," Patricia MacCormack writes, "She takes up the sex industry worker neither as post-modern false-consciousness pseudo-feminism nor as straightforward symbol of oppression, but both from the inside and the outside."[37] Tutti argues from the position of the pornographic model, without any illusions about the abuse involved in the business, but also with no distinct moral judgement of pornography per se. The facts that most sex workers are female and that the industry is replete with male chauvinism (and probably even more so, when we consider this was in the mid 1970s) are only addressed through subtext.

Tabea Blumenschein dances the pimp and prostitute

Another example of the lifestyle-art-music-sexuality medley, again from West Berlin: Tabea Blumenschein's cover design for Die Tödliche Doris' cassette *Tabea und Doris dürfen ja wohl noch Apache tanzen* (*Tabea and Doris Should at Least Still Be Allowed to Dance the Apache*, 1981, Figure 8.12). The simple black-on-white drawings mix Blumenschein's fashion sketching experience with punk's inclination toward strong symbols, and 1920s-style references. "Georg Grosz and all that was in Berlin of the 1920s, I really worshipped," says Blumenschein, "cabaret, Valeska Gert, Dada, Raoul Hausmann, and of course Max Beckmann."[38] On the West Berlin punk scene, the female provocateurs of the legendarily decadent 1920s and 1930s Berlin were admired. Nina Hagen's style—black shaggy bangs, black lipstick, dramatic black eyebrows—recalled that of the modern dancers of the Weimar Republic, such as Valeska Gert and Anita Berber. Both were known both for their avant-garde lifestyle and the eccentric, abstract themes of their dances; Valeska Gert danced "the traffic," Anita Berber danced "cocaine." Some 50 years later, such transgressive positions were admired in the punk milieu in West Berlin. This admiration was above all about a reconnection, aesthetically as well as thematically, with the excess and glamour, the madness and radicality of that era.

This interest in the Weimar period is likewise mirrored in Die Tödliche Doris' music (and, by the way, in Nina Hagen's too). On *Tabea and Doris Should at Least Still Be Allowed to Dance the Apache*, Thomas Groetz identifies several allusions to Bertolt Brecht and Kurt Weill, such as murder ballads and broadsheets, alienation effects, and amoral street criminal and bandit characters (recalling Mack the Knife and Pirate Jenny).[39] The

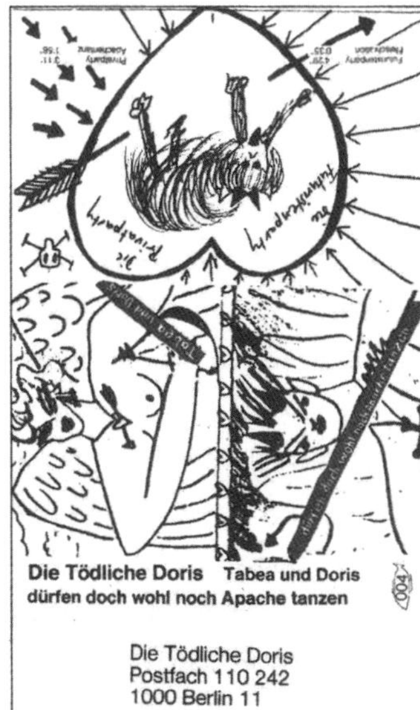

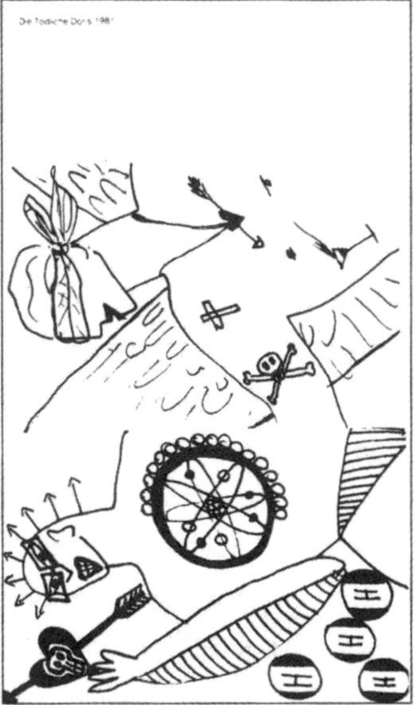

Figure 8.12: Die Tödliche Doris, Tabea und Doris dürfen ja wohl noch Apache tanzen (Tabea and Doris Should at Least Still Be Allowed to Dance the Apache), *1981. Archiv der Tödlichen Doris. Courtesy of Wolfgang Müller.*

background noise, which can be heard on Tödliche Doris' cassette—laughing, coughing, clinking glasses—increases this atmosphere. The effect is further reinforced by lyrical fragments, such as "Kannibalen in der Dunkelheit, stürmt das Café, sensationell" (in the darkness, cannibals storm the café, what a sensation).

The title, *Tabea and Doris Should at Least Still Be Allowed to Dance the Apache,* refers to the *Apache Dance,* a choreography which enacted an extremely brutal dance between a sex worker and a pander. The *Apache Dance* first appeared in Paris in the early twentieth century and became popular in the cabarets of Berlin in the 1920s and 1930s. Presumably due to their colorful clothing, youth gangs, pimps, and street criminals were sometimes called "Apaches," an expression coined by journalist Arthur Dupin in 1902 in a cultural stereotyping typical of the time.[40] Blumenschein's ties both to the female performers of the 1920s (Valeska Gert, for example, did dance *the Apache*) and to Max Beckmann coalesce in her drawings. Max Beckmann painted his version of the *Apachentanz* (*Apache Dance*) in 1938. In his painting, the element of violence is enhanced through the unnatural position of the female figure, who is slumped over the back of the central male figure. The pose in the painting depicts the quite dangerous climax of the *Apache Dance* choreography. This choreography is one long power struggle: full of desire and tension, of potential violence and potential sex.

The title *Tabea and Doris Should At least Still be Allowed to Dance the Apache* shows the importance of language in Tödliche Doris' work and how language was used for establishing a specific frame. First, the phrase "Should at least still be allowed to..." was (and is) often used by revisionists and racists to evade political correctness. For example: "One should at least still be allowed to say that Hitler built great motorways." The title thus makes use of a kind of suggestiveness, which passive-aggressively attacks the reflex of the viewer's expectations and preconceived notions. The way Die Tödliche Doris uses the phrase makes it two-edged: Who is trying to prevent Doris and Tabea from *Dancing the Apache*?

The title furthermore puts fantasy and reality side by side: The figures of (the actually fictive) Doris and (the actually existent) Tabea are treated as though they exist in the same dimension. Such an assertion ties in with other works by Die Tödliche Doris that juxtapose the imagined and the real. Because the title cites two women's names, it additionally raises the questions: Are the two dancers in a lesbian relationship? And who is performing which role in the *Apache Dance*: who dances the prostitute, who dances the pimp? Both notions—the passive-aggressive attack on preconceptions and the blurring of real and unreal—are quintessential of Die Tödliche Doris' artistic approach. What is specific to this work—and is an element that often reoccurs in Blumenschein's oeuvre—is the interest in sexual ambivalence, power plays, and all that is forbidden.

8.3 Sadism and submission

Throughout the twentieth century, avant-gardes and subcultures have drawn heavily on a tradition of cruelty-as-autonomy or amorality-as-autonomy, reaching back from Marquis de Sade over Friedrich Nietzsche to Sigmund Freud. Some of the best works of art are arguably about finding "badness" (or: lust, violence, rage ...) within oneself, relating to it, understanding, questioning, and exploring it. In punk art, this is the case too. We might find two sides of this autonomy: one side indeed in line with Sade: *Sadism*—here, however, a key question became, how women saw the Marquis, most prominently discussed in Simone de Beauvoir's *Must We Burn Sade?* (1955)—the other side being *submission*—but here, with an interesting turn: could submission be used for subversion? Both sides, sadism and submission, are vital to understanding how sexuality and autonomy were connected in punk culture, and thus also in punk art.

Oh, bondage!

Let us first take one step back to understand the influence of the writings of the Marquis de Sade. In the late eighteenth and early nineteenth centuries, Sade wrote his horrifying stories of sex, suffering, sickness, violence, pleasure, excrements, and extremes. They present a libertine philosophy through and through: Sade makes no concession, neither to religious moral, nor to public decency, nor to the law. In Sade's view, no (wo)man's value could stand over another. He was convicted, among other things, for sedating, for whipping, for anal sex, and for group sex. As he, himself wrote:

> Yes, I am a libertine, that I admit. I have conceived everything that can be conceived in that area, but I have certainly not practiced everything I have conceived and certainly never shall. I am a libertine, but I am neither a criminal nor a murderer.[41]

A majority of Sade's writings were burned and censored, and for many decades after his death in 1814, the texts were only read by very few (like Charles Baudelaire and Arthur Rimbaud). It was not until the early twentieth century, that Sade became more widely known. The manuscript of *The 120 Days of Sodom* was even believed to be lost, and wasn't published at all, until 1904 when Iwan Bloch got his hands on it and published it in Berlin. In 1909, Guillaume Apollinaire rescued de Sade from the "hell" of libraries (his words) and published *L'oeuvre du Marquis de Sade* (*The Works of the Marquis de Sade*). In the first centuries of the twentieth century, Sade was canonized by artists and poets as a hero of revolution.[42] Sade told tales of unthinkable terror. As Alyce Mahon describes it, artists in the first half of the twentieth century took up this idea of terror as their *cri-de-coeur* and a means of liberation, thus "aligning their terrifying art with revolutionary goals and discourse."[43] The Surrealists especially hailed Sade, for his power to unsettle, for his untamed transgressions, and for his revolt through sex. From Masson to Magritte, from Bataille to Buñuel, Surrealist film, artworks, and writings are full of Sadean references. André Breton called the Marquis a "Surrealist in sadism"[44] in the first *Surrealist Manifesto* of 1924, and this fascination with Sade carried on to the Lettrists in the 1950s and the Situationists in the 1960s, and further into punk in the 1970s.

Marquis de Sade stood for the exploration of the depravity of the human psyche and the exposure of the corruption of power. His name also came to signify the aestheticization of sexual violence, especially after 1886 when Richard von Krafft-Ebing introduced the conceptual pair, sadism (from the Marquis) and masochism (from Leopold von Sacher-Masoch), out of which Freud in 1905 coined "sadomasochism." *S&M* was born. In 1960s counterculture, Sade became popular for his agitation of absolute freedom and for his ability to upset. S&M aesthetics, for example, graced the book cover of Michael Leigh's *The Velvet Underground* (1963), with the teaser: "Here is an incredible book. It will shock and amaze you. But as a documentary on the sexual corruption of our age, it is a **must** [*sic*] for every thinking adult."[45]

As Alyce Mahon (leaning on fellow feminist Luce Irigaray) points out, Sade's writings had one simple advantage regarding women's sexuality: it takes place. His libertine stories incite women to enjoy their sexuality. Female pleasure was hardly written about at all, not in Sade's time, marginally in Surrealism (the infamous candid "conversations" of the Surrealists about sexuality, not published until 60 years later, stayed almost exclusively a male domain), and, in the 1960s, female pleasure was still widely a societal taboo. The female figures in Sade's writing have agency, they have their say: "The first fairy tale narrated by the fairy herself," as Mahon quotes Annie Le Brun's view of *Juliette*.[46] Furthermore, gender boundaries are bent in Sade's writings: the phallus is mocked, gender is queered; Madame de Volmar in *Juliette* has a three-inch clitoris that enables her to play the role of a man in the sexual games, and Durcet in *The 120 Days of Sodom* has feminine breasts, round hips, and a small penis.

> Sade's libertines certainly take jouissance to its extreme and embody the idea that the subject can situate him- or herself as sadist or masochist and revel in pleasure and pain as they undermine traditional gender roles and give the imagination free rein.[47]

These ideas of sexual liberation and queering made Sade a hit in the counterculture of the 1960s. Fittingly, it was Leonor Fini who illustrated *Histoire d'O* in 1962: in her extravagantly beautiful Surrealist paintings and costumes, Eros and Thanatos always seem present, as she plays with the erotic of torn clothes and with the inversion of expected gender roles: the female predator, the female gaze.

Whereas Simone de Beauvoir in *Must We Burn Sade?* had answered her own question with a *no* because of Sade's ability to describe the sickness of an unjust society, thus underlining his revolutionary quality, later feminist positions chose to focus on Sade's libertarian view on female sexuality. That women too should enjoy all pleasures and not be bound by morality was right down the alley for libertarian feminists, like Angela Carter (who wrote about it in her seminal book *The Sadeian Woman and the Ideology of Pornography* in 1978).[48]

In punk culture, then, both these arguments were articulated, as has been examined thoroughly by Matthew Worley, in his essay "Whip in My Valise: British Punk and the Marquis de Sade, c. 1975–85."[49] "Whip in My Valise" (1979) was the title of a song by Adam and the Antz, sung to a dominatrix, and starting with the lines: "When I met you, you were just 16 / Pulling the wings off of flies." Malcolm McLaren, drawing on his Situationist proficiency, argued that fetishism and sexual violence were extreme reactions to a suppressive cultural environment and that the shock value of Sade gave his

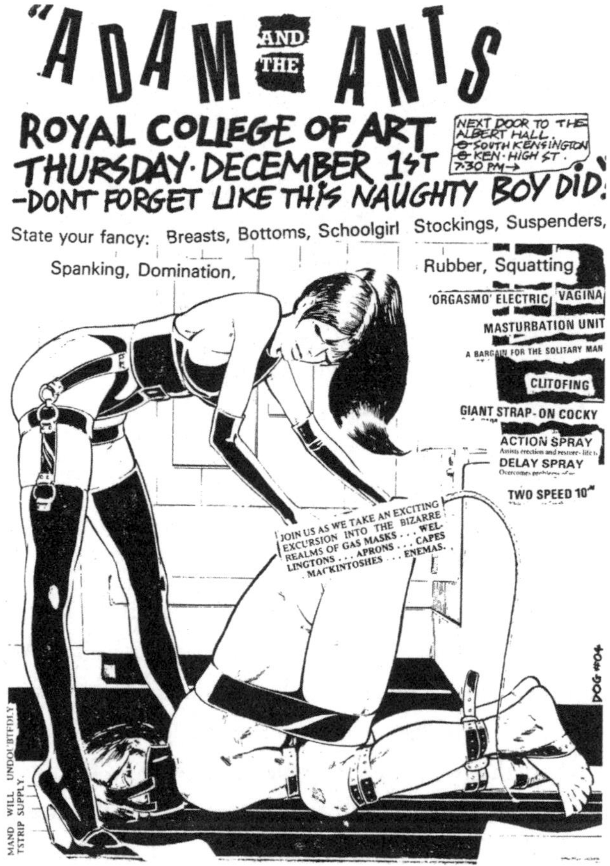

Figure 8.13: "Adam and the Ants, Royal College of Arts." Flyer, design by Adam Ant, 1977.

writings the power to stands against the numbing of mass culture, the oversaturation, the passivity. Sadean influences are on display in Derek Jarman's *Jubilee* (1978), in the track "Oh Bondage, Up Yours" (1977) by X-Ray Spex, and in punk's S&M style, the "rape" T-shirts, the rubber and leather and lace. In 1984, when Georges Bataille (whose 1928 novella *L'histoire de l'œil* (*Story of the Eye*) was almost like a Surrealist update of Sade's writing) was celebrated at London's Bloomsbury Theatre, both Cosey Fanni Tutti and Marc Almond contributed.[50]

Most directly, Adam and the Ants (sometimes Antz with a z) quoted Sadism, at one point even copying the iconic cover image of Angela Carter's *The Sadeian Woman*. Adam Ant (aka Stuart Godard) had attended Horsney College of Art, where Scottish artist Eduardo Paolozzi, one of the co-founders of British Pop Art, had been his teacher.[51] The imagery of Adam and the Ants, conveyed both through their live performances

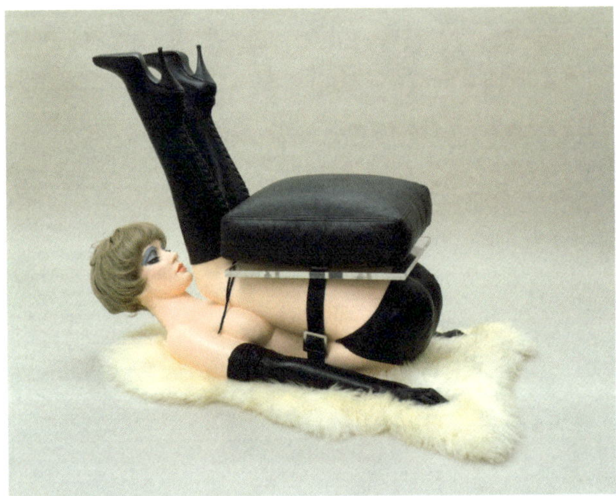

Figure 8.14: Allen Jones, Chair, *1969. Photograph by Tate. © Allen Jones. Courtesy of the artist.*

and diverse print matters (Figure 8.13), was full of sexual and violent fantasies, and art historical references from Dada, Futurism, and Pop Art, as well as Allen Jones' erotic furniture (Figure 8.14; which incidentally, Die Tödliche Doris also quoted in their live performance with the title *Hommage an / Homage to Allen Jones* in New York's The Kitchen in 1984, where the two male group members were on their knees and hands as the furniture, with the two female members sitting on them, thus reversing the gender roles in comparison to Jones).

Of the four artists groups in focus in this book, however, COUM Transmissions was the one most profoundly involved with the ideas of the Marquis de Sade. In 1973, P-Orridge had encountered the work of the Viennese Actionists, probably for the first time in original, at the Richard Demarco Gallery in Edinburgh, and they had made an impression, especially Otto Muehl. Around ten years earlier, in 1962, Otto Muehl had written:

> The free admittance of the true creative drives is the ethical intention of my apparatus: sadism, aggression, perversity, craving for recognition, avarice, charlatanry, obscenity, the aesthetics of the dungheap are the moral means against conformism, materialism and stupidity.[52]

Such a utilization of the declared depravity of human nature as a weapon against capitalist society fitted COUM's developing approach. Sadism as revolt, fighting evil with evil. "I found Muehl interesting because he was dealing with taboo and social behavior, whereas Fluxus was really a running battle and commentary with art itself," P-Orridge told Savage.[53]

In the following years, COUM's artwork became harder, more physical, and abject. The "social behavior" which P-Orridge cited as intriguing in the actions of the Viennese, came into focus. COUM's artistic explorations aimed at the abyss of human nature, including their own. In the context of the 1970s, theirs was a standpoint opposed to the socially critical, politically engaged art dominating the alternative, mostly left-wing art scene. COUM was less interested in day-to-day political struggle, and more engaged with base motives. COUM's attention was directed at something less comprehensible: both more abstract and more extreme. An artistic exploration of the darkest sides of humanity.

COUM became increasingly involved in the international art scene, and from 1974 to 1976 performed in Paris, Milan, Amsterdam, and Los Angeles, among other places.[54] Also in 1974, the group wrote their manifesto (see also Section 5.3: "Originality and appropriation"), in which they proclaimed an art that was in *all* ways independent: "COUM demonstrate that there are NO boundaries in any form," one line read.[55] A truly Sadean statement. At Art Meeting Place (AMP), an artist-run, co-operative space in Covent Garden, P-Orridge and Tutti performed *Filth*, which involved live anal sex. At this time, the group became more tight-knit, with fewer occasional contributors. Peter "Sleazy" Christopherson joined the group as a permanent member, and he enhanced the engagement of COUM in Sadism. In 1975, the group performed *Couming of Youth* at the hippie-turned-punk venue Melkweg in Amsterdam: Sleazy read out a text describing the callous castration of a young boy, then as a climax cut his own throat so badly that he had to apply a tourniquet. P-Orridge and Tutti spat at each other, and then licked the spittle off. P-Orridge also burned his hands with torches and urinated on Cosey, while "she stuck lighted candles up her vagina, so there were flames coming out of her vagina. Just ordinary everyday ways of avoiding the commercials on the television," P-Orridge later declared.[56]

In 1977, the group (by then TG) released a black-and-white 16mm movie (reminiscing an amateurish home sex film): "The first section was basically Chris being tied to a table and Cosey cutting his jeans off and apparently castrating him. The second section was [Soo] Catwoman being tied to an iron bed in a bare room," Christopherson summarized.[57] Soo Catwoman was a key figure in the early punk scene, and much like Jordan her body and style were living art (Figure 8.15). For this kind of performed sex and violence to reach a transgressive quality, a taboo break was required. Terror, causing distress and fear. With this approach, COUM thus re-connected with the artists of the early twentieth century and their "terrifying" art, as described above by Mahon. At the same time, they distanced themselves from the opposite idea of a moralist approach to art: "Expecting the artist to be a good person was a sentimental canard of Victorian moralism,"[58] as Camille Paglia points out.

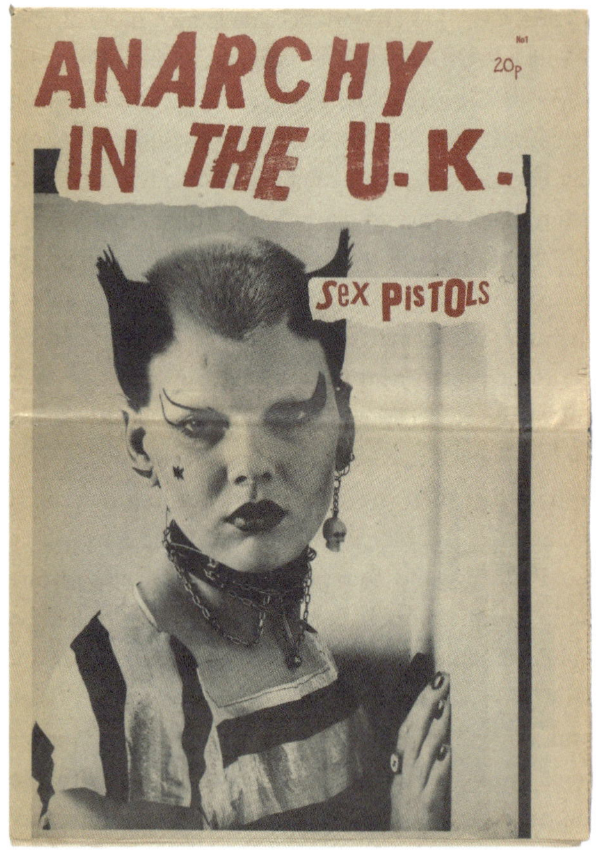

Figure 8.15: Jamie Reid, Sophie Richmond, Ray Stevenson and Vivienne Westwood, Anarchy in the UK, *no. 1 (Zine cover featuring Soo Catwoman), 1977. © Jamie Reid. Courtesy of John Marchant Gallery, UK.*

Subversion through submission

Punk protagonists did not only engage with Sadism; the other side of S&M came into play too. However, especially in punk art, this submission was often used in terms of the inverted power of playing the weak, the participation on one's own terms, a covertly subversive compliance. Cosey Fanni Tutti's "surrender" as she described it (see above) into the sex industry is one example. Another, similar example is how Tabea Blumenschein handled her role as a pin-up for the nude magazine *High Society* in 1984: when the photographer asked her to pose, she first made him demonstrate *exactly* the position she was supposed to do, "because usually, that is not how I sit on my bed," as she is actually quoted in the magazine.[59] Blumenschein's action is less comprehensive, but nonetheless compares to Cosey Fanni Tutti's exposure of the absurd, even comical, component of nude and porn magazines. Both Tutti and Blumenschein's approaches over-expose the circumstances of production, reveal its fakeness, and thus subversively regain control.

Curt Hoppe's collages for the magazine *Screw* (1979–81), in which he juxtaposed the faces of the rich, famous, and powerful onto pornographic photo, and which were shown in the *Punk Art* exhibition in Washington in 1978, go in the same direction. In the *Punk Art* exhibition were also an image series by photographer Jimmy DeSana, including a photo that showed himself hanged, with erect penis, variously titled *Noose* or *Self-Portrait* (1977). The way DeSana explores the dark sides of his own fantasies reminisces the violent, sexual works that COUM and TG were engaged in at the time. Incidentally, DeSana also co-edited the *FILE* magazine issue "Punk Til You Puke" in 1977, which comprised works by and with the Sex Pistols, Throbbing Gristle, Richard Hell, Patti Smith, Blondie, and Yoko Ono, among others.[60] In 1979, DeSana published the *Noose* or *Self-Portrait* images in his book *Submission* (1979).

In the 1970s, a position such as Tutti's in her *Magazine Actions* drew criticism from many feminists. Her ambiguousness is interconnected with her immersion in the role, which feminist critics at the time most often rejected.[61] Tutti's work was not unequivocally liberating—like Carolee Schneemann, who intimately filmed herself and her boyfriend having sex in *Fuses* (1964–67), thus retaining the autonomy of her own body—it was the opposite: a submission. In the mid 1970s, feminist art history and art theory were debated vigorously—it was only a few years after groundbreaking publications such as Shulamith Firestone's *The Dialectic of Sex: The Case for Feminist Revolution* (1970), John Berger's *Ways of Seeing* (1972), and Linda Nochlin's *Why Have There Been No Great Women Artists?* (1971), to name but a few. In such a battle, ambiguous positions were not welcomed by all.

As Hannah Wilke complained in *Art News* (October 1980),

> In the narrow politics of feminism, art is only a weapon, which may endanger women's art that is formally and humanly relevant but does not adhere to a specific political or commercial concept [...] There is an ethics as well as a warning in esthetic ambiguity.

Tutti, however, was not the first female artist to discover the power of subversion through submission. In her performance *Rhytm 0* (1974), Marina Abramović likewise offered herself passively to the invasion of spectators; she stood silently next to a table of objects, such as a gun, a bullet, a comb, lipstick, a whip, chains, and needles. A sign on the wall read: "There are seventy-two objects on the table that can be used on me as desired. I am the object."[62] Abramović's work might be viewed as an extended reiteration of Yoko Ono's *CUT PIECE*, which she performed, e.g. at DIAS in 1966. Ono placed scissors in front of herself and let audience members approach her to cut off pieces of her clothes. The snipping sound of the scissors was reinforced by contact microphones.[63] Jo Spence posed "as a Sex Object" in her self-portrait series (*Jo Spence as a Sex Object*, 1979), pushing her breasts toward the camera with a lascivious expression, wearing first dark, then blonde wigs, similarly to Sherman's *Untitled Film Stills* (1977–80) mentioned above. Wilke too, engaged with the topic of subversive objectification, for example in her series *S.O.S. Starification Object Series* (1974–82). These were topless photographs of Wilke with small labia-shaped gum-sculptures stuck to her skin; she had asked visitors of her exhibition to chew the gum and hand it back to her, before putting it on herself.

In this way, Spence, Wilke, Abramović, Ono, Sherman, and Tutti all address the objectification of women by becoming objects themselves, a method which artist Hito Steyerl describes as follows:

> Traditionally, emancipatory practice has been tied to a desire to become a subject. Emancipation was conceived as becoming a subject of history, of representation, or of politics. To become a subject carried with it the promise of autonomy, sovereignty, agency. To be a subject was good; to be an object was bad. [...] But as the struggle to become a subject became mired in its own contradictions, a different possibility emerged. How about siding with the object for a change? Why not affirm it? Why not be a thing?[64]

Such an inversion of power relations, such a taunting way of turning the tables, was very punk indeed. Punk women artists and musicians were interested in the dark sides, too. But, as Maggie Nelson observes in *The Art of Cruelty*:

> A woman who explores the depths of her despair or depression isn't typically valorized as a hero on a fearless quest to render any "darkness visible," but is instead perceived as a redundant example of female vulnerability, fragility, or self-destructiveness.[65]

In the late 1970s and early 1980s, punk feminism had to deal both with a misogynist society, sexism in the musical business as well as the artworld, and also gender-separatist second-generation feminists who were no fans of admitting that women too might have a dark side to explore, including cruelty, anger, violence, and depression (that were not solely caused by men). If for a second, we return to the beginning of this section on "Sadism and submission," however, then such a limitation to being "good" would arguably hinder women artists in understanding, questioning, and exploring the "badness" within themselves. Punk feminism in the late 1970s and early 1980s was thus often a kind of outsider feminism.

8.4 Punk feminism: Vamp up!

Whereas later punk iterations, such as the 1990s riot grrrls punk movement, took a clear stance on feminism, the first-generation punk women were often more ambiguous. Nonetheless, many of the women artists and musicians who emerged from the hybrid practices of the late 1970s and early 1980s came to be influential for later generations of feminists. Both chronologically and thematically, punk was situated between the second (roughly 1960s–70s) and third wave of feminism (roughly 1990s). This argument, that punk positioned itself between second-wave feminists, with whom both a generational and perspectival conflict loomed, and the third wave some twenty years later, has been proposed, but not much pursued—despite the notion that "[punk's] in-between position actually makes this generation a particularly interesting case through which to study situated performances of femininity," as Pauwke Berkers argues.[66]

Punk girls and women were often aware of the achievements of feminists before them but were at the same time critical of intolerant elements in the older feminist generation, such as gender separatism, trans-exclusion, or narrow-minded opinions on what was the "right" feminist way to dress and behave. The goals of the second wave feminists, such as equality, the right to contraception and abortion, were matters of course to most young punks. But they wanted to dress in S&M attire, wear lipstick, leopard print, over-knee lace-up boots, fishnet stockings, and skull earrings and whips as accessories. The getup and style of punk women often served a double role: both overtly affirming and undermining gendered attributes. Viv Albertine describes in her memoir how she and other punk girls dressed in Westwood's clothes, "Pippi Longstocking meets Barbarella meets juvenile delinquent," to provoke, excite, and feel free.[67] While pinpointing structural male oppression, personal choices and experiences were emphasized. Gender roles were simultaneously parodically affirmed and subverted. "It was so cool to see women in high heels and safety pins and leather jackets, getting off," says artist Sten-Knudsen.[68] Punk poet Søren Ulrik Thomsen likewise points in this direction, stating that it was new for women to present themselves as sexy, strong, and self-determined, and, at the same time, consciously and deliberately as "objects of desire."[69]

"It was important to us to be sexy. We wanted to sport tight-waisted styles, we wanted to wear high heels when walking through the squat courtyard, past construction sites, at nighttime, at demos," recalls Käthe Kruse of Die Tödliche Doris.[70] This meant

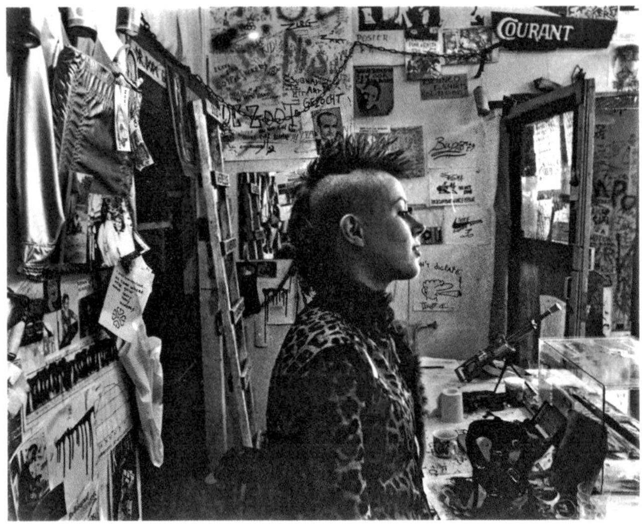

Figure 8.16: Diana Ozon at Gallery ANUS, Amsterdam, 1979. Photograph by Paul Tornado. Courtesy of Diana Ozon.

a certain detachment from the 'kill joy' reputation of feminism that prevailed at the time. The bra-burning of the second-wave feminists was rejected by the punks. "Women punks also reacted against second-wave feminism's uniform prescriptions on how to dress and sound," Berkers notes.[71] The feminist punk attitude echoes the (in)famous statement by the anarchist and feminist Emma Goldman—"If I can't dance, I don't want to be in your revolution."[72]

According to poet and artist Diana Ozon (Figure 8.16), the punk community in Amsterdam was characterized both by respect for the women's movement and a distance toward it, the roots of which were also of a generational nature:

> Many punks came from dysfunctional families. Many of them lived just with their mother. So, there was a sort of matriarchal dominance all around [...]. On International Women's Day, we punk girls went in the Melkweg to an event, or sometimes we would go to a women's pub, and these old feminists in their old purple feminist clothing would be there, with gardener's trousers and the women's sign hanging from their ear, no lipstick, very short hair, mine worker boots, you know. They were very amazed to see us with our 1950s styles, well, we had roughed it up, sure, but still it was a very feminine 1950s style. They were surprised to learn we had the same thinking in a lot of ways. We were almost all of us brought up by feminists.[73]

The recurring word here is "old," which points to how the conflict between second wave feminists and punks was just as much determined by generational issues as opinions. In the Netherlands, this discord is likewise demonstrated in younger women's criticism of what they called "klaagfeminisme" ("complaining feminism"). In spite of this criticism of strict gender dualism, complaining, and obduracy of the older second wave feminists, female punks were mostly aware of the important battles that had been fought, as might become clear in the fact that the "punk girls," as Ozon called herself and her friends, were indeed at the Melkweg on International Women's Day. There is a similarity here to the statement of Käthe Kruse: "Underneath our anti-attitude, we knew that we would not be where we were without the feminists before us."[74] The punk ideal was a self-determined and transgressive lifestyle, but the implementation was often sought on an individual level. "I liked the women teachers who had no children and no husband. They were independent. They were archetypes for me," Ozon recalls.[75]

Issues such as queerness and sex-positivity play a key role in punk feminism, and thus rather points forward in time, towards aspects showcased later by third wave feminism. As T. S. Høeg remarks on the punk scene in Denmark in the late 1970s and early 1980s:

> Inside of the milieu, there was a new relationship between boy and girl, which was highly interesting. And what it was, was mutual respect, which manifested itself in a way that you could almost dissolve gender. So, the boy role could be dissolved, the girl role could be dissolved […] There were new hybrids, also boy-boy and girl-girl.[76]

Punk's androgynous expression and questioning of fixed gender notions also corresponds to this proposition. In the COUM performance *Orange and Blue* (1975), for example, Tutti and P-Orridge swapped clothing, roles, and behavior in a slow and careful process. "It's a piece about the ambiguity between male/female, and thee way our visual responses are keyed by symbolic images," P-Orridge explained.[77]

Diana Ozon claims she did not at the time, experience a gender gap in the punk community in Amsterdam:

> We did not see the difference at all! Later on, people asked me about this, but at the time, it did not make a difference to me […] we were equal. You had Blondie, Nina Hagen, the Slits, the Runaways. They were sexy, but equal.[78]

Punk defined anew what feminism and femininity could be. Punk icon Nina Hagen (Figure 8.17), for example, combined women's emancipation with an attitude of youthful, uncontrollable defiance, unapologetic aggression, and sexuality. In "Unbeschreiblich

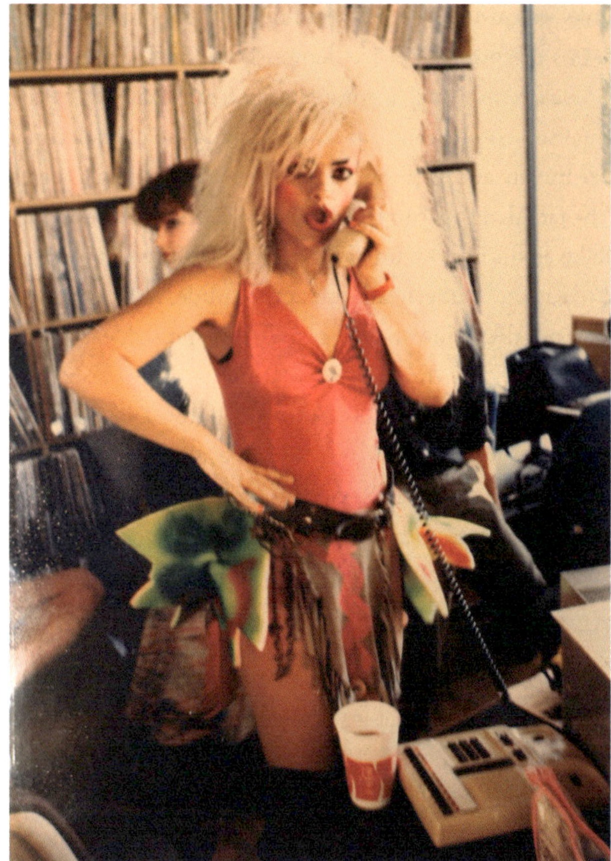

Figure 8.17: Nina Hagen on the phone, ca. 1986. Photograph by Bill DeRouchey. © Creative Commons.

Weiblich" ("Indescribably feminine"), Hagen sings about having an abortion and afterwards feeling miserable but "indescribably feminine," about freeing herself, about taking drugs, not wanting to have children, and not wanting to fulfill her womanly duties; she cites Marlene Dietrich ("she had other plans") and Simone de Beauvoir, and sneers: "Jetzt ist es Zeit, endlich mal aufzumotzen"[79] (Now it's time to finally ..., *aufmotzen* in German can mean to "vamp up," "beef up," or "rebel"). Punk artist and writer Caroline Coon is another example of this attitude, as was most recently to be seen in her show, *The Great Offender* at London's TRAMPS in 2019, a show simultaneously ripe with paintings of impressive penises and the destabilization of the patriarchy.

In the UK, many of the women who emerged out of the UK art schools—such as Linder Sterling, Caroline Coon, and Viv Albertine—were creating their own hybrid art forms and combining visuality and sound. The impact of this early generation of female punk artists, musicians, and film makers is currently a topic that is (finally!) being thoroughly studied, among others by Rachel Garfield in *Experimental Filmmaking and Punk: Feminist Audio Visual Culture in the 1970s and 1980s* (Bloomsbury, 2021) and Maria Elena Buszek in her forthcoming book *Art of Noise: Feminist Art and Popular Music in Since 1977*.

Linder and Ludus

One of the key feminist punk artistical positions from the late 1970s is aforementioned Linder, who combined notions of cut-up, soft porn, objectification, and sinister glam into biting imagery and caused a furor with her red tampon stage decorations for her band Ludus (Latin, play, game, fun). Linder studied art and design at Manchester Polytechnic in the late 1970s and got involved in the punk scene there, not only the zines, where she published not only her collages but also with her band. Since the 1970s, she has been known by Linder, an alteration of her birth name Linda Mulvey. In punk, Linder has often repeated in interviews, you could choose your own new identity, a kind of re-birth, and "one name seemed sufficient."[80] In changing her name from the mundane English Linda to the Germanic sounding Linder, she was also taking inspiration from Dadaists, who—in the Weimar time—had reversely anglicized their names (from Georg Groß to George Grosz, from Helmut Herzfeld to John Heartfield).[81]

Linder's characteristic magazine collages (Figure 8.18) have often been compared to the Dada collages of Hannah Höch (Figure 8.19). What they have in common is a subversive precision in taking apart modern print illusions, each artist in her own time. Both Linder and Höch also work with cut-out and displaced bodies and faces, particularly mouths and eyes, disturbingly distorting the appearances of the persons in their pictures.

Linder told Savage,

> I had two separate piles. One you might call women's magazines, fashion, romance, then a pile of men's mags: cars, DIY, pornography, which again was women, but another side. I wanted to mate the 'G-Plan' kitchens with the pornography, see what strange breed came out.[82]

In the 1970s and 1980s, such magazines were still very widely spread and culturally influential. Linder combines fragments from glossy consumer magazines: pornography and pies, cars and cosmetic, a remote control for penis, a TV for head. The weirdness of her juxtapositions affects a kind of Brechtian estrangement scheme with the purpose of obstructing comfortable consumption. As she told Peter Jones, her photomontages represent "configuration[s] of sex/consumer pathology."[83]

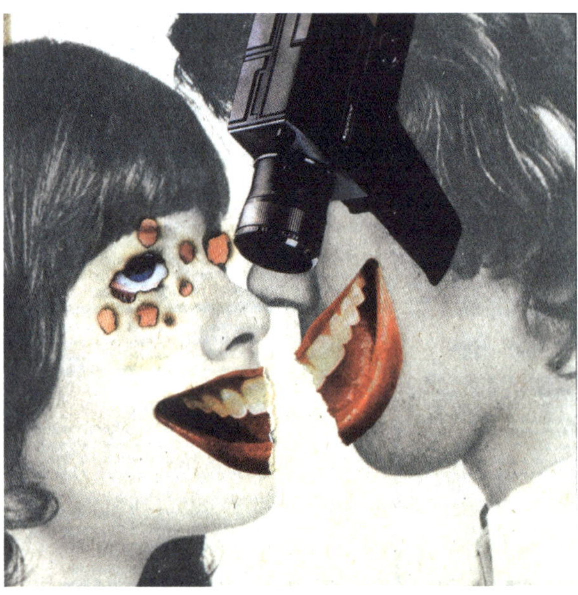

Figure 8.18: Linder, Untitled, *1977. © VG Bild-Kunst, Bonn 2022.*

The collage which was used on the cover of Buzzcocks' *Orgasm Addict* (1977) is typical of her style: the combination of nude, glistening perfect bodies, with weirdly placed smiling mouths (here: as nipples), and homemaker hardware, in the case of Buzzcocks cover a Morphy Richards iron. Her visual commentary on romantic clichés is well summed up in one image of a young couple in intimate embrace, while she stabs herself in the eyes with a dinner fork. This is Linder's détournement of romantic illusions. She attacks and caricatures conformist concepts of love, femininity, and beauty. Likewise, Hannah Höch developed a sardonic attitude towards the idealized bourgeois marriage of her own time: the dysfunctional couple is a recurring topic in Höch's collages. Her rejection of patriarchal conventionalist marriage and her critique of the commodification of sexual relations and particularly of the female body are expressed in several of her works. One image especially connects both in style and content with Linder's approach some 60 years later: in *Bürgerliches Brautpaar* (*Streit*) (*Bourgeois Married Couple* [*Quarrel*]) from 1919, we see a female and a male figure pasted over by magazine cutouts of domestic apparatuses, such as a slicing machine and a meat grinder. Each coming from and communicating for her own time, Höch and Linder both ripped open the domestic disharmony while simultaneously attacking the alienation of consumerism.

Video material of the performances with Ludus displays how Linder developed the same topics as in her collages for the stage. In a rebuttal of the famous Sigmund Freud quote (which claimed just the opposite), one Ludus song line goes: "Anatomy is *not*

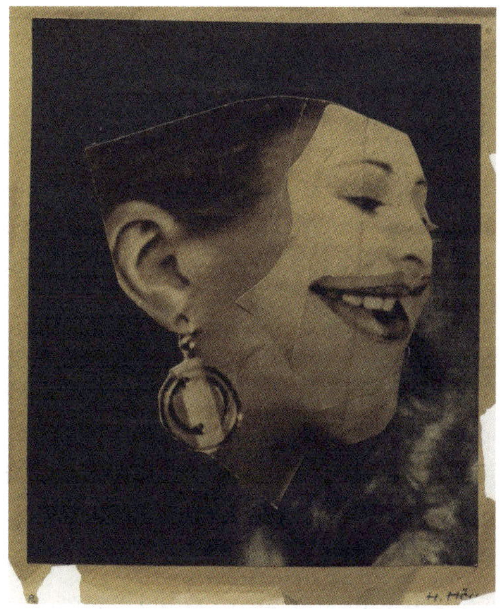

Figure 8.19: Hannah Höch, Fröhliche Dame, *1923.*
© VG Bild-Kunst, Bonn 2022.

destiny, so why persist in training me"[84]—released on the likewise tellingly named album *My Cherry Is in Sherry* (slang for menstruation). Linder was taking up the taboo topic, much like second generation feminists had done in the early 1970s, but her take was not serious menstruation lyrics, but rather teasing and provoking. At one particularly infamous Ludus show at the Hacienda in Manchester in 1982, the entire room was decorated with tampons, covered in dripping red paint. Linder (a vegetarian!) wore a dress made of discarded raw meat (nearly 30 years before Lady Gaga famously did too, at the MTV Video Music Awards 2010). At the end of the show, Linder tore of the dress, to disclose a big black strap-on dildo. Eight years before, in 1974, uncompromising Lynda Benglis had famously posed naked with a dildo in an artist's portrait published in *Artforum*, causing a controversy. Such works lead us to a specific feature of punk feminism: the role as the "black sheep."

Black sheep, femmes fatales, and female fighters

The expression "black sheep feminist artist"[85] was coined by Alison Gingeras, for a show of works by Cosey Fanni Tutti, as well as Joan Semmel, Anita Steckel, and Betty Tompkins. As Gingeras notes in an interview about the women artists she chose for the *Black Sheep Feminism* exhibition as well as a later show called *Sex Work*, they "made work that was doubly bound by their challenge to obscenity laws, as well as by the protests of the anti-pornography contingent of the feminist movements of the 1970s."[86] There is an overlap here with punk feminist work, perhaps most prominently Cosey Fanni Tutti and Vivienne Westwood, who both worked with fetishism and fantasy to reveal misogyny (surely)—but at the same time, because they were both fundamentally and artistically interested in sex and represented a libertine standpoint. If we take this idea by Gingeras further, we could understand black sheep feminism more widely as an outsider standpoint and as such, it played a role in punk too. Punks not only sided with the "black sheep" of society but recognized themselves as such. The direction of punk's societal criticism was always from the bottom up. Punk was often about staying true to oneself, including the dark sides. Patti Smith, for example, does so in her cover version of van Morrison's song "Gloria" (1975), over which she superimposed a part of her own poem "Oath" (1970), including the lines: "Jesus died for somebody's sins / But not mine / Melting in a pot of thieves / Wild card up my sleeve / Thick, heart of stone / My sins, my own, they belong to me / Me."[87] Patti Smith owns her sins and faults and that makes her strong. This is an outspokenly nonjudgmental position that focuses on individualism, self-exposure, and humor.

Looking back through (art) history, we might invoke Valentine de Saint-Point who wrote her "Manifesto of Futurist Woman" as an answer to Marinetti in 1912:

> Humanity is mediocre. The majority of women are neither superior nor inferior to the majority of men. They are all equal. They all merit the same scorn […] Women are Furies, Amazons, Semiramis, Joans of Arc, Jeanne Hachettes, Judith and Charlotte Cordays, Cleopatras, and Messalinas: combative women who fight more ferociously than males, lovers who arouse […] Woman, for too long diverted into morals and prejudices, go back to your sublime instinct, to violence, to cruelty.[88]

No less problematic than the rest of the Futurists, de Saint-Point thus points to a stance of energy and extremism. To her, moralism is the enemy. The women she invokes are warriors, queens, and murderers. The powerful Messalina is known for plotting against her husband Claudius, the emperor of Rome, and for her alleged promiscuity. Jeanne Hachette (French, "Joan the Hatchet") was the nom de guerre of Jeanne Laisné in the 1470s. Charlotte Corday killed Jean-Paul Marat in his bathtub during the French revolution, as famously depicted by Jacques-Louis David in 1793. With these femmes fatales, Valentine de Saint-Point, at the beginning of the century, argues against a feminism that she claims will "tame" women.

Sixty-something years later, female punks' search for emancipation and independence became linked with a "bad girl" attitude. In the very early years of punk, this attitude was often politically naïve and largely focused on getting a shock reaction. Examples of this trumping attitude—anything you can do, we can do better, including sadism and evil—can be seen in girls' vicious aliases, such as Ozon's "Gretchen Gestapo" and another girl of the Amsterdam scene, who was partly of Jewish origin and nonetheless called herself "Ilse Koch," the name of a murderous woman known for her brutality toward concentration camp prisoners in Buchenwald. Similar to the development of punk in London, the provocative and antithetical use of Nazi references, which was widespread among very early punks, became untenable when misuse and misunderstandings accumulated, and both girls stopped using these aliases.[89] In the context of a black sheep feminism, however, what comes through is the opposition to any sense of inferiority, even in the ways of violence. After all, figures such as Ilse Koch became a key reference for the case that women were exactly as depraved as men, and thus, indeed, miserably equal.

The stance of gender equality in every realm, including warfare, insurrection, and physical violence might also be seen in the art works of Nina Sten-Knudsen. In all her artworks in the late 1970s, physicality and violence (or symbols of violence) play a key role. Sten-Knudsen explains:

> The women in the punk milieu, we were not gentle and sweet, we were, in our expression, extremely angry and violent and aggressive. Back then, women were not allowed to be aggressive, not allowed to be fighters. But I was a blacksmith, damn it! I was standing with a sledgehammer and with axes and with machine guns! I had that strength and anger and aggression inside me.[90]

This physical element is strongly present in the works *Økser* (*Axes*, 1979; Figure 8.20) and *The Terrorist's Room* (original title in English, 1979). The installation of eighteen axes in the same-named work oscillates between severity and brutality. The seriality and weird orderliness of the hanging—three fastidious rows of six axes—contrast with the martiality and crudity of the blades, which are handmade, thus displaying slight variations, and spray-painted with red. "The headman's drying rack?" Frederik Stjernfeldt and Poul Erik Tøjner comment.[91] In its radical reduction, haptic materiality, energy, and sheer presence, *Axes* shows both a sensory quality and works with a kind of evocation of history. As Henrik Wivel notes, Sten-Knudsen's works are truly "loaded," recalling the concentrated acuity of cave painting or medieval sacred painting.[92]
Sten-Knudsen explains how she made the work:

> I forged the axes myself. I was very attracted to iron as a material: It was hard, you could melt it, you could use a cutting torch, the ember would fall, you could hammer it—Bang! Bang! Bang!—you could use all of your force. […] To me, that

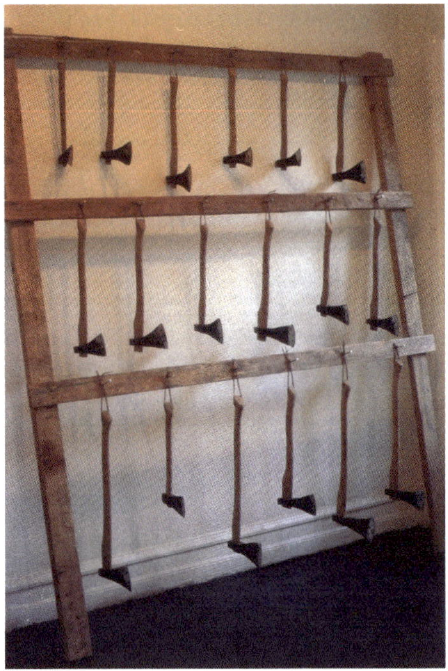

Figure 8.20: Nina Sten-Knudsen, Axes, *1979. Courtesy of Nina Sten-Knudsen.*

> was like punk. [...] It was the same energy as was in the sound. Steen [Jørgensen] and Knud [Odde] from the Sods, they were really interested in my work.[93]

In the same year, 1979, Nina Sten-Knudsen made *The Terrorist's Room* (Figure 8.21). It was a total installation in the Rådskælderen, the exhibition rooms in the basement of Charlottenborg in Copenhagen. Sten-Knudsen covered the walls in mud, crude drawings, and graffiti, such as LORT (SHIT) and SULT (HUNGER). On the floor lay gravel and sand, a dead rat, a blanket, caltrops, and imitations of the British submachine gun STEN.

Sten-Knudsen made the Sten guns and the caltrops herself at the metal workshop, using detailed drawings from her visits to Frihedsmuseet (The Museum of Danish Resistance, i.e. during the World War II) and the weapons collection of the civil defense. The Sten guns featured in Sten-Knudsen's work, due to their uncomplicated design, were typical weapons of insurgents. "I was born in '57, so to me, Sten guns were iconic, because the resistance used them," she says, "An old freedom fighter came to see the exhibition in Rådskælderen, he just nodded for a long time, then he looked at me and said: 'Yes, they are a pretty good likeness!'"[94] Sten-Knudsen recounts this anecdote with pride in her

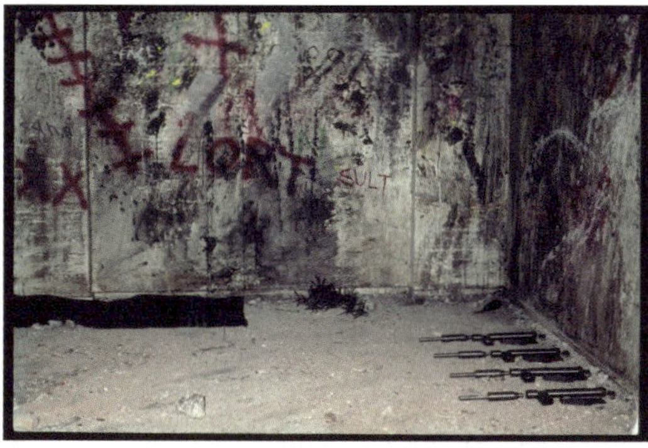

Figure 8.21: Nina Sten-Knudsen, The Terrorist's Room*, 1979. Courtesy of Nina Sten-Knudsen.*

voice, which underlines her identification with that resistance, with the sense of fighting. The theme of terror was of course extremely present at this time in the late 1970s. Sten-Knudsen recounts how well she felt she understood the motivation of Rote Armee Fraktion (RAF) and she was fascinated with how they had "taken it all the way." Parallel to the black sheep feminists endeavoring into pornography and toying with S&M, we thus also see an artist like Nina Sten-Knudsen who understood feminism as a question of showing how to be just as aggressive and hard as the male punks. "Back then, we were equal. We thought, we can do exactly what they can do. We thought, we are in no way different. We were pals," she explains.[95]

Notes

1. Viv Albertine quoted in Savage, *England's Dreaming*, 418.
2. Vivienne Westwood, interview with Len Richmond in *Forum*, June 1976, 20–25.
3. Talking Heads, "Not in Love" (Sire, 1978).
4. Bowie quoted in Savage, "Cut-Ups Go Pop," 42.
5. Christgau, "Punk England Report," n.p.
6. Matthew Worley, "Whip in My Valise: British Punk and the Marquis de Sade, c. 1975–85," in *Contemporary British History* 26, no. 2 (2022), 290–291.
7. Siouxsie Sioux quoted in Savage, *England's Dreaming*, 183.
8. Torres, "Traces of a Punk Attitude in Contemporary Art," 45.
9. "Queerpunk Manifesto," accessed January 16, 2018, http://www.queerpunk.org/manifesto.
10. See Liam Warfield, Walter Crasshole, and Yony Leyser, eds., *Queercore: How to Punk a Revolution: An Oral History* (San Francisco: PM Press, 2021) as well as Maria Katharina Wiedlack, *Queer-Feminist Punk: An Anti-Social History* (Vienna: zaglossus, 2015).
11. Hebdige, *Subculture: The Meaning of Style*, 2.
12. As one of his most famous quotes from *Lady Wintermere's Fan* goes (Act III).

13. See Kathryn Rosenfeld, "The End of Everything Was 20 Years Ago Today: Punk Nostalgia," in *New Art Examiner* 27, no. 4 (1999): 26–29.

14. Per Buhl Ács quoted in Poulsen, *Something Rotten*, 16.

15. TRB (Tom Robinson Band), "Glad to Be Gay" (UK: EMI, 1978).

16. Sami Sjöberg, *The Vanguard Messiah: Lettrism between Jewish Mysticism and the Avant-Garde* (Berlin: Walter de Gruyter, 2015), 36.

17. See Proll, *Goodbye to London*.

18. Savage, *England's Dreaming*, 139.

19. P-Orridge quoted in Ford, *Wreckers of Civilisation*, 5.13.

20. Bundeszentrale für Politische Bildung, "1994: Homosexualität nicht mehr strafbar," accessed April 4, 2018, http://www.bpb.de/politik/hintergrund-aktuell/180263/20-jahre-homosexualitaet-straffrei.

21. See Philipp Meinert, *Homopunk History: Von den Sechzigern bis heute* (Berlin: Ventil Verlag, 2018).

22. Müller, transcript of an interview with Slaski, 2017.

23. Tabea Blumenschein, interview with the author, October 30, 2017.

24. See Inka Graeve Ingelmann, ed., *Female Trouble: Die Kamera als Spiegel und Bühne weiblicher Inszenierungen* (Ostfildern: Hatje Cantz, 2008).

25. See Worley, "Whip in My Valise," 291.

26. Salomé quoted in "Die 80er: Figurative Malerei in der BRD," accessed April 4, 2018, http://80er.staedelmuseum.de.

27. Mott, *Showboat*, n.p.

28. Vivienne Westwood quoted in *The Guardian*, December 3, 1976, n.p.

29. Michael Kimmelman, "A Rendezvous with Manet in Paris," accessed March 29, 2018, http://www.nytimes.com/2011/05/17/arts/design/manet-the-man-who-invented-modernity-paris-exhibition-review.html.

30. Genesis P-Orridge quoted in Savage, *England's Dreaming*, 251.

31. Genesis P-Orridge quoted in Ford, *Wreckers of Civilisation*, 6.4. Emphasis added.

32. Karl Marx, "Economic and Philosophic Manuscripts [1844]," in *Prostitution and Pornography: Philosophical Debate about the Sex Industry*, ed. Jessica Spector (Palo Alto: Stanford University Press, 2006), 64.

33. Press release by COUM Transmissions.

34. Susan Sontag, "The Pornographic Imagination," in *L'Histoire de L'oeil / Story of the Eye*, ed. Georges Bataille (London: Penguin, 1982), 100.

35. Cosey Fanni Tutti, "Confessions" [postscript text, April 2002] (London: Cabinet Gallery, 2003).

36. "Cosey and Maria talk about Linguistic Hardcore," in *Cosey Complex*, eds. Maria Fusco and Richard Birkett (Cologne: Walter König, 2012), n.p.

37. Patricia MacCormack, "Mucosal Coseying," in *Cosey Complex*, 123.

38. Blumenschein, interview, 2017.

39. Groetz, *Doris als Musikerin*, 47–51.

40. Eva Fischer-Hausdorf, "Der Künstler als Theaterdirektor, Regisseur und Kulissenschieber: Das Welttheater bei Max Beckmann," in *Max Beckmann: Welttheater*, eds. Museum Barberini and Kunsthalle

Bremen (Munich: Prestel, 2017), 19.

41. Marquis de Sade in a letter to Madame de Sade, February 20, 1781. Quoted in Alyce Mahon, *The Marquis de Sade and the Avant-Garde* (Princeton: Princeton University Press, 2020).

42. Mahon, *The Marquis de Sade and the Avant-Garde,* 7.

43. Mahon, *The Marquis de Sade and the Avant-Garde,* 3.

44. André Breton, "First Manifesto of Surrealism [1924]."

45. Book cover of Michael Leigh's *The Velvet Underground,* 1963.

46. Mahon, *The Marquis de Sade and the Avant-Garde,* 21.

47. Mahon, *The Marquis de Sade and the Avant-Garde,* 17.

48. See Anna Watz, *Angela Carter and Surrealism: "A Feminist Libertarian Aesthetic"* (London: Routledge, 2017).

49. Worley, "Whip in My Valise."

50. Worley, "Whip in My Valise."

51. Bestley and Ogg, *The Art of Punk,* 54.

52. Otto Muehl quoted in Ford, *Wreckers of Civilisation,* 3.16. Muehl was later sentenced to seven years in prison for child abuse and violation of the narcotics law.

53. Jon Savage, "Throbbing Gristle," in *Search and Destroy* #6 [April 1978]. Quoted from *Search and Destroy, 1–6: The Complete Reprint,* ed. V. Vale (San Francisco: V/Search, 1996), n.p.

54. COUM action portfolio 1974–1976, Fales Library & Special Collections, New York.

55. COUM Transmissions Manifesto, quoted in Ford, *Wreckers of Civilisation,* 4.11.

56. P-Orridge quoted in *RE/search,* "Throbbing Gristle", 17.

57. Wreckers of Civilisation, 7.8

58. Camille Paglia, *Provocations* (New York: Pantheon 2018), 200.

59. *High Society D,* no. 1 (1984), n.p.

60. See *FILE* 3, no. 4 (Summer/Fall 1977).

61. See *Wreckers of Civilisation* for an overview of these discussions.

62. Tracey Warr, *The Artist's Body* (London: Phaidon, 2012), 125.

63. Miles, *London Calling,* n.p.

64. Hito Steyerl, "A Thing Like You and Me," in *e-flux Journal* #15 (April 2010), accessed March 30, 2018, http://www.e-flux.com/journal/15/61298/a-thing-like-you-and-me/.

65. Maggie Nelson, *The Art of Cruelty* (New York: W.W. Norton Company, 2011), 260.

66. Pauwke Berkers, "Rock Against Gender Roles: Performing Femininities and Doing Feminism Among Women Punk Performers in the Netherlands, 1976–1982," in *Journal of Popular Music Studies* 24, no. 2 (June 2012), 156.

67. Viv Albertine quoted in Sarah Jaffe, "Why Feminism Needs Punk," accessed April 1, 2018, https://www.dissentmagazine.org/article/why-feminism-needs-punk-viv-albertine-slits-autobiography.

68. Sten-Knudsen, interview, 2018.

69. Søren Ulrik Thomsen quoted in Poulsen, *Something Rotten,* 80.

70. Kruse, interview, 2017.

71. Berkers, "Rock Against Gender Roles," 168.

72. This now famous statement is actually a paraphrase of a much longer response by Emma Goldman to criticisms from her anarchist colleagues; see Kathy Davis, "Should a Feminist Dance Tango? Some Reflections on the Experience and Politics of Passion," in *Feminist Theory* 16, no 1 (2015): 3–21.

73. Ozon, interview, 2017.

74. Kruse, interview, 2017.

75. Ozon, interview, 2017.

76. T. S. Høeg quoted in Poulsen, *Something Rotten*, 232.

77. Ford, *Wreckers of Civilisation*, 4.15.

78. Ozon, interview, 2017.

79. Nina Hagen Band, "Unbeschreiblich Weiblich" (Berlin: Hansa Tonstudio, 1978).

80. Brian Dillon, "Linder, the artist with the hex factor," in *The Guardian*, accessed November 28, 2021, https://www.theguardian.com/artanddesign/2011/sep/02/linder-sterling-photomontage.

81. Amy Tobin, "Linderism: The Red Period," in *Linderism*, ed. Kettle's Yard (Cologne: Walther König, 2020), 42.

82. Savage, *England's Dreaming*, 403.

83. Peter Jones "Anxious Images: Linder's Fem-Punk Photomontages," in *Women: A Cultural Review* 13, no. 2 (2002): 168.

84. Ludus, "Anatomy Is not Destiny," on the album *My Cherry Is in Sherry* (Manchester: New Hormones, 1980). Emphasis added.

85. Exhibition *BLACK SHEEP FEMINISM: The Art of Sexual Politics*, Dallas Contemporary, January 16–March 20, 2016.

86. Rachel Middleman, interview with Alison Ginegeras: "Venus Envy," in *Frieze*, accessed December 29, 2021, https://www.frieze.com/article/venus-envy.

87. Patti Smith, "Gloria" (New York: Electric Lady Studios, 1975).

88. Valentine de Saint Point, "The Manifesto of Futurist Woman (Response to F. T. Marinetti)," 1912.

89. Voogd, "Punk in Amsterdam," n.p.

90. Sten-Knudsen, interview, 2018.

91. Stjernfeldt and Tøjner, *Billedstorm*, 56.

92. Henrik Wivel, *Nina Sten-Knudsen* (Copenhagen: Palle Fogtdahl, 1990), 5.

93. Sten-Knudsen, interview, 2018.

94. Sten-Knudsen, interview, 2018.

95. Sten-Knudsen, interview, 2018.

9 Pain and Presence

Hurting yourself and hurting others were recurring themes in punk (art). Pain was used to test one's own limits and to push oneself to a heightened sense of alert. "Punk was a protest against life that was not living," Tracey Warr writes: "It attacked the constructs of media, consumerism and capitalism with venom and passion to snap us out of it. Punk was edgy and ugly but not cynical."[1] The violence in punk was associated with the pain of living in an oppressive and power-abusing society; punk's melodramatic harmfulness was a response. In the first part of this chapter, "Performances and punches," we take a closer look at this staged and real hurtfulness.

Punk works of art were often concrete, tangible, physical: sometimes stinking, sometimes decaying, sometimes painful. Bodily fluids and ephemeral materials were engaged. That ephemerality is linked back to an understanding of making art for the here and now (not the future) and about being present and vigilant. The artists reacted against what they perceived as the domination of de-materialized, over-theorized, and esoteric art in the 1970s. These artworks link with the contemporary Body Art scene of the 1970s, and at the same time with extreme fashion and S&M sentiments. In the second part of this chapter—"It hurts and looks cool!" (a statement from Die Tödliche Doris)—examples of these artistic positions are presented.

The display of destruction, transcending any elaborate explanation, was an immediate way of communicating urgency. The underlying argument of Johnny Rotten's "I wanna destroy the passerby"[2] was thus akin to André Breton's in the "Surrealist Manifesto":

> The simplest Surrealist act consists of dashing down the street, pistol in hand, and firing blindly, as fast as you can pull the trigger, into the crowd. Anyone who, at least once in his life, has not dreamed of thus putting an end to the petty system of debasement and cretinization in effect has a well-defined place in that crowd with his belly at barrel-level.[3]

Pain arose in the realization that the response of the resistance could never be as effective as the system it opposed, or it would itself become equally cruel. Punk was inspired by the contemporary European wave of terror—Rote Armee Franktion, Brigate Rosse, Action directe—but its own terror was symbolic and its violence most often self-directed. This sentiment is echoed in Viv Albertine's depiction of Sid Vicious: "He could be a pain in the arse, but he was the type of person, like a lot of junkies, who are so idealistic that they can't handle life as it is."[4] Thus, in punk, destruction was just as often self-destruction. There is a dreamy madness in punk art. Because, in consequence, how could you show the madness of the world, if not by being (spectacularly!) mad yourself? In this poetic stance, there is again a philosophical proximity between punk and Surrealism. And a specific kind of melancholic Romanticism. In the last part of this chapter, thus, we see if punk might, in spite of itself, be—"Real Romance?"

9.1 Performances and punches

Punk as a lifestyle was per se performance. Theatricality became a part of every day, of walking on the street, taking the bus, going to a party. "Going out became a form of political action, a show of conviction," Tracey Warr observes, in comparing punk's clubs to Dada's cafés.[5] The Dadaists were the first to declare art not only what the artist *does* but what (s)he *is*. In punk, though, the old avant-garde idea of breaking the limits between art and life became, on top, staged. In Warr's observation about going out as a "show of conviction," the "show" part should be emphasized. As Jay Sanders writes about the contemporary New York loft scene: "these new performance practices sought to embody and enact the complex social, political, and media constructions that invisibly (and at times insidiously) define our reality."[6] In punk, such embodiments and enactments were taken to the max. The wearing of provocative punk attire was about a performed, often confrontational, expression; one that would get a strong reaction.

Kathryn Rosenfeld observes,

> Punk's reliance upon the visual—its earnest insistence upon the body as a canvas for self-expression-cum-visual terrorism—made it a logical home both for the performative, visually strategic tactics of contemporary queer culture, and for art students seeking a way out of the studio and the institutions and into the streets.[7]

Punk's style was a means of resistance, the regaining of signifying power, an escape. German punk Gudrun Gut did a parody of a magazine's "home-story" collage in 1977: "In the morning, when the punk awakes, and dresses up like a dream," it reads.[8] The outrageousness and colorfulness of the punk style was imaginative and evocative, full of roles and narratives from cabaret and burlesque to the Wild One, to the Last of the Mohicans. Like a Surrealist theater, performed on the street, in the bar, in the club.

Maria Elena Buszek has researched the Manhattan punk scene of the 1970s and 1980s and she describes the staged splatter violence for example at the *Live Lady Wrestling* events at Club 57, which spotted over-the-top caricatures with cartoonish costumes in fights: sadistic nuns vs. bored housewives. Such performances were an embrace of punk and post-punk's cross-disciplinary, dilettante culture, a pop- and trash-influenced performance art. In 1967, the formalist oriented art historian Michael Fried (famously, at least in the artworld) opinioned that art degenerates when it approaches the condition of theater. In 1981, Douglas Davis replied: "Art can eat theatre alive, and still survive."[9] In this context, the options crystalize that punk might be viewed as living art, as live art, as performance art. The place of this art, however, was most often not the gallery or the museum, but diverse places of the night life. And the self-serious earnestness of the art performance was undermined by elements of "low culture" from horror movie tricks to comic villains.

There were close connections between performance art groups and punk rock groups at the time, as their performances aimed at the same effects. One example might be seen in the Kipper Kids' support for the Sex Pistols at the Fine Art Department of the University of Reading on May 30, 1976, organized by Richard Boon (later manager of Buzzcocks and at the time a student at the Fine Art Department at Reading). The Kipper Kids were a key performance art group in the New York loft scene, and "a very bloody sight,"[10] earning them admiration from COUM Transmissions, among others. Boon describes them as "a performance art duo who used to work their way through a bottle of whiskey while bantering, cracking jokes, occasionally punching one another (or themselves) in the face."[11] Boon and Savage both note how Johnny Rotten integrated such ideas—insulting the audience, hurting himself by stubbing out cigarettes on himself—in his performances. "The power of performance art was it could act like a magnifying glass," Genesis P-Orridge told Jon Savage, "It was the reduction down to the critical moment between being dead and alive. Which is one feels totally alive but also under threat. That is expressed exactly in punk at the beginning: the same edge."[12] It was a verification of existence.

At early punk rock shows, there was hardly any separation between the performer and the audience, and the latter was not there to be pleased, but to be pushed, a duality of hurting and getting hurt. The safety of the audience as well as that of the artist or musicians was sometimes endangered. One famous example was when the Clash and Subway Sect played at the Institute of Contemporary Arts on October 23 in 1976, and one fan bit off a piece of another fan's ear, prompting the *New Musical Express* to use the headline "CANNIBALISM AT CLASH GIG."[13] The sensationalist depiction of punk's destructive instincts, however, often overlooked how much of it was theatrical. "By far the most violent in appearance and rhetoric of any musical movement, punk was probably the least violent in fact—though by far the most violence was directed against it," Marcus asserts.[14] The assertion "by far most violent in appearance" could also be questioned, if we consider dark metal, heavy metal, death metal, or other musical movements. Punk, however, attained a more immersive cultural influence and was thus perceived differently.

Diana Ozon tells how she sometimes exasperated at the incomprehension of cultural critics in the Netherlands, who depicted punk as inciting physical brutality: "We were not condoning violence by showing it, we were just mirroring it! It was ridiculous that it should be understood any other way!" she exclaims.[15]

The punk live art/music shows were cheaply done and accessible, which was ultimately the same reason why performance art had been on the rise in the 1960s and 1970s, as more traditional artistical media were being challenged. Among the reasons for the rise of performance art were thus its impermanence (one time, one place, one situation) and its accessibility (it could often be done with cheap materials or no materials, and the artist's own body). Performance art goes back to the Futurists and the Dada cabarets of the 1910s; with Fluxus, performance had become an important element in the art of the 1960s. In the 1970s, however, performance art became more violent and confrontational than it had been before. Time and again, the performances were deviant, on edge, with themes of sexuality, aggression, humiliation, domination, vulnerability. The artists used and hurt their own body or the bodies of colleagues. In *Reading Position for a Second Degree Burn* (1970), Dennis Oppenheim exposed himself to the burning sun for hours. In *Pryings* (1971), Vito Acconci tried to force open Kathy Dillon's eyes, while she attempted to keep them shut. In *Trans-fixed* (1974), Chris Burden let himself be nailed to a Volkswagen Beetle.

The violent fight against others and oneself is a recurring theme in 1970s performances: boxing specifically emerges as a cultural reference that is invoked again and again. In *Boxing Match* (1972), one of the Kipper Kids—the duo opening for the Sex Pistols at the University of Reading in 1976 and one of whom got into a fight at COUM's ICA opening—bloodied himself up while the other took the role of referee. In another boxing-themed work, Paul McCarthy's *Rocky* (1976), the artist—dressed up and mumbling like Rocky Balboa of the famed movies—repeatedly punches himself in the face, falls to the floor, gets up again, smears ketchup on his genitals, masturbates, then continues hitting himself. It is a display of trash and transgression, horror and humor, dysfunction and deadpan. McCarthy's boxer is the counter-projection to Stallone's heroically manly projection; he is the punk version, both ridiculous and scary, sad and true. Tom Otterness, one of the artists shown in the *Punk Art* exhibition in 1978, was himself an amateur boxer and he exhibited recordings of his own Golden Gloves fights in various art settings (Figure 9.1).

In these works, the Kipper Kids, Paul McCarthy, and Tom Otterness all open a double space where they align the performance of the boxer and the performance of the artist: the violence and (self-)destruction as excitement within a certain agreed-

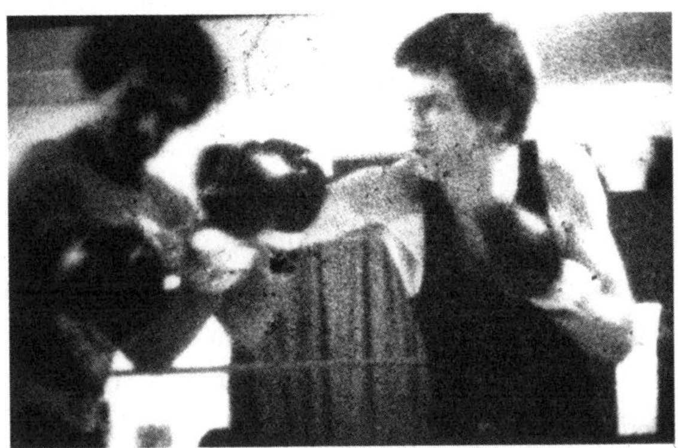

Figure 9.1: Tom Otterness, still from Golden Gloves fight film, 1978. Courtesy of Tom Otterness.

upon-space; even the expectance of the spectators, the anticipation of extreme behavior. In a way, these performers move in that overlapping space between punk and performance art, and between entertainment and assault, too, as Martin von Haselberg told Dominic Johnson:

> There was certainly a lot of edge and a distinct sense of danger when we would do our shows, not just for the audience, but for each other, through physical injuries and things like that. We wanted to entertain but—I don't want to sound too pompous—we also wanted to wake people up [*sic*].[16]

This sentiment is echoed by Tom Otterness as he is interviewed by the curator of the *Punk Art* exhibition, Marc H. Miller. When Miller asks Otterness, why he wants to assault the audience, Otterness shoots back: "You understand that. That's not a question you would ask me if the tape wasn't going. It's SoHo, you know. People sleep a lot. They are not often awake."[17] SoHo, at that time, being *the* art gallery district on Manhattan. The power balance here, however, is a fragile one. The boxer is a blur between machismo and masochism (as evident in Stallone's *Rocky*) and the boxing match as a performance medium is enthralling, potentially sexually loaded, and in the end, perhaps *too* entertaining to wake anybody up?

9.2 "It hurts and looks cool!": Fetish fashion

The self-expression of punks was often paired with physical and aesthetical modification, in a combination of Body Art, style, and everyday performance. But, as Kevin Mattson points out, punk is more easily mainstreamed, if viewed primarily—or even solely—as a style.[18] The importance of Dick Hebdige's analysis in his seminal *Subculture: The Meaning of Style* is thus in the expansion of the understanding of "style": As Hebdige indicates, such expressions "take on a symbolic dimension, becoming a form of stigmata, tokens of a self-imposed exile."[19]

This depiction of punk as a community in exile from the rest of society, recognizing each other by certain style tokens, is also in line with the conception of punks as an "urban tribe," a term coined by Michel Maffesoli.[20] Punk's gestures of naïvety, wildness, and primitivism were means to express an anti-civilization view. There is thus a close connection between punk and the later *Modern Primitive* community, as can for example be seen by the many (former) punks participating in the defining zine issue *RE/Search* #12 in 1989. In this light, mohawk haircuts and safety pins might be viewed as (more playful) versions of scarification, cutting, flesh hooks, and extensive tattoos. Surely, in the stylistic "primitivism" we also see yet another expression of the punk scepsis of the tale of modern progress. Identification with the "primitive" is at the same time a manifestation of an anti-modernist stand, a criticism of the glorifying depiction of the advancing western civilization. This time, punk's style implied, the "barbarians" are not at the gate; they grew up in your house.

Of course, "primitivism" was not the only realm from which the punk style borrowed. As we have seen, punk-style influences came from many different times and places: 1950s American bikers' gangs and diner waitresses, Berlin 1920s decadent dancers, mid nineteenth century extravagant English dandies, and so on. With their designs, figures such as Vivienne Westwood and Linder moved in the space between fashion and politics, sex and art. Westwood's T-shirts with pictures of boobs on them, her mesh stockings and studded bracelets were toying with fetishization and fantasy, while subversively sticking it to conservative moralists. In the late 1970s, Linder designed a series of lingerie and leather masks (Figure 9.2) under the brand name Limiting Accessories LTD. The masks were designed to be worn by men—Devoto from Buzzcocks stood model—and the designs twisted fixed gender expectations. After all, it occurs more often that women are the ones wearing "limiting accessories." The designs also highlight the extensiveness of Linder's artwork, so typical for punk in its multidisciplinary approach. Her art takes place not only in the art gallery but also in the bedroom or on the stage or on the runway.

Weaving together art, fashion, and (sometimes subtle) subversion was of course not new. In Surrealism, the art-fashion connection reached a high, perhaps most prominently incorporated by fashion designer Elsa Schiaparelli and her the eccentric *trompe l'oeil* designs, her insect accessories and black monkey fur shoes.[21] With a hint to the rebellious connection between style and insubordination, which would, later in

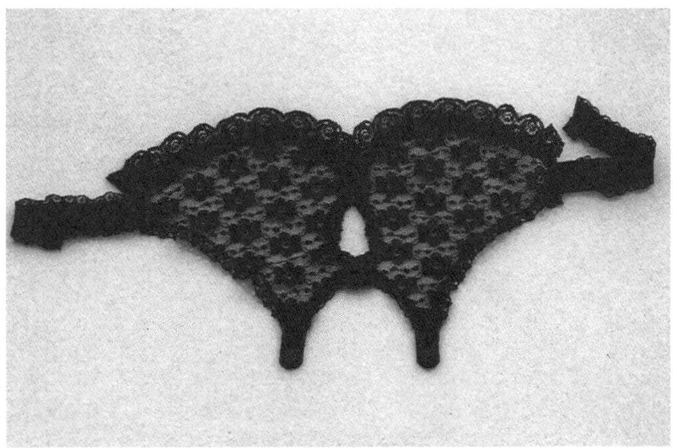

Figure 9.2: Linder, Mask III, *1977. © VG Bild-Kunst, Bonn 2022.*

the century, become a teenage culture classic, Schiaparelli also designed a dress with a hidden pocket for a small flask of your chosen liquor during the prohibition in the United States (1920–33). In Surrealist fashion, the fetish was key, as can be observed in some of Schiaparelli's most infamous designs, such as the Tear Dress, the Shoe Hat, and the Skeleton Dress, all in collaboration with Salvador Dalí, or the fur-lined metal cuffs which Schiaparelli created in collaboration with Meret Oppenheim. In the 1930s fashion industry, clothing was psychologized following the sexual symbolism of Sigmund Freud and J. C. Flügel, interpreting ties and hats as phallic symbols and girdles and garter as clitoral or vaginal symbols.[22]

In punk, such Freudian symbols were present, too, but rather executed by way of pastiche. What does indeed compare to the Surrealists is the combination of fashion and fetishism into artistic objects. Punk artists and designers toyed with the borders of the body, the point where body becomes image. Many of these ideas we can see as linked to Surrealist imagery, but crossed-over with a sense of a bodily counterculture of the youth, which was not present to the same degree in the 1920s–30s. What both the elements of S&M style as well as the body scarification brought to the punk style was a sense of physicality and of pain. In several punk works of art from the late 1970s and early 1980s, these notions of physicality and pain were thematized too, often with a reference, direct or indirect, to punk style, too.

The use of safety pins, in Westwood's fashion (word is, she got it from Richard Hell) and in Jamie Reid's collages (see Section 2.3: "Punk precursors: 1919, 1966, 1968"), has a prehistory in the 1950s Surrealist photo collages of Leo Dohmen (see Figure 9.3). Dohmen was involved first with the Belgian Surrealists, and later in the Situationist

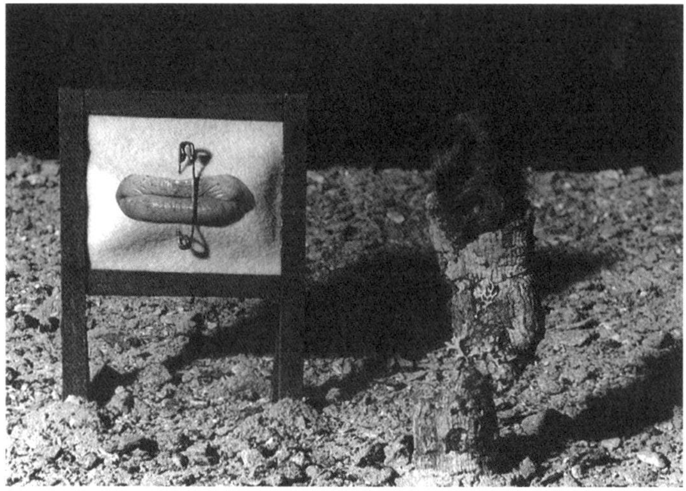

Figure 9.3: Leo Dohmen, Revanche de la Nuit, *1958. Courtesy of the estate of Leo Dohmen, Antwerp.*

International, thus underpinning (no pun intended) that Surrealists–Situationists–punks lineage. The juxtaposition of red lips (in Dohmen's collage, the mouth seems almost clownish) with the shiny object of the safety pin evokes both pain, fetishism, and, since the lips are thus sealed, forced restrain. With the title *Revanche de la Nuit* (Revenge of the night), this confliction between soft flesh and pointy object, between expression and restraint seems to become emphasized.

From the late 1970s punk era, we will examine two examples: one work complex (comprising a shoe, braces, and a hairdo) by Die Tödliche Doris group in West Berlin and another a work by Nina Sten-Knudsen (a very dangerous necklace). First: the *Schmuckzahnspange* (*Jewelry-Braces*, Figure 9.4), *Knochenknorpelschuh* (*Bone-Gristle-Shoe*), and the *Teppicheinlagefrisur* (*Carpet-Tile-Hair-Do*) by Die Tödliche Doris. These artwork/styles are taken out of a more complex affair, Tödliche Doris' first LP, called *"   "* (that is: quotation marks surrounding blank text) released on ZickZack records in 1982. Characteristically of Die Tödliche Doris, this debut took place in several media: there are the recordings themselves, the cover, a Super 8 film, a supplementary zine, and thirteen fashion styles (one for each track). The record sleeve furthermore is filled with a ludicrously brutal, seemingly maniacal sex description, which made Germany's Federal Department for Media Harmful to Young Persons put the album on its list.[23]

The inserted zine was the black-and-white photocopied *Boingo Osmopol* no. 2. The first issue of *Boingo Osmopol* was published by Blixa Bargeld in an edition of five (!) in 1980. These two issues, Bargeld's no. 1 and Die Tödliche Doris' no. 2, were the only ones.[24] The titles of the West Berlin zines mirror the scene's admiration of both Dada

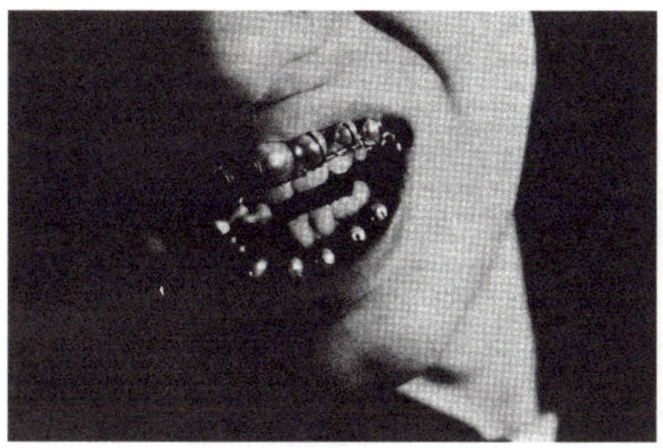

Figure 9.4: Die Tödliche Doris, Schmuckzahnspange (Jewelry-Braces)*, 1982. Archiv der Tödlichen Doris, Courtesy of Wolfgang Müller.*

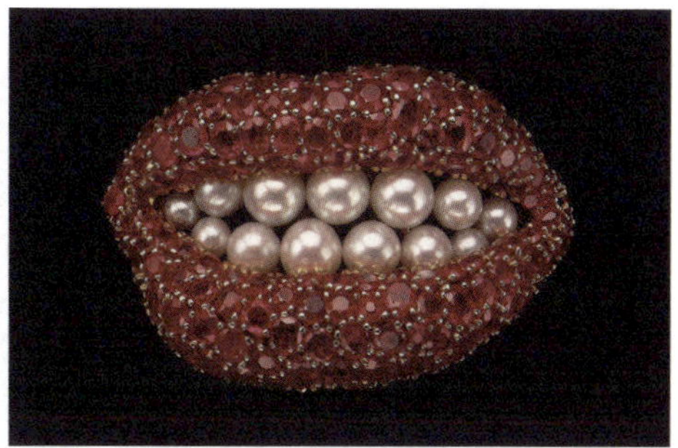

Figure 9.5: Salvador Dalí, Ruby Lips Brooch*, 1949.* *© VG Bild-Kunst, Bonn 2022.*

and Futurism: apart from the neologism *Boingo Osmopol*, it comes across in other titles such as *Y-KLRMPFNST* and *Clonk Clonk Clonk*, both of which sound almost as if they are straight out of Luigi Russolo's *L'Arte dei Rumori* (see Section 2.3: "Punk precursors: 1919, 1966, 1968").

On the cover, *Boingo Osmopol* no. 2 shows one of the thirteen fashion styles that the group had devised for their songs: the *Jewelry-Braces*, which corresponded to the track "Stümmel mir die Sprache" (Maltreat my language). The *Jewelry-Braces* can be seen as related to punk band X-Ray Spex's front woman Poly Styrene's dental braces: a physical protest against a specific beauty stereotype. Seen as an object, braces are associated with youth and physical restraint to achieve a desired ideal. The pain associated with wearing ordinary braces is exaggerated in Die Tödliche Doris' mouth-maltreatment: the pearl brackets are so big they force open the lips, gagging the wearer (and thus, corresponding to the song title, maltreating his/her language). A clear reference for Die Tödliche Doris' *Jewelry-Braces* is Salvador Dalí's *Ruby Lips Brooch* with pearl teeth (1949; Figure 9.5).

Dalí modeled his brooch after Hollywood's original bleach-blonde diva, Mae West's lips and had it executed in eighteen-carat yellow gold, natural rubies, and pearls.[25] Again, we see an example of an image with which the Surrealists only played, and which is weird, yet also expensive and aesthetically pleasing, is, in punk, made manifest, is made physical, and is made base and sordid (see Section 5.2: "Modernity in extremis").

Bodily modifications and mutable appearances, often accompanied with just a touch of injury, were a focal point of punk. The text accompanying these styles in *Boingo Osmopol* parodies the rhetoric and style of cheap self-help and how-to books, with comments like "The corrective teeth retainer so unpopular among the young in their puberty, adorned with lovely gems? It hurts and looks cool!" and "The glue for your hair is easy to make, just mix flour and water, but be careful that it doesn't go lumpy!"[26]

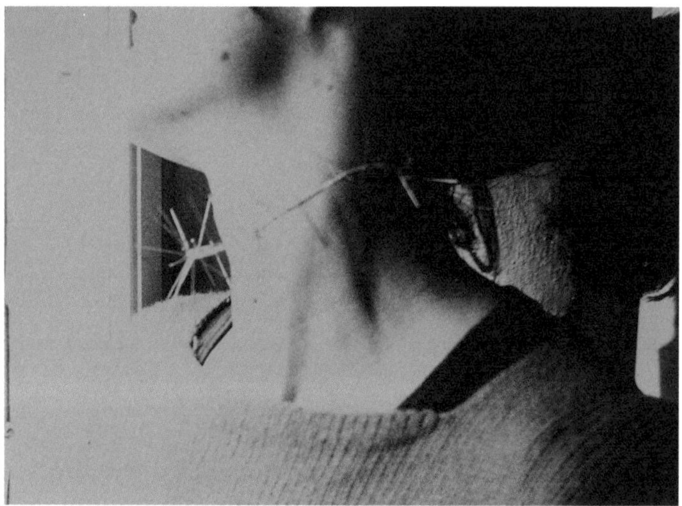

Figure 9.6: Nina Sten-Knudsen, Smykker *(Jewelry), ca. 1979–80. Courtesy of Nina Sten-Knudsen.*

The "fashion" elements were an acknowledgment of Vivienne Westwood and SEX. "We were trying to think one step further [...] what comes after the spiked dog collar? The jewelry brace,"[27] says Müller. The styles thus ironize fashion's hype impulse but also celebrate its subversive potential. The unwearable, high-heeled, pointed *Bone-Gristle-Shoe* was made of gristle, mold, bones, remains of animal tissue, and scraps of fur, thus displaying an ephemeral material aesthetic somewhere between Dieter Roth and Joseph Beuys. Die Tödliche Doris' works also share a lot with works by Meret Oppenheim, such as *Fur Gloves with Wooden Fingers* (1936), *Sugar Ring* (1936–37), or the stitched-together shoes of *The Couple* (1956): tangibility, impossibility, absurdity, corporeality, subversion, and (dark) humor.

Like *Jewelry-Braces, Carpet-Tile-Hair-Do* encourages readers to maltreat themselves, this time with a sharp scraping knife and self-made glue. "Similar to sound and language, hair and nails were also considered by us to be a form of bodily dissociation," writes Müller.[28] Through these foreign matters—language, sound, hair, nails—a modification of perception and reputation becomes possible. The haircut has a long tradition as a symbolic rite of passage into a certain societal status or cultural stance; the queue, the pompadour, the jar head, the tonsure, the afro, the mohawk, etc. Die Tödliche Doris, however, primarily uses the hairdo as a sardonic remark on the absurdities of appearance.

The second example is a necklace by Nina Sten-Knudsen. It is part of a series of art objects which she called *Smykker* (Jewelry), of which none remain, leaving only a few blurred photos (Figures 9.6 and 9.7).

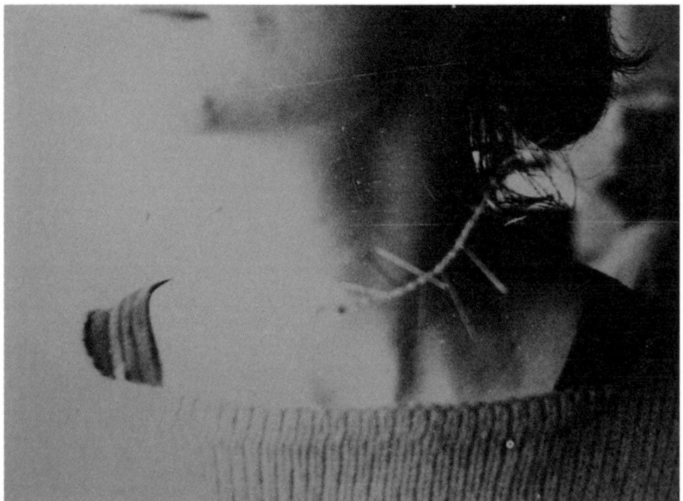

Figure 9.7: Nina Sten-Knudsen, Smykker *(Jewelry), ca. 1979–80. Courtesy of Nina Sten-Knudsen.*

> One was a necklace made out of rope yarn with needles protruding from all sides, and then I would wear it. So it would sting my neck, but also sting, if someone tried to touch me. That was how I felt, back then. That was how the time was, back then.[29]

The duality of hurting and getting hurt is present in this jewelry. There is a strong connection with the works of Die Tödliche Doris, in the juxtaposition of pain and fashion, softness and hardness, metal and skin. Sten-Knudsen's jewelry is less absurd and more direct than that of Doris, but they share a sense of impossible physicality (which incidentally can also be connected with both Meret Oppenheim and Vivienne Westwood).

The difference between the pearl braces of Die Tödliche Doris and Nina Sten-Knudsen's needle necklace is a matter of irony vs. solemnity. Die Tödliche Doris is displaying a far more distanced and drier attitude toward the prospect of dressing up in your agony: "It hurts and looks cool!"—what a subversion of the subversion. Sten-Knudsen, on the other hand, is expressing her inner state through self-harming. This is a recurring field of tension in punk: the movement fluctuates between the poles of distance and depth, seriousness and satire. At this time, Sten-Knudsen made several works that focused on her hurt body: "I started using my own body, I made a whole series of Body Art. I laced my body with twine, I used steel wire," Sten-Knudsen explains: "It was about hurting yourself to express something that was present at the time, something you could feel, but which was invisible," she says."[30] Nina Sten-

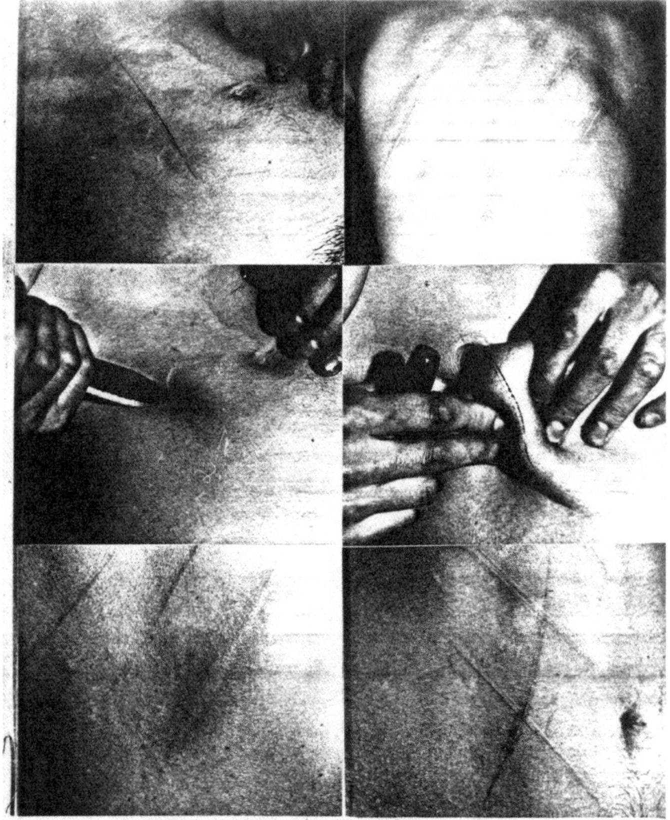

Figure 9.8: Nina Sten-Knudsen, Knife and Skin, *ca. 1979–80. Courtesy of Nina Sten-Knudsen.*

Knudsen uses double-edged (self-)destruction (she is herself both the perpetrator and the victim) in these images as a means to make her pain visible.

The scarification work *Knife and Skin* (Figure 9.8) is also part of this series, as is the image used by Thomsen for the cover of *City Slang* (see Section 4.2: "Punk poetry"). It shows a mouth, lips drawn back, with wooden stakes rammed between the teeth: "I found these wood pieces on the ground and I took my knife—I always carried a knife back then—and sharpened them and stuck them between my teeth. And that was the picture that became the cover of *City Slang*." Thomsen, giving his view of the image, writes that it displays, "an ambiguity of aggression and pain, which is congenial with the self-staging of the punk period."[31] Sten-Knudsen's image also alludes to Die Tödliche Doris' song "Maltreat My Language" and the accompanying *Jewelry-Braces* artwork. This link becomes even clearer in the further explanation by Thomsen, "both poems and slang are language, and language comes from the mouth, especially slang, which is more spoken word than written word." Thomsen understands both language and body as means of awareness, and this awareness is connected to agony. It is the same awareness which Sten-Knudsen describes. In Thomsen's poems, we might find a similar link—a kind of existentialist sadness—for instance in *Levende* (*Alive*) which ends with the reduced repetition, "jeg græder / jeg er levende / græder / levende" ("I am crying / I am alive / crying / alive"). Says Sten-Knudsen about the mood of the time: "Darkness, obscurity, melancholy."[32]

9.3 Real romance?

The overarching theme of this chapter is "Pain and Presence"—such an unironic sense of gravity comes with that! Is that really punk? Yes and no. It is a side of punk. As a movement, punk is full of such internal contradictions. We just saw it, in the last section: Die Tödliche Doris' intelligent wryness and Sten-Knudsen's physical expressions of felt agony, so different, and none the less connected. With that tension in mind, it is possible to look at punk as deeply romantic too. Indeed, in *Vacant: A Diary of the Punk Years 1976–79*, Nils Stevenson (first-generation punk, Sex Pistols' road manager, producer for Siouxsie and the Banshees) quotes Isaiah Berlin's *The Roots of Romanticism*, but he crosses out "Romanticism" and replaces it with "PUNK," so that the quote reads:

> PUNK ~~Romanticism~~ is the primitive, the untutored, it is youth, life […] but it is also pallor, fever, disease, decadence […] the Dance of Death, indeed Death itself […] it is the confused, teeming fullness and richness of life, […] turbulence, violence, conflict, chaos, but it is also peace […] it is the strange, the exotic, the grotesque, […] the irrational, the unutterable […] [*sic*].[33]

If Romanticism was to some degree a reaction against Enlightenment, a turn away from the rationalization of all aspects of life, a turn toward irrationality, imagination, emotionality, then we might view punk as a kindred outburst of radicality and inexplicability. The image of the outcast artist, not understood, but also not dependent on being understood, was a prevailing feature in Romanticism, and this idea was revisited in punk. We have seen aspects of Romanticism in punk throughout this book: the role of the child in punk, for example, or the attitude toward playful dilettantism (see Chapter 6: "Children Run Riot: The Art of the Infantile" and Chapter 7: "Work vs. Play"). Take the following quote by Gavin Grindon:

> Radical aspects of Romanticism had already formulated a celebration of creative vitality as an "impossible" return to play, childhood, or nature contra capital, the

> urban centre and work, yet coupled to a cult of paralysed retreat into isolation, poverty, madness, and death.[34]

It is Peter Pan and the Lost Boys all over again: a fantasy land for the outcasts, an impossible return to childhood (as Gavin Grindon writes of Romanticism).

Of course, punk was not having any Jean-Jacques Rousseau "Retour à la nature!" (Return to nature) cliché. *Au contraire*. German punk band S. Y. P. H. even recorded a song called "Zurück zum Beton" ("Return to concrete," 1980). The natural habitat of punk was the city. The Zeitgeist was tabloids, teenage subculture, tutti-frutti-rock-n-roll reenactments. Not standing alone on a mountain top. However, there is a longing for authenticity in punk, or perhaps a longing for a state of innocence (the child, the playful improvisation), as well as a melancholic dreamfulness. We might again invoke the Surrealists too, who—in the name of youth—strived to give poetry a revolutionary character, who—in the middle of urban life—dedicated to the idea of the magnificent. A sense of the irrational flows through Romanticism, Surrealism, and punk.

Punk could even be romantic, in the sense of loving—it was just a different kind of love than the old-fashioned romantic cliché that had in late-capitalist society been wrapped into a whole package of a house and a mortgage and a regular life of defining yourself through the size of your consumer goods. Still, punk's romantic side is only understandable when the movement's overall negative judgement of the state of society is considered. Punk was and is "a minority culture for outcasts, for those willing to make and live in their own embattled but special world, for those who didn't fit into society or who saw society as unfit for themselves," as Greil Marcus writes.[35] The romantic madness, which comes through in that Isaiah Berlin quote, which Stevenson summons, points to the incongruity of punk, its inbuilt inability to achieve. Punk was in many ways an impossible quest, a downbound trip, not destined, not designed to "go well." At the same time, that very impossibility, that romantic madness, crystalizes as the power of punk: punks revealed the madness of the world by acting mad themselves.

As an example of how that punk sense of madness and darkness was expressed in artworks, we might look to Copenhagen: there is a nocturnal darkness, an almost tangible nakedness in the (combined) visual and lyrical expression of this time (perhaps Scandinavian melancholia plays a role here, too). This is the case in the collaborations between the poet Søren Ulrik Thomsen and artist Nina Sten-Knudsen, or the poet Michael Strunge working together with the painters Dorte Dahlin and Lars Nørgård. Likewise, the Sods (who also worked closely with Søren Ulrik Thomsen, using his poem for the track "Marble Station" in 1980) tended toward the dark, dreamy, and deep. The Sods embodied an experimental crossover take on punk. "It was more the images, the

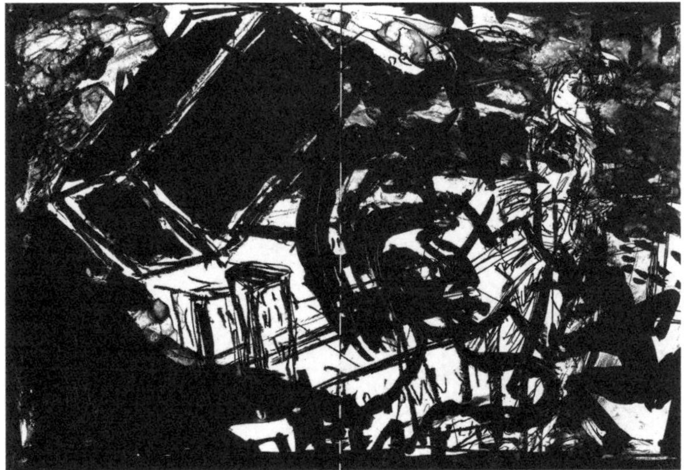

Figure 9.9: Christian Lemmerz, drawing for the catalogue Græsset malker koens ben (The Grass Milks the Leg of the Cow)*, 1983. Courtesy of Christian Lemmerz.*

iconography of punk, that I was attracted to [...] the aesthetics," Knud Odde, an artist in his own right, by the way, explains.[36] The Sods worked together closely with the theater collective Billedstofteatret (roughly: ImageMaterialTheater), transforming their live concerts into visual performances with elaborate scenography and choreography.[37] The disposition of the Sods' aesthetics was imbued with the poetic, giving all their work an air that at its core seemed more melancholic than raging.

The small black-and-white catalogue for the exhibition *The Grass Milks the Leg of the Cow* in 1983 at Værkstedet Værst is a testament to this dark Romanticism in Copenhagen at this time: Christian Lemmerz and Nina Sten-Knudsen's works, for examples. Lemmerz' drawing (Figure 9.9) is a semi-abstract whirlwind of black forms, lines, and figures. It takes a while to orient ourselves within the image. A large coffin hovers in the upper left corner. In the lower right corner squats the dark silhouette of a figure. The image oscillates between floating gray areas and hard black lines, some of which appear to have been scratched, revealing the white underneath: a pandemonium of darkness and fragments, a face, inscriptions, possible signs. The world is a place of chaos. "We wanted to rediscover the archaic, the existentialist image," says Christian Lemmerz, "Better a scream than a beautiful sentence. Better to vomit on the floor than paint something deep. That was like punk. Three chords are enough, if your mode of expression is honest."[38]

Sten-Knudsen's drawing for the catalogue shows an amorphous figure; a dark torso with a disfigured, blurred head (Figure 9.10). The outlines of a mouth and nostrils, and a line of black spikes around the figure's neck, contrast with the lightness of the cobweb-like

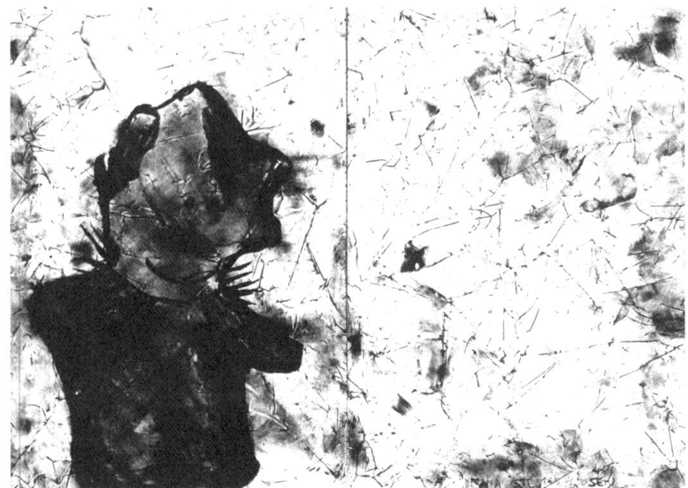

Figure 9.10: Nina Sten-Kudsen, drawing for the catalogue Grœsset malker koens ben (The Grass Milks the Leg of the Cow), *1983. Courtesy of Nina Sten-Knudsen.*

background. In the early 1980s, Sten-Knudsen repeated such compact, physical, eyeless figures in her work: other examples are *Kædemand* (*The Chain Man*, 1982) and *Graffiti* (1982). The figure seems much too massive for its surroundings, as though it does not belong, an imagery of alienation and vulnerability.

Together, the drawings by Lemmerz and Sten-Knudsen transport a sense of both youthful uproar and tragedy, of confusion and existentialism. Other images in the small catalogue were less naked in their expression, some of them self-ironically reciting the contemporary neo-Expressionist painter scene in Düsseldorf (Jiří Georg Dokoupil, Walter Dahn, e.g.), whose style they were "borrowing." As often throughout this book, we look at punk that is art and art that is punk, and ascertain: that it is like that, and it is not like that. That punk (art) is deep and superficial, ironic and innocent, authentic and fake. In the next and final chapter, we take a deep dive into these punk paradoxes. It is: "Dystopian with a Twist."

Notes

1. Warr, "Feral City", 116.
2. Sex Pistols, "Anarchy in the UK" (UK: EMI, 1976).
3. Breton, "Second Manifesto of Surrealism" [1930], 125.
4. Viv Albertine quoted in Savage, *England's Dreaming*, 194–95.
5. Tracey Warr, "Feral City," in *Panic Attack! Art in The Punk Years*, eds. Mark Sladen and Ariella Yedgar (London: Merrell, 2007), 117.

6. Jay Sanders, "Love Is an Object," in *Rituals on Rented Island*, 28.

7. Rosenfeld, "The End of Everything," 29.

8. Gudrun Gut, 1977. See Kunstalle Düsseldorf, *Zurück zum Beton*, 5.

9. Quoted in Maria Elena Buszek, "Ladies Auxiliary of the Lower East Side: Post-Punk Feminist Art and New York's Club 57," in *Punk & Post-Punk* 9, no. 3 (2020), 426.

10. Genesis P-Orridge quoted in Savage, *England's Dreaming*, 250. See also Tutti, *Art Sex Music*, 205.

11. Matthew Worley, "The Sex Pistols at Reading, May 30, 1976," accessed January 8, 2018, https://unireadinghistory.com/2016/05/27/sex-pistols-at-reading.

12. Genesis P-Orridge quoted in Savage, *England's Dreaming*, 250.

13. *New Musical Express*, November 6, 1976, n.p.

14. Marcus, "Punk (1979)."

15. Ozon, interview, 2017.

16. Martin von Haselberg quoted in Johnson, *The Art of Living*, 79.

17. Tom Otterness quoted in *Punk Art*, n.p.

18. Mattson, "Did Punk Matter?", 69–97.

19. Hebdige, *Subculture*, 2.

20. Michel Maffesoli, *The Time of the Tribes: The Decline of Individualism in Mass Society* [French version: 1985] (Thousand Oaks: SAGE Publications, 1996).

21. See Dilys Blum, *Shocking: The Art and Fashion of Elsa Schiaparelli* (New Haven: Yale University Press, 2004).

22. Ghislaine Wood, *The Surreal Body: Fetish and Fashion* (London: V&A Publications, 2007), 62.

23. The complete letter of argumentation is reproduced in *Die Tödliche Doris – Kino*, 99.

24. See http://www.punkfanzines.de, accessed April 5, 2018.

25. Wood, *The Surreal Body*, 82.

26. *Boingo Osmopol*, no. 2 (1982). Die Tödliche Doris Archive, Berlin.

27. Müller, interview, 2017.

28. Wolfgang Müller, *Die Tödliche Doris – Performance. Band* 5 (Berlin: Hybriden Verlag, 2017), n.p.

29. Sten-Knudsen, interview, 2018.

30. Sten-Knudsen, interview, 2018.

31. Thomsen, "Om Forsiden til City Slang."

32. Sten-Knudsen, interview, 2018.

33. Stevenson, *Vacant*, 18.

34. Grindon, "Surrealism, Dada, and the Refusal of Work," 83.

35. Marcus, "Punk (1979)."

36. Knud Odde quoted in Poulsen, *Something Rotten*, 16.

37. See Elmer, *Billedstofteater 1977–85: Et Billedteater skabt af Per Flink Basse og Kirsten Dehlholm, et billedforløb* (Copenhagen: Christian Ejlers, 1995).

38. Lemmerz, interview, 2018.

10 Dystopian with a Twist

This is the last chapter of this book (well, almost, the last chapter before we get to the attempt of summarizing the laws of the lawless, of holding down this *Punk Art History*, which was always bound to be fragmented and somewhat disorderly). So, at the end of this book, we will be looking at: The end. In punk, the sense of being in the closing stages of *something* (history? human existence? the world as we knew it?) was omnipresent. The general dystopian outlook of the late 1970s was celebrated in punk art and music. Johnny Rotten's lyric "Your future dream has sure been seen through"[1] set the tone. Punks were not about to mourn the death of a dream that had never been their own. Still, the disposition of punk was never unequivocal: Punk was dystopian, yes, but with a twist.

We analyze punk's hedonistic mixture of crashing-cum-roistering in three steps: first, in the section "It's the end of the world," we look at punk artworks and punk music which in different ways thematize collapse and dystopia. In the second section, we focus on The Grand Downfall Show (original: Die Große Untergangsshow), which was a one-day festival organized by the Ingenious Dilettantes in West Berlin's Tempodrom, a building reminiscent of a huge circus tent, which underlines punk's link between doom and fête. And finally, in the third section, "Broken heroes, aces of failure," we think over punk's own ending. This consideration is linked with the conceptualization of failure in punk culture. Faults and fiasco were held high in many punk artworks. Indeed, it seems the anticipated failure of the punk movement itself was integrated into the movement from the start. If no one here was expecting to get out alive (as Jim Morrison sang it back it 1963), then how could success be a criterion?

10.1 It's the end of the world

"We were really convinced the world was coming to an end," Alexander Hacke of Einstürzende Neubauten recalls.[2] In punk culture, this imagination of a looming apocalypse mixed with a more general pessimistic assessment of the contemporary state of society. The city was often used as a symbol for decay and destruction, as we have seen in the "Burning Babylon" allegory (see Section 7.1: "Punk's Homo Ludens"). The name of Hacke's band, Einstürzende Neubauten, that is: collapsing new buildings, contains the same dystopian schadenfreude, as does the pyromaniac satisfaction with the smoldering of Babel. Many artists and writers, who were connected to punk, took up the theme of the damaged city. In *Day's End* (1975), Gordon Matta-Clark intervened in a deserted warehouse in New York, removing sections of its walls to change the light, in an attempt, as

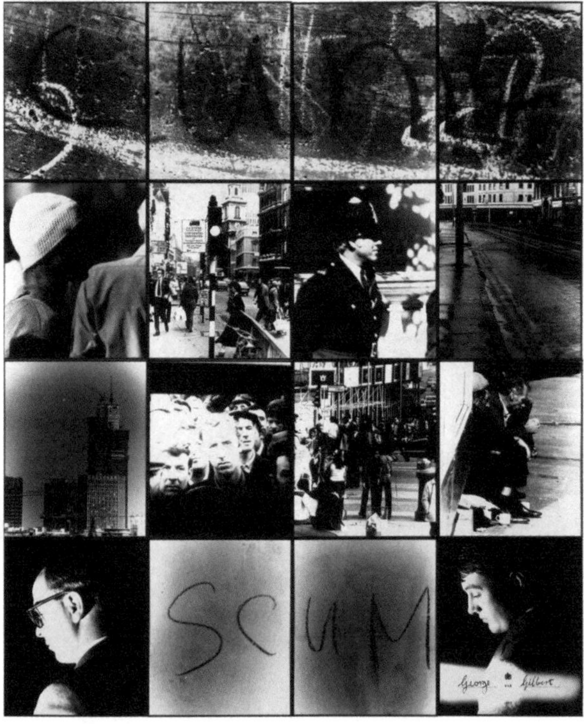

Figure 10.1: Gilbert & George, CUNT SCUM *(from the series* Dirty Words Pictures*), 1977. © Gilbert & George. Courtesy of the artists and White Cube.*

he put it himself, to draw attention to "social economic and moral conditions" in the city.[3] In the UK, Stephen Willats's collages titled *Every Day and Every Night* (1984) juxtapose social housing constructions, concrete, combat boots, photos of young punks or skinheads, and slogans such as "A COMMON HATE IS JUST AS BINDING AS A COMMON LOVE." Dystopic visions of urbanity were also present in J. G. Ballard's *High Rise,* which was published in 1975, and was, according to Jon Savage, "the big book that autumn"—that is 1976—in the punk milieu.[4] On edge between criticism of the social conditions and a fascination with downfall, punk drew inspiration from the ruins of the city.

In their large-scale black, white, and red *Dirty Words Pictures* (1977), the artists Gilbert & George show social tensions, brokenness, and abuse in London. Each image carries a photo of a graffiti at the top, such as *QUEER, BOLLOCKS, PROSTITUTE,* or *CUNT SCUM* (Figure 10.1). One picture carries the sprayed slogan: "Are you angry or are you boring?" (Figure 10.2). The artists contrast self-portraits both with images of broken windows, damaged facades, street riots, homeless people, and symbols of power, such as

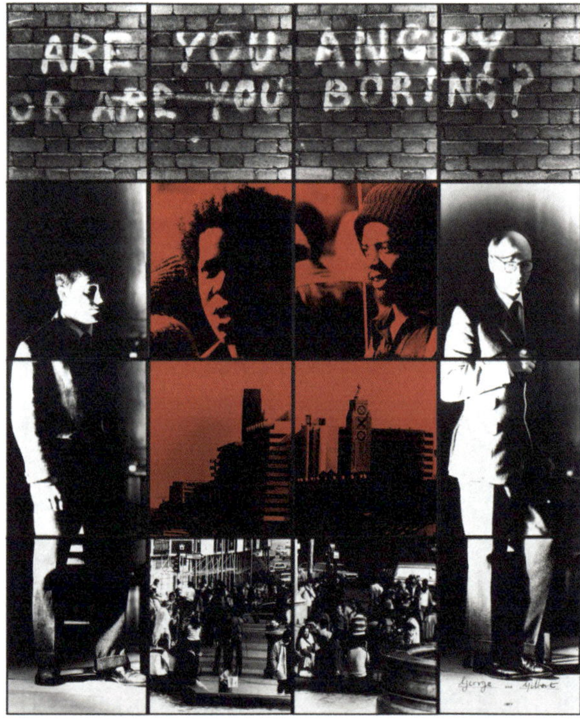

Figure 10.2: Gilbert & George, ARE YOU ANGRY OR ARE YOU BORING? *(from the series* Dirty Words Pictures*), 1977. © Gilbert & George. Courtesy of the artists and White Cube.*

the Palace of Westminster and armed military and police personnel. London is depicted as a brutal place in these images. In their pictures, Gilbert & George take on the blunt directness of graffiti and transfer it into their own work. "Violent social realism," Michael Bracewell calls the series.[5] As we have seen in several artworks and songs throughout this book (see e.g. Section 8.1: "Queer punks and dykes in high heels"), the topic of police violence was a constant in punk. The musical counterpart to Gilbert & George's imagery can for example be found in The Jam's track "In the City" which was likewise released in 1977: "In the city there's a thousand men in uniforms / And I've heard they now have the right to kill a man."[6]

The broken city thus became a symbol of inner demise, whereas the threat of an escalation in the Cold War stood for a more literal demise: the atomic end of the world. There is a longing for destruction among punk artists: in May 1978, for example, Hugo Kaagman produced a poster insert for the *KoeCrandt* zine with the slogan "Drop de Neutron Bomb," an alternative to the "Stop the Neutron Bomb" campaign of the Dutch

Interchurch Peace Council. Such a message from the church (!) about peace (!) triggered a reflex denouncement from the punks, and the phonetical similarity between stop-the-bomb and drop-the-bomb did the rest.

In Berlin, the possibility of such an escalation was more concretely present than elsewhere. It had been less than twenty years since US and Soviet tanks stood opposite each other at Checkpoint Charlie, threatening a World War III, and the Berlin Wall was a constant reminder of that tension. This sentiment that World War III and, with it, collective death in a nuclear mushroom cloud might be coming any time soon was thus especially pronounced, even cultivated, in West Berlin. Around 1980, writes Martin Schmitz about the West Berlin scene, "there was a lot of talk about the end of the world."[7] Berlin signified that potential mushroom cloud, but also a decadent sense of partying, like the last days of Rome. In one Einstürzende Neubauten song called "Ich stehe auf Berlin" ("I am into Berlin," 1981), Blixa Bargeld murmurs and cries:

> Ich steh auf Feuer
> Ich steh auf Rauch
> Ich steh auf Krach
> Ich steh auf Steine
> Ich steh auf Zerfall
> Ich steh auf Krankheit
> Ich steh auf Niedergang
> Ich steh auf Ende.
>
> (I am into fire
> I am into smoke
> I am into noise
> I am into stones
> I am into decay
> I am into sickness
> I am into demise
> I am into the end.)[8]

Sure enough, the song was the answer to the Neue Deutsche Welle song "Ich steh auf Berlin" (1980) by Ideal which sported a much more positive attitude.

The outlook to Armageddon was met with both weltschmerz and cynicism in punk music and punk art. Sometimes, the romance of disaster was countered by a cooler, wryer approach. In the work of Die Tödliche Doris, for example, there is no melodramatic longing toward death. Instead, the deadly catastrophe arrives in a laconic and impassive form: In their song "Sieben tödliche Unfälle im Haushalt" ("Seven Deadly Household Accidents," 1981),[9] a catalogue of mishaps—all leading to death—is presented. A can of hairspray is transformed into a flamethrower by a tired morning cigarette; a falling pane of glass from a shop window guillotines a drunken young man who accidentally stumbles on the pavement in front of it; and so on. These stories are recited in a flat voice with an annoyingly loud cacophony of instruments playing in the foreground. The title "Seven Deadly..." reminds us of the Bible's seven deadly sins, but the scenarios in Tödliche Doris' song are just the bad practical jokes of everyday life. Such a sardonic and bizarre dealing with the hardships of life (and death) was typical of the work of Die Tödliche Doris. On the spectrum of apocalyptic moods of the late 1970s, Die Tödliche Doris' random deadly household accidents signify a counterpoint to the thespian end of the scale.

As we have seen, COUM Transmissions were likewise engaged in a base assessment of the human condition, both life and death. With this skeptical disposition, COUM fitted well to *VILE*, where they published several works over the years among others the above-mentioned collage *L'ecole de l'art infantile* (1974, see Section 6.3: "Infancy conforms to nobody"). The collage was printed in the (rather infamous) *VILE* no. 1, which was published in 1974, but was deliberately dated wrongly February 14, 1985. The cover carried the note "Happy Valentine's Day" and featured a manipulated photo of Monte Cazazza holding his own ripped-out heart toward the viewing eye (Figure 10.3).

Cazazza's photocollage, with its bloody accuracy, might have fit right into Georges Bataille's *DOCUMENTS* (1929–30), which underscores that link between the "evil" side of punk and the "evil" side of Surrealism. Concerning the wrong date, George Orwell's novel *1984* was often referenced in punk art, and Banana did so by placing *VILE* into a framework that was even *post*-dystopia: "I linked it with Orwell and made it the year AFTER his famous tome."[10] This dystopian notion of a *1984* society was likewise taken up by Hugo Kaagman, who, for a number of years, dated all of his works 1984, until Diana Ozon convinced him to stop, because it was so difficult to keep track of.[11] In itself, this bespeaks an interesting internal conflict between a "No Future" impulse and the requirements of archiving, which after all only makes sense if there is indeed a future.

Along these lines, dystopia was treated ambivalently in punk: in Western Europe, the United Kingdom, and the United States, at least, punk artists and musicians were getting ready to dance on the grave of "Western Civilization." There was no remorse for the expected downfall of what punks viewed as a war-mongering and unjust system.

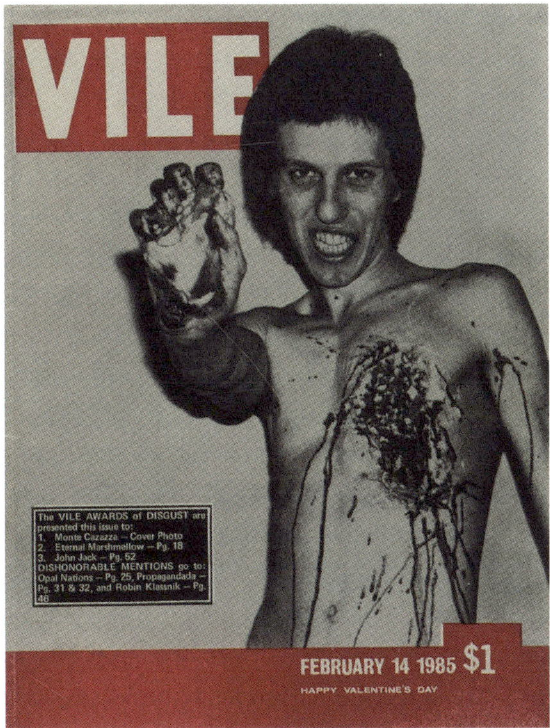

Figure 10.3: Anna Banana & Bill Gaglione, cover of VILE, *no. 1, 1974 [dated 1985]. Photo collage by Monte Cazazza. The Museum of Modern Art Library, New York. Courtesy of Anna Banana.*

There was no "give peace a chance" either—it was: Drop the Neutron bomb! The apocalyptic mood was instead used for a decadent celebration: *après nous, le deluge*—after us, the flood.

10.2 The Grand Downfall Show

In the half-city of West Berlin in particular, these threads of doom and celebration intertwined. West Berlin was the over-subsidized western frontier, a small island lying isolated in the middle of the German Democratic Republic surrounding it on all sides. The risks and inaccessibility of West Berlin resulted in most large German companies moving away, leaving few to no career opportunities. Due to its special political status, West Berlin instead became the city where maladjusted West-German youth went to avoid military service. In the late 1970s and early 1980s, it was also the only European city with no mandatory curfew for bars. In the words of David Bowie (who lived together with Iggy Pop in West Berlin from 1976 to 1978), it was "the heroin capital of Europe,"[12] a reputation only reinforced by Christiane F. and *Wir Kinder vom Bahnhof Zoo* (*Zoo Station:*

The Story of Christiane F.; book 1978/film 1981). In the early 1980s, there were around 170 squat houses in Berlin, a result both of real-estate speculation and of the misguided "Flächensanierung" (mass renovation), sometimes referred to as "Kahlschlagsanierung" (eradication renovation), which sought to redevelop Berlin by tearing down whole blocks of older and often still war-damaged buildings.[13] The squatters moved into these unrenovated buildings, with some putting a lot of effort into renewing them and others just enjoying the free (and decaying) space.

The artists and musicians in Berlin sought to reconnect with the radical modernity and hedonism of the inter-war avant-garde, with Berlin-Dada, cabaret, Mack the Knife. The Weimar period was seen as that glittery and eccentric period just before catastrophe, and parallels were drawn. The late 1970s–early 1980s scene in West Berlin was hybrid: in squat houses and in night clubs, bars, and off-off cinemas, such as Chaos, RISIKO, Schizzo, Exzess, Dschungel, Frontkino, Punk House, and SO36, different media mixed. Ursula Block's Gelbe Musik was both a gallery and a record shop. Bettina Köster and Gudrun Gut's Eisengrau was both a fashion store and a DIY cassette music label. The apparel and the varying window displays at Eisengrau were reminiscent of Vivienne Westwood and Malcolm McLaren's SEX and Peter Christopherson's installations for BOY in London. Among other things, you could buy knitted punk sweaters with large holes in them, or wallets made from old pornographic magazines in see-through plastic wrap. In the store front sat a mannequin chained to a table decked out with a bowl of puke, or the mannequin hung from the ceiling with a noose around its neck.[14] (The Berlin Dadaists' use of a mannequin hanging from the ceiling at the opening of the First International Dada Fair in Berlin in 1920 springs to mind, see Section 7.2: "Ingenious Dilettantes").

In punk culture, Berlin was a myth, a symbol of decadence. As the Ramones song goes: "Jackie is a punk / Judy is a runt / They both went down to Berlin, joined the Ice Capades."[15] Nils Stevenson writes about the ironic and glamorous fishnet stockings and swastikas in the outfits of early London punks that they "signified the decadence of pre-war Berlin and pissed off your parents."[16] The Sex Pistols wrote "Holidays in the Sun" (1977) in West Berlin, with the lines: "I didn't ask for sunshine / And I got World War Three / I'm looking over the Wall / And they're looking at me."[17] Many years later, Johnny Lydon explained how the Pistols had looked to escape London, where "there was hatred and constant threat of violence." Lydon captures the mood:

> Berlin and its decadence was a good idea. The song came about from that. I loved Berlin. I loved the wall and the insanity of the place. The communists looked in on the circus atmosphere of West Berlin, which never went to sleep, and that would be their impression of the West.[18]

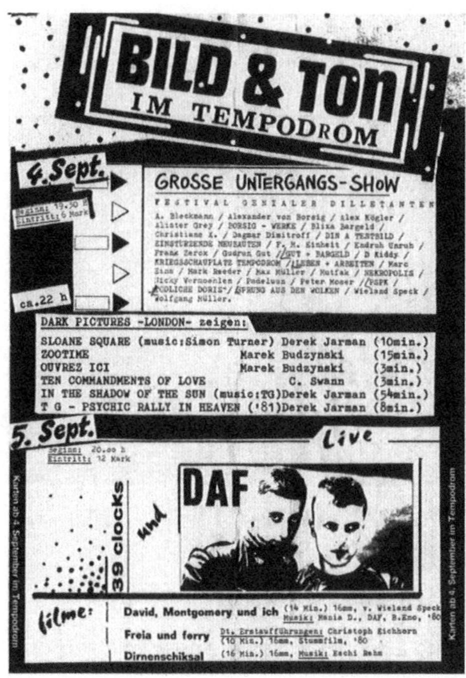

Figure 10.4: Poster for Die Große Untergangsshow (The Grand Downfall Show), 1981. Archiv der Tödlichen Doris. Courtesy Wolfgang Müller.

That "circus atmosphere," which Lydon describes, became gloriously expressed four years later, at the Festival der Genialen Dilletanten (Festival of Brilliant Dilettantes), a one-day festival of music and art, which took place on September 4, 1981 (Figure 10.4). The festival's title, Die Große Untergangsshow (The Grand Downfall Show) expresses exactly that hedonistic doomsday-relishing, packed in extravaganza ambience. The Grand Downfall Show took place in the Tempodrom, an entertainment arena that resembles a circus tent and stands in what was then a deserted area close to the Berlin Wall. Wieland Speck (later program curator of the Berlin Film Festival) was the *compère*, the grand show master. Among the performances at The Grand Downfall Show were Din A Testbild, Sprung aus den Wolken, Einstürzende Neubauten, a spontaneous duet between Gudrun Gut and Blixa Bargeld, one-man-show Frieder Butzmann (with whom Genesis P-Orridge recorded a track the same year)[19] and the lavishly dressed-up members of Die Tödliche Doris, who posed as ironic allegories of the "women's movement" (Dagmar Dimitroff), the "peace movement" (Wolfgang Müller), and "individuality" (Nikolaus Utermöhlen) (Figure 10.5).

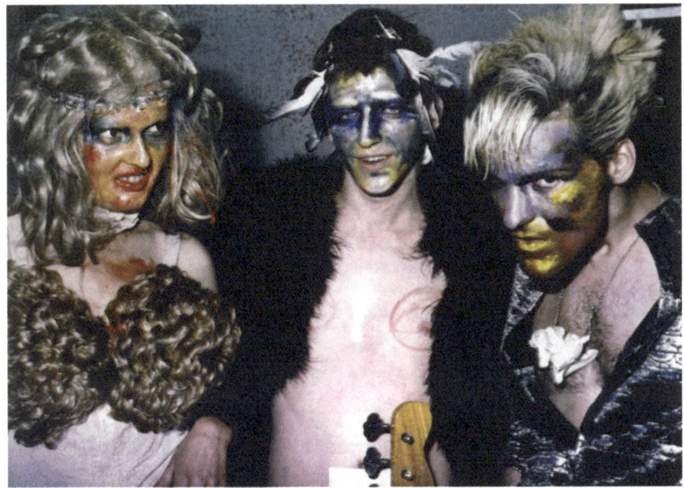

Figure 10.5: Die Tödliche Doris in their stage outfits for the Geniale Dilletanten Festival, 1981 (Dagmar Dimitroff, Wolfgang Müller, Nikolaus Utermöhlen), West Berlin, 1981. Courtesy of Wolfgang Müller.

Another act at The Grand Downfall Show was the duo Sentimentale Jugend (Sentimental youth). The name itself was a sarcastic statement. One half of the duo was then 16-year-old Alexander Hacke (of Einstürzende Neubauten), who performed under the pseudonym Alexander von Borsig, an ironic mix of the aristocratic "von" and "Borsig," from the Borsig Machine Factory in Berlin-Tegel where his father worked. The other half was the then 19-year-old Christiane X., better known as the child heroin addict Christiane F. in *Zoo Station: The Story of Christiane F.* At The Grand Downfall Show, this "sentimental youth," aka von Borsig, sang: "Hiroshima, wie schön es war, damals da schlug der BLITZ ein!" (Hiroshima, how beautiful it was, back then the lightning STROKE) then widened his eyes and laughed. Von Borsig underscored his lyrics with waltzing tones and the sound of children screaming, and had combed forward his hair, which had been bleached ash-blonde.[20] One might recall the Sex Pistols' song "Belsen Was a Gas," which begins as a horribly misconceived joke about the concentration camp Bergen-Belsen, then ends with the lines: "Be a man, kill someone, kill yourself."[21] Both songs take on the most extreme shock topic to be found with a youthful ruthlessness and an inclination for both destruction and self-destruction.

This dark outlook of The Grand Downfall Show—its "No Future" component—was combined with show and circus components, which gave it a both absurd and spectacular ambience. At The Grand Downfall Show images and sound, performance and stage coalesced. The background of the no-man's-land that was Potsdamer Platz at that time reinforced the sense of absurdity. The Ingenious Dilettantes and the punks performing at and attending the event, however, treasured that sense of absurdity. What was so intrinsically punk about it all, were the antithetical aspects: how the ugly was the beautiful, doom was drive, fiasco was triumph. In the last part of this chapter, "Broken heroes, aces of failure," we explore this innate punk feature of the adversative.

10.3 Broken heroes, aces of failure

Rather than a hunger for success, there is a hunger for failure in punk. About the band Subway Sect, Savage writes that "The idea was to work, not with power, but weakness and introversion."[22] Punks did not present themselves as confident winners, but as maladaptive losers. Fragility meant sensitivity; brokenness meant honesty. "Guess my race is run," the Clash sang: "I fought the law and the law won."[23] Within music as well as art, failure was a concept consciously applied and was regarded as far more interesting than success. In interviews, Westwood and McLaren emphasized failed rebellions as their inspiration and aspiration: the Gordon Riots of the 1780s and the machine-wrecking Luddites, fighting the inevitable.[24] In punk, being a loser can mean simply: not accepting the rules of the game.

It seems the punk movement anticipated and staged its own downfall from the very beginning. "The Sex Pistols were a fiasco. A farce," said Lydon.[25] "All punk codes were always intended to fail," Mark Sinker argues;[26] at its core, punk imagery bore the oblivion of its own effect. At the funeral of Malcolm McLaren in 2010, his coffin, among many other slogans, bore a part of the advice of Samuel Beckett—"Ever tried. Ever failed. No matter. Try again. Fail again. Fail better."[27] The lesser-known continuation of that famous Beckett quote, however, goes like this: "Try again. Fail again. Better again. Or better worse. Fail worse again. Still worse again. Till sick for good. Throw up for good."[28] That possibility, not of becoming better and learning from past mistakes, but of just continuing the failing, the worsening, until it is sickening, is present in punk, too. To get too motivational about "trying again" would be a gross misinterpretation.

Many punk names were initially intended as insults—Rat Scabies, Johnny Rotten—differently, for example, to the glamorous pseudonyms of Warhol's superstars. As Jon Savage notes, "identity was thus created and reinforced by hostility."[29] The word "punk" itself was a similar circumvolution of connotations of weakness, youth, and misconduct. Neither were punks interested in a culture of exaltation. Servando Rocha describes how both the Futurists and Dadaists would respond to applause with punches and insults "because there was nothing more humiliating than receiving the gratitude of the audience."[30] The fighting and spitting ("gobbing") at punk shows comes to mind. "The true Dadas are against Dada," wrote Tristan Tzara.[31] Perhaps, in a sense, the true punks were against punk, too.

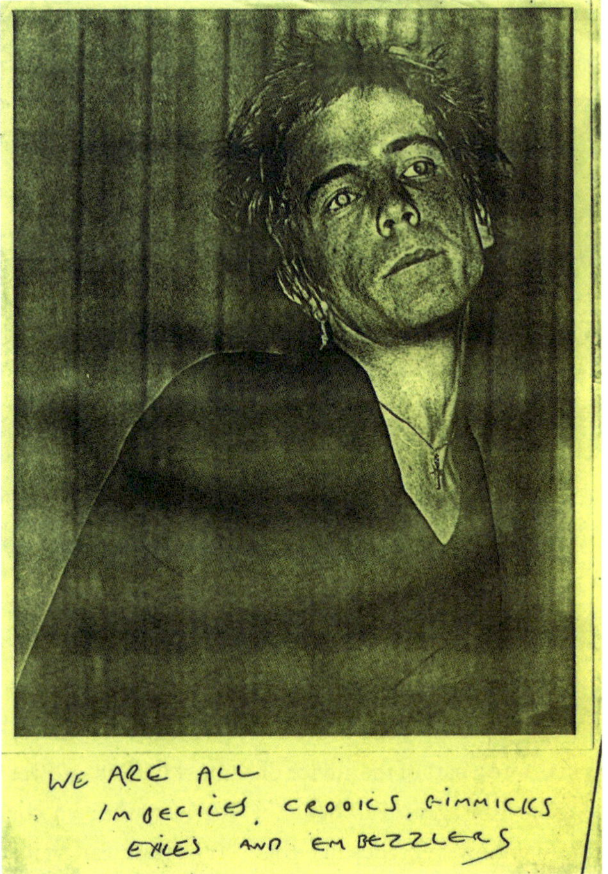

Figure 10.6: Jon Savage, photocopy on yellow paper of a photograph of Johnny Rotten by Joe Stevens juxtaposed with writing by Jamie Reid, 1979 or 1980. Courtesy of Jamie Reid and Jon Savage.

No idolization of punk protagonists, however, did not mean a lack of spectacular anti-heroes. Like Arthur Cravan, the self-proclaimed Dada King of Failures (see Section 7.3: "'The Baby Wagner Lullaby,' or: Brilliance blackout"), punks were surely the crowned heads of *something*. Their demeanor had the grandezza of the exceptional, out of reach, out of range. It was emancipation through negation, a self-chosen social exclusion, an identification with anyone outside the norm. "We are all imbeciles, crooks, gimmicks, exiles and embezzlers," Jamie Reid scribbled down on a piece of paper in 1979. Savage juxtaposed Reid's note with a photo of Rotten, "for my own amusement in 1979 or early 1980"[32] (Figure 10.6).

Dada and Surrealism, too, had been reactions to modernity in crisis. Louis Aragon and André Breton both worked at the Val-de-Grâce military hospital in Paris, where they were confronted with dismembered and traumatized veterans of World War I.[33] This was what modern warfare could do, yet the dominant nationalist parties both in France and Germany were in denial about the horrors caused by the war. The Surrealists worked to draw attention to the broken state of contemporary civil society and to make a stand against authoritarianism by casting themselves as the deviants. Punk artists comparably posed as the outsiders, the lowlifes, the fools.

In punk culture, there is sympathy for the outsider, who is perceived as the truthful one, or the mentally ill, who are perceived as the sane ones, in a world gone mad. This is the frame of reference in punk band names such as the Epileptics, the Idiots, the Insane, the Mental, or the Newtown Neurotics. In the poetry of Michael Strunge, we see this aspect as well, in a poem such as "ALLE DE GALE" ("ALL THE CRAZY PEOPLE"), or this one called "HJERTERNES TERRORIST" ("THE TERRORIST OF HEARTS"):[34]

Jeg er en verdenssøn.
Kølig og klar
Diamanten der ridser dit øje.
Jeg er den store hader
Alt i verden er mig fremmed
Og min angst er kun kendt af mig selv
Som kun tigeren kender sit bur.

Det guld der flænser sin ild i mig
Har intet med verden at gøre.
Jeg blev smidt herind
Med et bål af et skrig
Altid nede og ude af mig selv.

(I am a son of the world.
Cool and clear
The diamond that scratches your eye.
I am the great abhorrer
Everything in the world is alien to me
And only I know my fear
As only the tiger knows his cage.

The gold whose fire tears me apart
Has nothing to do with the world.

I was thrown in here
With a fire by a scream.
Always down and beside myself.)

The great abhorrer, the diamond that scratches your eye: Strunge paints the image of a splendid lunatic. In punk, the role of the artist was the refusal of the role of artist. Rather, the artist (who could be a musician or a poet) was a jester, or a mad king, or the parody of a rock star.

For a moment, let us return to Die Tödliche Doris' film *The Life of Sid Vicious* (see Section 6.2: "The life of Sid Vicious: The sad, dead boy"). Apart from deriding conventional docudramas, the title also sounds like the promise of an idol movie. In their artists' statement, Die Tödliche Doris cited The Stranglers' "No More Heroes," noting how Sid Vicious eventually turned out to be the very last hero.[35] The Stranglers' song has often been interpreted as a rejection of late-hippie self-satisfied music heroes (the "rock gods": the Beatles, the Stones, Pink Floyd), and consequently "no heroes!" is often connected with punk's battle cry for equality in music as well as art. However, the text simply goes "Whatever happened to the heroes? No more heroes any more."[36] That can also be understood as an expression of regret, rather than a claim. Such a notion would fit punk's understanding of failure-as-heroism. Perhaps punks still wanted heroes, but different ones, broken ones. A good argument can be made for this interpretation, first, because of the (anti)heroes mentioned in the Stranglers' song—Leon Trotsky, Lenny Bruce, and Sancho Panza—and second, because Hugh Cornwell has indicated this reading in interviews with Diedrich Diedrichsen.[37]

Artists, like poets, and punks, often cast themselves in the role of society's outcasts, the misunderstood, the poètes maudits (see Section 4.2: "Punk poetry"). There is an identity overlap here, a pride taken in being the ones who dare to fail. As Lisa Le Feuvre has noted, the concept of failure is deeply embedded in what it is to be an artist:

> To strive to fail is to go against the socially normalized drive towards ever increasing success […] When failure is released from being a judgemental term, and success deemed overrated, the embrace of failure can become an act of bravery, of daring to go beyond normal practices and enter a realm of not-knowing.[38]

This embrace of failure is connected to punk's exaltation of both the figure of the child (punk Peter Pan!) and the figure of the sinner (remember Patti Smith's "my sins, my own, they belong to me / me."[39]). We can view these strategies of glorified imperfection as a protection against pressure, against the (capitalist) ideology of success. We can also view imperfection as part of the punks' depiction of the world, as they saw it: as a place full of failure, flaws, and faults. As "bad painting"/neo-Expressionist artist Julian Schnabel stated in 1978, a time when he was deeply involved with the punk/post-punk scene in New York: "I am not making some things. I am making a synonym for the truth with all its falsehoods, oblique as it is. I am making icons that represent life in terms of our death. A bouquet of mistakes."[40]

As we have seen, mistakes and coincidences were revered in punk art, a trait that throws a fishing hook all the way back through the twentieth century to pull up Marcel Duchamp's *Erratum Musical* (Musical mistake, 1913; see Section 2.3: "Punk precursors: 1919, 1966, 1968"). Another example: to Die Tödliche Doris the artist Dieter Roth was a particularly important influence. In the late 1970s and early 1980s, Roth was often present at Exil (Exile), a pub started up by Oswald Wiener, who had fled from Vienna to West Berlin in 1969 to avoid approaching prosecution for profanity. At Exil, Wiener arranged poetry and music workshops together with Dieter Roth and others. Roth can be seen as a kind of proto-punk, an affinity which manifests itself in the materiality of his works, such as his *Schimmelbilder* (Mold pictures) and *Scheiße-Gedichte* (Shit poems) from the 1960s. One of the leitmotifs of Roth's oeuvre was failing, but he did not want it to be too intellectual (like Cage or Duchamp) and he did not want it to be too melodramatic (like the Viennese Actionists).[41] He wanted his failings to be tragi-comical, anarchic, odd—a feeling which Die Tödliche Doris was likewise conveying in their art. Both *The Life of Sid Vicious* and *Seven Deadly Household Accidents* are about the tragicomical failings of human beings, about our randomness, our lack of control.

Punk's conception of failing—art-as-a-gamble, life-as-a-hazard, madness-as-a-lifestyle—throws up the question if punk, as a movement, can be judged to have failed or not. To ponder this question, if punk was a failure, however, does seem futile; it seems beside the point. If we have looked at punk as an art movement, too (not only!)—then did that movement try to achieve something that could be deemed either a success or a failure? Punk, to a degree, tried to break through the cultural hegemony of the establishment, sure, punk was anything that questioned the status quo. Nonetheless, the understanding of art in punk was neither utilitarian, nor idealistic. Thinking in categories of "failure" or "success" leans into a perception of history as progress, of moving forwards, and punk did not. Punk after, let us say, late 1979, around the time when punk turned away from pure negation (see Section 2.1: "The short version: From proto to post") could perhaps more easily be reviewed on such terms. In *PUNK: Its Traces in Contemporary Art*, David Torres writes of the possibility of punk's failure, because "dissidence is nothing other than the entropy required for the system to continue functioning."[42] Did punk let off steam, thereby preventing an explosion, rather than causing one? Maybe, but as Torres himself notes, punk strategies survived, first and foremost in the form of DIY resistance. Or, as Brian Cogan has noted: "[P]unk is best seen as a virus, one that mutates constantly."[43]

At any rate, punk changed, already in the period we have been dealing with here. Even in the late 1970s, the first punks began to move on, while somewhere else, punk had just freshly arrived. In different cultures and at different times, punk manifested itself differently (yet consistently) and was mixed up. Conditions changed; cities changed. Over time, punk artists, poets, and musicians adapted their strategies, and to a certain degree, punk split, manifesting itself in new forms: industrial, hardcore, new wave, no wave, and so on. The inner contradictions, which were present from the beginning in punk, protruded. Roughly, we might imagine, the melancholic and romantic inclinations of punk continued into dark wave and post-punk, while the bleaker, harder stream of punk continued into industrial, and the minimal, noisy aspects were continued in no wave.

In 1983, in *RE/Search #6-7: Industrial Culture Handbook*, the most influential early account of industrial culture, Jon Savage writes: "In the gap caused by the failure of punk rock's apocalyptic rhetoric, 'industrial' seemed like a good idea."[44] There were many direct links between punk and industrial. "The people involved with *RE/Search*, who were all punks […] wanted to set aside—or at least not talk directly about—music, and get back to that stronger Surrealist-Dada tradition," Nat Trotman describes, "They felt they were facing, the 'failure of punk,' the assimilation of that movement into the mainstream and the rising feeling of its impossibility. Noise music and industrial music tried to break through that."[45] Industrial thus also signified a further drawing away from the idea of usurping mainstream culture from within, instead abandoning it altogether: "I never understood alienation. Alienation from *what*? You have to *want* to be part of something in order to feel alienated from it,"[46] as Non aka Boyd Rice stated, likewise in the *Industrial Culture Handbook*.

With the founding of their Industrial Records label (likewise in 1976), Throbbing Gristle were among the first to define themselves as "industrial." Others were Cabaret Voltaire, the French record label Sordide Sentimental, and artists Monte Cazazza, Mark Pauline, Johanna Went, and Z'EV. According to P-Orridge, the idea at first was to name the label "Factory Records" after Andy Warhol's factory, but then Cazazza suggested "Industrial Music for Industrial People" instead.[47] That emphasis on working can even to a certain extent be seen as a refutation of the playful dilettante construct in punk. Returning to work. The playtime of punk, however subversive it might have been for some years, was no longer feasible. "[I]t was about working with yourself and others […] and life, rather than being passive," Cosey Fanni Tutti

emphasizes, "You can actually create something yourself or go in a different direction. That's what we meant by industrial. It was about working. Working to create something new and something that would inspire everybody." Chris Carter added: "Maybe, we should've called it industrious."[48]

Notes

1. Sex Pistols, "Anarchy in the UK" (UK: EMI, 1976).

2. Alexander Hacke quoted in Max Dax, *Nur was nicht ist ist möglich: Die Geschichte der Einstürzenden Neubauten* (Berlin: Bosworth Music, 2006), 15.

3. Gordon Matta-Clark, "My Understanding of Art" [1975], quoted in Sladen, "Introduction," in *Panic Attack! Art in The Punk Years*, 12.

4. Savage, *England's Dreaming*, 232.

5. Michael Bracewell, "Writing the Modern World," in *Gilbert & George: Dirty Word Pictures 1977* (London: Serpentine Gallery, 2002), 9.

6. The Jam, "In the City," *In the City* (Germany: Polydor, 1977).

7. Schmitz, "Reunification through Dematerialization," 7.

8. Einstürzende Neubauten, "Ich stehe auf Berlin" (Oxford: ZickZack, 1983).

9. All title translations from *Die Tödliche Doris – Kunst / The Deadly Doris – Art: Band 3* (Berlin: Martin Schmitz Verlag, 1999) and *Die Tödliche Doris – Kino*.

10. Banana, e-mail to the author, November 27, 2017. Emphasis in original.

11. Ozon, interview, 2017.

12. David Buckley, *Strange Fascination: David Bowie: The Definitive Story* (London: Virgin Books, 2005), 269.

13. Daniel Kulle, "Alle Macht der Super 8," 263.

14. Käthe Kruse, *Lob des Imperfekts: Kunst, Musik und Wohnen im West Berlin der 1980er Jahre* (Berlin: mikrotext, 2017), Kindle 228–30.

15. The Ramones, "Jackie is a Punk," *Ramones* (US: Warner, 1976). "Ice capades" can refer to anal sex without lubricant or a meth-amphetamine-fueled crime spree, see https://www.urbandictionary.com/, accessed April 4, 2018.

16. Stevenson, *Vacant*, 113.

17. Sex Pistols, "Holidays in the Sun" (New York: Universal Music, 1977).

18. See https://www.sexpistolsofficial.com/nmtb-track-by-track, accessed December 29, 2021.

19. Frieder Butzmann with Genesis P-Orridge, "Just Drifting/Tales of Death" (Germany: ZENSOR, 1981).

20. Kruse, *Lob des Imperfekts*, 233–40.

21. Sex Pistols, "Belsen Was a Gas" (UK: Virgin Records, 1979).

22. Savage, *England's Dreaming*, 419.

23. The Clash, "I Fought the Law" (Copenhagen: CBS, 1979). Original by Sonny Curtis, 1958.

24. "Malcolm McLaren im Gespräch mit Gerald Matt," 200.

25. Marcus, "Punk (1979)."

26. Mark Sinker, "Concrete, so as to Self-Destruct: The Etiquette of Punk, Its Habits, Rules, Values and Dilemmas," in *Punk Rock: So What?*, 136.

27. Torres, "Traces of a Punk Attitude in Contemporary Art," 66.

28. Samuel Beckett, *Worstward Ho* (New York: Grove Press, 1983), 7.

29. Savage, *England's Dreaming*, 193.

30. Rocha, "Great Negative Work," 284.

31. Tristan Tzara, "Dada Manifesto 1918," 92.

32. Jon Savage, e-mail to the author, June 16, 2018.

33. Amy Lyford, *Surrealist Masculinities: Gender Anxiety and the Aesthetics of Post-World War I Reconstruction in France* (Berkeley: University of California Press, 2007), 47.

34. Strunge, *A Virgin from a Chilly Decade*, 51, 78–79.

35. Müller, *Das Leben des Sid Vicious*, 29.

36. The Stranglers, "No More Heroes" (Fulham: United Artists, 1977).

37. Diedrich Diedrichsen, "Intensität – Negation – Klartext: Simultanes und Inkommensurables zwischen Theorie, Bildender Kunst und Musik im deutschen Punk," in *Zurück zum Beton*, 141.

38. Lisa Le Feuvre, "Introduction: Strive to Fail" in *Failure: Documents of Contemporary Art*, ed. Lisa Le Feuvre (London: Whitechapel Gallery, 2010), 12, 13. Emphasis in original.

39. Patti Smith, "Gloria" (New York: Electric Lady Studios, 1975).

40. Julian Schnabel, "Statement, 1978," quoted in Le Feuvre, ed., *Failure*, 131.

41. See Mathias Haldemann, ed., *Dieter Roth und die Musik/and Music: Und weg mit den Minuten* (Luzern: Edizioni Periferia, 2014), 204.

42. Torres, "Traces of a Punk Attitude in Contemporary Art," 65.

43. Cogan, "'Do They Owe Us a Living?", 79.

44. Jon Savage, "Introduction," in *RE/Search #6-7: Industrial Culture Handbook*, 4–5.

45. Nat Trotman quoted in Meg Santisi, "Interview: Nat Trotman on *RE/Search* magazine," accessed March 28, 2018, http://blogs.colum.edu/caa/interview-nat-trotman-on-research-magazine.

46. Non quoted in *RE/Search #6-7*, 52. Emphasis in original.

47. P-Orridge quoted in *RE/Search #6-7*, 10. Three years later, in 1979, an independent label "Factory Records" was indeed established, in Manchester, by Tony Wilson and Alan Erasmus.

48. Tom Doyle, "Throbbing Gristle 'Hamburger Lady'," accessed March 28, 2018, http://www.soundonsound.com/people/throbbing-gristle-hamburger-lady.

11 The Laws of the Lawless

It is not of importance to label punk an art movement. That is not the raison d'être of this book. But much is lost if we look at punk too narrow mindedly. Punk extends beyond music, art, poetry, theater, fashion; it was and is a way of life and both a social and a cultural movement. Nonetheless, the view taken here was art historical, and out came just how much punk has to do with art and with art history. The analyzed artworks showed us how the punk movement engaged with classical art historical topics such as work vs. play, surface vs. depth, originality vs. copy—but the artists involved with the punk movement did so on their own terms. Artists involved with the punk movement took on art history; they engaged with their heroes and anti-heroes, made art and anti-art; they processed the works of the past and made their own of it. Oscillating between nostalgia and parody, punk artists chewed up the past and spat it out as something new.

And now? As Max Ernst told Patrick Waldberg in an interview in 1970: "Dada was a bomb. Can you imagine someone, half a century after the explosion of a bomb, intent on collecting the shards, pasting them together and displaying them?"[1] Well, yes, that is kind of what we do. Punk was a bomb too, and we as historians are in a way collecting the shards. Sometimes, that might seem absurd, but on the other hand, those small, bruized scraps of culture, if put into context, might tell us something important. I for one am very content being an art historian living in a world where art is *not* defined, as Arthur C. Danto puts it, as "treasures that have passed the test of time."[2] Artworks do not have to be made for eternity. But displaying the genesis, the meaning, and the impact of art in its own time seems significant to me.

Wolfgang Müller says,

> People say: Punk in the museum, isn't that a contradiction? Then I say: What nonsense, that is terrific, do you want to throw it in the garbage, or what? That is terrific, if it is put into a glass showcase, and then everyone comes and looks at it. Everyone should have the opportunity to see it.[3]

Hugo Kaagman argues similar to Müller but is more critical:

> It is a question of conservation, of documentation. Of course, street art really should always be outside, and punk should not be in a museum. But these things disappear. And then, where can you see it? Only in the shops, or what? But make a good documentation of it! Not just a fetishized jacket. Then you can inspire people.[4]

Kaagman, noting that the commercialization of the punk style is widespread, apparently considers public archives and public exhibitions to be the lesser evil. Furthermore, there are a number of archives which seek to maintain the do-it-yourself (DIY) ethos. For instance, May Day Rooms in London is run collectively, as an "archive from below."[5] If the road taken is thus not the one of Joe Corré, burning punk memorabilia on the Thames, but a more engaged, even inspirational, approach is sought, then the answers lie in genuineness of purpose and in accessibility for all. As punks and Rosalind Krauss knew, "original" is just another word for an inspired copy.

Maybe some kid is out there, ready to take a hard look at some punk art, chew it over, and spit out some of it as new art for our time. The "No Future" generation of the late 1970s and the teenage generation today are linked by a sense of "late stage" (what is coming: the end of capitalism? or the end of humankind?). The "Extinction Rebellion," "Last Generation," and "Fridays for Future" movements of today thus do seem connected to "No Future," even if invertedly so. Perhaps that jump is like the one from punk's "No Future" back to the Futurists' radical judgement of all musings from the past. In essence, all these different youth (and art) movements and each way of looking at the past *and* the future dissect quite sharply the historic point in time we are at. At each of these historical junctures—the Futurists' 1910s (and connected, the Dadaists and Surrealists of the 1920s), punks' 1970s, or today—we are dealing with a sense of disruption, a clash of perceptions about reality, and a need for action. Thus, both sides of the punk medallion—destructive negation and creative DIY—seem excruciatingly relevant these days.

In that spirit, let us take another and summarizing look at what this book established about punk art history. This is punk, so these are not rules. Let's call them the ten laws of the lawless:

One

True punks were against punk. Punk is antithetical. Contrasting manifestations not only occur side by side but are even sometimes mutually dependent. These inner contradictions of punk art are linked with the movement's anti-hierarchical impulse, its resistance to classification, its refusal to be understandable. That was part of what was perceived as alarming about the punk movement: A youth rebellion had been seen before, but one that refused to state its progressive claims, less so (if any art movement comes close, it would indeed be Dada).

As Wolfgang Müller wrote in his contribution to the *Ingenious Dilletantes*: "The rationale of progress is obsolete."[6] Progress, however, might be "the ultimate mystification behind post-industrial Western society itself," as Greil Marcus observed.[7] Punk was a youth movement that was not only against the status quo, but also against the future. This pessimism of the youth put a splinter in the self-conception of the society that had brought it into being.

Furthermore, in punk culture, mistakes are honored, tensions are included, and battles are welcomed. A last short anecdote to drive the point home: the Sods, relatively well-known in West Berlin, where their music was sold at Heino's Scheiß-Laden, often as a cassette copy of a cassette copy, were set to play at SO36. Here, the Sods played not only their fastest and hardest numbers but also some slow atmospheric songs with saxophone, resulting in outrage from the Berlin crowd, who attacked the Sods on stage. The band had to break off the concert. The Sods were surprised by the aggressive atmosphere, but Blixa Bargeld and Alexander von Borsig both came backstage to applaud the Sods for being able to get such a strong reaction so quickly.[8] Artist Nina Sten-Knudsen had joined the Sods at their concert in SO36:

> I was with the Sods in Kreuzberg at the SO36, there was huge trouble! It is probably one of the most extreme things I have ever experienced, concert-wise [...] Those were the wildest people, so angry! So, I thought: I should move here![9]

Punk in the late 1970s and early 1980s was elusive and self-contradictory. In writing this book, thus, it became crucial to grasp these inner conflicts, because punk in the years in question was all about the tension. Already in the first chapter, we saw this: Kippenberger in the hospital, the stolen Kango-Hammer of N.U. Unruh, and the threatening letter on the door of Art Something in Amsterdam all bear witness to a punk × art culture of clashes.

Two

In tracing the art origins in the history of punk, two historical periods emerge as significant: the early twentieth century that is Dada (especially Berlin Dada) and Surrealism, and 1960s art and counterculture. Whereas Dada has often been emphasized, and rightfully so, the analysis in this book has put forward many links to Surrealism, too. Both Surrealism and punk moved between poetry, politics and pain, both revered in sexuality, dreams and violence, both engaged with absurd humor, madness, exorbitance, and kitsch. Furthermore, there is a chain of personage from Surrealists to Situationists to ex-Situationists to punks.

Concerning the 1960s, we could look at punk art as a splatter version of Pop Art or a doom version of the hippies or a hedonistic, amphetamine-infused version of the Situationist International. Even the Ramones took their name from the Beatles' Paul

McCartney, who had used the pseudonym "Paul Ramon" to check into hotels back in the days of the Silver Beatles.[10] (Of course, that was also before the Beatles became hippies). In punk art, many 1960s preoccupations were extended in a crasser version, and they impacted beyond the artworld context. This is, for example, the case if we look at Yoko Ono, Dieter Roth, and Gustav Metzger as proto punks.

The punk movement drew on the counterculture of the (late) 1960s. We have seen the degree to which punk's stance was connected with that of artists who had been refused by or excluded from the Situationist International: for instance, the protagonists in King Mob, Drakabygget, and Ben Morea of the Motherfuckers (who had requested to meet with Raoul Vaneigem in New York in 1967 and was rejected).[11] This connection to radical 1960s groups also highlights punk's practice of hyper-spectacle (instead of anti-spectacle), as we have seen it applied in several instances, perhaps most prominently in the cases of COUM Transmissions and the Sex Pistols.

With this connection to the harder side of 1960s counterculture, it is also possible to gain a more nuanced perspective on the apparent punk hatred towards the hippie generation. This rejection of hippiedom stems from punk's call-out of what by the mid 1970s had become an empty promise and a pretentious mindset. Punks were reassessing reality: "Face the coldness surrounding you!"[12] is how Diedrich Diedrichsen expressed this sentiment. Punks stood in opposition to the maintenance of the hope of love and peace that had obviously not been fulfilled. But "punk vs. hippie" is too superficial a paradigm. Indeed, punk, in each of its manifestations, drew on elements of the hippie counterculture of the 1960s: from DIY, squatting, and activism to personal liberation and subversion through youth culture.

The initiative to do-it-yourself—DIY: the DNA of punk—was thus connected to 1960s alternative and hobo culture, but in the 1970s came to be expressed in a more marked way through the accessibility of Xerox, Super 8, aerosol cans, and so on. In his article of the same name about the anarcho-punk movement, Rich Cross argues: "The Hippies Now Wear Black,"[13] (where black in this image might equally convey sorrow as anarchy). Likewise, the "peace punk" sub-genre exemplifies the links between both movements. Much of what the hippies propagated was pushed in a darker and more aggressive version in the late 1970s. To Sabin, this "raises the question whether punk was, indeed, the last gasp of the 1960s counterculture."[14]

Three

Andy Warhol was the hero of the punks. Warhol stood for a provocative commercialization of culture, a hedonistic attack on High Art, a cool lifestyle, and a deep dive into all things low and profane. Warhol, and Pop Art in general, stood for a strategy of affirmation of the cheap product, the exaltation of superficiality and fakeness.

Peter Bürger famously ridiculed the notion of a subversive potential in Warhol's artwork:

> [T]he painting of 100 Campbell soup cans contains resistance to the commodity society only for the person who wants to see it there. The Neo-Avant-Garde, which stages for a second time the avant-gardiste break with tradition, becomes a manifestation that is void of sense.[15]

In contrast to this opinion, punk art quasi fulfilled that subversive potential of Pop Art.

Punk's strategies of affirmation thus effectively originated in Pop Art, but—characteristically—they were taken even further (or, even lower) in punk. This affirmation relates to the effect of the hyper-spectacular: It is inversion through assertion, or—one step further—negation through escalation. Pop Art's preoccupation with the copy was likewise integrated into punk, as multiplication, replication, and reiteration became standard features of punk art.

Four

Language was of the utmost importance in punk. Language was seen as a weapon against the establishment; language was used to hack the system of power. We can see this in the "Coumalphabet" used by COUM Transmissions and we can see it in punk's use of propaganda as well as poetry. This importance of language again links with both the Dadaists (the nonsensical) as well as the Surrealists (supralogical word/image games). Michael Strunge, for example, identified several of his own poems as Surrealist, noting how they were "pure psychic automatism," as described by Breton and that his poetry, like Surrealist poetry, came from compulsion, not inclination.[16]

Punk created semantic images against institutions of authority, like when Howard Smith wrote that the *Punk Art* exhibition in Washington was within "throw-up distance from the White House,"[17] thus echoing P-Orridge's words from 1976, about the ICA being within "spitting distance"[18] of Buckingham Palace. Connected to these alternative means of resistance (the weapons of the underdog) was also the exploration of crime-as-art and scandal-as-art. To artists and poets involved with the punk movement, this was indeed counterpropaganda, mixed up with a great deal of absurd humor, because centuries of resistance bear witness, a joke can be more subversive than most of all other things.

Five

Punks positioned themselves as the rear-guard, not the avant-garde. Punk refused to become yet another new ism. In this refusal lay, a critique of the concept of originality as well as a critique of the notion of (art) history as a progression, as an evolutionarily tinted development toward the more refined. No wonder then, that the collage was so central in punk art: the cut-up method likewise destabilizes established narratives and breaks habitual thinking. Punks might have agreed with Peter Bürger's criticism of the compliance of the neo-avant-garde (e.g. Fluxus) and they moved closer to what Bürger viewed as the only true avant-garde: Futurism, Surrealism, and—most importantly—Dada.[19]

To a certain degree, Bürger's reproach of the neo-avant-garde leans on Adorno's analogy that the artist's craving to create the new was comparable to the consumer's craving for the new in a capitalist society. With its "No Future" watchword and its rejection of progress, punk art effectively broke through that craving for the new. Not fitting into linear art history poses another link to Surrealism, too: like punk, Surrealism did not fit into the linearly progressing story of modern art, exasperating formalist critics such as Clement Greenberg, who struggled to fit Surrealism into the modern canon.

Punk's appropriations are conscious copies, oftentimes realizing a new potential in old art and music. These reiterations, however, were not postmodern in the sense of nothing new can be expressed, all signs are equal, all is now *simulacra.* The message was rather the one in COUM's manifesto: "It has NOT all been done before, and that which has, can still bear valid reinterpretation."[20] Such a valid reinterpretation might be an acid test, a parody, an homage, a critical review, or the fulfillment of a hidden potential, in either way an active involvement with these references. When Sid Vicious sings Frank Sinatra's "I Did It My Way" (and then shoots the audience), he is making fun of Sinatra and the discrepancy between the free-spirit lyrics of the song and the old crooner, but he is also using the song for his own purpose. Analogously, the way Cosey Fanni Tutti usurps Manet's *Olympia* fortifies the inherent position of that figure, Tutti is mocking the circumlocution as well as the male viewpoint of the image, while at the same time celebrating the underlying subversion that is indeed present in the old painting. After having seen Tutti's reinterpretation, our perception of the original painting is irrevocably altered, what Mieke Bal calls "an active reworking"[21] of the older piece. Punk's concept of originality was thus (knowingly or unknowingly) drawing on Rosalind Krauss and her dismantling of the modernist myth of originality: "the ever-present reality of the copy as the underlying condition of the original."[22]

We could even go back to early modernism: Gustave Courbet can be seen as a key figure in punk art, as Jerry Silk argued in the *Punk Art* catalogue in 1978: "Courbet therefore established subversion, negation, and provocation both as viable components of art and as a crucial current within the development of modernism."[23] These modern features—subversion, negation, provocation—are at the heart of punk artwork too, but in amplified form. Very often, the artists involved with punk took up modern art motifs but exaggerated them or made the implicit *explicit*. Punk realizes all suggestions, concretizes all metaphors, takes any stance to the extreme. By and large, punk art went into the extreme: it was "modernity *in extremis*"[24]—a fin-de-siècle mannerism, the sound and look of the dying twentieth century.

Six

"Infancy conforms to nobody."[25] In punk art and music, the childish is conceptualized as nonconformity and candor. Childhood, however, also stands for vulnerability, the escape into infantilism as a way to cope with the corruption of grown-up society. In punk's inclination toward infantility, there are echoes both of the innocent child, in the sense of Jean-Jacques Rousseau, and of the wicked child, in the sense of Sigmund Freud. Either way, the childish is the free. This conceptualization also links in with a preference of the nonsensical over the sensible, irrationality over rationality. Creatively, infantilism was directed against opportunistic and refined art pour l'art. Much like in Dada, the primitiveness of infancy was understood as cathartic.

The child is perceived as the only truthful one, and fantasies and fairytales are invoked to display that quality, from Peter Pan and his Lost Boys to Hans Christian Andersen's fairy tale "The Emperor's New Clothes." Here, the child is the only one who goes against vanity, authority, and greed, to say: "But he hasn't got anything on." At the end of the story, Andersen writes: "The Emperor shivered, for he suspected they were right. But he thought, 'This procession has got to go on.' So he walked more proudly than ever, as his noblemen held high the train that wasn't there at all."[26] There is a subversive undertone here: Those in power never change. But that kid putting truth to power in the fairy tale? He is pure punk. This punk feature is still being invoked: In their 2017 "Punk Manifesto," the Russian performance art group Pussy Riot wrote: "Take your beatings as a badge of honour. When you say that the emperor is naked, you may end up being punched in the face by the emperor's bodyguards."[27] In that context, Russian president Vladimir Putin would be the emperor.

Seven

Punk artists leaned on Johan Huizinga's seminal ideas of the *Homo Ludens*, the playing human. There is a consistent line going from the Surrealists and Lettrists through the

Situationists, the Provos and CoBrA to punk. Aesthetic play was cast as the alternative to capitalist work, and this conception spilled over into an idea of the dilettante or the amateur as the more autonomous artist.

Punks were tired of the over-refinement and self-regarding seriousness that in their perception dominated both in music and art at the time. Amateurism and playfulness were ways to break through that. The concept of the brilliant exceptional artist was ridiculed. The Ingenious Dilettantes in West Berlin, the KoeCrandt artists in Amsterdam, and Værkstedet Værst in Copenhagen set up the genius vs. the idiot—and chose to identify with the latter. Accordingly, mistakes and distortions were seen as creatively more productive than overly perfect and smooth renditions, be it in art or in music. Furthermore, the de facto very high youth unemployment was turned around to proclaim recreation and hedonistic exuberance: "Waste your youth!"[28] Thus, the artist in punk was rather conceived as a connoisseur of the art of living, someone like Dadaist Arthur Cravan, the King of Failures.

Eight

In punk, sex was a vehicle to liberation. Challenging conservative notions about sex was like an immediate shortcut to a thorough rattling of the whole cage. Punk art thematized gender fluidity, sexual orientation, female sexual pleasure, as well as questions about sexual power structures. Artists, who were associated with the punk movement, took on the topic of sex with a high sense of defiance. From Salomé, Luciano Castelli, and Tabea Blumenschein to Cosey Fanni Tutti and Genesis P-Orridge, these artists incorporated an overt sexuality. The explicitness of their work combined societal criticism with seditious impudence.

Prostitution and porn were clipped together with art historical references from Édouard Manet to Max Beckmann. Visually, the punk movement went overboard with sexual references: it was chains and leather and feathers and leopard print, corsets and fishnet stockings and high heels and obscene T-shirts with print-on naked breasts. Or it was perplexingly asexual and androgynous. Either way, punk provoked not only the rightwing asserters of the status quo but often enough the leftwing moralists too.

The libertarian strain in punk thus accounts for the movement's involvement with the Marquis de Sade. In punk, Sade was a key reference, as he had been in Surrealism too, especially that "evil" side of Surrealism, represented by Georges Bataille or Hans Bellmer. Not only the sexual aspects of Sadean thought were represented in punk, but the notion of cruelty-as-autonomy. Georges Bataille incorporated the idea of transgression as a way (the only way) to find dark truths. Susan Sontag put it like this: "That discourse one might call the poetry of transgression is also knowledge. He who transgresses not only breaks a rule. He goes somewhere that the others are not; and he knows something the others don't know."[29] Again we might think of Walter Benjamin's analysis of the Surrealist movement, and his reflection on "the cult of evil as a political device, however romantic," which has the ability "to disinfect and isolate."[30] Such explorations into evil are present in punk, too, as we have seen for example in the cases of COUM Transmissions' infatuation with Thomas De Quincey and indeed the Marquis de Sade, Alexander von Borsig's Hiroshima shocker, or the Sex Pistols' "Belsen Was a Gas."

For punk women, de Sade was insofar of relevance, as that he regarded women to be capable of both pleasure-seeking and cruelty on the same level as men. The female artists involved with the punk movement positioned themselves as black sheep feminists. Or, in the words of Futurist Valentine de Saint-Point: "They are all equal. They all merit the same scorn."[31] Whereas later iterations of the punk movement, such as the 1990s riot grrrls, were very outspoken about feminism, the punk women of the late 1970s and early 1980s generally lived it out, more than they spoke about it. Unapologetically, the women of the hybrid punk art/music scene of this time represented queerness, sassiness, and sex-positivity. Historically as well as substantially, they were positioned in-between the second and the third wave of feminism.

Nine

There is a kind of existentialist awareness in punk art. Existentialist in the sense that the world makes no sense, and we are not born with a preconceived purpose. Existentialist in the sense of being fully aware of your own existence and understanding freedom. Punk art is thus about being present in the now; punk art is often *live*, as in active performance, and always *alive*. This sensation comes through in the statement by P-Orridge, when he asserts that both in punk and in performance art, "one feels totally alive but also under threat."[32] In punk, corporeality was also used to express vulnerability, injury, and (self) harm. More often than not, however, the violence in punk was of a theatrical nature. It also became clear that punk (art) was both romantic and cynical, both escapist and realistic. For every hardcore realization of existentialist pain, was a moment of dreamful madness to counter it.

This fantasy was intertwined with the self-conception of punks as children. "When I see the price that you pay," sang the Ramones still many years later: "I don't wanna grow up."[33] The colorful Mohawks, the spiky hair, and the face paint were in their own way elements of a childish escapist masquerade too. The old dream of the avant-garde—to merge life and art—became reality in punks' everyday extravagant costumes and parties that were like surreal theater shows. Bodies, behaviors, and appearances were turned into artworks.

In punk culture, bodily modifications, as well as accessories and costumes, were a kind of tribal tokens of a shared code. Especially in the juxtaposition of physicality and fashion, the link between punk and Surrealist artworks manifests itself again. Both in punk art and Surrealist art, we have the subjects of pearl bracelets as/on teeth and safety pins through lips: "It hurts and looks cool!"[34]

Ten

The perceived gloomy outlook was met with a dance on the volcano. If the end of the world was coming that meant a spectacular staging of the downfall was apt. There were varying perceptions of that doomsday atmosphere; some were more romantic about it than others. Comparably, the resistance of punk was often enough merged with humorous elements. The visuality of contemporary terror groups, such as the Rote Armee Franktion, was copied, but induced with a sense of jesting. Punk in the late 1970s and early 1980s was more invested in visual terror, then in real. "We were amateur terrorists," says Hugo Kaagman.[35] Or: "We were playing Russian Roulette, but with a children's toy pistol," as Christian Lemmerz asserts.[36]

Punk artists, punk musicians, and punk poets were casting themselves as the kings and queens of failure. Embedded in their roles as lowlifes was a sense of mythical grandezza, a larger-than-life air, outlaw glamour. If failing was the only option, punks were going to fail stunningly. The power of the punk movement thus came from embracing powerlessness. Punk inverted, or better: broke the scale on which success was measured. Yes, punk was an "impossibility," as Nat Trotman noticed.[37] Perhaps that was part of what made the movement so special, at least for a while. The punk revolution did not devour its own children, but perhaps they did grow up. Over time, punk strategies had to change because times changed, because society changed.

Punk is dead, long live punk.

Notes

1. Quoted in Adamowicz, *Dada Bodies*, 5.

2. Arthur C. Danto, *Unnatural Wonders: Essays from the Gap Between Art and Life* (New York: Columbia University Press, 2005), xv.

3. Müller, interview, 2013.

4. Kaagman, interview, 2017.

5. See http://maydayrooms.org/, accessed August 8, 2018.

6. Müller, "Die wahren Dilletanten," 12.

7. Marcus, "Punk (1979)."

8. Poulsen, *Under en Sort Sol*, 132.

9. Sten-Knudsen, interview, 2018.

10. Exhibition flyer, "Hey! Ho! Let's Go: Ramones and the Birth of Punk," Queens Museum, New York, April 10–July 31, 2016.

11. Cooper, *The Situationist International in Britain*, 102.

12. Diedrichsen, "Intensität – Negation – Klartext" in *Zurück zum Beton*, 141.

13. Rich Cross, "The Hippies Now Wear Black: Crass and the Anarcho-Punk Movement, 1977–1984," in *Socialist History*, no. 26 (2004), 25–44.

14. Sabin, "Introduction," 4.

15. Peter Bürger, *Theory of the Avant-Garde* (trans. Michael Shaw) (Minneapolis: University of Minnesota Press, 1984), 62.

16. Strunge, *A Virgin from a Chilly Decade*, 16.

17. Smith, "Clash Bash." See Section 4.2.

18. Metzger, "Nothing Short of a Total War," 43.

19. Bürger, *Theory of the Avant-Garde.*

20. COUM Transmissions Manifesto 1974.

21. Bal, *Quoting Caravaggio*, 1.

22. Krauss, "The Originality of the Avant-Garde," 11.

23. Jerry Silk, "Punk Precedents," in *Punk Art* exhibition, n.p.

24. Bracewell, "Some Notes for the Exhibition," 13; emphasis in original.

25. COUM Transmissions, *COUM Decoumposition: Schlimm* [Rottweil 1974]. MoMA Archive: MoMA Queens Artists' Books.

26. Hans Christian Andersen, "The Emperor's New Clothes" [1837], transl. Jean Hersholt.

27. Nadya Tolokonnikova/Pussy Riot, "Punk Manifesto," July 2017, i-D VICE.

28. See Teipel, *Verschwende Deine Jugend* and Diederichsen, "Wie ich mal meine Jugend verschwendete," in *Zurück zum Beton.*

29. Sontag, "The Pornographic Imagination," 116.

30. Benjamin, "Surrealism: The Last Snapshot of the European Intelligentsia (1929)."

31. Valentine de Saint Point, "The Manifesto of Futurist Woman."

32. Genesis P-Orridge quoted in Savage, *England's Dreaming*, 250.

33. Released on the Ramones' final LP *¡Adios Amigos!* in 1995. Track written Kathleen Brennan and Tom Waits.

34. *Boingo Osmopol*, no. 2 (1982). Die Tödliche Doris Archive, Berlin.

35. Kaagman, interview, 2017.

36. Kaagman, interview, 2017.

37. Trotman quoted in Santisi, "Interview: Nat Trotman on RE/Search Magazine."

List of interviews and Archives

Interviews (all translations of the interviews appearing in this book are by the author)

Tabea Blumenschein, interview in Berlin, October 30, 2017 (in German)

Elmer, interview via phone, May 24, 2018 (in Danish)

Hugo Kaagman, interview in Amsterdam, November 22, 2017 (in English)

Käthe Kruse, interview in Berlin, October 23, 2017 (in German)

Christian Lemmerz, interview via phone, March 27, 2018 (in German)

Marc Miller, interview in New York, April 16, 2018 (in English)

Wolfgang Müller, interview in Berlin, May 23, 2013 and October 25, 2017 (in German)

Lars Nørgård, interview via phone, March 28, 2018 (in Danish)

Diana Ozon, interview in Amsterdam, November 24, 2017 (in English)

Nina Sten-Knudsen, interview via phone, May 17, 2018 (in Danish)

E-mail correspondence

Anna Banana, November 27, 2017

Jon Savage, June 16, 2018

GENESIS BREYER P-ORRIDGE, October 26, 2018

Further background talks

Jeannette Dekeukeleire (Amsterdam), Markus Müller (Berlin), Jan Poulsen (Copenhagen), Harry Ruhé (Amsterdam), GENESIS BREYER P-ORRIDGE (via phone), David G. Torres (Barcelona), Cosey Fanni Tutti (London), Andrew Wheatley (London)

Visited or consulted archives and collections

US: Fales Library & Special Collection, New York University, Marc Miller Private Archive, The Museum of Modern Art Archives

UK: British Library, Cabinet Gallery, Cosey Fanni Tutti private collection, May Day Rooms, Tate Archive, The Jon Savage Archive, John Moores University, Online collection of the UK National Archives, London and Kew

Germany: Die Tödliche Doris Archive, Online archive of the Neue Gesellschaft für bildende Kunst (New Society for Visual Arts), Berlin

Netherlands: Diana Ozon private collection, Hugo Kaagman private collection

Denmark: Det Kongelige Bibliotek, Danmarks Kunstbibliotek, Nina Sten-Knudsen private collection, Online archive of Rigsarkivet (The Danish National Archives), Copenhagen

Bibliography

Adamowicz, Elza. *Dada Bodies: Between Battlefield and Fairground*. Manchester: Manchester University Press, 2019.

Adriani, Götz and Museum für Neue Kunst Karlsruhe, eds. *Obsessive Malerei – ein Rückblick auf die Neuen Wilden*. Ostfildern: Hatje Cantz, 2003.

Ambrosch, Gerfried. *The Poetry of Punk: The Meaning Behind Punk Rock and Hardcore Lyrics*. London: Routledge, 2018.

Andreotti, Libero. "Architecture and Play." In *Guy Debord and the Situationist International: Texts and Documents*, edited by Tom McDonough, 213–40. Cambridge: MIT Press, 2002.

Baker, Simon. "Crime." In *Undercover Surrealism: Georges Bataille and DOCUMENTS*, edited by Dawn Ades and Simon Baker, 102–05. Cambridge: MIT Press, 2006.

Bal, Mieke. *Quoting Caravaggio: Contemporary Art, Preposterous History*. Chicago: University of Chicago Press, 1999.

Ball, Hugo. "Dada Fragments 1916–1917." In *The Dada Painters and Poets: An Anthology*, 2nd ed., edited by Robert Motherwell, 49–54. Cambridge: Harvard University Press, 1981.

Banana, Anna. *About VILE: Mail Art, News and Photos from the Eternal Network*. Vancouver: Banana Productions, 1983.

Barr, Alfred. "Preface." In *Fantastic Art, Dada, Surrealism*, edited by Alfred H. Barr and Georges Hugnet. New York: The Museum of Modern Art, 1947.

Battino, Freddy and Luca Palazzoli. *Piero Manzoni: Catalogue Raisonné*. Milan: Vanni Scheiwiller, 1991.

Baudrillard, Jean. *Simulacra and Simulation*. Translated by Sheila Faria Glaser. University of Michigan Press, 1994.

Beckett, Andy. *When the Lights Went Out: What Really Happened to Britain in the Seventies*, London: Faber & Faber, 2009.

Beckett, Samuel. *Worstward Ho*. New York: Grove Press, 1983.

Beil, Ralf and Peter Kraut. *A House Full of Music: Strategien in Musik und Kunst*. Cologne: Hatje Cantz, 2012.

Benjamin, Walter. "Surrealism: The Last Snapshot of the European Intelligentsia [1929]". In *Modernism: An Anthology*, edited by Lawrence Rainey, 1087–95. Malden: Blackwell Publishing, 2005.

Berkers, Pauwke. "Rock Against Gender Roles: Performing Femininities and Doing Feminism Among Women Punk Performers in the Netherlands, 1976–1982". *Journal of Popular Music Studies* 24, no. 2 (June 2012): 155–75.

Bestley, Russ and Alex Ogg. *The Art of Punk: The Illustrated History of Punk Rock Design.* London: Voyageur Press, 2012.

Blum, Dilys. *Shocking: The Art and Fashion of Elsa Schiaparelli.* New Haven: Yale University Press, 2004.

Boehlke, Michael and Henryk Gericke, eds. *Too Much Future: Punk in der DDR.* Berlin: Verbrecher Verlag, 2007.

Bracewell, Michael. "Some Notes for the Exhibition." In *Red White and Blue: Pop Punk Politics Place,* edited by Chelsea Space, 8–20. London: University of the Arts, 2012.

Breton, André. "First Manifesto of Surrealism [1924]." In *Manifestoes of Surrealism.* Translated by Richard Seaver and Helen Lane. Ann Arbor: University of Michigan Press, 1969.

Breton, André. "Second Manifesto of Surrealism [1930]." In *Manifestoes of Surrealism.* Translated by Richard Seaver and Helen Lane. Ann Arbor: University of Michigan Press, 1969.

Buckley, David. *Strange Fascination: David Bowie: The Definitive Story.* London: Virgin Books, 2005.

Buffet-Picabia, Gabrielle. "Arthur Cravan and American Dada [1938]." In *The Dada Painters and Poets: An Anthology,* 2nd ed., edited by Robert Motherwell, 13–17. Cambridge: Harvard University Press, 1981.

Burgess, Paul. "'Cut' – The Punk Use of Collage." Paper, *The Art of Punk Conference,* University of Northampton, November 25, 2016.

Bürger, Peter. *Theory of the Avant-Garde.* Translated by Michael Shaw. Minneapolis: University of Minnesota Press, 1984.

Buszek, Maria Elena. "Ladies Auxiliary of the Lower East Side: Post-Punk Feminist Art and New York's Club 57." *Punk & Post-Punk* 9, no. 3 (2020): 425–42.

Buttgereit, Jörg, ed. *Nekromantik.* Berlin: Martin Schmitz Verlag, 2007.

Callesen, Jørgen. "Dunst i ungeren: kønspolitik, punk og sexuelt anarki." In *69,* edited by Helle Hansen, 122–23. Copenhagen: Verve Books, 2008.

Christgau, Robert. "Avant-Punk: A Cult Explodes . . . and a Movement Is Born." In *Village Voice,* October 24, 1977. Accessed December 10, 2017. https://www.robertchristgau.com/xg/music/avantpunk-77.php.

Christgau, Robert. "'We Have to Deal with It'. Punk England Report." In *Village Voice,* January 9, 1978. Accessed January 5, 2018. https://www.robertchristgau.com/xg/rock/punk-78.php.

Christie, Stuart and Albert Meltzer. *The Floodgates of Anarchy.* Oakland: PM Press, 1970.

Christopherson, Peter. *Photography.* Cugnaux: Timeless, 2016.

Coatman, Anna. "Watch These Spaces: The Future of Art Schools." *RA Magazine*, Spring 2016. Accessed December 8, 2017. https://www.royalacademy.org.uk/article/future-of-art-schools.

Cogan, Brian. "'Do They Owe Us a Living? Of Course They Do!' Crass, Throbbing Gristle, and Anarchy and Radicalism in Early English Punk Rock." *Journal for the Study of Radicalism* 1, no. 2 (2008): 77–90.

Cohen, Stanley. *Folk Devils and Moral Panics* [1972]. London: Routledge Classics, 2002.

Considine, Liam. "Screen Politics: Pop Art and the Atelier Populaire." *Tate Papers,* no. 24, Autumn 2015. Accessed February 20, 2018. http://www.tate.org.uk/research/publications/tate-papers/24/screen-politics-pop-art-and-the-atelier-populaire.

Cooper, Sam. *The Situationist International in Britain: Modernism, Surrealism, and the Avant-Gardes*. New York: Routledge, 2017.

COUM Transmissions. *COUM Decoumposition: Schlimm* [Rottweil 1974]. MoMA Archive: MoMA Queens Artists' Books.

COUM Transmissions. *G.P.O. vs. G.P.-O. – A Chronicle of Mail Art on Trial Coumpiled by Genesis P-Orridge and COUM* [1976]. MoMA Archive: MoMA Queens Artists' Books.

Crane, Michael and Mary Stofflet, eds. *Correspondence Art.* San Francisco: Contemporary Arts Press, 1984.

Cross, Rich. "The Hippies Now Wear Black: Crass and the Anarcho-Punk Movement, 1977–1984." *Socialist History,* no. 26 (2004): 25–44.

Danto, Arthur C. *After the End of Art: Contemporary Art and the Pale of History.* Princeton: Princeton University Press, 2014.

Danto, Arthur C. *Unnatural Wonders: Essays from the Gap Between Art and Life.* New York: Columbia University Press, 2005.

Dany, Hans-Christian. "Im Kohlenkeller eines neuen Dekadenzbewußtseins." In *Lieber zu viel als zu wenig: Kunst, Musik, Aktionen zwischen Hedonismus und Nihilismus (1976–1985),* edited by Neue Gesellschaft für Bildende Kunst e.V., 42–59. Berlin: NGBK, 2003.

Davis, Kathy. "Should a Feminist Dance Tango? Some Reflections on the Experience and Politics of Passion." *Feminist Theory* 16, no. 1 (2015): 3–21.

Dax, Max. *Nur was nicht ist ist möglich: Die Geschichte der Einstürzenden Neubauten.* Berlin: Bosworth Music, 2006.

De Chassey, Éric. "Bazooka, Pistols and Other Visual Weaponry." In *Europunk: The Visual Culture of Punk in Europe [1976–1980],* edited by Éric de Chassey, 127–39. Rome: Drago, 2011.

De Chassey, Éric. "Introduction." In *Europunk: The Visual Culture of Punk in Europe [1976–1980]*, edited by Éric de Chassey, 8–10. Rome: Drago, 2011.

Dekeukeleire, Jeanette and Harry Ruhé, eds. *Punk in Holland: God Shave the Queen.* Amsterdam: Cult Club Productions, 2011.

Diederichsen, Detlef. "Wie ich mal meine Jugend verschwendete." In *Zurück zum Beton: Die Anfänge von Punk und New Wave in Deutschland 1977–'82*, edited by Kunsthalle Düsseldorf and Ulrike Groos, 111–19. Cologne: Walther König, 2002.

Diedrichsen, Diedrich. "Geniuses and Their Noise." In *Brilliant Dilletantes: Subculture in Germany in the 1980s*, edited by Leonhard Emmerling, Mathilde Weh, and Goethe Institut e.V., 10–22. Ostfildern: Hatje Cantz, 2015.

Diedrichsen, Diedrich. "Intensität – Negation – Klartext: Simultanes und Inkommensurables zwischen Theorie, Bildender Kunst und Musik im deutschen Punk." In *Zurück zum Beton: Die Anfänge von Punk und New Wave in Deutschland 1977–'82*, edited by Kunsthalle Düsseldorf and Ulrike Groos, 137–46. Cologne: Walther König, 2002.

Duncan, Michael and Kristine McKenna. *Semina Culture: Wallace Berman & His Circle.* Santa Monica: Santa Monica Museum of Art and New York: D.A.P., 2007.

Duncombe, Stephen. "White Riot?" In *White Riot: Punk Rock and the Politics of Race*, edited by Stephen Duncombe and Maxwell Tremblay, 1–17. Brooklyn: Verso, 2011.

Eburne, Jonathan P. *Surrealism and the Art of Crime.* Ithaca: Cornell University Press, 2008.

Ehrensmann, Nina. *Paint Misbehavin': Neoexpressionismus und die Rezeption und Produktion figurativer, expressiver Malerei in New York zwischen 1977 und 1984.* Berlin: Peter Lang, 2005.

Elkins, James. *Stories of Art.* London: Routledge, 2002.

Elmer. *Billedstofteater 1977–85: Et Billedteater skabt af Per Flink Basse og Kirsten Dehlholm, et billedforløb.* Copenhagen: Christian Ejlers, 1995.

Engelhardt, Katrin. "Die Ausstellung 'Entartete Kunst' in Berlin 1938: Rekonstruktion und Analyse." In *Angriff auf die Avantgarde: Kunst und Kunstpolitik im Nationalsozialismus*, edited by Uwe Fleckner, 98–197. Berlin: Akademie Verlag, 2007.

Le Feuvre, Lisa. "Introduction: Strive to Fail." In *Failure: Documents of Contemporary Art*, edited by Lisa Le Feuvre, 12–21. London: Whitechapel Gallery, 2010.

Fischer-Hausdorf, Eva. "Der Künstler als Theaterdirektor, Regisseur und Kulissenschieber. Das Welttheater bei Max Beckmann." In *Max Beckmann: Welttheater*, edited by Museum Barberini and Kunsthalle Bremen, 10–21. Munich: Prestel, 2017.

Ford, Simon. "Myth Making." *Art Monthly*, no. 194 (March 1996): 3–9.

Ford, Simon. *Wreckers of Civilisation: The Story of COUM Transmissions & Throbbing Gristle*. London: Black Dog Publishing, 1999.

Freud, Sigmund. *A General Introduction to Psychoanalysis*. Translated by G. Stanley Hall. New York: Boni and Liveright, 1920.

Fusco, Maria and Richard Birkett, eds. *Cosey Complex*. Cologne: Walter König, 2012.

Garnett, Robert. "Too Low to Be Low: Art Pop and the Sex Pistols." In *Punk Rock: So What? The Cultural Legacy of Punk*, edited by Roger Sabin, 17–30. London: Routledge, 1999.

Gilroy, Paul. *There Ain't No Black in the Union Jack: The Cultural Politics of Race and Nation*. London: Routledge, 2002.

Gingeras, Alison, M. *The Avant-Garde Won't Give Up: Cobra and Its Legacy*. Los Angeles: Blum & Poe, 2015.

Goossens, Jerry. "A Black and White Statement: The Imagery of Dutch Punk." In *Europunk: The Visual Culture of Punk in Europe [1976–1980]*, edited by Éric de Chassey, 198–204. Rome: Drago, 2011.

Goossens, Jerry and Jeroen Vedder. *Het Gejuich was massaal: Punk in Nederland 1976–1982*. Amsterdam: Schilt Publishing, 1996.

Graham, Dan. "Punk as Propaganda." In *Sympathy for the Devil: Art and Rock and Roll since 1967*, edited by Dominic Molon, 122–33. Chicago: Museum of Contemporary Art, 2007.

Greene, Shane. "Introduction: ¿Otro Punk es Posible?" In *Punk! Las Américas Edition*, edited by Olga Rodríguez-Ulloa, Rodrigo Quijano, and Shane Greene, 11–31. Bristol: Intellect Books, 2021.

Grindon, Gavin. "Poetry Written in Gasoline: Black Mask and Up Against the Wall Motherfucker." *Art History* 38, no. 1 (February 2015): 170–209.

Grindon, Gavin. "Surrealism, Dada, and the Refusal of Work: Autonomy, Activism, and Social Participation in the Radical Avant-Garde." *Oxford Art Journal* 34 (2011), no. 1: 79–96.

Groetz, Thomas. *Doris als Musikerin: Die Tödliche Doris, Band 2*. Berlin: Martin Schmitz Verlag, 1999.

Groetz, Thomas. *Kunst – Musik: Deutscher Punk und New Wave in der Nachbarschaft von Joseph Beuys*. Berlin: Martin Schmitz Verlag, 2002.

Groos, Ulrike. "Zurück zum Beton." In *Zurück zum Beton: Die Anfänge von Punk und New Wave in Deutschland 1977–'82*, edited by Kunsthalle Düsseldorf and Ulrike Groos, 109. Cologne: Walther König, 2002.

Gruen, Bob. *The Clash*. London: Omnibus Press, 2001.

Haas, Martijn. *Dr. Rat, godfather van de Nederlandse graffiti*. Amsterdam: Lebowski Publishers, 2011.

Hackett, Pat and Andy Warhol. *POPism: The Warhol Sixties*. Boston: Mariner Books, 1980.

Haldemann, Mathias, ed. *Dieter Roth und die Musik / and Music: Und weg mit den Minuten*. Lucerne: Edizioni Periferia, 2014.

Hansen, Helle, ed. *69*. Copenhagen: Verve Books, 2008.

Hansen, Kamma Overgaard. "'Vi har ikke noget at sige, men vi gør det så koncentreret som muligt': De Unge Vilde i dansk kunst." PhD dissertation, Aarhus: Aarhus Universitet, 2017.

Hebdige, Dick. *Subculture: The Meaning of Style*. London: Routledge, 1979.

Hebdige, Dick. "Contemporizing 'Subculture': 30 Years to Life." *European Journal of Cultural Studies* 15, no. 3 (2012): 399–424.

Heylin, Clinton. *Babylon's Burning: From Punk to Grunge*. London: Penguin, 2007.

Higgins, Hannah. *Fluxus Experience*. Berkeley: University of California Press, 2002.

Hollins, Paul. "Never Mind the Paradox: 'Situationists', the Sorbonne and Ongoing Influence of Atelier Populaire on Punk Art and Culture." *The Art of Punk Conference*, University of Northampton, 25 November 2016.

Hopkins, David. "Oz Magazine and British Counterculture: A Case Study in the Reception of Surrealism." In *Radical Dreams: Surrealism, Counterculture, Resistance*, edited by Elliott King and Abigail Susik, 190–206. University Park: The Pennsylvania State University Press, 2022.

Huelsenbeck, Richard. "En Avant Dada: A History of Dadaism (1920)." In *The Dada Painters and Poets: An Anthology*, 2nd ed., edited by Robert Motherwell, 22–47. Cambridge: Harvard University Press, 1981.

Hussey, Andrew. "Mapping Utopia: Debord and Constant between Amsterdam and Paris." In *Paris-Amsterdam Underground: Essays on Cultural Resistance, Subversion, and Diversion*, edited by Andrew Hussey and Christoph Lindner, 37–48. Amsterdam: University Press, 2013.

Huxley, David. "'Ever Get the Feeling You've Been Cheated?' Anarchy and Control in The Great Rock 'n' Roll Swindle." In *Punk Rock: So What? The Cultural Legacy of Punk*, edited by Roger Sabin, 81–99. London: Routledge, 1999.

Ingelmann, Inka Graeve, ed. *Female Trouble: Die Kamera als Spiegel und Bühne weiblicher Inszenierungen*. Ostfildern: Hatje Cantz, 2008.

Jackson, Matthew Jesse and Robert Slifkin. *Towards a Rock and Roll History of Contemporary Art*. Los Angeles: CAA session, February 23, 2012.

Jacobsen, Signe Marie Ebbe. "Centrifugal Transformations: Looking at Lars Nørgård's Works." In *Lars Nørgård: Luxury Visions*, edited by Gitte Ørskou, 26–35. Aalborg: KUNSTEN. Museum of Modern Art, 2011.

Jahnke, Robin. "Merhaba S.O. 36." In *SO36: 1978 bis heute*, edited by SUB OPUS 36 e.V., 99–107. Berlin: Ventil Verlag, 2016.

Jameson, Fredric. *Postmodernism, or, The Cultural Logic of Late Capitalism*. Durham: Duke University Press, 1991.

Jensen, Carsten. "Christian Lemmerz og hans usømmelige omgang med verden," October 16, 2010. Accessed June 29, 2018. https://www.information.dk/moti/2010/10/christian-lemmerz-usoemmelige-omgang-verden.

Jensen, Grethe. "Folkets Hus." In *69*, edited by Helle Hansen, 8–13. Copenhagen: Verve Books, 2008.

Jeppesen, Simon. "Einstürzende Ungdomshus." In *69*, edited by Helle Hansen, 44–45. Copenhagen: Verve Books, 2008.

Johnson, Dominic. *The Art of Living: An Oral History of Performance Art*. London: Palgrave, 2015.

Johnson, Dominic. *Unlimited Action: The Performance of Extremity in the 1970s*. Manchester: Manchester University Press, 2019.

Jonker, Leonor. "Introduction." In *Punk in Holland: God Shave the Queen*, edited by Jeanette Dekeukeleire and Harry Ruhé, n.p. Amsterdam: Cult Club Productions, 2011.

Jonker, Leonor. *NO Future NU: Punk in Nederland 1977–2012*. Amsterdam: Lebowski Publishers, 2012.

Jones, Peter. "Anxious Images: Linder's Fem-Punk Photomontages." *Women: A Cultural Review* 13, no. 2 (2002): 161–78.

Kane, Daniel. *Do You Have a Band? Poetry and Punk Rock in New York City*. New York: Columbia University Press, 2017.

Karker, Andreas. *Jagtvej 69: Historien om et hus*. Copenhagen: Lindhardt og Ringhof, 2007.

Karpantschof, René and Flemming Mikkelsen. "Kampen om Byens rum: Ungdomshuset, Christiania og husbesættelser i København." In *Kampen om Ungdomshuset. Studier i Oprør*, 21–44. Copenhagen: Frydenlund og Monsun, 2009.

Karschnia, Alexander. "OUT OF JOINT: The 'New Spirit of Capitalism', Creative Class Struggle and the Ghosts from the Future." Key note talk, *Impossibility of Novelty? (Re)Creating the Old and Consuming the New*, Freie Universität Berlin, November 7, 2013. Accessed February 5, 2018. https://alextext.wordpress.com/2013/11/11/out-of-joint.

Kelley, Mike. "I Rip You." In *Hungry for Death: Destroy All Monsters,* edited by Cary Lohen, n.p. Boston: Boston University Art Gallery, 2011.

Kempton, Richard. *The Provos: Amsterdam's Anarchist Revolt.* New York: Autonomedia, 2013.

Kippenberger, Susanne. *Kippenberger: Der Künstler und seine Familien.* Berlin: Berlin Verlag, 2007.

Klotz, Heinrich. *Die Neuen Wilden in Berlin.* Stuttgart: Klett-Cotta, 1984.

Krauss, Rosalind. "The Originality of the Avant-Garde [1981]." In Krauss, *The Originality of the Avant-Garde and Other Modernist Myths.* Boston: MIT Press, 1986.

Kruse, Käthe. *Lob des Imperfekts: Kunst, Musik und Wohnen im West Berlin der 1980er Jahre.* Berlin: mikrotext, 2017.

Kugelberg, Johan and Jon Savage, eds. *Punk: An Aesthetic.* New York: Rizzoli, 2012.

Kugelberg, Johan and Philippe Vermès, eds. *Beauty is in the Street: A Visual Record of the May '68 Uprising.* London: Four Corners Books, 2011.

Kulle, Daniel. "Alle Macht der Super-8: Die West Berliner Super-8-Film-Bewegung und das Erbe des Punks." In *Punk in Deutschland: Sozial- und Kulturwissenschaftliche Perspektiven,* edited by Philipp Meinert and Martin Seeliger, 261–81. Bielefeld: Transcript, 2013.

Kunsthalle Düsseldorf and Ulrike Groos. *Zurück zum Beton: Die Anfänge von Punk und New Wave in Deutschland 1977–'82.* Cologne: Walther König, 2002.

Kunzru, Hari. "The Mob Who Shouldn't Really Be Here." In *Tate Etc.* 13 (Summer 2008). Accessed January 23, 2018. http://www.tate.org.uk/context-comment/articles/mob-who-shouldnt-really-be-here.

Kølster, Sune 'Køter' Carlsson. "Punk." In *69,* edited by Helle Hansen, 24–28. Copenhagen: Verve Books, 2008.

Laing, Dave. *One Chord Wonders: Power and Meaning in Punk Rock.* London: Open University Press, 1985.

Laxton, Susan. *Surrealism at Play.* Durham: Duke University Press Books, 2019.

Lemmerz, Christian. *Das Zeug.* Copenhagen: Galleri Specta, 1986.

Lerner, Adam and Steven Wolf. *Punk Rock and Contemporary Art on the West Coast.* Los Angeles: CAA Session, 23 February 2012.

Letts, Don and David Nobakht. *Culture Clash: Dread Meets Punk Rockers.* London: SAF Publishing, 2008.

Lewisohn, Cedar. *Street Art: The Graffiti Revolution.* London: Tate Publishing, 2008.

Lohman, Kirsty. *The Connected Lives of Dutch Punks: Contesting Subcultural Boundaries.* London: Palgrave Macmillan, 2017.

Lowey, Ian and Suzy Prince. *The Graphic Art of the Underground: A Countercultural History*. London: Bloomsbury Visual Arts, 2014.

Lydon, John, Keith Zimmerman, and Kent Zimmerman. *Rotten: No Irish, No Blacks, No Dogs*. London: Picador, 1994.

Lyford, Amy. *Surrealist Masculinities: Gender Anxiety and the Aesthetics of Post-World War I Reconstruction in France*. Berkeley: University of California Press, 2007.

MacCormack, Patricia. "Mucosal Coseying." In *Cosey Complex*, edited by Maria Fusco and Richard Birkett, 123–28. Cologne: Walter König, 2012.

Madura, Joe and Dominic Molon. "A Timeline." In *Sympathy for the Devil: Art and Rock and Roll since 1967*, edited by Dominic Molon, 252–67. Chicago: Museum of Contemporary Art, 2007.

Maffesoli, Michel. *The Time of the Tribes: The Decline of Individualism in Mass Society*. Thousand Oaks: SAGE Publications, 1996.

Mahon, Alyce. *The Marquis de Sade and the Avant-Garde*. Princeton: Princeton University Press, 2020.

Marcus, Greil. "Gulliver Speaks." In *Artforum* (November 1983). Accessed December 10, 2017. https://www.artforum.com/print/198309/gulliver-speaks-35454.

Marcus, Greil. *Lipstick Traces: A Secret History of the Twentieth Century*. Cambridge: Harvard University Press, 1989.

Marcus, Greil. "Punk (1979)" [first published in *The Rolling Stone Illustrated History of Rock & Roll*, ed. Jim Miller 1979]. Accessed December 17, 2017. https://greilmarcus.net/2014/09/08/punk-1979.

Margulies, Leo, ed. *The Young Punks*. New York: Pyramid Books, 1957.

Markey, Dave, director. *1991: The Year Punk Broke*, DVD. New York: Geffen Records, 2011.

Marx, Karl. "Economic and Philosophic Manuscripts [1844]." In *Prostitution and Pornography: Philosophical Debate about the Sex Industry*, edited by Jessica Spector. Palo Alto: Stanford University Press, 2006.

Matt, Gerald. "Vorwort." In *Punk: No One Is Innocent: Kunst – Stil – Revolte*, edited by Kunsthalle Wien, Gerald Matt, and Thomas Mießgang, 6–7. Nuremberg: Verlag für Moderne Kunst, 2008.

Mattson, Kevin. "Did Punk Matter? Analyzing the Practices of a Youth Subculture During the 1980s." *American Studies* 42, no. 1 (Spring 2001): 69–97.

McNeil, Legs and Gillian McCain. *Please Kill Me: The Uncensored Oral History of Punk*. New York: Grove Press, 1996.

Meinert, Philipp. *Homopunk History: Von den Sechzigern bis heute*. Ventil Verlag, 2018.

Metzger, Richard. "Nothing Short of a Total War" [first printed in *World Art Magazine*].

In *Painful But Fabulous: The Lives & Art of Genesis P-Orridge*, edited by Nick Mamatras, Maggie Balistreri, Ellen Moynihad, and Don Goede, 43–49. Brooklyn: Soft Skull Press, 2002.

Mießgang, Thomas. "No One Is Innocent." In *Punk: No One Is Innocent; Kunst – Stil – Revolte*, edited by Kunsthalle Wien, Gerald Matt, and Thomas Mießgang, 10–13. Nuremberg: Verlag für Moderne Kunst, 2008.

Miles, Barry. *London Calling: A Countercultural History of London since 1945*. London: Atlantic Books, 2011.

Miles, Barry. "The Future Leaks Out: A Very Magical and Highly Charged Interlude." In *Cut-Ups, Cut-Ins, Cut-Outs: The Art of William S. Burroughs*, edited by Kunsthalle Wien, Colin Fallows, and Synne Genzmer, 22–31. Nuremberg: Verlag für Moderne Kunst, 2012.

Miller, John. "Excremental Value: Piero Manzoni's 'Merda d'artista.'" In *Tate Etc.* 10 (Summer 2007). Accessed January 5, 2018. http://www.tate.org.uk/context-comment/articles/excremental-value.

Miller, Marc H. and Bettie Ringma. *Punk Art Exhibition: The Catalogue*. Washington, DC: Washington Project for the Arts, 1978.

Molon, Dominic. "Experimental Jet Set: The New York Scene." In *Sympathy for the Devil: Art and Rock and Roll since 1967*, edited by Dominic Molon, 10–19. Chicago: Museum of Contemporary Art, 2007.

Molon, Dominic, ed. *Sympathy for the Devil: Art and Rock and Roll since 1967*. Chicago: Museum of Contemporary Art, 2007.

Morell, Lars. *Broderskabet: Den Eksperimenterende Kunstskole 1961–69*. Copenhagen: Thaning & Appel, 2009.

Mott, Toby. *Showboat: Punk/Sex/Bodies*. New York: Dashwood Books, 2016.

Müller, Wolfgang. "Das Chaos reist mit dem Schönen Wochenende." In *Punk: No One Is Innocent; Kunst – Stil – Revolte*, edited by Kunsthalle Wien, Gerald Matt, and Thomas Mießgang, 154–62. Nuremberg: Verlag für Moderne Kunst, 2008.

Müller, Wolfgang. "Das Leben des Sid Vicious." In *Die Tödliche Doris – Kino*, edited by Wolfgang Müller and Martin Schmitz, 29–33. Berlin: Martin Schmitz Verlag, 2004.

Müller, Wolfgang. *Die Tödliche Doris – Performance: Band 5*. Berlin: Hybriden Verlag, 2017.

Müller, Wolfgang. "Die wahren Dilletanten." In *Geniale Dilletanten*, edited by Wolfgang Müller, 11–14. Berlin: Merve, 1982.

Müller, Wolfgang. "No Future now! Das SO36: Beitrag zum Experiment der Selbstmumifizierung (Sokushinbutsu)." In *SO36: 1978 bis heute*, edited by SUB OPUS 36 e.V., 64–72. Berlin: Ventil Verlag, 2016.

Müller, Wolfgang. "Produktion West 1980: Punk, Kunst, Aura: Die wilden Jahre, bevor die Großwildjäger kamen." *Lettre International*, no. 86, (Herbst 2009): 115.

Müller, Wolfgang. *Subkultur Westberlin 1979–1989: Freizeit*. Hamburg: Philo Fine Arts, 2013.

Müller, Wolfgang and Martin Schmitz, eds. *Die Tödliche Doris – Kunst / The Deadly Doris: Art*: *Band* 3. Berlin: Martin Schmitz Verlag, 1999.

Müller, Wolfgang and Martin Schmitz, eds. *Die Tödliche Doris – Kino / The Deadly Doris: Cinema: Band* 4. Berlin: Martin Schmitz Verlag, 2004.

Munuera, Iván López. "I Don't Know Where I am Going But I Promise It Won't Be Boring: The Political Specificity of Punk." In *PUNK: Its Traces in Contemporary Art*, edited by David G. Torres, 194–214. Barcelona: Museu d'Art Contemporani de Barcelona, 2016.

Nelson, Maggie. *The Art of Cruelty*. New York: W. W. Norton Company, 2011.

Nickas, Bob. "Komplaint Dept: Never Mind the Bollocks, Here's Anna Wintour," posted August 1, 2013. Accessed February 28, 2018. https://www.vice.com/en_us/article/kompbrlaintbrdeptbr-never-mind-the-bollocks-anna-wintour.

Nielsen, Jens-Emil. *Ung i 80'erne*. Copenhagen: Her&NU, 2005.

Nieuwenhuys, Constant. "New Babylon: Outline of a Culture [1974]." In *Constant's New Babylon: The Hyper-architecture of Desire*, edited by Mark Wigley. Rotterdam: Witte de With Center for Contemporary Art/010 Publishers, 1998.

Ølholm, Marianne. "Traces of Avant-Garde Strategies in Danish Poetry of the 1980s." In *A Cultural History of the Avant-Garde in the Nordic Countries 1975–2000*, edited by Benedikt Hjartarson, Camilla Paldam, Laura Schultz, and Tania Ørum, 831–45. Leiden & Boston: Brill Rodopi, 2022.

Ørum, Tania. *De eksperimenterende tressere: kunst i en opbrudstid*. Copenhagen: Gyldendal, 2009.

Ozon, Diana. *Laag Bij De Gronds*. Amsterdam: Guus Bauer, 1982.

Paglia, Camille. *Provocations*. New York: Pantheon, 2018.

Palmer, Alan. *East End: Four Centuries of London Life*. London: Faber & Faber, 2011.

Papenfuß, Bert. "Kunsterziehung durch Punk." In *Lieber zu viel als zu wenig: Kunst, Musik, Aktionen zwischen Hedonismus und Nihilismus (1976–1985)*, edited by Neue Gesellschaft für Bildende Kunst e.V., 60–63. Berlin: NGBK, 2003.

P-Orridge, Genesis. "To Be Ex-Dream: Photographic Sources of COUM Actions." In *Painful But Fabulous: The Lives & Art of Genesis P-Orridge*, edited by Nick Mamatras, Maggie Balistreri, Ellen Moynihad, and Don Goede, 155–69. Brooklyn: Soft Skull Press, 2002.

P-Orridge, Genesis and Peter Christopherson. "Annihilating Reality." *Studio International* 192, no. 982 (July/August 1976): 44–48.

Porta, Eloy Fernández. "The Artist in the Mosh Pit." In *PUNK: Its Traces in Contemporary Art*, edited by David G. Torres, 156–72. Barcelona: Museu d'Art Contemporani de Barcelona, 2016.

Poulsen, Jan. *Something Rotten! Punk i Danmark: Maleri, Musik og Litteratur*. Copenhagen: Gyldendal, 2010.

Poulsen, Jan. *Under en Sort Sol: Fra Pisserenden til Statens Museum for Kunst*. Copenhagen: Aschehoug, 2002.

Proll, Astrid, ed. *Goodbye to London: Radical Art and Politics in the Seventies*. Cologne: Hatje Cantz, 2010.

Proll, Astrid. "Hello London." In *Goodbye to London: Radical Art and Politics in the Seventies*, edited by Astrid Proll, 8–11. Cologne: Hatje Cantz, 2010.

Punk Scholars Network. "Documenting Punk in Academia." Accessed July 8, 2017. http://www.punkscholars.net.

Rasmussen, Mikkel Bolt. "Raping the Whole World in a Warm Embrace of Fascination: Drakabygget's Anti-Authoritarian Artistic Endeavors." In *A Cultural History of the Avant-Garde in the Nordic Countries 1950–1975*, edited by Tania Ørum and Jesper Olsson, 593–602. Leiden: Brill Rodopi, 2016.

Rasmussen, Mikkel Bolt. "The Fantasy of a Powerful Myth: The Situationist International After Surrealism." In *Radical Dreams: Surrealism, Counterculture, Resistance*, edited by Elliott King and Abigail Susik, 128–41. University Park: The Pennsylvania State University Press, 2022.

Ratcliff, Carter. "Snakes & Ladders: The COBRA Group, Sons of the Surrealists." In *Tate Etc.*, no. 4 (April 2003). Accessed May 1, 2018. http://www.tate.org.uk/context-comment/articles/snakes-and-ladders-the-cobra-group.

Reichensperger, Petra. "Schlau sein – dabei sein." In *Lieber zu viel als zu wenig: Kunst, Musik, Aktionen zwischen Hedonismus und Nihilismus (1976–1985)*, edited by Neue Gesellschaft für Bildende Kunst e.V., 18–33. Berlin: NGBK, 2003.

RE/search. "Throbbing Gristle." In *RE/search Issue 6-7: Industrial Culture Handbook*, edited by V. Vale and Andrea Juno, 6–19. San Francisco: RE/search Publications, 1983.

Reynolds, Simon. "Ono, Eno, Arto: Nonmusicians and the Emergence of Concept Rock." In *Sympathy for the Devil: Art and Rock and Roll since 1967*, edited by Dominic Molon, 80–91. Chicago: Museum of Contemporary Art, 2007.

Reynolds, Simon. *Rip It Up and Start Again: Postpunk 1978–1984*. London: Faber & Faber, 2005.

Richter, Angelika. *Das Gesetz der Szene: Genderkritik, Performance Art und Zweite Öffentlichkeit in der späten DDR.* Bielefeld: transcript, 2019.

Rocha, Servando. "A Great Negative Work of Destruction to Be Accomplished." In *PUNK: Its Traces in Contemporary Art*, edited by David G. Torres, 280–300. Barcelona: Museu d'Art Contemporani de Barcelona, 2016.

Rombes, Nicholas. *A Cultural Dictionary of Punk: 1974–1982.* London: Bloomsbury, 2009.

Rosenfeld, Kathryn. "The End of Everything Was 20 Years Ago Today: Punk Nostalgia." *New Art Examiner* 27, no. 4 (December 1999): 26–29.

Ross, Trine. *Lars Nørgård: Maleri.* Copenhagen: Aschehoug, 2004.

Rushkoff, Douglas. "Good Trip or Bad Trip? The Art and Heart of Genesis P-Orridge." In *Painful But Fabulous: The Lives & Art of Genesis P-Orridge*, edited by Nick Mamatras, Maggie Balistreri, Ellen Moynihad, and Don Goede, 19–28. Brooklyn: Soft Skull Press, 2002.

Sabin, Roger. "Introduction." In *Punk Rock: So What? The Cultural Legacy of Punk*, edited by Roger Sabin, 1–13. London: Routledge, 1999.

Sabin, Roger, ed. *Punk Rock: So What? The Cultural Legacy of Punk.* London: Routledge, 1999.

Sanders, Jay. "Love Is an Object." In *Rituals of Rented Island: Object Theater, Loft Performance, and the New Psychodrama. Manhattan 1970–1980*, edited by Jay Sanders, 27–39. New York: Whitney Museum of American Art, 2013.

Sanders, Jay, ed. *Rituals of Rented Island: Object Theater, Loft Performance, and the New Psychodrama: Manhattan 1970–1980.* New York: Whitney Museum of American Art, 2013.

Santisi, Meg. "Interview: Nat Trotman on RE/Search Magazine," posted March 2, 2014. Accessed March 28, 2018. http://blogs.colum.edu/caa/interview-nat-trotman-on-research-magazine

Savage, Jon. "Cut-Ups Go Pop: William S. Burroughs and a Mashed-up Future." In *Cut-Ups, Cut-Ins, Cut-Outs: The Art of William S. Burroughs*, edited by Kunsthalle Wien, Colin Fallows, and Synne Genzmer, 38–44. Nuremberg: Verlag für Moderne Kunst, 2012.

Savage, Jon. "Don't Just Watch." In *Europunk: The Visual Culture of Punk in Europe [1976–1980]*, edited by Éric de Chassey, 190–96. Rome: Drago, 2011.

Savage, Jon. *England's Dreaming: The Sex Pistols and Punk Rock.* London: Faber & Faber, 2005.

Savage, Jon. "Introduction." In *RE/Search #6-7: Industrial Culture Handbook*, 4–5. San Francisco: RE/search Publications, 1983.

Savage, Jon. "London Subversive." In *Goodbye to London: Radical Art and Politics in the Seventies,* edited by Astrid Proll, 12–31. Cologne: Hatje Cantz, 2010.

Savage, Jon. "The World's End: London Punk 1976–1977." In: *Punk: No One Is Innocent: Kunst – Stil – Revolte,* edited by Kunsthalle Wien, Gerald Matt, and Thomas Mießgang, 40–47. Nurnberg: Verlag für Moderne Kunst, 2008.

Savage, Jon. "Throbbing Gristle." *Search and Destroy,* no. 6 (April 1978).

Schaefer, Dirk. "City of Projections: The West Berlin Super-8 Movement between Punk and Art School." In *Who Says Concrete Doesn't Burn, Have You Tried? West Berlin Film in the '80s,* edited by Stefanie Schulte Strathaus and Florian Wüst, 26–35. Berlin: b books, 2008.

Schmitz, Martin. "Reunification through Dematerialization." In *Die Tödliche Doris – Kunst / The Deadly Doris – Art: Band 3,* edited by Wolfgang Müller and Martin Schmitz, 6–7. Berlin: Martin Schmitz Verlag, 1999.

Schmitz, Martin. "The Medium Was the Message." In *Berlin Super-80: Music & Film Underground West Berlin 1978–1984* [DVD, CD, and booklet], 7. Berlin: Monitorpop, 2005.

Schnabel, Julian. "Statement (1978)" In *Failure: Documents of Contemporary Art,* edited by Lisa Le Feuvre, 131. London: Whitechapel Gallery, 2010.

Schneider, Frank Apunkt. *Als die Welt noch unterging: Von Punk zu NDW.* Mainz: Ventil, 2007.

Schneider, Martin. "Shane MacGowan perpetrates 'Cannibalism at Clash gig,' 1976," January 2, 2016. Accessed March 4, 2018. http://dangerousminds.net/comments/shane_macgowan_perpetrates_cannibalism_at_clash_gig_1976.

Schönberg, Arnold. "Probleme des Kunstunterrichts [1911]." In *Stil und Gedanke: Aufsätze zur Musik 1909–1950,* edited by Arnold Schönberg. Frankfurt am Main: S. Fischer, 1976.

Schröter, Melani and Steffen Pappert. "Der Punk-Diskurs in der DDR." In *Politische Wechsel, Sprachliche Umbrüche,* edited by Bettina Bock, Ulla Fix, and Steffen Pappert, 171–94. Berlin: Frank & Timme, 2011.

Schütz, Heinz. "Excess of Ruins, Cult of Catastrophe: Jencks, Einstürzende Neubauten and Punk and Tödliche Doris and." In *Brilliant Dilletantes: Subculture in Germany in the 1980s,* edited by Leonhard Emmerling, Mathilde Weh, and Goethe Institut e.V., 130–41. Ostfildern: Hatje Cantz, 2015.

Silk, Jerry. "Punk Precedents." In *Punk Art Exhibition: The Catalogue,* edited by Marc H. Miller and Bettie Ringma. Washington, DC: Washington Project for the Arts, 1978.

Sinker, Mark. "Concrete, so as to Self-Destruct: The Etiquette of Punk, Its Habits, Rules, Values and Dilemmas." In *Punk Rock: So What? The Cultural Legacy of Punk*, edited by Roger Sabin, 120–40. London: Routledge, 1999.

Sjöberg, Sami. *The Vanguard Messiah: Lettrism between Jewish Mysticism and the Avant-Garde*. Berlin: Walter de Gruyter, 2015.

Skai, Hollow. *PUNK: Versuch der künstlerischen Realisierung einer neuen Lebenshaltung* [1979]. Wissenschaftliche Reihe, vol. 3. Berlin: Archiv der Jugendkulturen Verlag, 2008.

Skov, Marie Arleth. "Dominas & Paradisvögel: Sexyness, Spiel und Subkultur im Leben der Claudia Skoda." In *Claudia Skoda. Dressed to Thrill*, edited by Britta Bommert and Staatliche Museen zu Berlin, 31–49. Dortmund: Verlag Kettler, 2020.

Sladen, Mark. "Introduction." In *Panic Attack! Art in The Punk Years*, edited by Mark Sladen and Ariella Yedgar, 9–17. London: Merrell, 2007.

Smith, Donald. "Curators Foreword." In *Red White and Blue: Pop Punk Politics Place*, edited by Chelsea Space, 3–4. London: University of the Arts, 2012.

Smith, Pauline. "Corpse Club [1977]." In *About VILE: Mail Art, News and Photos from the Eternal Network*, edited by Anna Banana, 59–60. Vancouver: Banana Productions, 1983.

Sofianos, Lisa, Robin Ryde, and Charlie Waterhouse. *The Truth of Revolution, Brother: An Exploration of Punk Philosophy*. London: Situation Press, 2014.

Sontag, Susan. "Notes On 'Camp'" [first published in *Partisan Review* 1964]. In *Against Interpretation and Other Essays*, edited by Susan Sontag, 275–92. London: Penguin Modern Classics, 2009.

Sontag, Susan. "The Pornographic Imagination." In *L'Histoire de L'oeil / Story of the Eye*, edited by Georges Bataille, 83–118. London: Penguin, 1982.

Stevenson, Nils and Ray Stevenson. *Vacant: A Diary of the Punk Years 1976–1979*. London: Thames & Hudson, 1999.

Steyerl, Hito. "A Thing Like You and Me." In *e-flux Journal* #15, April 2010. Accessed March 30, 2018. http://www.e-flux.com/journal/15/61298/a-thing-like-you-and-me/.

Stiles, Bradley J. *Emerson's Contemporaries and Kerouac's Crowd: A Problem of Self-location*. London: Associated University Press, 2003.

Stjernfeldt, Frederik, and Poul Erik Tøjner. *Billedstorm: Om dansk kunst og kultur på det seneste*. Copenhagen: Amadeus, 1989.

Strunge, Michael. "Revolt [1981]." In *A Virgin from a Chilly Decade*. Translated by Bente Elsworth and edited by Michael Strunge, 41. Todmoren, Lancs: Arc Publications, 2000.

Strunge, Michael. *SAMLEDE STRUNGE: Digte 1978–85*. Copenhagen: Borgen, 1995.

Suárez, Juan A. "Warhol's 1960s' Films, Amphetamine, and Queer Materiality." *Criticism* 56, no. 3 (Summer 2014): 623–51.

Susik, Abigail. *Surrealist Sabotage and the War on Work*. Manchester: Manchester University Press, 2021.

Sussman, Elisabeth. "Introduction." In *On the Passage of a Few People through a Rather Brief Moment in Time: The Situationist International 1957–1972*, edited by Elisabeth Sussman, 2–16. Cambridge: MIT Press, 1989.

Symons, Arthur. *Selected Writings*, edited by Roger Holdsworth. New York: Routledge, 2003.

Teipel, Jürgen. *Verschwende Deine Jugend. Ein Doku-Roman über den deutschen Punk und New Wave*. Frankfurt: Suhrkamp, 2001.

Thomsen, Søren Ulrik. "Om forsiden til City Slang." Accessed June 27, 2018. http://www.soerenulrikthomsen.dk/sut/boeger/city-slang/city-slang-om-forsiden.html.

Tobin, Amy. "Linderism: The Red Period." In *Linderism*, edited by Kettle's Yard, 39–48. Cologne: Walther König, 2020.

Torres, David G. "Traces of a Punk Attitude in Contemporary Art." In *PUNK: Its Traces in Contemporary Art*, edited by David G. Torres, 40–66. Barcelona: Museu d'Art Contemporani de Barcelona, 2016.

Torres, David G., ed. *PUNK: Its Traces in Contemporary Art*. Barcelona: Museu d'Art Contemporani de Barcelona, 2016.

Tutti, Cosey Fanni. *Art Sex Music*. London: Faber & Faber, 2017.

Tutti, Cosey Fanni. "Confessions" [postscript text, April 2002]. London: Cabinet Gallery, 2003.

Tzara, Tristan. "Dada Manifesto 1918". In *The Dada Painters and Poets: An Anthology, 2nd ed.*, edited by Robert Motherwell, 76–82. Cambridge: Harvard University Press, 1981.

Van der Steen, Bart, Ask Katzeff, and Leendert van Hoogenhuijze. "Introduction." In *The City Is Ours: Squatting and Autonomous Movements in Europe from the 1970s to the Present*, edited by Bart van der Steen, Ask Katzeff, and Leendert van Hoogenhuijze, 1–19. Oakland: PM Press, 2014.

Verhagen, Marcus. "There's No Success Like Failure: Martin Kippenberger (2006)." In *Failure: Documents of Contemporary Art*, edited by Lisa Le Feuvre, 43–46. London: Whitechapel Gallery, 2010.

Voogd, Fanta. "Punk in Amsterdam." *Ons Amsterdam*, no. 3 (March 2013). Accessed May 8, 2018. http://www.onsamsterdam.nl/tijdschrift/jaargang-2013.

Wagner, Gretchen L. "Fluxkit." In *Thing/Thought: Fluxus Editions 1962–1978*, Museum of Modern Art New York, September 21, 2011–January 16, 2012. Accessed May 1, 2018. https://www.moma.org/interactives/exhibitions/2011/fluxus_editions/category_works/fluxkit.

Wagner, Gretchen L. "Riot on the Page: Thirty Years of Zines by Women." In *Modern Women: Women Artists at the Museum of Modern Art*, edited by Cornelia Butler and Alexandra Schwartz, 444–61. New York: Museum of Modern Art, 2010.

Walker, John A. *Left Shift: Radical Art in 1970s Britain*. London: I.B. Tauris, 2002.

Walker, John A. "Panic Attack!" *The Art Book* 15, no. 1 (2008): 14–15.

Warr, Tracey. "Feral City." In *Panic Attack! Art in The Punk Years*, edited by Mark Sladen and Ariella Yedgar, 116–21. London: Merrell, 2007.

Warr, Tracey. *The Artist's Body*. London: Phaidon, 2012.

Wiedlack, Maria Katharina. *Queer-Feminist Punk: An Anti-Social History*. Vienna: zaglossus, 2015.

Wien, Kunsthalle, Gerald Matt and Thomas Mießgang, eds. *Punk: No One Is Innocent: Kunst – Stil – Revolte*. Nurnberg: Verlag für Moderne Kunst, 2008.

Willmann, Fran. *Leck mich am Leben: Punk im Osten*. Berlin: Neues Leben, 2012.

Wilson, Julie. "As It Is." In *Painful But Fabulous: The Lives & Art of Genesis P-Orridge*, edited by Nick Mamatras, Maggie Balistreri, Ellen Moynihad, and Don Goede, 51–110. Brooklyn: Soft Skull Press, 2002.

Wise, David, ed. *King Mob: A Critical Hidden History*. London: Bread and Circusses, 2014.

Wivel, Henrik. *Nina Sten-Knudsen*. Copenhagen: Palle Fogtdahl, 1990.

Wolfe, Tom. *The Electric Kool-aid Acid Test* [1968]. London: Picador, 2008.

Wollen, Peter. "Bitter Victory: The Art and Politics of the Situationist International." In *On the Passage of a Few People through a Rather Brief Moment in Time: The Situationist International 1957–1972*, edited by Elisabeth Sussman, 20–61. Cambridge: MIT Press, 1989.

Wood, Ghislaine. *The Surreal Body: Fetish and Fashion*. London: V&A Museum, 2007.

Worley, Matthew. "Whip In My Valise: British Punk and the Marquis de Sade, c. 1975–85." In *Contemporary British History* 36, no. 2 (2022): 277–303.

Zapperi, Giovanna. "Marcel Duchamp's 'Tonsure': Towards an Alternate Masculinity." *Oxford Art Journal* 30, no. 2 (2007): 291–303.

index

Page numbers in roman represent figures.

A

13AB (exhibition space) *73*
1984 (book) *19, 76, 183, 258*
A Clockwork Orange (film) *107, 170–71*
Abramović, Marina *221–22*
abstraction *161*
Acconci, Vito *133, 240*
Achternbusch, Herbert *103–04*
Adam and the Ants *62, 217*
agitprop *120*
Albertine, Viv *62, 172,197, 223, 226*
anarchism *25*
anarcho-punk *51, 60, 274*
Anderson, Laurie *53*
anti-art *13, 33, 43, 45, 63, 109, 185, 271*
antimodernism *160*
ANUS Gallery *38–39, 224*
apocalypse *52, 55–56, 183, 254*
Art Something *37, 39, 273*
Atelier Populaire *13, 67, 68–69*
auto-destructive art *65*
autodidactic *177–78, 189*
automatism *157, 275*
autonomy *61, 64, 72, 176, 180, 194, 214, 221–22, 278*

B

bad painting *23, 106, 267*
Ball, Hugo *133, 166*
Banana, Anna *15, 20, 71, 174, 258, 259*
Bargeld, Blixa *146, 187, 244, 257, 261, 273*
Barr, Alfred *161*
Bataille, Georges *215, 217, 278*
Baudelaire, Charles *62, 113, 215*
Bazooka *12–13*
Beat Generation *52, 70, 108, 122, 177*
Beauvoir, Simone de *214, 216, 226*
Beckmann, Max *212–13, 278*
Bellmer, Hans *155, 278*
Benglis, Lynda *43, 229*
Berber, Anita *212*
Berlin Wall *75, 109, 257, 261*
Berman, Wallace *44, 71*
Bestley, Russ (artist) *69*
Beuys, Joseph *29, 102, 109, 188–89, 246*
Black Flag *24*
Block, Ursula *92, 260*
Blondie *26–27, 53, 221, 225*
Blumenschein, Tabea *15, 157, 203, 212, 213, 214, 220, 278*
Body Art *14, 23, 43, 89, 95, 126, 237, 241, 247*
Borum, Poul *159*
boxing *240–41*
BOY (the store) *164, 168, 260*
Brassaï *77*
Brecht, Bertolt *147, 212*
Breyer, Jackie *155*
Brisley, Stuart *209*
Burroughs, William S. *51, 70–71, 105, 114, 133, 152, 170*
Buttgereit, Jörg *43, 110*
Buzzcocks *44, 60, 87, 90, 105, 228, 239, 242*

C

cabaret *212, 213, 238, 240, 260*
Cabaret Voltaire (band and Dada bar) *20, 62, 268*
Cage, John *17, 64, 267*
camp *85–86, 100–01*
Caravaggio *148, 173, 206*
Carson, Neke *85, 88, 89*
cartoon *33, 41, 53, 87, 146*
Castelli, Luciano *205, 206, 278*
Catwoman, Soo *204, 219–20*
Cazazza, Monte *258, 259, 268*
CBGB *32, 53*
Christopherson, Peter "Sleazy" *19, 133–34, 167, 168,* 169, *170,* 201, *202, 219*
Clark, Larry *186*
Clash, the *21, 22, 25, 36, 55, 58, 62, 115, 123, 135, 239, 263*
Cobain, Kurt *71, 100*
CoBrA *18, 64, 147, 149–52, 161–63, 180–81, 192, 278*
Constructivism *106*
Coon, Caroline *87, 226*
corporeality *64, 155, 246, 279*
Corré, Joe *45, 272*
COUM Transmissions *13, 15, 16–17,* 18, *19–20, 43–44, 55, 71–72, 79, 94, 96, 107–09, 113, 118,* 119, *131–34, 136,* 137, 139, *140, 147–48,* 150, *153, 164, 174, 175, 176–77, 192, 201, 210, 218, 239, 258, 274–75, 279*
Coumalphabet *118, 181, 275*
counterculture *52, 57, 108, 215–16, 243, 273–74*
counterpropaganda *113, 140, 275*
Courbet, Gustave *154, 276*
Cragg, Tony *43*
Crass *44, 51, 60–61, 114–15*
Cravan, Arthur *185, 194, 264, 278*
Crone, Ulrik *31*
cruelty *166, 176, 214, 222, 230, 278–79*

D

Dada *13–14, 20, 24–25, 38, 62–65, 70, 94, 114, 118, 135, 147, 149, 151–53, 161, 166, 174, 180–84, 185, 187, 212, 218, 227, 240, 244, 260, 263–64, 268, 271–73, 276–77*

Dahlin, Dorte *125, 250*
Dalí, Salvador *12, 154,* 155, *243,* 245
De Stijl *161*
Death Factory *55, 138*
Debord, Guy *67–68, 94–95, 148, 166, 180*
decadence *11, 138, 249, 260*
Denney, Alice *32,* 33
DeSana, Jimmy *221*
Destroy All Monsters *12, 96*
détournement *69–70, 110, 118, 140, 146, 148, 152, 228*
Devo *27, 70, 159*
Dickens, Charles *56, 170*
Die Große Untergangsshow *254,* 261, *262*
Die Tödliche Doris *15–17, 44, 85, 91–94, 102, 109–110, 150, 153, 157–59, 164,* 165, *171–74, 186–87, 203, 212–14, 218, 223, 237, 244–49, 257–58, 261, 262, 266–67*
Dietrich, Marlene *193–94, 226*
dilettantism *70, 180, 184–85, 188, 192, 194, 249*
Dimitroff, Dagmar *157, 261–62*
Divine *86,* 101, *198*
DIY *43, 51, 57, 60–61, 71–75, 96, 180, 184, 194, 199, 227, 260, 268, 272, 274*
Dohmen, Leo *68,* 204, *243–44*
Dr Rat *38, 79, 127*
Drakabygget *95, 274*
Dreier, Chris *157*
Duchamp, Marcel *12,* 19, *20, 36, 63, 116,* 117, *148, 267*
dyke *60, 198, 256*
dystopian *138, 162, 170, 180, 184, 254, 258*

E

Einstürzende Neubauten *27, 30–31, 119, 186–87, 254, 257, 261–62*
Eisengrau *74, 260*
Eken, Rose *31*
Elmer *15, 73, 116–17*
Emin, Tracey *100, 208,* 211
Eno, Brian *69–70*
escapism *11, 57, 115, 171, 279*
existentialist/existentialism *122, 249, 251–52, 279*
EXPORT, VALIE *44, 205, 208,* 209
exquisite corpse *156–58*
Ex–Situationist *95, 115, 131, 146–47*

F

fantasy *99, 164, 166, 193, 206, 214, 242, 250, 279*
Fekner, John *78–79*
feminism *40, 198, 212, 221–25, 229–31, 233, 279*
femme fatale *198, 206, 229–30*
fetishism *101–02, 146, 155, 216, 230, 243–44*
fin-de-siècle *145, 152, 159, 183, 277*
Fluxus *14, 18, 65, 70, 91–92, 94, 108–09, 117, 145, 147, 149–50, 188–89, 192, 218, 240, 276*
Freddie, Wilhelm *155*
Friedman, Ken *108–09, 150*
futurism/futurist *13, 20, 63, 94, 168, 218, 230, 240, 245, 263, 272, 276, 279*

G

gay *24, 26, 53, 62, 75, 198–202*
Genet, Jean *198–99*
Gert, Valeska *212–13*
Gilbert & George *255–56*
Goldin, Nan *44, 186*
Gordon, Douglas *44*
graffiti *14, 18, 31, 38, 58, 61, 66, 68, 73, 76–80, 88, 91, 115–16, 118, 122, 126, 173, 232, 252, 255–56*
Graham, Dan *27, 44, 115*
Grootveld, Robert Jasper *90*
Grosz, George *25, 64, 77, 212, 227*
grunge *15, 52*
Guerrilla Girls *44*
Gut, Gudrun *12, 73, 238, 260–61*
Gysin, Brion *70–71, 105*

H

Hagen, Nina *79, 225,* 226
Harry, Debbie *26*
Hausmann, Raoul *149, 182, 187, 212*
hedonism *11, 27, 85, 94, 260*
Heino, the true *110, 157*
Hell, Richard *53, 86, 113, 221, 243*
Hilsberg, Alfred *158*
Höch, Hannah *227–29*
Høiby, Camilla *159*
Holck, Henrik S. *73, 122*
Holmstrom, John *27, 32, 37, 53*
Hoppe, Curt 34, *36–37*
Hugo, Victor (the NYC artist) *87*

I

ICA (Institute of Contemporary Arts, London) *133, 135–38, 140, 192, 210, 239, 275*
Ignorant, Steve *61*
industrial (music/culture) *51, 94, 109, 268–69*
infantilism *11, 77, 93, 164, 166, 176–77, 194, 277*
Ingenious Dilettantes *184, 186–88, 194 , 254, 262*
Isou, Isidore *181*

J

Jarman, Derek *43, 53–54, 70, 74, 217*
Jones, Allen 218
Jorn, Asger *67,* 151–*52, 180*
Jürgenssen, Birgit *205*

K

Kaagman, Hugo *15, 17, 38–39, 41, 62, 71, 78–79, 90–91, 127–28, 149–52, 183, 256, 258, 271–72, 280*
Kanstadt, Kristian *38, 127*

Kelley, Mike *44, 53, 96*
King Mob *51, 64, 66–68, 95–96, 115, 140, 146, 152, 274*
Kippenberger, Martin *27, 28–30, 32, 74–75, 273*
Kipper Kids, the *53, 100, 138, 192, 239–40*
Kirkegaard, Michael *73*
Kitchen, the (venue) *61, 218*
Klüver, Billy *85, 87–88*
KoeCrandt *15, 17–18, 37–39, 41, 58–59, 79, 89–90, 93, 109, 126–28, 149, 150–52, 182–83, 194, 256, 278*
Kruse, Käthe *15, 71, 110, 131, 157, 186, 223, 225*
Kvernenes, Karen *37*
Kvium, Michael *102–03*

L

L'Hotsky, Tina *37*
le Rat, Blek *79*
Lemmerz, Christian *15, 23, 102–04, 190, 251–52, 280*
Lenin, Wladimir Iljitsch *31*
Lesbian *203, 214*
Lettrists/Lettrism *14, 146, 215, 277*
LGTBQ *40, 201*
libertarian/libertine *215, 216, 230, 278*
Longo, Robert *43*
Lost Boys *170–71, 250, 277*
Luddites, the *107, 263*
Ludus *227–29*
Lulu Zulu & the White Guys *38, 59, 127*
Lunch, Lydia *73, 152*
Luxemburg, Rosa *31*
Lydon, Johnny (see also: Rotten) *17, 54, 164, 260–61, 263*

M

Maciunas, George *91*
madness *206, 212, 237–38, 250, 267, 273, 279*
Magritte, René *132, 153, 215*
Malaria (band) *73*
Manet, Édouard *207–08, 276, 278*
Mania D *73*
mannerism *145, 153, 159, 277*
Manzoni, Piero 101, *175*
Mapplethorpe, Robert *37, 40, 186*
Marten, Ruth *37*
Marx, Karl *53, 67, 101, 146, 182*
Marxist *68, 162, 210*
Matta-Clark, Gordon *43, 254*
McCarthy, Paul *43, 240*
McLaren, Malcolm *24, 45, 53–55, 59, 61–62, 65–66, 87, 96, 107, 115, 146–47, 170, 173, 202, 216, 263*
McNeil, Legs *27, 32, 36–37*
Merry Pranksters *107*
Metzger, Gustav *51, 65, 274*
Mickey Mouse *161*
Middendorf, Helmut 21, *23*
Miller, Marc H. *15, 32–41, 88, 241*
Minor Threat *60*
modernism *145, 147, 149, 160, 208, 276–77*
Mooney, Jordan *12, 53, 54, 194, 219*
Moore, Thurston 71
Morea, Ben *68, 151, 274*
Motherfuckers, the *51, 68, 151, 152, 161, 274*
Movemente Arte Nucleare *192*
Muehl, Otto *218*
Müller, Wolfgang (artist) *15–20, 28, 93–94, 102, 104, 157, 165, 172–73, 186, 188, 194, 203, 245, 261–62, 271–72*

N

Nash, Jørgen *67–68, 95*
negation *24–25, 57, 60, 67, 72, 86, 95, 122, 148, 194, 264, 267, 272, 275, 277*
neo-avant-garde *14, 85, 94–95, 150, 275–76*
Neo-Dada *13, 63, 149, 151, 161*
neo-expressionist *23, 106, 206, 252, 267*
Neo-Nazism *26, 59, 109*
Neue Deutsche Welle *16, 257*
Neue Wilde *23, 205*
New Babylon *181–84*
New York Dolls *53, 170, 198*
Nieuwenhuys, Constant *180–81*
no future *11, 13, 24, 40, 57–58, 61, 68, 79, 104, 130, 138, 145, 160, 258, 262, 272, 276*
Noise Art *63*
Nørgård, Lars *15, 86, 105–06, 125–26, 190–92, 250*
Nouveau Réalisme *94*
Nuttall, Jeff *52*

O

Odde, Knud *121, 232, 251*
Oi! *59*
Ono, Yoko *69–70, 109, 221–22, 274*
Oppenheim, Meret *204, 243, 246–47*
Orwell, George/Orwellian *19, 160, 258*
Otterness, Tom *37, 240–41*
Oursler, Tony *43*
outsider art *152*
Ozon, Diana *15, 38–39, 79, 89, 90–91, 113, 127, 182, 224–25, 231, 240, 258*

P

Pan, Peter *11, 170, 250, 266, 277*
Panic, Peter *18*
Papenfuß, Bert *113, 129, 131*
Paradiso (venue) *58, 91*
performance art *12, 23, 238–41, 277, 279*
performativity *64, 198, 205*
Piper, Adrian *43*
Pippi Longstocking *223*
Pirroni, Marco *26*

poetry *11–12, 14–15, 18, 23–24, 51, 56–57, 63, 71, 77, 91, 113, 120–23, 126–29, 159, 164, 181, 250, 265, 267, 271, 273, 275, 278*
Poison Girls, the *60*
Polack, Lilian *73*
Pop Art *32, 69, 85–86, 88–89, 91, 94–95, 147, 149, 161, 217–18, 273, 275*
Pop, Iggy *165, 259*
P-Orridge, Genesis (Breyer) *13, 15–19, 71–72, 86–87, 94, 101, 107–08, 118–19, 131–39, 150, 153–56, 164, 174–77, 202, 209, 218–19, 225, 239, 261, 268, 275, 278–79*
postmodernism/postmodern *160, 276*
Presley, Elvis *21, 26, 97–100, 206*
propaganda *107, 110, 113, 115, 117, 119–20, 275*
PROSTITUTION (exhibition) *131, 133, 135–40, 153, 192, 207, 209–10*
Provo (movement) *79, 126, 128, 149, 152, 181*
Punk Scholars Network *41, 68–69*
Pussy Riot *277*

Q
queercore *51, 198*

R
Raincoats, the *60*
Ramone, Joey *52*
Ramones *53, 106, 165, 201, 260, 274, 279*
Rat Jenny *27–29, 32*
Ratinger Hof *92*
Ray, Man *19, 20, 155*
realism *11, 44, 89, 256*
Rebel Dykes *60*
Reed, Lou *53, 71, 104, 198*
reggae *26, 58–59, 149, 183*
Reid, Jamie *20, 43–44, 55, 61, 64, 66–68, 115, 146, 171, 220, 243, 264*
Resnick, Marcia *37, 168*
Ridder, Willem de *91*
Rimbaud, Arthur *113, 215*
Rimbaud, Penny *61, 115*
Ringma, Bettie *32, 34, 36–41*
riot grrrls *51, 223, 279*
RISIKO (night club) *186–87, 202, 260*
Romanticism *44, 238, 249–51*
Rondos, the *79, 200*
Rote Armee Fraktion (RAF) *233, 237, 280*
Roth, Dieter *70, 246, 267, 274*
Rotten, Johnny (see Lydon) *54, 57, 59, 72, 99, 104, 115, 136, 146, 201–02, 239, 263, 264*
Rubin, William *161*
Rupp, Christy *79*
Ruppert, Ilse *129–30*
Russolo, Luigi *63, 245*

S
S&M *53, 146, 155, 198, 215, 217, 220, 223, 233, 237, 243*
Sade, Marquis de *133, 214–16, 218, 278–79*
Saint-Point, Valentine de *230, 279*
Salomé (artist) *43, 200, 205–06, 278*
Savage, Jon (artist) *57, 264*
Schiaparelli, Elsa *242–43*
Schleime, Cornelia *129–30*
Schnabel, Julian *267*
Schulhoff, Erwin *51, 64*
Schwitters, Kurt *38, 146*
Scott B & Beth B *35–36*
Screaming Mad George *37*
SEX (the store) *53–55, 146, 197, 246, 260*
Sex Pistols *14, 16–17, 20, 24–25, 44, 54–55, 60, 62, 67–68, 85, 87, 96–97, 99–100, 113–15, 123, 132, 135–36, 138, 140, 146, 158, 170–71, 197, 201–02, 221, 239–40, 249, 260, 262–63, 274, 279*
sexuality *41, 154–55, 169, 194, 197–98, 202, 204, 206–07, 212, 214, 216, 225, 240, 273, 278*
Sherman, Cindy *210, 222*
Sickie *159*
simulacra *160, 276*
Sioux, Siouxsie *114, 138, 198, 205*
Situationist International *14, 64, 66–67, 85, 180–82, 274*
Skinhead *25, 51, 59, 255*
Skoda, Claudia *73–75*
Slits, the *60, 62, 146, 197, 225*
Smith, Jack *53*
Smith, Patti *53, 113, 126, 221, 230, 266*
Smith, Pauline *174*
Smith, Pennie *21–22*
SO36 (venue) *16–17, 21, 23, 28, 61, 157–158, 260, 273*
Sods, the *73, 105, 121–23, 152, 159, 191, 232, 250–51, 273*
speed *12, 23, 78, 85, 104–06, 123, 190*
Spence, Jo *222*
Spungen, Nancy *60, 99, 165, 171*
Squatting *40, 57, 71, 91, 104, 129, 149, 180, 184, 186, 189, 200, 274*
Stein, Chris 26
Sten-Knudsen, Nina *15, 32, 105, 126–27, 223, 231–33, 244–52, 273*
Sterling, Linder (aka Linder) *43–44, 146, 156, 226–29, 242–43*
Steyerl, Hito *222*
Stezaker, John 43
street art *14, 31, 71, 76–79, 92, 95, 116, 271*
Strummer, Joe *57–58, 62*
Strunge, Michael *113, 122–26, 164–65, 250, 265–66, 275*

Styrene, Poly *245*
submission *198, 204, 214, 220–22*
Suprematism *106*
Surrealism/Surrealists *13, 20, 24–25, 38, 52, 63–65, 77, 94, 113–14, 133–35, 145, 147, 151–52, 157–58, 160–61, 166, 180, 184–86, 198, 215–16, 238, 242–45, 250, 258, 264–65, 272–73, 275–76, 278*
Swindle *25, 40, 97, 99, 108, 114, 171, 173, 193*
symbolism *125, 132, 205, 243*
Symons, Arthur *134*

T
Tapehead (band) *191–92*
Temple, Julien *114, 140, 171*
Tempodrom (venue) *254, 261*
theatricality *238*
Thomsen, Søren Ulrik *32, 122, 126–27, 191, 223, 248–50*
Throbbing Gristle (TG) *15–17, 55, 122, 136, 176, 221, 268*
Tom Robinson Band (TRB) *58, 199*
Townsend, Pete *65–66*
Townson, Ian 200
transgression *18, 63, 65, 67, 101, 113, 131, 207–08, 215, 240, 278*
trash *11, 20, 41, 85–86, 89, 94, 96, 100–01, 104, 107, 109, 122, 130, 174, 238, 240*
Turk, Gavin 97–*100*
Twist, Oliver *11, 170*
Tzara, Tristan *25, 263*

U
unemployment *56, 180, 182–84, 278*
Ungdomshuset (Youth House) *27, 30–32*
Unruh, N.U. *31*
Utermöhlen, Nikolaus *157, 261–62*
utopian *161–62, 180–81, 184*

V
Værkstedet Værst *15, 17, 102, 105, 180, 189–194, 251, 278*
VÆRST *102–03*
Vaneigem, Raoul *68, 95, 274*
Vaucher, Gee *44, 146*
Vega, Arturo *37*
Venus *153–55, 161, 202, 204, 206–07*
Vicious, Sid *14, 57, 60, 97–100, 146, 161, 164–65, 171–74, 237, 266–67, 276*
Vienna Actionists *20, 134*
VILE (magazine) *20, 71, 174, 209, 258–59*
Voigt, Torben *73*

W
Warhol, Andy *12, 85–89, 91, 95–98, 101, 105, 149, 274–75*
Washington Projects for the Arts *33*
Waters, John *86, 101*
Weltschmerz *121, 257*
Westwood, Vivienne *43, 45, 53, 55, 87, 146, 172, 197, 202, 207–08, 220, 230, 242, 246–47, 260, 263*
Who, the *65*
Wild Boys *70, 170*
Wilde, Oscar *56, 199, 206*
Wilke, Hannah *221–22*
Willat, Stephen *255*
Wojnarowich, David *43*
Woodrow, Bill *43*
Wulz, Wanda 203

X
Xerox art *71, 73*
X-Ray Spex *58–59, 217, 245*

Y
Young British Artists (YBA) *100*